THE CAMBRIDGE COMPA
'LYRICAL BALLAD

C000051389

Lyrical Ballads (1798) is a work of huge cultural and literary signifi-cance. This volume of poetry in which Coleridge's *The Rime of the Ancyent Marinere* and Wordsworth's *Lines Written above Tintern Abbey* were first published lies at the heart of British Romanticism, establishing a poetics of powerful feeling that is, nonetheless, expressed in direct, conversational language and explores the everyday realities of common life. This engaging, accessible collection provides a comprehensive overview of current approaches to *Lyrical Ballads*, enabling readers to find fresh ways of understanding and responding to the volume. Sally Bushell's introduction explores how the Preface to the second edition (1800) became a potent manifesto for the Romantic movement. Broad in scope, the *Companion* includes accessible essays on Wordsworth's experiments with language and metre, ecocritical approaches, the reception of the volume in America and more, furnishing students and scholars with a range of entry points to this seminal text.

SALLY BUSHELL is Professor of Romantic and Victorian Literature and Co-Director of the Wordsworth Centre in the Department of English Literature & Creative Writing, Lancaster University. She has long had an interest in Wordsworth. Her first book, *Re-reading the Excursion* (2002), sought to open up the text to new readings, followed by her co-editing of the Cornell edition of *The Excursion* (2007) and her second monograph, *Text as Process: Creative Compos-ition in Wordsworth, Tennyson and Dickinson* (2009), which explored the margins of textuality by developing a method for interpreting works in a state of process. A strong interest in place and space in literature has recently led her into research around the question of how the reader spatialises literature with a forthcoming monograph (Cambridge, 2020), *Reading and Mapping Fiction*. She is also inter-ested in digital and spatial projects for the mapping of literature. She is the PI on the AHRC-Funded project, *Chronotopic Cartographies*, and has developed an educational project using Minecraft to map literary worlds (*LITCRAFT*).

THE CAMBRIDGE COMPANION TO 'LYRICAL BALLADS'

EDITED BY

SALLY BUSHELL

Lancaster University

CAMBRIDGE
UNIVERSITY PRESS

CAMBRIDGE
UNIVERSITY PRESS

University Printing House, Cambridge CB2 8BS, United Kingdom

One Liberty Plaza, 20th Floor, New York, NY 10006, USA

477 Williamstown Road, Port Melbourne, VIC 3207, Australia

314–321, 3rd Floor, Plot 3, Splendor Forum, Jasola District Centre, New Delhi – 110025, India

79 Anson Road, #06–04/06, Singapore 079906

Cambridge University Press is part of the University of Cambridge.

It furthers the University's mission by disseminating knowledge in the pursuit of
education, learning, and research at the highest international levels of excellence.

www.cambridge.org
Information on this title: www.cambridge.org/9781108416320
DOI: 10.1017/9781108236300

© Cambridge University Press 2020

First published 2020

Printed in the United Kingdom by TJ International Ltd, Padstow Cornwall

A catalogue record for this publication is available from the British Library.

Library of Congress Cataloging-in-Publication Data
NAMES: Bushell, Sally, editor.
TITLE: The Cambridge companion to 'lyrical ballads' / edited by Sally Bushell, Lancaster University.
DESCRIPTION: Cambridge ; New York : Cambridge University Press, 2019. | Includes
bibliographical references and index.
IDENTIFIERS: LCCN 2019038196 (print) | LCCN 2019038197 (ebook) |
ISBN 9781108416320 (hardback) | ISBN 9781108402835 (paperback) |
ISBN 9781108236300 (epub)
SUBJECTS: LCSH: Wordsworth, William, 1770–1850. Lyrical ballads.
CLASSIFICATION: LCC PR5869.L93 C35 2019 (print) | LCC PR5869.L93 (ebook) |
DDC 821/.709–dc23
LC record available at https://lccn.loc.gov/2019038196
LC ebook record available at https://lccn.loc.gov/2019038197

ISBN 978-1-108-41632-0 Hardback
ISBN 978-1-108-40283-5 Paperback

For Jeff Cowton at the Wordsworth Trust,
and for John Beer, in memoriam.

Contents

Contributors

POLLY ATKIN is working on a monograph, exploring connections between Romantic legacies, ecopoetics and tourism emerging from her collaborative PhD on Dove Cottage undertaken at Lancaster University and The Wordsworth Trust. Her debut poetry collection, *Basic Nest Architecture* (2017), is followed by a pamphlet, *With Invisible Rain* (2018), drawing on Dorothy Wordsworth's late journals. She is a Penguin Random House *WriteNow* mentee, 2018, for a non-fiction book on place, belonging and chronic illness.

ANDREW BENNETT is Professor of English at the University of Bristol. With Cambridge University Press he has published *Suicide Century: Keats, Narrative and Audience* (1994), *Romantic Poets and the Culture of Posterity* (1999), *Wordsworth Writing* (2007), *William Wordsworth in Context* (editor, 2015) and *Literature and Suicide from James Joyce to David Foster Wallace* (2017). His other books include *Ignorance: Literature and Agnoiology* (2009) and with Nicholas Royle, *An Introduction to Literature, Criticism and Theory* (5th ed., 2016).

SALLY BUSHELL is Professor of Romantic and Victorian Literature and Co-Director of The Wordsworth Centre in the Department of English Literature & Creative Writing, Lancaster University. Her first two books (*Re-reading the Excursion*; *The Excursion* for the Cornell Series) were on Wordsworth's second long poem, while her third (*Text as Process: Creative Composition in Wordsworth, Tennyson and Dickinson* (2009)) sought to articulate a method for interpreting works in a state of process. She is also co-editing (with Damian Walford Davies and Julia S. Carlson) a second forthcoming collection with Cambridge University Press: *Romantic Cartographies* (2019).

FRANCES FERGUSON is Professor in the Department of English Language and Literature at the University of Chicago. She has published

Wordsworth: Language as Counter-Spirit (1977), *Solitude and the Sublime: Romanticism and the Aesthetics of Individuation* (1992) and *Pornography, the Theory: What Utilitarianism Did to Action* (2004), as well as various articles on eighteenth-century and Romantic topics, literary theory and aesthetic theory.

PAUL H. FRY is the William Lampson Professor of English and former Head of Ezra Stiles College at Yale University. His books include *The Poet's Calling in the English Ode* (1980), *The Reach of Criticism* (1983), *William Empson: Prophet Against Sacrifice* (1991), *A Defense of Poetry: Reflections on the Occasion of Writing* (1995), an edition of 'The Rime of the Ancient Mariner' (1999), *Wordsworth and the Poetry of What We Are* (2008) and *Theory of Literature* (2012).

TIM FULFORD is Professor of English at De Montfort University, Leicester. Among his books are *The Late Poetry of the Lake Poets* (Cambridge, 2013), *Wordsworth's Poetry 1815–45* (2018) and *The Collected Letters of Sir Humphry Davy* (2019).

NIKKI HESSELL is Associate Professor in the English Programme at Victoria University of Wellington in New Zealand. She works on the intersections of Romanticism, indigeneity and print culture. Her latest book is *Romantic Literature and the Colonised World: Lessons from Indigenous Translations* (2018), which considers Pacific and Indian translations of texts by Wordsworth, Hemans, Burns, Keats and Scott.

JAMES C. MCKUSICK is Dean of the Honors College and Professor of English at the University of Missouri–Kansas City. He received a PhD in English from Yale University. His research and teaching interests include British Romanticism, ecocriticism and the history of science. He is the author of *Coleridge's Philosophy of Language* (1986) and *Green Writing: Romanticism and Ecology* (2000). He is co-editor of *Literature and Nature: Four Centuries of Nature Writing* (2001) and *Faustus: From the German of Goethe, translated by Samuel Taylor Coleridge* (2007).

PETE NEWBON is a senior lecturer in Romantic and Victorian literature at Northumbria University. He is the editor of *The Charles Lamb Bulletin*. His monograph, *The Boy-Man, Immaturity and Masculinity in the Long Nineteenth Century*, was published in 2019. His research addresses representations of childhood, child psychology, children's literature and Romantic masculinities. He has published on Wordsworth, Coleridge, Lamb, Southey and De Quincey.

BRENNAN O'DONNELL has served as President of Manhattan College in New York since 2009, where he also holds an appointment as Professor of English. Previous appointments include five years as Professor and Dean of Fordham College, Fordham University, New York, and seventeen years as Professor of English at Loyola University, Maryland. Among his publications are two studies of Wordsworth's versification, *Numerous Verse* (1989) and *The Passion of Meter* (1995).

JOEL PACE is Professor of English at the University of Wisconsin–Eau Claire, and Associate Editor of *Symbiosis*. He is co-editor of *Transatlantic Romanticism: An Anthology, 1767–1867*; *Wordsworth in American Literary Culture*; and *Studies in Romanticism*'s special issue on Black Romanticism (April 2017). He has appeared as a guest on BBC Radio and BBC Two to discuss literature, race and music. Also a vocalist, trumpeter and songwriter, he has shared bills with Wyclef Jean, The Wailers and The Meditations.

ALEXANDER REGIER is Professor of English at Rice University and editor of the scholarly journal *SEL Studies in English Literature 1500–1900*. He is the author of *Exorbitant Enlightenment: Blake, Hamann, and Anglo-German Constellations* (2018) and *Fracture and Fragmentation in British Romanticism* (Cambridge University Press, 2010). He co-edited *Wordsworth's Poetic Theory: Knowledge, Language, Experience* (2010) and has edited special journal issues on 'Mobilities' and 'Genealogies'. His articles on Romanticism, rhetoric, William Wordsworth, Walter Benjamin, ruins, contemporary poetry, the aesthetics of sport and other topics have appeared in a wide variety of journals.

PHILIP SHAW is Professor of Romantic Studies at the University of Leicester where he maintains research interests in Romantic poetry and prose and visual culture. His publications include *Waterloo and the Romantic Imagination* (2002), *The Sublime* (2005; 2nd ed., 2017), *Suffering and Sentiment in Romantic Military Art* (2013), as editor, *Romantic Wars: Studies in Culture and Conflict, 1789–1822* (2000), and as co-editor, *Visual Culture and the Revolutionary and Napoleonic Wars* (2016). He is currently working on a study of Wordsworth's later poetry.

SUSAN J. WOLFSON is Professor of English at Princeton University and most recently the author of the prize-winning *Reading John Keats* (Cambridge University Press, 2015). Her publications on Wordsworth(s) include a unit in *Romantic Interactions* (2010), 'The Poem on the Wye' in *The Oxford Handbook of William Wordsworth* (2015) and 'Wordsworth's Craft' in *The Cambridge Companion to William Wordsworth* (2011). A chapter in *Romantic Shades and Shadows* (2018), 'What's in a Name? Will + Words + Worth,' reflects an article by the same name in *ELH* (2017).

Acknowledgements

I would like to thank: my colleagues at Lancaster University, particularly the Romanticists (Simon Bainbridge; Keith Hanley and Sharon Ruston); those at the Wordsworth Trust, particularly the director, Michael McGregor, and Jeff Cowton, the curator; at Cambridge University Press, Linda Bree for inviting me to edit this collection, the anonymous readers for their helpful advice and Bethany Thomas for seeing it through the Press; and last, but by no means least, the wonderful Kate Ingle – best editorial assistant anyone ever had.

Chronology

1770   William Wordsworth (WW) born 7 April in Cockermouth, Cumberland (now the Lake District), second of five children.

1771   Dorothy Wordsworth (DW), the poet's sister, born 25 December, Cockermouth.

1772   John Wordsworth (JW), the poet's younger brother, born 4 December, Cockermouth.
        Samuel Taylor Coleridge (STC) born 21 October, Ottery St Mary, Devonshire. Youngest of ten children.

1776   4 July 1776: American Declaration of Independence. War with Britain begins.
        France recognises American Independence.

1778   WW's Mother, Ann Wordsworth, dies 6 March. DW sent to live with cousins in Halifax, WW to Penrith.

1779   In May, WW and his brother Richard sent to Hawkshead Grammar School (they lodge with Ann Tyson).

1781   Death of STC's father, Rev. John Coleridge, October.

1782   STC sent to Christ's Hospital School, London.

1783   WW's father, John Wordsworth, dies, 30 December.
        3 September 1783, Treaty of Paris ends the Revolutionary War.

1787   WW goes to St John's College, Cambridge.
        25 May 1787, American Constitution adopted.

1789   In Paris, storming of the Bastille, 14 July. Declaration of 'The Rights of Man', 26 August. Start of the French Revolution.

1790   WW undertakes a walking tour of France and Switzerland with Robert Jones during the long vacation.

1791   WW goes on a walking tour of Wales with RJ. WW in London. November, WW goes to live in France, meets Annette Vallon. STC attends Jesus College, Cambridge.

1792   WW's illegitimate daughter, Caroline, born 15 December in France.

1793   WW returns to England (unable to return to France for next nine years because of war).
Publication of 'An Evening Walk' and 'Descriptive Sketches'.
Unpublished radical 'Letter to the Bishop of Llandaff'.
STC Enlists in the 15th Light Dragoons under the false name 'Silas Tomkyn Comberbache'. Discharged April 1794.
Execution of Louis XVI, 21 January 1793.
War declared between France and England. 'Reign of Terror' commences.

1794   WW reunited with DW in Keswick after many years apart.
STC returns to Cambridge. Meets Robert Southey, plans pantisocracy in America. Both become engaged to the Fricker sisters. STC collaborates with Southey on *The Fall of Robespierre*.
Execution of Robespierre, 28 July 1794. End of the Terror.
Treason Trials in London.

1795   WW and STC meet for the first time in Bristol in September.
WW is left £500 by his friend Raisley Calvert, enabling him to pursue a poetic career.
STC marries Sara Fricker, 4 November.
Directory takes power in France.

1796   STC publishes *Poems on Various Subjects* and 10 issues of *The Watchman* (a political journal).
Hartley Coleridge born 19 September 1796.
Coleridge family moves to Nether Stowey, Somerset, in December.
Napoleon Bonaparte leads campaign in Italy.

1797   WW and DW move to Alfoxden, Somerset, in July to be near Coleridge.
WW writes play *The Borderers* and tries to get it put on in London.
STC writes play *Osorio* and tries to get it put on in London.
Walking tour of Quantocks in Somerset. First composition of 'The Rime of the Ancyent Marinere'.
Switzerland and Italy declared Republics.

1798   Often called the *annus mirabilis*. WW finishes 'The Ruined Cottage' and writes most of the poems for *Lyrical Ballads* (*LB*)

1798. Walking tour of the Wye valley in July with DW results in 'Tintern Abbey'.

***Lyrical Ballads with a Few Other Poems (anon)* printed in September by Joseph Cottle, Bristol; pub. in London 4 October, J & A. Arch.**

STC pub. 'Fears in Solitude' with 'Frost at Midnight' and 'France, An Ode'. Birth of second son, Berkeley, in May.

WW, DW and STC travel to Germany together, then split up. WW and DW go to Goslar. WW writes first episodes of *The Prelude*, drawing on childhood memories. STC goes to Ratzeburg and Göttingen.

Napoleon invades Egypt.

Nelson destroys French fleet at the Battle of the Nile, 3 August 1798.

1799   WW and DW return to England. WW writes up early *Prelude* material (Bks I and II).

On walking tour of Lake District with STC and JW, WW sees Dove Cottage, Grasmere; moves there with DW in December.

Death of Berkeley in February. STC returns to England in July. Works for *The Morning Post*. Walking tour with WW and JW in October, meets Sara Hutchinson (SH).

Napoleon overthrows Directory and is elected First Consul, 12 December.

1800   WW writes 'Preface' for *LB*. **Second edition *Lyrical Ballads with Other Poems in Two Volumes by W. Wordsworth* (with Preface) pub. January 1801.** Writes 'Home at Grasmere'.

STC moves to Greta Hall, Keswick, to live near the Wordsworths. Birth of Derwent, 14 September.

1802   WW writes lyrical poetry towards **third edition of *Lyrical Ballads with Pastoral and Other Poems in Two Volumes by W. Wordsworth* (with revised Preface). Pub. April 1802.**

Temporary peace Treaty of Amiens allows WW and DW to visit Annette and Caroline.

WW marries Mary Hutchinson (MH) 4 October.

Birth of STC's daughter, Sara, 23 December.

Napoleon established as First Consul for life, 2 August.

1803 — Birth of WW's first son, John. Scottish tour with WW, DW, STC.

STC becoming ill, decides to travel abroad.

Britain declares war on France, 18 May.

1804 WW works on *The Prelude*, enlarging it from 2 to 5 to 13 books.
Daughter Dora Wordsworth born 16 August.
STC visits Sicily and works as Acting Public Secretary to
Alexander Ball in Malta.
Napoleon crowned Emperor by the Pope, 2 December.

1805 John Wordsworth drowns as captain of his ship, *The Earl of
Abergavenny*, off Portland harbour, 5 February. WW completes
The Prelude in a state of mourning.
Nelson defeats the French navy and is killed at the Battle of
Trafalgar, 21 October.

1806 WW's son Thomas born 15 June 1806.
STC returns to Keswick, separates from his wife.

1808 WW's daughter Catherine born 5 September. With four
children the WW family move from Dove Cottage to Allan
Bank, Grasmere.
STC also moves to Allan Bank, Grasmere. Begins to publish *The
Friend* (28 numbers).
Peninsular War begins. Convention of Cintra signed 30 August
1808, allowing French evacuation from Portugal.

1809 Wordsworth pub. *The Convention of Cintra*.

1810 Son William born 12 May.
Select Views of Cumberland, Westmoreland and Lancashire pub.
WW and STC fall out and their friendship ends. Coleridge goes
to London to live with the Montagues.

1811 In May, the WW family leaves Allan Bank for rectory opposite
Grasmere Church.
STC gives famous lectures in London sponsored by the
Philosophical Institution.
Napoleon's son born 20 March.

1812 Death of Catherine Wordsworth, aged 3, 4 June.
Death of Thomas Wordsworth, aged 6, 1 December.
Napoleon's disastrous Russian Campaign.

1813 Wordsworth appointed Distributor of Stamps for
Westmoreland.
WW family move to Rydal Mount.
STC's play *Remorse* is staged at Drury Lane.

1814 WW's second long poem *The Excursion* published.
Napoleon abdicates 4 April; Louis XVIII is restored to the
throne.
Napoleon is exiled to Elba, 4 May.

1815   *Poems in Two Volumes* (first collected edition) pub. with poems arranged by WW and a new 'Preface'.
        Napoleon escapes and arrives in Paris, 20 March; marks beginning of the 'Hundred Days'. Napoleon finally defeated at the Battle of Waterloo, 18 June. King is restored 8 July. NB is exiled to St Helena, 16 October.

1816   STC pub. *Christabel; Kubla Khan; The Pains of Sleep; The Statesman's Manual.*

1817   STC pub. *Biographia Literaria; Sibylline Leaves; Zapolya.*

1819   WW pub. *Peter Bell* and *The Waggoner*, both written many years earlier.

1820   WW pub. *The River Duddon: A Series of Sonnets.*

1821   Napoleon dies on St Helena, 5 May.

1822   WW pub. *Description of the Scenery of the Lakes.*
        Henry Nelson Coleridge begins recording STC's conversation for *Table Talk.*

1825   STC pub. *Aids to Reflection.*

1828   Pub. of *The Poetical Works of Samuel Taylor Coleridge*, 3 vols., ed. Henry Nelson Coleridge.

1829   STC pub. *On the Constitution of Church and State.*

1834   STC dies at Highgate, London, 25 July.

1843   WW becomes Poet Laureate on death of Robert Southey.

1847   Death of Dora, 9 July.

1850   WW dies 23 April. Posthumous pub. of *The Prelude.*

Abbreviations

BL	Coleridge, Samuel Taylor. *The Collected Works of Samuel Taylor Coleridge, Biographia Literaria or Biographical Sketches of My Literary Life and Opinions.* Eds. James Engell and W. Jackson Bate. Princeton: Princeton University Press, 1983.
CL STC	Coleridge, Samuel Taylor. *The Collected Letters of Samuel Taylor Coleridge.* 6 vols. Ed. Earl Leslie Griggs. Oxford: Clarendon Press, 1956. (Identified by volume number.)
CN STC	Coleridge, Samuel Taylor. *The Notebooks of Samuel Taylor Coleridge.* 5 vols. Ed. Kathleen Coburn. Princeton: Princeton University Press, 1957–2002. (Identified by volume number.)
Cornell LB	*Lyrical Ballads and Other Poems 1797–1800.* Eds. James A. Butler and Karen Green. Ithaca and New York: Cornell University Press, 1993.
CW STC	Coleridge, Samuel Taylor. *The Collected Works of Samuel Taylor Coleridge.* Ed. James Engell and W. Jackson Bate. 16 vols. Routledge & Kegan Paul, 1983.
DWJ	Dorothy Wordsworth. *The Grasmere and Alfoxden Journals.* Ed. Pamela Woof. Oxford: Oxford University Press, 1991. Rpt. 2002.
Letters EY	*The Letters of William and Dorothy Wordsworth: The Early Years 1787–1805.* Ed. Ernest de Selincourt. Oxford: Clarendon Press, 1967.
Letters MY	*The Letters of William and Dorothy Wordsworth.* Ed. Ernest de Selincourt. *The Middle Years Part I 1806–1811.* Rev. Mary Moorman. Oxford at the Clarendon Press, 1969; 2nd ed. *III. The Middle Years Part II. 1812–1820.* Revd. Mary Moorman and Alan G. Hill. Oxford: Clarendon Press, 1970. (Identified by volume number.)

Letters	*The Letters of William and Dorothy Wordsworth: The Later*
LY	*Years 1821–1853.* Ed. Ernest de Selincourt. 4 vols. Revd. Alan G. Hill. Oxford: Clarendon Press, 1978–1988. (Identified by volume number.)
LB	Wordsworth, William. *William Wordsworth and Samuel Taylor Coleridge: Lyrical Ballads 1798 and 1802.* Ed. Fiona Stafford. Oxford: Oxford University Press, 2013.
Owen	Owen, W. J. B. Ed. *Wordsworth's Literary Criticism.* London: Routledge & Kegan Paul, 1974.
Prelude	*The Prelude, 1799, 1805, 1850.* Ed. Jonathan Wordsworth, M. H. Abrams and Stephen Gill. New York: W.W. Norton & Co., 1979.
Prose	*The Prose Works of William Wordsworth.* Ed. W. J. B. Owen and Jane Worthington Smyser. 3 vols. Oxford: Clarendon Press, 1974. (Identified by volume number.)
PW	*The Poetical Works of Samuel Taylor Coleridge.* Ed. J. C.
STC	C. Mays. 3 Parts; 6. vols. Princeton: Princeton University Press, 2001. (Identified by part and volume numbers.) *The Collected Works of Samuel Taylor Coleridge*, Vol. 16.
WSCW	William Shakespeare: The Complete Works. Compact Edition. Ed Stanley Wells, Gary Taylor, John Jowett and William Montgomery. Oxford: Clarendon Press, 1988.

Introduction

Sally Bushell

Fools have laughed at, wise men scarcely understand, them.
(William Hazlitt on Lyrical Ballads)[1]

From the row of first editions in The Jerwood Centre at the Wordsworth
Trust, Grasmere, the curator, lovingly takes down one of his favourite
items. It is not much to look at, a slim volume still in its original card
covers; cheap stained covers that should have been removed and thrown
away when it was bound in leather to match the designs of a gentleman's
library. The curator tells the paradoxical tale of an object so ordinary that it
has become a rarity; the book whose pages remain untrimmed; the book
that can never be read: a first edition of *Lyrical Ballads* (1798). But *Lyrical
Ballads* has always been a volume of paradoxes, from its contradictory title,
to the tensions between poems and prose, to the variable accounts by its
two authors of its aims and origins, to the difficulty readers have with
grasping how such slight poems can be accorded such high status. Perhaps
it is *just this* sense of it – as something unable to be quite pinned down –
that has made this unassuming volume such a major, lasting work of
British Romanticism.

The tale of the volume's progress from inception to first (1798) and
subsequent publication (1800, 1802, 1805) has been told many times but,
for readers coming to the collection for the first time, a brief outline is
sketched here.[2] Two young men, Coleridge and Wordsworth (aged
twenty-five and twenty-eight, respectively) came up with the idea for the
volume together while on a walking tour in 1797 during a period of
intense symbiotic creative activity ('the *annus mirabilis* of English Romanticism' (*Cornell LB* 4)) when they were living as neighbours in Somerset.
Accounts of origins vary to some degree, and are all retrospective and thus
open to misremembering, but all agree that the 'The Rime of the Ancyent
Marinere' was the first poem planned and composed. Other poems were
written over the spring of 1798 and the volume of nineteen poems by

Wordsworth and four by Coleridge was in preparation when William and Dorothy went on a walking tour of Wales in July. Returning to Bristol, Wordsworth finished 'Lines Written a Few Miles above Tintern Abbey', which was then added at the back of the edition. The volume was printed in five hundred copies by a friend, Joseph Cottle, in Bristol in September 1798 – Dorothy writes '[William's poems are] printed, but not published' on 13 September (*Letters EY* 227) – but, due to financial difficulties, Cottle sold the rights and the copies to a London firm, J & A. Arch, who finally published an octavo edition for 5 shillings on 4 October 1798. The second edition was enlarged considerably by the addition of a 'Preface' by Wordsworth and a second volume of thirty-seven poems also written by him in Goslar, Germany (October–February 1798–99), and then in Grasmere, where William and Dorothy settled from 20 December 1799. Poems in Volume I remained largely the same ('The Convict' was removed and replaced with Coleridge's poem 'Love' and 'Lines written near Richmond, upon the Thames, at Evening' split into two poems) but were re-arranged in terms of order. This edition was published in January 1801 for 10 shillings by Longman. The third edition (with some enlargement of the 'Preface') was published in June 1802 and the final edition in October 1805, after which the poems were separated and published by each poet in separate collections.

Does it really deserve all the acclaim? And how can it continue to be relevant to us today? In his perceptive essay on 'Mr. Wordsworth' in *The Spirit of the Age*, critic and writer William Hazlitt succinctly explains the way in which Wordsworth and *Lyrical Ballads* are both profoundly of their time, yet also universal. As he makes clear, the political fervour of the 1790s finds its focus in this volume:

> The political changes of the day were the model on which he formed and conducted his poetical experiments. His Muse . . . is a levelling one. It proceeds on a principle of equality, and strives to reduce all things to the same standard. (139)

So, the 'experimental' nature of the poetic collection, declared in the 'Advertisement' to the 1798 volume, is an experiment not just of form or language but also of social values, validating the ordinary life, the everyday, in ways that we might take for granted but that find their roots in the democratic principles of the French Revolution. Hazlitt goes on to describe the poems as:

> a test to prove that nature is always interesting from its inherent truth and beauty . . . Hence the unaccountable mixture of seeming simplicity and real

abstruseness in the *Lyrical Ballads*. Fools have laughed at, wise men scarcely understand, them. He takes a subject or a story merely as pegs or loops to hang thought and feeling on; the incidents are trifling . . . the reflections are profound. (140)

Again, Hazlitt touches on something significant here – how easy it is to miss the point of these poems because 'the incidents are trifling'. This has always been a problem for readers coming new to them. Where the subject and the style are slight, it is easy to undervalue the true message of the poem and it leaves those poems open to parody because if the emotion that underlies the action is forced or insincere, then poetry falls into bathos.

It is worth pausing to look more closely at an example of what Hazlitt is describing. 'The Childless Father' is a poem to which few readers today pay much attention. In the 1802 'Preface', Wordsworth states:

> it is proper that I should mention one other circumstance which distinguishes these Poems from the popular Poetry of the day; it is this, that the feeling therein developed gives importance to the action and situation, and not the action and situation to the feeling. My meaning will be rendered perfectly intelligible by referring my Reader to the Poems entitled POOR SUSAN and the CHILDLESS FATHER, particularly to the last Stanza of the latter Poem. (*LB* 99)

This is a central concept for *Lyrical Ballads*, 'that the feeling therein developed gives importance to the action and situation, and not the action and situation to the feeling'. In other words, the primary effect is internal, unseen, but it is then played out in a certain scenario or directed towards a particular object which is made important only by the human story in which it participates. The subject matter is *deliberately* understated. Using extremely simplistic, largely monosyllabic language, and emphasising the song-like rhythms of the ballad, 'The Childless Father' is centred on a familiar micro-moment: locking the door as you leave the house. The old man, Timothy, sets off to take part in the excitement of the hunt that all the village are involved in:

> Old Timothy took up his staff, and he shut
> With a leisurely motion the door of his hut.
> (Lines 13–14)

The father goes out, as he has done many times before, but suddenly he realises that this time he must take the house key *with* him. He has never before had to do this. Previously, he has left the house with his daughter in it, knowing she will be there when he comes home, but now things are irrevocably changed, just as his identity has changed (he is now defined only by a lack). The last stanza reads:

> Perhaps to himself at that moment he said
> 'The key I must take, for my Ellen is dead.'
> But of this in my ears not a word did he speak,
> And he went to the chase with a tear on his cheek.
>
> (Lines 16–20)

The poem focuses on a small event – even half negates it in the utterance (perhaps he didn't think any of this) – but one that represents for this individual the absolute and terrible change that has occurred in his life. Wordsworth, as he often does, loads an ordinary everyday object (the house key) and an act that we all do every day without thinking (locking up) with a weight of human emotion. From the outside, looking on, there is literally nothing to see. The core event is entirely undramatic and relies on a highly receptive reader and poet-narrator, reading between the unemotive lines of the poem to sense the depths of loss beneath. The old man may not have the sophistication to express what he feels, he may need someone else to speak on his behalf, but nonetheless we can recognise that this is how life is – still, today. It's the little things that break our hearts.

***

Thus far I have focused on Wordsworth but, of course, the first edition of *Lyrical Ballads* was published anonymously and it had *two* authors: William Wordsworth and Samuel Taylor Coleridge. Another reason for lasting interest in this volume then, is its identity as a joint venture by two major figures of the period working together in a powerfully symbiotic relationship that brought out the best in both men early on (each often stimulated by and writing *for* the other), but that also already contained the seeds of its later destruction.[3] From the start Coleridge recognised Wordsworth's powers as a poet ('The Giant Wordsworth – God love him' [*CL STC* I. 391]) but that very admiration destabilised his own ambition, as he made clear in a letter to Southey: 'Wordsworth is a very great man – the only man, to whom *at all times* & in *all modes of excellence* I feel myself inferior'(*CL STC* I. 334). A perceived inequity in the relationship present from the outset could only worsen over time and lead to resentments. However, rather than focus on the differences between Wordsworth and Coleridge here, I want to look at what their accounts of the origins of the collaborative project have *in common*. Famously, the first poem to be composed was 'The Rime of the Ancyent Marinere' and close attention to Wordsworth's account of the organic way in which the entire volume developed *out of* this first poem (recalled much later in *The Fenwick Notes*) is illuminating. First, Wordsworth makes it clear that walking and writing were closely intertwined, indeed the motivation for writing together came from the need to cover the costs of a walking tour:

> In the Spring of the year 1798, he [STC], my sister, & myself started from Alfoxden, pretty late in the afternoon, with a view to visit Linton & the Valley of Stones near it, and as our united funds were very small we agreed to defray the expence of the tour by writing a Poem to be sent to the *New Monthly Magazine*.[4]

Wordsworth then famously describes the shared conceptual origins of 'The Rime of the Ancyent Marinere' in which Coleridge provides the core, Wordsworth the key elements of agency and the two poets begin by attempting to write the work together. However, the fantasy of literal co-composition is rapidly revealed as such, as Wordsworth makes clear:

> As we endeavoured to proceed conjointly (I speak of the same evening) our respective manners proved so widely different that it would have been quite presumptuous in me to do anything but separate from an undertaking upon which I could only have been a clog. (3)

As interesting, however, as this well-known account of the writing of the first poem, is the development of the larger project out of it:

> The Ancient Mariner grew & grew till it became too important for our first object ... and we began to talk of a volume, which was to consist as Mr Coleridge has told the world, of Poems chiefly on supernatural subjects taken from common life but looked at, as much as might be, through an imaginative medium. Accordingly I wrote The Idiot Boy, Her Eyes are wild &c., We are Seven, The Thorn & some others. (3)

What this comment makes clear is the ad hoc nature of the volume as a whole (which is again both problematic and part of its charm) and the way in which 'The Rime of The Ancyent Marinere' determines the subject, viewpoint and purpose of many of the other ballad poems. The core of the original 1798 volume is succinctly given here: 'Poems chiefly on supernatural subjects taken from common life but looked at ... through an imaginative medium'. Such a statement, as Wordsworth rather sharply notes, concurs with Coleridge's (also retrospective) account in *Biographia Literaria*. Coleridge takes the same core, shared idea but articulates two different ways of dealing with it (the first relating to Coleridge's contributions, the second to Wordsworth's):

> The thought suggested itself (to which of us I do not recollect) that a series of poems might be composed of two sorts. In the one, the incidents and agents were to be, in part at least, supernatural ... to consist in the interesting of the affections by the dramatic truth of such emotions, as would naturally accompany such situations, supposing them real. ... For the second class, subjects were to be chosen from ordinary life ... to give the charm of novelty to things of every day, and to excite a feeling analogous to the supernatural, by awakening the mind's attention from the lethargy of custom. (*BL* II. 5–7)

The two poets thus address the same issue from two opposing directions, both reliant on the differing powers of imaginative creativity in each of them. Coleridge's challenge is to present supernatural events so convincingly that they can be experienced as if real; conversely, Wordsworth's is to show that everyday interactions and events between ordinary people (particularly in states of emotional and psychological extremes), can be as fascinating and elicit as strong an emotion as more exciting or titillating forms of writing. These two stances are potentially contradictory – and difficulties emerge as a result between the collaborators that indirectly bear upon their personal relationship. The relocation of 'The Rime of the Ancyent Marinere' from the opening poem in 1798 to the penultimate poem of the volume in 1800 is the most obvious and problematic outcome – understandably offensive to Coleridge when we see how the entire project evolved out of this poem (which was also presumably the reason it was initially positioned first).

Wordsworth's note to 'The Thorn' is also worth consideration here as an example of the original principles in action:

> Arose out of my observing, on the ridge of Quantock Hill, on a stormy day a thorn which I had often past in calm and bright weather without noticing it. I said to myself, Cannot I by some invention do as much to make this thorn permanently an impressive object as the storm has made it to my eyes at this moment. (*LB* 14)

The poem finds its origins in an entirely ordinary natural object that would normally be overlooked. That object is imbued with a certain distinctiveness – a symbolic power – as a result of extreme weather conditions, and this leads the poet to develop a human narrative that corresponds to the natural. Without the power of the poet's imagination, of course, nothing can come of this. But with it, with Wordsworth's binding together of the insensate and the sentient, a new way of understanding the world and the dynamic between human and environment can be uncovered.

***

Previous collections of critical essays on *Lyrical Ballads* have been strongly centred upon how inclusive a critical volume should attempt to be and on *which Lyrical Ballads* is to be the focus: 1798 as the first edition but only including one volume; 1800 in two volumes with the 'Preface'; 1802 as the fullest version with significant additions to the 'Preface'.[5] It is certainly important to be aware that the 1798 volume is a different beast from the later editions, indeed the only volume that can truly be said to be *shared*. The earliest edition contained around 3,000 lines (roughly one-third of which were Coleridge's), was published anonymously and was counter-gothic in focus – defining itself, in part at least, in relation to that mode of popular writing.[6] In 1800 the emphasis and weight of the contributions shifted considerably, as did the generic focus – felt in Coleridge's description of it as 'a second Volume of Lyrical Ballads, & Pastorals' (*CL STC* I. 585). Wordsworth added that second volume and a 'Preface' and decided *not* to include a second, long poem of Coleridge's ('Christabel') which would have proportionately increased the latter's contribution to the second edition.[7] When the volume was published in *Wordsworth's* name the move away from a joint collection was formally and publicly signalled.

Rather than being distracted by the need to hierarchize, this collection of essays has chosen to consider the three major editions of *Lyrical Ballads* quite fluidly as three parts within one whole, or as different versions. The contents of this collection of critical essays, then, are not determined by privileging one version of the text over another but determined strongly by the needs of the Companion reader. If you knew nothing about this collection and came to it cold what would you want to learn? In the light of this, the volume is organised into five main parts centred upon the most innovative and 'experimental' ideas at the heart of the poetic collection and on what Wordsworth calls 'the perception of similitude in dissimilitude' (*LB* 111) which he describes as 'the great spring of the activity of our minds' (111); a series of complex dialectics which run through the collection as a whole.

So, Part I, 'Part and Whole', draws attention to the constructed nature of the volume over time and the tensions that exist between different elements; authorial contributions; prose and poetry; different poetic forms. The opening chapter picks up where the introduction leaves off to lead the reader through essential questions concerning the relationship between different editions of *Lyrical Ballads* and its reception, while those of Atkin and Fulford look at the writing of the volume as a collaborative act, not only with Coleridge, but within the larger Wordsworth circle of men and women. Atkin focuses on the domestic process of poetic production and the role of Dorothy Wordsworth as creative partner, as well as the support of John Wordsworth in a 'co-mingling' that brings the work into being. Fulford considers the collection specifically from a Coleridgean point of view as a typical project of co-writing for him (whereas for Wordsworth this was highly unusual) but also notes that when the collection was 'claimed' by Wordsworth as author in 1800 this damaged Coleridge considerably. The final chapter in Part I is centred on the titular contradiction. Newbon offers a full analysis of the distinction between lyric and ballad voice in the context of their separate traditions and of the ballad revival in the late eighteenth century.

In contrast to the inward-looking approach of Part I, the final section, Part V, of the book looks forward and outward, considering the wider impact and influence of the collection from a twenty-first-century global perspective. What happens when we release *Lyrical Ballads* from its canonical status in Britain? How did it fare in other cultures and traditions, for readers who had no knowledge or understanding of its subjects? McKusick provides an illuminating overview of the popular eco-critical approach to Romanticism that emerged in the late twentieth century and applies such a reading to the 'Rime' as 'a parable of ecological transgression', while his interpretation of 'Expostulation and Reply' as a 'radical credo of ecological awareness' opens into a larger exploration of human experiences of the wild across the collection. The next chapter, by Pace, takes us across the Atlantic, grounding the American perspective in the publication of the 1802 American edition of *Lyrical Ballads* by James Humphreys and the adaptation of the volume's original political resonances to a post-Revolutionary United States. The final chapter in Part V, and of the whole volume, takes us the furthest afield as Hessell considers the shaping of the canon in the colonies and the status of *Lyrical Ballads* in relation to indigenous print culture. As Hessell makes clear: 'indigenous translations *of Lyrical Ballads* did not merely transmit or imitate; they *indiginised*'. *Lyrical Ballads* becomes something else, something new, for a different culture.

Between these two framing parts, three internal parts delineate core concerns that lie at the centre of the collection ('Subjects and Situations from Common Life'; 'Feeling and Thought'; and 'Language and the Human Mind'). In the 1800 'Preface' Wordsworth declares:

> The principal object, then, which I proposed to myself in these Poems was to chuse incidents and situations from common life, and to relate or

describe them, throughout, as far as was possible, in a selection of language really used by men. (*LB* 96–97)

In the account of his aims given here, Wordsworth positions the poet as mediator, a scribe acting on behalf of others – relating or describing their stories for them in language as close as possible to actual utterance (exactly as the poet-narrator does for 'Timothy' in 'The Childless Father'). The poet is not raised above other men but speaks on their behalf, employing his skills for the good of others. As we have seen, such a stance aligns Wordsworth with the radical principles of the French Revolution – most obviously that of 'Egalité'. Not only is the middle-class writer associating himself with the ordinary man, he is willing to allow that figure and the language of that figure to determine the subject and style of his verse.

The three chapters in 'Subjects and Situations from Common Life' explore the different ways in which *Lyrical Ballads* is centred upon reciprocity between individuals or between men and women and their environment. In the first chapter Ferguson compares the model of conversation within *Lyrical Ballads* with earlier eighteenth-century forms of 'conversational poetry' and explores the ways in which various poems explore multiple voices and differing dynamics between speakers. In the next, Fry considers Wordsworthian interest in the power of things for humans, when they engage with them knowingly as objects, but also in ways that try to get at the 'thingness' of things – the essential attributes of things beyond and above the mind's attempts to know them. Poems such as 'Lines Written a Few Miles above Tintern Abbey' or the 'Lucy Poems' perfectly embody this 'sense sublime of / Something far more deeply interfused' (Lines 96–97) in the most transcendent moments when the boundary between outer and inner worlds, between material and ideal, collapse into a unity of being. In the third chapter in Part II, Shaw focuses on encounters with those marginalised by society and the way in which the collection seeks to recentre them and compel readers to engage with the overlooked. Running across all three volumes of *Lyrical Ballads*, the chapter uncovers the socio-economic causes that themselves lie half-hidden within the text through an exploration of 'biopower' – the use of technologies and disciplinary structures to increase the productive force of the human body.

The title of Part III, 'Feeling and Thought', takes us to one of the most famous statements of the 'Preface':

> For all good poetry is the spontaneous overflow of powerful feelings: but though this be true, Poems to which any value can be attached, were never produced on any variety of subjects but by a man, who being possessed of more than usual organic sensibility, had also thought long and deeply. (98)

Poetry is redefined as primarily expressive – proceeding directly from the self and as an outpouring ('overflow') of emotion. However, the statement not only immediately qualifies itself ('but though this be true'), it complicates its own initial account of poetry as the external expression of the inner self, upwelling from an act of heightened mental activity. Not everyone is capable of this kind of utterance and there is a need for a prior context of preparation, a grounding of the imagination. As Andrew Bennett makes clear, feeling, in the form of sympathy (or the lack of it), is a 'central organising impulse of almost every poem in the collection' as well as a core element in Wordsworth's definition of the role of the poet. Bennett works out of the pre-existing eighteenth-century context not only to explore the origins of such ideas, but also to show the ways in which *Lyrical Ballads* moves beyond the straightforward to complicate feeling with thought. Silent sympathy, in particular, becomes a disruptive force that challenges and subverts in situations where the feeling that should be present is absent. Alongside and following on from this, Wolfson's chapter considers the importance of domestic ties and family feeling, not just locally, but politically and nationally, with *Lyrical Ballads* drawn into an idealised depiction of hearth and home as 'the patriotic heart of England'. However, in a way comparable to Bennett, she goes on to reveal how 'Homebody-Wordsworth' actually takes this concept and pushes it to its limits, or inverts it, in repeated portraits of homelessness and dispossession.

The final core concept drawn upon here – 'Language and the Human Mind' – concerns the relationship between human universals and the connection between mind and world, the 'deep impression of certain inherent and indestructible qualities of the human mind, and likewise of certain powers in the great and permanent objects that act upon it' (100) but also the choice of certain forms of language to express higher ideas as directly as possible. This part therefore moves into a more abstract territory, albeit one that returns us to the human collaboration that underpins the volume. What *exactly* was the difference between Wordsworth and Coleridge in terms of their understanding of poetic language, metre and principle? O'Donnell leads us masterfully through this complex territory that many readers struggle to understand. He seeks to show that Coleridge's influential critique of Wordsworth in terms of metre should be set against the democratic principles that underlie linguistic communication in the poems, allowing for a complex dynamic between speakers (in ways that look back to Ferguson's chapter). Following on from him, Regier teases out another tricky concept implicit in the differences between co-creators: the relationship between poetry and philosophy. What kind of *un*systematic philosophy is this? Regier argues that the collection ultimately puts forward a relationship of awkwardness, a 'deeper dimension that never quite fits' so that poetry itself becomes a kind of philosophy, one that gives awkwardness meaning; that is self-consciously 'strange'.

What has always struck me about *Lyrical Ballads* is its capacity to touch upon almost all of the concerns of the age, as the wide-ranging chapters of this collection so clearly demonstrate. It doesn't set out to do this, and it doesn't do things in a particularly orderly way. Parts are thrown together and contradict each other – 'Lines Written a Few Miles above Tintern Abbey' is written last and so it surprises at the end of the volume instead of standing nobly at the start; 'The Rime of The Ancyent Marinere' is moved from opening poem to penultimate; the second volume has significantly different aims and tone from the first; the principles of the 'Preface' neither map directly onto the poems nor stand for the ideas of both its authors. But in the end, this collection both stands for, and itself embodies, the ordinary made extraordinary, the valuing of what otherwise might be overlooked. This is where we began. And this is what *Lyrical Ballads* is all about.

Endnotes

1 William Hazlitt, 'Mr Wordsworth', *The Spirt of the Age or Contemporary Portraits*, ed. E. D. Mackerness (Plymouth: The Guernsey Press, 1969), 139.
2 For a full and thorough account see 'Introduction', *Cornell LB* 3–33.
3 After a period of strained relations, Wordsworth and Coleridge finally fell out irrevocably in 1810 as a result of miscommunication between the two men by means of a third party (Basil Montagu). See Stephen Gill, *Wordsworth: A Life* (Oxford: Oxford University Press, 1990), 287–293.
4 *The Fenwick Notes of William Wordsworth*, ed. Jared Curtis (London: Bristol Classical Press, 1993), 2.
5 See discussion in 'A Guide to Further Reading' at the back of this book.
6 Michael Mason, 'Introduction,' *Lyrical Ballads*, ed. Michael Mason (London and New York: Longman, 1992), 4.
7 We know exactly when the decision was made thanks to Dorothy Wordsworth's Journal which records the Wordsworths' pleasure in 'Christabel' on 4 and 5 October 1800, followed by the decision: 'Determined not to print Christabel with the LB' (*DWJ* 24). See also *Cornell LB* 29–30.

PART I

Part and Whole

CHAPTER I

Wordsworth's 'Preface': A Manifesto for British Romanticism

Sally Bushell

A kind of manifesto that preceded one of their more flagrant acts of hostility . . .

(Francis Jeffrey, Review of 'Thalaba')[1]

This chapter follows the principles outlined in the introduction by responding to the three early editions (1798, 1800, 1802) of *Lyrical Ballads* as a combined totality: three parts that make up one whole. It uses the historicity provided by the reception of the 'Preface' in each of the three parts to pull out defining features of response to the volume in its own time. John E. Jordan states of *Lyrical Ballads*, 'For so long now we have thought of the work as a literary landmark, forgetting that many of the characteristics of that monument are the accumulation of age or the effects of perspective'.[2] By looking at what the volume was assumed to be without (before) the 'Preface,' as well as once this prose essay is added, we can begin to understand its intended and actual impact within its own time. Approaching the volume in this way allows us to see how the work itself accumulates over time and in conjunction with its reception, as well as drawing out for us the core principles it was understood to embody.

There are three problems that readers coming new to the collection encounter: obvious contradictions between what the 'Preface' argues for in terms of universal poetic principles and the actual poems in the collection; how a poem such as 'Tintern Abbey' can be a 'lyrical ballad'; and the question of what is really 'new' about the volume and its underlying principles. The first two of these can be quite easily answered when we look across all three editions.

1798
Prose: 'Advertisement'
Poetry: *Lyrical Ballads with a Few Other Poems*

1800
Prose: 'Preface'

Poetry: *Lyrical Ballads with Other Poems in Two Volumes by W. Wordsworth*, 2 vols.

1802
Prose: 'Preface'
Poetry: *Lyrical Ballads with Pastoral and Other Poems in Two Volumes* by W. Wordsworth

What this simple chronology makes clear is how fluid the volume is across the three publications in terms of what it contains and how it presents its contents. We can immediately see that there is a strong potential for contradiction inherent in the order of publication, since the 'Preface' is written after the first volume has already been published. As important, however, the full (changing) title clearly signals that 'lyrical ballads' are only *one form* within the collection and do not constitute the entirety of it. This immediately answers many readers' confusion when faced with the most famous poem in the collection, 'Lines Written a Few Miles above Tintern Abbey', which clearly is not in ballad form or simple language. In fact, Robert Southey, in a negative review of the 1798 collection (a review that angered Wordsworth since he felt it would damage sales) strongly distinguished between 'experimental poems' for which he considered 'the experiment ... has failed' and the poems of which he approved, 'With pleasure we turn to the serious pieces, the better part of the volume'.[3] These include 'Lines Written a Few Miles above Tintern Abbey' which he directly compares with the experimental ballads (to their detriment):

> the author seems to discover still superior powers in the Lines written near Tintern Abbey. On reading this production it is impossible not to lament that he should ever have condescended to write such pieces as the Last of the Flock, the Convict, and most of the ballads. (203)

When we compare the titles of the editions we can see that for the 1798 volume the distinction between poems in terms of form is very clearly signaled, but, once the 'Preface' is added in 1800 as well as the second volume of poems, the principles of the collection become far more universalized and seem to apply to the *whole* volume in a way that is clearly misleading (and that confuses later readers). So what we really have is a miscellany – a mixture of different kinds of poetic forms, some of which are undertaking a more radical experiment than others. Thus, two of the problems that new readers find disturbing are immediately partly resolved: there are significant contradictions between prose and poetry because the prose explanation is written *after* the poetic content of Volume I; some poems do not at all conform to the definition of a 'lyrical ballad' but they were never intended to – these are defined in the first title as 'A Few Other Poems'.

The third problem, how to grasp what is 'new' about *Lyrical Ballads* and its underlying principles, is a little more difficult. To try and address this the first half of this chapter will analyse reviewers' responses to each collection, paying particular attention to the critical reception of the prose explanation offered by the poet. The second half of the chapter will consider the extent to which the 'Preface' can be considered as a 'Manifesto' and the extent to which reception of it as such is built into the core principles of the 'Preface'. Such an approach partly looks back to an early influential article by Robert Mayo entitled 'The Contemporaneity of the *Lyrical Ballads*' in which he approached the collection both through comparison with other popular verse collections of the day and through the reviews.[4] However, unlike Mayo and others who have returned to his approach, I will also be drawing upon 'reception aesthetics' (*rezeptionästhetik*) as articulated by Hans Robert Jauss as a way of allowing a well-known text to be seen afresh.

In *Toward an Aesthetic of Reception* Jauss set out to establish a new model for literary history which recognised that the literary work is not merely mimetic (representing reality) but can also actively shape and act upon reality through its effect on its audience. An ongoing, open dialogue is created between work and reader through an aesthetics of influence. He asserts:

> In the triangle of author, work, and public the last is no passive part, no chain of mere reactions, but rather itself an energy formative of history. The historical life of a literary work is unthinkable without the active participation of its addressees.[5]

Thus, literature is understood to be an event, rather than a fact. Building on Hans Georg Gadamer's account of understanding as a constantly shifting horizon, Jauss articulates a 'horizon of expectations' for literature through which readers anticipate future works and which establishes the bounds of genre categories. A strikingly new work, which has the potential to challenge generic categories or change the way we read, does so through this horizon:

> the new text evokes for the reader (listener) the horizon of expectations and rules familiar from earlier texts, which are then varied, corrected, altered, or even just reproduced. Variation and correction determine the scope,

whereas alteration and reproduction determine the borders of a genre-structure. (23)

Equally, the new work is capable of preparing its audience for the fact that it will alter the horizon in the future, to enable it to do so:

> A literary work, even when it appears to be new, does not present itself as something absolutely new in an informational vacuum, but predisposes its audience to a very specific kind of reception by announcements, overt and covert signals, familiar characteristics, or implicit allusions. (23)

In both the 'Advertisement' and the 'Prefaces' we see Wordsworth doing exactly this. He alerts his readership to unexpected elements and thus predisposes them to accept rather than reject these and so allow 'horizonal change' (25) to occur. In the 'Advertisement' he explicitly asks readers to 'consent to be pleased in spite of that most dreadful enemy to our pleasures, our own pre-established codes of decision' and to 'temper the rashness of decision' (*LB* 3).

Jauss's argument for the importance of reception is essentially open-ended since it is concerned with the continuous and ongoing openness of the literary work, which will have influence for as long as it is read anew by each generation. The danger here, however, is that a work which was striking and had impact when first published becomes far less so over time: 'the original negativity of the work has become self-evident and has itself entered into the horizon of future aesthetic experience, as a henceforth familiar expectation' (25). *Lyrical Ballads* is a work that potentially suffers in just such a way for many readers. Its call for an expressive poetics that is accessible to all has long since ceased to be a revelation and therefore the power and force of that call are lessened. However, if we focus solely on one 'closed' period of reception – that of first publication – then perhaps we can use the determining features of first reception to reassert 'newness' rather than being unable to understand the 'change in horizon' that the work so successfully brought about. Jauss advocates such a reading:

> The reconstruction of the horizon of expectations, in the face of which a work was created and received in the past, enables one . . . to pose questions that the text gave an answer to, and thereby to discover how the contemporary reader could have viewed and understood the work. (28)

Understanding the intervention that such a work represents becomes easier if we analyse the first reactions to it but, more than this, the reader in the present needs to realise that meaning and interpretation are not absolute or static but involve 'the successive unfolding of the potential for meaning that is embedded in a work' (30). Each fresh context of lived experience must find a new relevance (if the work is to go on having significance).

Interpreting the Preface through the Context of the Reviews

Let us turn to the context of first reception. On reading the reviews of 1798 it is surprising how many of Wordsworth's larger principles in the 'Preface' are captured by them. While it is easy to overlook the shorter statement of 1798 entitled 'Advertisement' in favour of the 'Preface', it does concisely encompass core principles of the later, longer essay. Reviewers pay careful attention to Wordsworth's concise statement of his aims and seem happy to accept them at face value. Many responses to the poems, personally expressed in letters or more publicly in the reviews, are strongly influenced by the author's rationale and carefully adhere to his description of how to read the collection, often reproducing a substantial section of his prose. The following key points made in the 'Advertisement' are all echoed sympathetically in the reviews:

> The majority of the following poems are to be considered as experiments. They were written chiefly with a view to ascertain how far the language of conversation in the middle and lower classes of society is adapted to the purposes of poetic pleasure.
>
> Readers ... will perhaps frequently have to struggle with feelings of strangeness and aukwardness ...
>
> they should ask themselves if it contains a natural delineation of human passions, human characters, and human incidents ...
>
> Readers of superior judgment may disapprove of the style in which many of these pieces are executed it must be expected that many lines and phrases will not exactly suit their taste. ... An accurate taste in poetry ... is an acquired talent ('Advertisement', *LB* 3)

In a succinct way then, Wordsworth covers many of the anticipated criticisms of the collection and prepares his readership not to judge too rapidly or harshly. That the poems are introduced as 'experiments' excuses the poet to some extent and suspends judgment: no great claim is to be made for them. Robert Mayo goes even further here and suggests that, in a transitional period of experimentation in poetic form, such a claim would be attractive: 'even the word *experiments* in the Advertisement would be more likely to invite rather than repel readers' (307). These experiments recentre both the *language* and *subject* of poetry on the lower classes and do so in order to represent human experiences 'naturally' (while the use of the term also signals the kind of intervention into an existing debate that Jauss describes). The *style* in which such poems seek to communicate their low subjects is of a piece, so that the reader of fashionable taste accustomed to a more ornate and gentlemanly poetry is asked to allow for adjustment to this. These three points concerning the accessibility of the poems in terms of language, subject and style are at the heart of the collection and of its importance to Romanticism. Poetry is for all and should be able to be read by all. Its aim is to speak universal truths simply and directly.

Although, as already noted, Southey's influential review of the poems in *The Critical Review* deemed that 'the experiment we think has failed', his view was by no means universally held. The poems certainly have an impact and stand out from other prior collections. Many readers register the poems as 'strange' initially but then dutifully follow Wordsworth's advice and undertake further readings that enable them to adjust to the new style: 'Readers will perhaps frequently have to struggle with feelings of strangeness and awkwardness', declares *The Analytical Review*, directly quoting Wordsworth's own words.[6] There is an eagerness to engage in a new way and an openness to having one's 'taste' redefined (confirming Mayo's account).

At the same time, by far the most dominant concept that emerges from the early reviews is *not* explicitly present in Wordsworth's 'Advertisement'. 'Simplicity' is the key word of the 1798 reviews and one that lies at the heart of the contemporary debate around the nature, subject and language of poetry. As Robert Mayo makes clear: 'The new poets of the day were everywhere striving for artless expressions of simplicity' (494). *The Analytical Review* approves of the poems as models of 'studied simplicity' (583) while *The British Critic* asserts 'the endeavour of the author is to recall our poetry, from the fantastical excess of refinement, to simplicity and nature'.[7] This review suggests a contrast between two models of poetic expression: one civilised to a point of extreme ornateness, one plain and direct (a contrast which Wordsworth later builds upon in his attack on 'Poetic diction'). A more critical response in the *New London Review* enlarges upon this, noting that 'We have had a multitude of rhimers who … seem to have thought, that rudeness was synonimous [*sic*] with simplicity'. The article goes on to distinguish 'a *simple* style' from 'a style of *simplicity*'.[8] The first of these is negative; it describes a rude, debased or vulgar style. The second is positive and outlines a conscious affectation of simplicity in order to achieve elegance. The second remains within the accepted parameters of the prior eighteenth-century definition of poetry as a gentlemanly pursuit, shared between those with the civilised taste to appreciate it. The first moves beyond it. While the collection is undoubtedly capable of being read through this contemporary frame, which helped to make it palatable, Wordsworth's understanding of the power of 'simplicity' is not limited to the terms of fashionable debate.

In an extended discussion of simplicity in *Why the Lyrical Ballads?* John E. Jordan postulates that 'What Wordsworth does is to deny the trivially simple, but value the *essentially* simple'.[9] He goes on: 'Thus the simple was for Wordsworth not, as Jeffrey complained ... a repudiation of art, but rather the quintessence of art' (99). In other words, what Wordsworth is trying to do is to strip away all kinds of constructed and predetermined responses to poetry and get back to a universal core of meaning at the heart of the human condition. Underlying this we can strongly identify a Rousseauvian influence. Civilised man in all his refinement requires complexity of language to meet his sophisticated needs; as *The Monthly Review* wittily puts it: 'None but savages have submitted to eat acorns after corn was found'.[10] Poetry has achieved a certain level of advanced civilisation so why would it go backward? On the Wordsworthian (Rousseauvian) side though, Poetry has become a corrupt, degenerate form of language that no longer allows the poet to speak truly because of *over*-refinement. Only by returning to core human concerns, those of 'natural' man, can it once again speak the truth to all in a language that all can understand. This is a much larger, more ideologically charged position in relation to 'simplicity' than that of the straightforward poetic debate.

Mayo argues that in its engagement with the debate around simplicity *Lyrical Ballads* was not as original a collection as has been claimed and was 'less a revolution, therefore, than the excess of a new orthodoxy' (495). He goes on:

> The more one reads the minor poetry of the magazines from 1788 to 1798, the more it is impossible to escape the impression that the concept of the 'lyrical ballad' does not represent a significant innovation in 1798. (511)

However, if it is true to say that the collection is of its time, it is also clearly the *absolute epitome* of its time: the best example of what others were attempting to do far less effectively and with underlying principles that from the start clearly exceed the fashionable stance of the day.

If we move on to the reviews for the enlarged 1800 and 1802 volumes which now contain the 'Preface' (as well as the new poems in Volume II) it is perhaps surprising to find that, as first published, the prose introduction is largely uncontroversial. The dominant mode of critical response to the much fuller argument of the 'Preface' is one that views it positively as an enlargement and extension of the previous 'Advertisement'. There is little argument with the principles of the 'Preface' itself and a stronger restatement of the 'true taste' that this collection represents – its universal appeal – as John Wilson's letter to Wordsworth makes clear:

> You have seized upon the feelings that most deeply interest the heart ... You do not write merely for the pleasure of philosophers and men of improved taste, but for all who think – for all who feel.[11]

The contrast between a more affected false language for poetry and that achieved by Wordsworth in order to express true feeling as directly as possible emerges increasingly strongly and is consolidated in the reviews:

> His style is now wholly changed, and he has adopted a purity of expression, which, to the fastidious ear, may sometimes sound poor and low, but which is infinitely more correspondent with true feeling than what, by the courtesy of the day, is usually called poetical language.[12]

The use of 'natural language' is understood in and through the rationale for pure and genuine expression of feeling in terms of 'modes of speech which are prompted by the natural flow of passion' (127). The early reviews then remain strongly focused on elements of feeling and the nature of emotional transmission, willing to redefine the larger taste debate in these terms (and thus adjusting their horizon, in Jauss's terms).

It is not until the very end of the reviewing period that reviewers begin to question or challenge the wider implications of the 'Preface'. The *American Review and Literary Journal* makes an important point (the same that Coleridge makes privately) that the universalization of Wordsworth's principles to *all* forms of poetry weakens his position by taking it too far: 'This is indeed stripping poetry at once of half her plumage ... the laws prescribed by Mr W. may suit a particular species of poetry like his own'.[13] But, famously, by far the most damaging attack is that of the highly influential editor of *The Edinburgh Review*, Francis Jeffrey.

The Critical Turn: Jeffrey and Coleridge

Jeffrey is the only one of the reviewers who responds to the threat that *Lyrical Ballads* represents, not only as a disturbing redefinition of the nature and subject of poetry and of poetic language, but as a politically charged act with dangerously radical undertones and an implicit social agenda. In the first article of the first volume of his new journal (October 1802–January 1803), Jeffrey was supposed to be reviewing Robert Southey's long poem 'Thalaba' but instead he used this as a platform to mount his attack on the '*sect*' of modern poets, '*dissenters* from the established systems in poetry and criticism' who have 'broken loose from the bondage of antient authority' (63). Right at the heart of Jeffrey's attack was a redetermining of critical response to the 'Preface' not as an enlarged account of experimentation but as something with far greater ambition: 'A kind of manifesto that preceded one of their more flagrant acts of hostility' (65). In Jeffrey's eyes the previously perceived strengths of the volume now become its weakness as the aims of the 'Preface' are underpinned by French sympathies – 'the antisocial principles, and distempered sensibility of Rousseau' (64) – so that it works as a devil's document to 'seduce many into an admiration of the false taste . . . in which most of their productions are composed' (64) playing to 'a perverted taste for simplicity' (68).[14] Jeffrey uses the larger ambition of the 'Preface' against itself to imply a de-stabilising agenda being promoted on behalf of a sinister poetic cabal.

What is a manifesto? It's a term that we associate strongly with contemporary politics and the attempt to win an election. Samuel Johnson's dictionary of 1785 describes it as 'Publick proclamation; declaration' and The *OED* similarly defines it as:

> A public declaration or proclamation, written or spoken; *esp.* a printed declaration, explanation, or justification of policy issued by a head of state, government, or political party or candidate, or any other individual or body of individuals of public relevance, as a school or movement in the Arts.

A manifesto is a deliberate utterance by more than one individual, or by an individual on behalf of a group, that feel themselves to be 'of public relevance'. To want to write such a document one needs to have a strong sense of audience, of speaking to others ('proclaiming' or 'declaring') and a strong sense of the importance of what is being said and of one's personal commitment to it. In other words, it is a highly self-conscious utterance, directed towards future action and change, which it seeks to bring about.

In what sense does the 'Preface' to *Lyrical Ballads* fit such a definition? Wordsworth himself did not call the 'Preface' a 'manifesto' but the conditions of writing it *do* gesture towards this conception of it. In Wordsworth's own self-defensive first presentation of the 'Preface' he states that:

> Several of my Friends are anxious for the success of these Poems from a belief, that, if the views with which they were composed were indeed realized, a class of Poetry would be produced, well adapted to interest mankind permanently, and not unimportant in the multiplicity, and in the quality of its moral relations: and on this account they have advised me to prefix a systematic defence of the theory, upon which the poems were written.[15]

We can see that the way Wordsworth describes the writing of the 'Preface' does accord very much with the definition of a manifesto. The desired 'declaration' is seen to be of public relevance to the Arts – and indeed beyond to the entirety of mankind – and the writing of it by an individual is motivated by the explicit desire of a group who want to get across a clear message articulated as 'a systematic defence'.

For Coleridge, as for Jeffrey, the status of the 'Preface' as manifesto is troubling. As co-creator of the volume, the 'Preface' remains unproblematic as long as it embodies shared personal aims relating to the poems in this *particular* collection, but becomes so once it starts to want to make greater claims for itself. Such concerns are expressed first privately and later publicly (my italics):

> altho' Wordsworth's Preface is half a child of my own Brain & so arose out of Conversations, so frequent, that with few exceptions we could scarcely either of us perhaps positively say, which first started any particular thought – I am speaking of the Preface as it stood in the second Volume – yet *I am far from going all lengths with Wordsworth.* . . . On the contrary, I rather suspect that some where or other there is a radical Difference in our theoretical opinions respecting Poetry. (*CL STC* II. 830)

> To the second edition he added a preface of considerable length; in which notwithstanding some passages of apparently a contrary import, he was understood to contend for the *extension of this style to poetry of all kinds,* and to reject as vicious and indefensible all phrases and forms of style that were not included in what he (unfortunately, I think, adopting an equivocal expression) called the language of *real* life. From this preface, prefixed to poems in which it was impossible to deny the presence of original genius, however mistaken its direction might be deemed, arose the whole long continued controversy. (*BL* 8–9)

Coleridge's critique of Wordsworth's principles in *Biographia Literaria* (1817), particularly in terms of the desire to write in 'the language of *real* life', is based largely on the grounds of his claim to make them universal, which Coleridge actively counters: 'in any sense this rule is applicable only to certain classes of poetry' (42). In the longer term, Coleridge's powerful entry into the reception history of the 'Preface' has the effect of distorting ongoing readings of it. In an article on Coleridge's response Don H. Bialostosky declares:[16]

> Coleridge's rhetoric has been so effective that it has not merely refuted the Preface but re-created it. His argument has drawn the bulk of subsequent critical commentary to the question of poetic diction, though that topic is subordinate in Wordsworth. (912)

As Bialostosky goes on to say of Wordsworth: 'what he is trying to do is not, like Coleridge, to prove a thesis about the *causes* of rustics' sentiments and language but to justify his choice of these subjects to exemplify human emotions' (915). Coleridge's detailed critique of Wordsworth's statement that there can be 'no essential difference' between the language of prose and metrical language means that the 'Preface' becomes entangled in a debate around the language of poetry, but this was only ever relevant to Wordsworth as a means of communicating feeling and human psychology most powerfully and directly.

Thus, at the very heart of the meta-narrative to the poems that the 'Preface' provides, there is a model of enlargement from the core principles of the earlier 'Advertisement,' that related *only to these particular poems*, into a much larger claim for an entire 'class of Poetry' – indeed into an entire redefinition of the language, form and subject of poetry itself. It is this *enlargement* of poetic principles from the particular to the universal that both Jeffrey and Coleridge object to – those aspects of the 'Preface' that function most like a 'manifesto' – since those who seek to resist the change of definition for Poetry recognise the danger that it represents to the prior model (a valid fear since it does eventually supplant it entirely). The two later critical interventions shift the focus of reception away from acceptance and assimilation of the original authorial aims to a highly sceptical denial and then a counter-reading of them.

Rezeptionsästhetik *and the Principles of the 'Preface'*

My purpose in drawing upon the approach of *rezeptionsästhetik* was to clear the ground – to try and understand the core principles of the 'Preface' in a fresh way. As we have already seen, such an approach is helpful in making it clear that in the twenty years following first publication that reception history involves three main phases of reading: an unproblematic acceptance of the author's intended aims; a resistance to those aims as a major challenge to the literary and social establishment; a problematizing of those aims in terms of poetic language.

In his account of the ways in which television viewers interpret representations on the screen, Stuart Hall (building on Jauss) adapts reception theory to mass communication. In a famous article entitled 'Encoding/Decoding' he notes three ways in which televisual discourse may be received: the *dominant-hegemonic position*; the *negotiated position*; and the *oppositional*.[17] In the first of these 'the viewer is *operating inside the dominant code*' (137) taking it at face value. The second involves a more complex interpretation. 'It accords the privileged position to the dominant definitions of events while reserving the right to make a more negotiated application to 'local conditions' (138). The third deliberately sets itself against the dominant code. Hall's account of the ways in which meaning is transformed across discourses is strongly centred upon the viewer (the reader) but also acknowledges that production is not a closed system but draws upon larger shared meanings so that 'the audience is both the "source" and the "receiver" of the television message' (130). He continues: 'Production and reception of the television message are not, therefore, identical, but they are related: they are differentiated moments within the totality' (130).

Such a model can easily be adapted to the reception of the 'Preface' for *Lyrical Ballads* in more than one way. First, Wordsworth's framing methods strongly present his ideas as requiring a negotiated position from the reader who must be willing to move outside the dominant mode of reading. In the 'Preface' he states: 'Now these men would establish a canon of criticism which the Reader will conclude he must utterly reject, if he wishes to be pleased with these volumes' (75). Second, Wordsworth's development of ideas for the prose 'Preface' over time occurs alongside and *in dialogue with* the reviews of his work (which we know he scrutinised carefully).[18] The cautiousness with which Wordsworth first presents his materials to the public means that between the brief anonymous 'Advertisement' of 1798 and the authored 'Preface' of 1800 there is the possibility of incorporating and building upon the comments of the reviewers (which themselves largely validated those core principles). We might speculate that if the initial reception of 1798 had not been so positive then Wordsworth might not have gone on to enlarge his ideas at all and the 'manifesto' might never have been written. However, with each accretion the volume moves more and more towards an *oppositional* model, making greater claims for itself and the new poetics. This in turn provokes opposition *to* it by those representing the dominant-hegemonic position as exemplified by Jeffrey – who begins his review with an assertion that there is no need for change: 'Poetry has this much, at least, in common with religion, that its standards were fixed long ago' (63).

We could go even further and suggest that the development of the volume over three different publications involves such a high level of self-conscious awareness of readership that the *nature of reception* becomes for Wordsworth an essential part of the core principles. Within the 1802 'Preface' Wordsworth refers to 'the Reader' *thirty-seven times* with a strong sense of anticipating the 'horizon of expectation'. He conceives of the relationship between Author and Reader as a kind of 'promise' or contract between them:

> It is to be supposed, that by the act of writing in verse an Author makes a formal engagement that he will gratify certain known habits of association; that he not only thus apprizes the Reader that certain classes of ideas and expressions will be found in his book, but that others will be carefully excluded. ... I will not take upon me to determine the exact import of the promise which by the act of writing in verse an Author, in the present day, makes to his Reader; but I am certain it will appear to many persons that I have not fulfilled the terms of an engagement thus voluntarily contracted. (*LB* 96)

Later in life Wordsworth becomes aggressively hostile towards critics of his poetry, famously turning away from the critical readership of his day (the PUBLIC) to an imagined future 'PEOPLE' in the 'Essay, Supplementary to the Preface,' 1815.[19] But the accumulating prose frames of 1798, 1800 and 1802 feed off and respond to their readership with a strong sense of whom they are trying to convert and how essential this is as part of the aims of the volume.

What are those aims? What core statements emerge for the collection in the full 'Preface' of 1800? In fact, after an extended qualifying statement at the start, loaded with various disclaimers, Wordsworth gets to the point quite explicitly:

> The principal object, then, which I proposed to myself in these Poems was to choose incidents and situations from common life, and to relate or describe them, throughout, as far as was possible, in a selection of language really used by men;

> and at the same time, to throw over them a certain colouring of imagination, whereby ordinary things should be presented to the mind in an unusual way;

> and further, and above all, to make these incidents and situations interesting by tracing in them, truly though not ostentatiously, the primary laws of our nature: chiefly, as regards the manner in which we associate ideas in a state of excitement.

> Low and rustic life was generally chosen because in that condition, the essential passions of the heart find a better soil ... and speak a plainer and more emphatic language; because in that condition of life our elementary feelings co-exist in a state of greater simplicity and, consequently, may be more accurately contemplated, and more forcibly communicated. (*Owen* 71)

Wordsworth is at his most Rousseauvian here. Those who have lived their lives in proximity to nature, and without the effects of civilisation acting upon them, are somehow purer than others, and 'elementary feelings co-exist in a state of greater simplicity'.[20] In other words, man is naturally good and the 'civilised' reader can be returned to a purer moral state – the essence of what it is to be human – by sharing the emotions and reading the language of such a being. Natural man can be 'more accurately contemplated' but also 'more forcibly communicated' to the reader.

Wordsworth goes on to assert the importance of his poetry 'having a worthy *purpose*' (72) and he provides two clear articulations of what that purpose is and how it is different from other poetry of the day:

> to follow the fluxes and refluxes of the mind when agitated by the great and simple affections of our nature . . . to sketch characters under the influence of less impassioned feelings . . . of which the elements are simple, belonging rather to nature than to manners, such as exist now, and will probably always exist . . .
>
> the feeling therein developed gives importance to the action and situation, and not the action and situation to the feeling. (73)

The collection is strongly psychological: interested in exploring a particular aspect of the mind by tracing the effects of deep emotion upon it, as well as depicting ordinary (but universal) activities and it strongly incorporates 'feeling' into its own ambitions for reception, directed towards its reader. Right at the heart of Wordsworthian principles, then, is an expressive but also an *empathetic* model for poetry. It makes the subject itself that of emotion under pressure but also extends this out by sympathetic association to the reader in a way that is crucial if the poems are to *achieve* their 'purpose'. Other elements – the choice of subject, the language and form – are employed only insofar as they support and reinforce this core concern.

In *Toward an Aesthetic of Reception*, Jauss describes the need for reception to be continuously active:

> For it is only through the process of its mediation that the work enters into the changing horizon-of-experience of a continuity in which the perpetual inversion occurs from simple reception to critical understanding; from passive to active reception, from recognised aesthetic norms to a new production that surpasses them. (19)

The concept of 'active reception' is crucial for any work of literature but what we see in the 'Preface' is that Wordsworth has a heightened awareness of this and builds it into the very heart of his principles. In other words, the 'Preface' does not just anticipate and seek to manipulate its reception; rather, a model of sympathetic identification of reader with subject and content is right at the heart of the poetics it advocates. Jauss notes of literature:

> It also can make possible a new perception of things by preforming the content of a new experience first brought to light in the form of literature. The relationship between literature and reader can actualise itself . . . in the ethical realm as a summons to reflection. (41)

This is exactly what Wordsworth attempts to do. His ultimate aim is to 'preform' the social and moral attitudes of his readers towards his lowly subjects not only in the poems but also out in the world and thus, in a way characteristic of the optimism of the 1790s, to transform the world, and society, by changing each individual from within.

Conclusion

A manifesto is, by its nature, introducing something new and forward-looking but it is also not entirely trustworthy and subject to change and interpretation by others. We don't always do what we state that we intend to do (as global politics repeatedly reminds us). This is worth remembering in relation to Wordsworth's 'Advertisement' of 1798 and 'Preface' of 1800 and 1802. On the one hand, we have seen that Wordsworth's prose explanation was partly at odds with both the original aims and motivation for the collection and with many of the poems contained in it. The joint nature of the venture (intellectually and philosophically if not in terms of contribution of material) was also immediately put under threat by the extent to which Wordsworth moved beyond shared principles and the 'Preface' is not a clear and well-ordered argument, its language containing many self-qualifying and indistinct elements – often at points where greatest clarity is needed. The open question of which poems are even definable as 'lyrical' ballads further muddies the water.

On the other hand, the 'Preface' is a declaration of intent that is charged with a strong desire to communicate directly to its readership now and in the future. Ultimately it extends far beyond the individual author to encompass the principles of a literary generation because it redefines poetry as a kind of living ('natural') alternative to philosophy – 'its object is truth carried alive into the heart by passion' (79) – that allows language to connect author to reader through feeling. Wordsworth's broader aims and intentions – to write for all in a way that all can understand; to redefine poetry as an effusive expression of individual power and feeling – end up vitally underpinning writing by later poets with whom he may have had little sympathy and who define themselves in, through and against him. When, in his definition of the role and function of the poet, Wordsworth declares that 'Poetry is the breath and finer spirit of all knowledge' (80) he anticipates Shelley in *A Defence of Poetry*. When he describes the Poet losing his sense of self in sympathy with others as he 'brings his feelings near to those of the persons whose feelings he describes, nay, for short spaces of time perhaps, to let himself slip into an entire delusion, and even confound and identify his own feelings with theirs' (78) he sounds remarkably like Keats in his *Letters* defining 'negative capability'. The debate around 'Simplicity' and 'Rudeness' in relation to the 1798 volume could just as well find its focus in a writer like John Clare – a writer unaware that he embodies Wordsworthian principles and one whose ungrammatical dialect writing Wordsworth himself may even have found vulgar.[21] In other words, the 'Preface' speaks not only on behalf of those for whom it is written but for poets yet to come. We can allow Coleridge to have the last word:

> Not only in the verses of those who have professed their admiration of his genius but even of those who have distinguished themselves by hostility to his theory, and depreciation of his writings are the impressions of his principles plainly visible. (*BL* 41)

Endnotes

1 Francis Jeffrey, 'Art. VIIII. Thalaba the Destroyer: A Metrical Romance. By Robert Southey', *The Edinburgh Review*, 1 (1802–03): 63–83; 65.

2 John E. Jordan, 'The Novelty of the Lyrical Ballads', in *Bicentenary Wordsworth Studies in Memory of John Alban Finch*, ed. Jonathan Wordsworth (Ithaca and London: Cornell University Press, 1970), 340–358; 349.

3 Unsigned (Robert Southey), 'Lyrical Ballads, with a Few Other Poems', *The Critical Review* (October 1798): 197–204; 201.

4 Robert Mayo, 'The Contemporaneity of the *Lyrical Ballads*', *PMLA*, 69.3 (1954): 486–522.

5 Hans Robert Jauss, *Toward an Aesthetics of Reception*, trans. Timothy Bahti (Minneapolis: University of Minnesota Press, 1982), 19.

6 Unsigned, 'Lyrical Ballads, with a Few Other Poems', *The Analytical Review*, 28.6 (December 1798): 583–587; 583.

7 Unsigned, 'Art VI. Lyrical Ballads, with other Poems: in Two Vols. By W. Wordsworth. Second Edition', *The British Critic*, 17 (February 1801): 364.

8 Unsigned Review, *New London Review*, I (1799): 33–35; 34.

9 John E. Jordan, *Why the Lyrical Ballads: The Background, Writing and Character of Wordsworth's 1798 Lyrical Ballads* (Berkeley and London: University of California Press, 1976), 98.

10 Unsigned, 'Art. XIX. Lyrical Ballads, with a Few Other Poems', *Monthly Review, or, Literary Journal* (June 1799): 202–210; 203.

11 Mary Wilson Gordon, *'Christopher North': A Memoir of John Wilson* (Edinburgh and London: Hamilton, Adams and Co., 1879), 28.

12 'Art VI. Lyrical Ballads', 125–131; 125.

13 Unsigned Review, *American Review and Literary Journal*, 2 (January 1802): 118–119; 119.

14 Rousseau's works, particularly *The Social Contract* and *Émile*, were key texts for the Revolution and he was honoured by the Revolutionary government.

15 Although the standard edition for this Cambridge Companion is the Oxford World Classics edition, ed. Fiona Stafford, this does not include the 'Preface' of 1800. Since my concern in this chapter is with the first published edition, here I am referencing this as reproduced in *Owen* 69.

16 Don H. Bialostosky, 'Coleridge's Interpretation of Wordsworth's Preface to Lyrical Ballads', *PMLA*, 93.5 (October 1978): 912–924.

17 Stuart Hall, 'Encoding/Decoding', in *Culture, Media, Language*, ed. Stuart Hall, Dorothy Hobson, Andrew Love and Paul Willis (Hutchinson: London, 1980), 128–138; 137.

18 See Wordsworth's letter to Sara Hutchinson of February – early March 1801 in which 'for Coleridge's entertainment' he humorously lists comparable positive and negative responses to the same poem in a collection (*Letters EY* 319).

19 Wordsworth famously ends the 'Essay Supplementary to the Preface' by stating: 'Still more lamentable is his error who can believe that there is any thing of divine infallibility in the clamour of that small though loud portion of the community, ever governed by factitious influence, which, under the name of the PUBLIC, passes itself, upon the unthinking for the PEOPLE. Towards the Public, the Writer hopes that he feels as much deference as it is entitled to: but to the People, philosophically characterised ... his devout respect, his reverence, is due' (*Owen* 214).

20 In *Émile*, Rousseau states: 'Let us lay it down as an incontestable maxim rule that the first movements of nature are always right; there is no original perversity in the human heart. There is not a single vice to be found in it of which it cannot be said how and whence it entered' (*Emile or On Education*, trans. Allan Bloom (London: Penguin Books, 1979), Book II, 92).

21 See Johanne Clare, *John Clare and the Bounds of Circumstance* (Kingston and Montreal: McGill-Queens University Press, 1986), 152.

CHAPTER 2

Collaboration, Domestic Co-Partnery and Lyrical Ballads

Polly Atkin

Lyrical Ballads is well established as a work of literary collaboration, co-conceived, co-authored and 'rooted in friendship'.[1] Jack Stillinger calls it 'the most famous co-authored book in English literature'.[2] The 'most famous' literary collaborators are of course Samuel Taylor Coleridge and William Wordsworth, 'twins almost in genius and mind' as Wordsworth phrases it in his *Prelude*.[3] However, the volume's various, complex print histories point to the role of multiple collaborators in creating the texts we know as *Lyrical Ballads*. This chapter begins with a re-examination of the original project of creating an anonymous, collaborative poetry collection, taking into account the 1798 print variants, and moves towards a wider examination of what collaboration may mean in the production of the 1798 and 1800 editions. In so doing, it reconsiders the role of literary friendships and influences, as well as the domestic processes of poetic production. More importantly, this chapter re-centres Dorothy Wordsworth as a key collaborator, drawing on Elizabeth Fay's conception of Wordsworth the poet as 'William and Dorothy Wordsworth combined'.[4] Nicola Healey calls *Lyrical Ballads* 'a symbol of their collaborative textual union'.[5] However, even in the introduction to the authoritative Cornell edition of *Lyrical Ballads*, Dorothy appears only as a companion, a copyist, and as a commentator on the publication prospects of the male poets' work. This chapter therefore follows on from the work of Fay and Healey in repositioning Dorothy as a principal creative partner, as 'part of William's writing self', as well as considering the importance of the presence of John Wordsworth at Dove Cottage during the production of the 1800 edition (Healey, 167).

Conjoint Proceedings

The back-and-forth of collaborative thinking is often unseen and goes unrecorded, leaving little evidence. As Lisa Ede and Andrea Lunsford recognise, even 'the meaning of the term *collaborative writing* is far from self-evident', arguing that scholarship has 'traditionally ignored or under-valued the numerous complex intellectual and social processes that consti-tute an important part of most writing activities'.[6] For literary criticism which revolves around 'traditional notions of creativity and originality', collaborative work provides a particular challenge.[7] There has been much focus in Romantic scholarship on attempting to unravel the work done by each of the two men on *Lyrical Ballads*, usually in terms of the authorship of the poems. Domsch highlights the uncertainty about 'the exact nature of collaboration, and the extent to which the collection was created according to a plan' which troubles reception and criticism of *Lyrical Ballads* (345). Attempting to titrate collaborative work into the work of individuals risks misunderstanding creative practice, confusing and con-flating authorship, ownership and instigation of intellectual property, and attribution of work.

The 1798 edition of *Lyrical Ballads* was published anonymously, with the intention that no reader would be able to uncover the authorship of the poems. Dividing ownership of parts of the volume into William's or Coleridge's is complicated by the print history of the volume, and the passing of copyright from Joseph Cottle of Bristol to J. and A. Arch of London mid-production. Verbal and non-verbal errors in the printed version of 1798 vary from the manuscript prepared for the printer (*Cornell LB* xii). Early, cancelled versions made under Cottle co-exist with the later corrected London versions. The editors of the Cornell edition of *Lyrical Ballads*, James Butler and Karen Green, note that 'Coleridge's contribu-tions to the 1798 edition of *Lyrical Ballads* vary according to the state of the copy consulted' (43–44). Still, the canonical 1798 edition contains four poems whose authorship is now attributed primarily to Coleridge ('The Rime of the Ancyent Marinere', 'The Foster-Mother's Tale', 'The Nightingale', 'The Dungeon'), and nineteen whose authorship is attrib-uted to William.

Four known copies – all with the Bristol imprint – contain the poem 'Lewti; or, The Circassian Love Chant', which in other copies was replaced by 'The Nightingale' (44). There is also extant 'a copy of the Bristol imprint in the British Library [which] contains "The Nightingale" … and, inserted before it, Thomas Beddoes' "Domiciliary Verses"' (44). Beddoes is not generally considered part of the collaborative production team, despite this rogue copy. Several culprits have been accused of producing this variant, including William, with an intention of replacing 'Lewti'; Cottle attempting to appease Beddoes; and Beddoes himself, who may have 'had this leaf printed to insert into his copy as part of a joke' (44). A 1971 facsimile edition reproduces a copy held by the British Museum which was 'one of those privately distributed and ... unique in its make-up' and contains both 'The Nightingale' and 'Lewti'.[8] G. H. Healey lists thirteen copies of this particular alternative version in existence; however, none of these variants was ever offered for sale to the general public: 'only with the London title-lead, the cancellans Table and "The Nightingale" was the book finally issued for publication and general sale' (LB 1798).

While the bare number of poems Coleridge submitted is many fewer than those by William, the balance of pages is not so uneven as those numbers suggest, due to the scope and length of Coleridge's contributions. The five pages of 'Lewti' were replaced by the seven pages of 'The Nightingale', while 'The Ancyent Marinere' commandeers the first fifty-one pages of the printed volume, approximately a quarter of the whole book (Cornell LB 44). It is also worth considering the order of the poems in the 1798 edition, with 'The Ancyent Marinere' given prime position, opening and setting the tone for the reader. It seems the 1798 edition at least attempts to give equal weighting to the two standard co-creators, who in the anonymous advertisement are referred to in one person, as the 'author'.

Some of the complications around the project of Lyrical Ballads can be elucidated through re-considering its origins. The project began with the plotting of 'The Ancyent Marinere'. William recorded his version of the events around its composition in The Fenwick Notes, under his recollections of the poem 'We Are Seven'.[9] According to William, 'The Ancyent Marinere' began very much as a joint composition, with the practical aim of paying for a shared excursion:

> In the Spring of the year 1798, he [Coleridge], my sister & myself started from Alfoxden ... and as our united funds were very small we agreed to defray the expense of the tour by writing a Poem to be sent to the New Monthly Magazine. (FN 2)

William recalls that while 'much the greatest part of the story was Mr. Coleridge's invention', some of it was definitely his. Examples he gives include the figure of the albatross and its role in the narrative, as well as 'the navigation of the ship by the dead men' (FN 2).

William notes how not only some of the ideas, but also some of the particular wording came from him, recalling how when they 'began the composition together on that to me memorable evening: I furnished two or three lines at the beginning of the poem' (*FN* 2). In what would now be dubbed a humblebrag, William calls these 'trifling contributions', and presents the handing of the project wholly into Coleridge's hands as stemming from a realisation of his own poetic limitations:

> as we endeavoured to proceed conjointly . . . our respective manners proved so widely different that it would have been quite presumptuous in me to do anything but separate from an undertaking upon which I could only have been a clog. (*FN* 3)

In his notes to the 1834 edition, Coleridge marks the following lines as entirely William's: 'And thou art long, and lank, and brown / As is the ribbed sea-sand' (*PW STC* I. i. 391). He concedes:

> For the last two lines of this stanza, I am indebted to Mr. Wordsworth. It was on a delightful walk from Nether Stowey to Dulverton, with him and his sister, in the autumn of 1797, that this poem was planned, and in part composed. (*PW STC* I. i. 391)

In this phrasing, it seems that while William supplied these particular lines, the planning and composition may have been an individual project of Coleridge's undertaken while merely in the company of the others. In the *Fenwick Notes* William is keen to point out those contributions he feels Coleridge has 'slipt out of his mind' and thus omitted from literary history, and to reposition himself as co-congenitor of the poem (*FN* 3). These might include the phrase 'alone on a wide wide sea' which is written in William's hand in the Racedown Notebook (*DCMS* 11) (*PW STC* I. i. 391). Similarly, there is a confluence of phrasing between the closing lines of 'The Ancyent Marinere' – the 'sadder and a wiser man' – and an abandoned 1798 ending of William's 'The Ruined Cottage', in which the listener considers himself 'a better and a wiser man' for hearing that other old man's tale (*PW STC* I. i. 401). This flow of ideas, images and influences is neither abnormal in William and Coleridge's wider creative practice, nor remarkable or unusual in poetic composition more generally. Gene Ruoff refers to this interflow between the two men as 'intertextual genetics'.[10] It only becomes significant when unravelling responsibility and ownership is prioritized, as it has been in critical consideration of the *Lyrical Ballads*.

Some of this blurring of authorship can be seen in other poems of the same period written by the two men. The editor of the Bollingen edition of Coleridge's *Poetical Works*, J. C. C. Mays, notes how Coleridge 'had been involved in continuing and rewriting several of [William's] poems' in

the winter of 1797–1798' (*PW STC* I. i. 453). For example, in February
1798, Coleridge's poem 'Modification of *Translation of a Celebrated Greek
Song* by William Wordsworth' was published in *The Morning Post*. Published under the pseudonym 'PUBLICOLA', Mays concludes 'that the
variants in the *Morning Post* version are due to [Coleridge's] intervention'
(I. i. 449). Mays notes the influence of both William and John Thelwall on
Coleridge's 'Frost at Midnight', written the same month: 'the beginnings
of the poem might lie in an early version of Thelwall's poem to his son,
"To the infant Hampden" . . . but the poem also mingles enthusiasms
deriving from conversations with WW' (452–453). He even goes so far as
to suggest '"Frost at Midnight" might be said to be [Coleridge's] version of
a Wordsworthian poem that [William] was then only on the verge of
writing' (I. i. 453).

The interflow of ideas seems to have been particularly central to
Coleridge's poetic output. When Mays writes that 'The Ancyent Marinere' 'was begun with WW', he adds 'that is, it began as a collaboration in the same form as "The Three Graves", i.e. a poem which
originated with an idea of William's, but which was taken over and
completed by Samuel' (I. i. 365–356). 'Lewti' is another 'reworking [by
Coleridge] of a schoolboy poem by William, expanded and re-figured to
refer to Coleridge's biography (I. i. 457). Butler and Green refer to
'Lewti' as a poem 'in which Coleridge re-wrote and nearly tripled the
length of Wordsworth's "Beauty and Moonlight, and Ode, Fragment"'
(*Cornell LB* 44). The 111-line version published in *The Morning Post* in
April 1798 is a blending of both poets' work by Coleridge. Again it was
published under a pseudonym, NICAS ERYTHROEUS, which was
also used for 'The Old Man of the Alps'. Mays records that 'both
poems appear to be reworkings of WW juvenilia revised to different
extents' by Coleridge, reducing any claim Coleridge might have to
authorial ownership of either (*PW STC* I. i. 444). 'Lewti' presents an
interesting case model for thinking about co-labour on these poems, as
it was withdrawn from the canonical version of *Lyrical Ballads*. Its
replacement, 'The Nightingale', is less obviously a version of William's
work, but as Lucy Newlyn notes 'also participates in a dialogue' with
his poetry and ideas, with Paul Magnuson calling it 'one of his most
Wordsworthian poems'.[11] In this sense, all of the poems Coleridge
included in the *Lyrical Ballads* can be said to be co-authored with
William, with a great deal of the creative impulse also originating
with him.

How far the feed went both ways is hard to quantify. Mays' note on 'We Are Seven' may serve as a summary of the futility of trying to disentangle the work and ideas of William and Coleridge:

> The present single stanza stands for an entire category of assistance contributed by C to WW's poetry that is not as easily quantifiable. Other stanzas and revisions are in his hand in WW's mss, but he never claimed them, nor did WW specify him as their author. (*PW STC* I. i. 515)

Mays concludes, inarguably, that 'in general, in ways that have long been recognized, the relation between WW and C cannot be measured by detached passages but is symbiotic and entire' (I. i. 515). Daniel Robinson similarly refers to their collaboration as a symbiosis, adding that 'although they co-wrote only one or two poems' the two men 'would be a presence in each other's work as long as they both lived'.[12]

The expanded 1800 edition contains five poems by Coleridge, with his 'Love' replacing William's badly reviewed 'The Convict'. 'The Ancyent Marinere' is edited in response to criticism, and its position shunted to twenty-third. Meanwhile, William's contribution grows to include the first version of the famous 'Preface', and fifty-six poems, spreading the collection over two volumes. More importantly, William is now named as the author. Coleridge's poetic contributions are listed in the 'Preface' and attributed anonymously to 'a Friend' (*Cornell LB* 741). In 1802 William extends the 'Preface', adds the 'appendix on poetical diction' to further guide the critical reader, and in 1815 adds a 'supplementary essay'.

It is not surprising that many critics have hence made a distinction between the 1798 *Lyrical Ballads* as a work of collaboration, and the later editions as authored by William. Robinson claims the 1798 edition 'is the only *Lyrical Ballads* that may be said to be Wordsworth and Coleridge's *Lyrical Ballads*'.[13] This seems to follow Coleridge's own lead. In a letter to Francis Wrangham in December 1800, Coleridge reports that Wordsworth 'has even now sent off the last sheet of the second Volume of his Lyrical Ballads' (*CL STC* I. 658). James Chandler takes this as a sign that all collaboration has ended, and the men are 'no longer partners'.[14] Later, in the *Biographia Literaria*, Coleridge reconstructs the situation around the production of the 1800 edition as clearly placing prime authorship with William:

> Mr. Wordsworth's industry had proved so much more successful, and the number of his poems so much greater, that my compositions, instead of forming a balance, appeared rather an interpolation of heterogeneous matter.[15]

Michael Gamer implies that the shift in weighting and the naming of William as author in the 1800 edition has more to do with William's new awareness of 'literary property, publication and bookselling' after the copyright problems surrounding the 1798 printing, than to do with any creative schism with Coleridge.[16] Gamer summarises that 'the task of re-collecting *Lyrical Ballads* also converted him into a writer determined to maintain critical control over his texts and over the authorial self projected through them' (121–122).

It is easy from the Wordsworth siblings' perspective to see the 1800 edition as essentially William's work. They seem to work day after day in the summer and autumn of 1800 to prepare the second edition, while Coleridge is contributing little or nothing. Dorothy writes on 17 October that 'Coleridge had done nothing for the LB', and on 22 October, 'Coleridge came into dinner. He had done nothing' (*DWJ* 27–28).[17] There seems no bad feeling about this at the time. The ensuing sentence states 'we were very merry', which belies the sense that there was a deep resentment. At this time, Coleridge certainly considered the volume as conceptually collaborative work beyond the simplistic measuring of poetic output. As Stillinger argues, the 'Preface' might have been published under William's name, but it 'grew out of mutual conversation', like the rest of the project (71). At the time, Coleridge writes to Daniel Stuart that 'The Preface contains our joint opinions on Poetry' (*CL STC* I. 627). To Robert Southey, two years later, Coleridge affirms the 'Preface' as 'half a child of my own Brain / & so arose out of Conversations, so frequent, that with few exceptions we could scarcely either of us perhaps positively say, which first started any particular Thought' (*CL STC* II. 830). Stillinger takes this as evidence that the 1800 *Lyrical Ballads* is every bit as much a 'multiply-authored book' as the 1798 edition, moreover adding that it produced 'a multiply-authored preface of enduring critical importance' (71).

Conversely, Dorothy's letters imply she thought of the book as primarily William's, with some co-authored pieces, even in 1798. Of the famous co-creation of the Mariner, she simply writes in November 1797: 'William and Coleridge [are] employing themselves in laying the plan of a ballad, to be published with some pieces of William's' (*Letters EY* 194). William produces new poems quickly, writing to Cottle in April 1798: 'I have gone on very rapidly adding to my stock of poetry' (*Letters EY* 215). Dorothy repeatedly refers to *Lyrical Ballads* in letters at this time as 'William's Poems', though this is predominantly when presenting them as a symbol of creative success, so it may reflect more on what she wanted to present to the recipients of the letters than what she really believed about the ownership of the project. She writes, for example, to their brother Richard in May 1798: 'William has sold his poems very advantageously – he is to receive the money when the printing is completed' (*Letters EY* 219). She does not mention co-authorship, or the poems being published in a shared volume.

Literary Co-Partnery

For Robinson the 1798 *Lyrical Ballads* is 'if not a true collaborative, a shared endeavour' which 'the two men worked on as "joint labourers"' ('Wordsworth and Coleridge's *Lyrical Ballads*' 169). However, it is not only William and Coleridge who are working on these poems and helping them reach their conclusions. At various stages of production, they are read aloud to friends, whose comments are used to edit and redraft the poems, much as a contemporary creative writing workshop functions. For example, William's doubts about his capacity to work with Coleridge on 'The Ancyent Marinere' seem to have grown 'when it was read to Hazlitt [which] brought the divergence into the open' (*PW STC* I. i. 366). William's note to 'The Ancyent Marinere' also raises the question of wider collaboration and influence on both the poem, and the project of *Lyrical Ballads*. He recalls the idea behind 'The Ancyent Marinere' came from 'a dream, as Mr. Coleridge said, of his friend Mr. Cruikshank' (*FN* 2). His own suggestion of the albatross came from reading Shelvocke's *Voyages* (*FN* 2). These details highlight the difficulty in claiming ownership over any one of the ideas, as Mays argues: 'the conscious use of books of travel is particularly evident in the earlier sections of the poem, but there are debts of every kind and degree of significance, many of them unconscious' (*PW STC* I. i. 368). Details about the composition of some of the other ballads hint at the interflow of ideas and phrases between various people. For example, William notes that the last stanza of his 'The Idiot Boy' which 'was the foundation of the whole' was 'reported to be by my dear friend Thomas Poole' (*FN* 10).

Felicity James makes a case for consideration of the roles of Thelwall and Lamb in the collaborative atmosphere that feeds into *Lyrical Ballads*, noting how while Lamb 'has always been acknowledged as an important friend of Wordsworth . . . his contribution to the poetry has also remained relatively little discussed'.[18] Sharon Ruston has built on earlier work by Roger Sharrock to argue for the influence of Humphrey Davy on *Lyrical Ballads*, as well as on 'Romantic-period culture, both literary and scientific' more widely.[19] Davy proofread the 1800 edition, and the extent of his influence on the project, and particularly on the 1800 and 1802 'Prefaces', is now being recognised. Interestingly, for a discussion of what collaboration might mean for such a project, it should be noted that although Coleridge and Southey met Davy in person in 1799, Davy and Wordsworth did not meet until 1804. Prior to that, all their joint labour was managed through reading and writing: letters, manuscripts and the published volumes (Ruston 21). Meanwhile, Coleridge dreamed of Davy living with them in 'a little colony', and being fully part of the poetic collective (*CL STC* I. 556).

The greatest influence on the volume, aside from William and Coleridge, must be attributed to Dorothy Wordsworth. Dorothy is present during the whole walk on which 'The Ancyent Marinere' is proposed and begun. She is part of the core 'mutual conversation' of the collaboration: a collective group walking, thinking and creating from the beginning of the project to its end. Evidence to consider Dorothy an active collaborator in the composition of *Lyrical Ballads* includes her presence during important discussions and conversations; her presence during the incidents that inspired the poems; her role in writing down the work; the use of her journals to record incidents, and to source key images and phrases in the poems, by both William and Coleridge; and her vital role in all of Williams' poetry – in giving him poetic vision – shared for a time by Coleridge. The second half of this chapter will question how far we can trace Dorothy's role in the planning and production of *Lyrical Ballads*, and her role as one part of the sibling co-construction, 'The Poet Wordsworth', before finally considering whether this construct might be made of three siblings, not two.

The role of Dorothy's journals in the composition of William's poems has long been acknowledged. William's ardent Victorian admirers, such as Stopford Brooke, favoured Dorothy's journals as 'records' from which grew 'the roots ... of his most sensitive poems.'[20] William Knight uses the phrase 'literary co-partnery' to describe William and Dorothy's collaborative working practices.[21] He notes how 'many sentences in the journals present a curious resemblance to words and phrases which occur in the poems', concluding 'the co-partnery may have extended to more than the common use of the same MS' (Knight I. ix). Edmund Lee described Dorothy as 'a moulding and educating power' on William, and recognised the literary importance of how 'they read and thought and talked together'.[22] This strong influential relationship was so accepted that by 1927 Catherine MacDonald Maclean was able to call Dorothy 'the most poetical woman of her generation'.[23] Thomas De Quincey laid the groundwork for an understanding of Dorothy as instrumental to her brother's work within her own lifetime – so that 'the admirers and the worshippers through every age of this great poet, are become equally her debtors' – but also as subject to internalised sexism, suggesting she self-restrained her own creativity 'in obedience to the decorum of her sex and age'.[24] Coleridge wrote famously in August 1833 that she was 'a Woman of Genius, as well as manifold acquirements, and but for the absorption of her whole Soul in her Brother's fame and writings would, perhaps, in a different style have been as great a Poet as Himself' (*CL STC* VI. 959).

The prevailing notion that Dorothy was oppressed by her closeness to William – that, as Harriet Martineau suggested in 1861, 'she had sacrificed herself to aid and indulge her brother' – underpins much of her appearance in scholarship.[25] Even where her creativity is acknowledged, it is most often as a '"hidden" role in the collective authorship from which William Wordsworth's public work emerged.'[26] Healey notes that in portraying her as 'fully invest[ing] her life and identity in her brother' critics tend to follow De Quincey in 'emphasiz[ing] the *negative* element of this', which in turn has 'nullified rigorous critical engagement with her work' (171–172). This is particularly apparent in considerations of the production of *Lyrical Ballads*.

Healey posits that 'critical fascination with the collaboration of William Wordsworth and Coleridge may have caused Dorothy's influence to become ... sidelined' where *Lyrical Ballads* is concerned (167). Domsch corrects his own fascination with *Lyrical Ballads* as a 'joint production, a collaboration of *two* minds who drift apart at the same moment that they fertilize each other's thoughts' (357) with a parenthetical nod to Dorothy: '1798 was a meeting of two minds (three, since one should acknowledge the multi-faceted influence of Dorothy Wordsworth)' (346). He knows one should acknowledge Dorothy's multifaceted influence, yet to do so is rare. Even Newlyn's 'first literary biography of the Wordsworths' creative collaboration' tends to sideline Dorothy.[27] Newlyn positions Dorothy as one of three equal partners in the creation of the 1798 *Lyrical Ballads*: 'the names of Coleridge, Dorothy and William are missing from the title page – but all three writers were involved in collaboration and there was no competition for ownership' (62). Despite this 'partnership in writing', she still gives William and Coleridge priority as forming 'a collaboration which would transform English poetry' (44).

In *Becoming Wordsworthian* Fay called for a reassessment of 'Wordsworth' the poet as 'a consensual being composed of William and Dorothy':

the result of 'the collaborative artistic endeavour on which the Wordsworths embark when they decide to live together' (6–7). This echoes Lee's
assertion that 'she *was* him – a second pair of eyes to see, a second and
more delicate intuition to discern, a second heart to enter into all that
came before their mutual observation' (23). Fay conceives of the Wordsworths as undertaking 'a poetic project which, for the Wordsworths, is the
making both of poetic texts *and* of the poetic life' (2). Fay dubs this poetic
project – both creative, created and 'self-composing' – the 'Wordsworthian
Life' (16).

Fay's theory of 'the Wordsworthian Life' explicitly draws on Alan Liu's
cognitive mapping of the 'worlding' of Grasmere as operating over two
intersecting axes, representing the four compass directions:

> Poetic Composition (William) stands at the north point; Housework
> (Dorothy) at the south; and Textual Work and Walking in Nature at the
> west and east.[28]

In his spatial construction of this 'dome of labour', Fay argues, Liu not
only leaves out 'conversation and social visits . . . [but] also leaves out the
daily activity of Dorothy's own writing, its process and concerns' (19). He
does, however, place 'Walking' and 'Housework' on the same level as
'Textual Work' and 'Poetic Composition', despite the gendering of these
activities through fixing their association with William or Dorothy. These
four activities that Liu places at opposing compass points are in fact deeply
interconnected, and impossible to separate into the role of one person or
another. The housework – the literal making of home – allows a centre
from which to walk out into nature, which enables the poetic composition
(which takes place while walking, mostly to and fro), which is written
down to become poetry inscribed on a page (the textual work), back in the
home. This textual work in Dorothy's life seems an intrinsic element of her
housework. Anne Wallace notes how this is reflected in Dorothy's textual
output:

> In Dorothy Wordsworth's journals, and in the poetry of her commonplace
> book . . . women's domestic work reappears as public business, cognate with
> the work of the male poet; and women themselves may speak and compose
> as they walk.[29]

For Fay the creation of poetry becomes 'domestic routine', combining the
work of the housewife/gardener with the work of the poet in one performative, collaborative role (26). Fay thereby allows a way of examining
the work of brother and sister as part of the same process, continuous

through acts of housework, gardening, walking (often perceived as separate to the literary process), and the more straightforwardly literary acts of composing poetry and writing journals.

Healey builds on this to make an extensive case for Dorothy's involvement in the 'joint labour' of the ballads, and for her own awareness of her role as part of an 'entire collaborative literary process', arguing that Dorothy 'understood herself as half of the Wordsworthian enterprise' (176). Healey pays close attention to the language Dorothy uses to describe the work she is doing. Dorothy's own perception of her collaborative role can be traced in her shifts between the use of the single person pronoun 'I' and 'we' in both directions (177). Although she often talks of shared work done in partnership (e.g. 'We corrected the last sheet'; 'Wm & I were employed all the morning in writing an addition to the preface') this shifts into and out of her solo work (*DWJ* 24). She makes a keen distinction when referring to William's work between 'composing' and 'altering', and in her own between 'altering' and 'copying', where the creative element diminishes with each grade. William is seen to be 'composing' or 'working at' poems, followed by a process of 'altering' and 'writing', which often involves reading the poem aloud and taking on comments. Dorothy herself is often 'writing', also 'altering': never composing. It seems the word 'writing' for Dorothy is used literally: it means putting marks on paper and does not cover the aspects of composing and drafting, as it tends to be used to do now. On 2 October 1800, she writes, 'I wrote – the last sheet of notes & preface', and it is unclear whether she means she wrote out (as in copied) or whether there is altering and editorial input involved (*DWJ* 23).[30] Either way it is clear from her journals that the process of composition involves both of them. Over February and March 1802, when Dorothy writes, 'William left me at work altering some passage of the Pedlar', and later, 'we sate by the fire in the evening and read the Pedlar over' it paints a picture of a creative partnership; two people working towards a shared goal, in conversation (*DWJ* 68, 76). In Healey's reading, such entries show that while Dorothy may be the 'willing amanuen[sis]' (Stillinger 71) she is so often reduced to, she also 'constructs herself as primary editor of William's compositions in progress' (Healey 176), noting the number of instances in which she records how her opinion on a poem or its subject altered the finished product. More importantly, at times 'Dorothy presents herself overtly as co-author of William's work announcing his literary endeavour as a shared industry and vision' (Healey 176). Bushell argues for the recognition of the process of reading aloud as collaborative in itself:

> Whilst Dorothy records no active input on her part, the process of reading
> his work to her stimulates action in the poet. In this way the act of reading
> aloud is a critical process in which they are both involved.[31]

This interflow between poetry and journal is not limited to William and
Dorothy. Mays notes the confluences or 'coincidences of observation'
between many lines in 'Christabel' and Dorothy's Alfoxden Journal,
suggesting that in those early days of the *Lyrical Ballads* project her journal
and the practice of reading aloud from it were functioning in a similar way
for Coleridge as they did for her brother (*PW STC* I. i. 483). Her journal
thus can be seen as an essential part of the drafting and compositional
process for both men. Knight picked out the image from the Alfoxden
Journal (7 March 1798) of a leaf, questioning 'did this suggest the lines in
Christabel?' (13), indicating that early Wordsworthians recognised this
co-partnery as an essential part of the construction of *Lyrical Ballads*.
A letter to the printers in July 1800 with instructions for the new edition
of *Lyrical Ballads* is co-written by all three of them. Griggs notes it is 'entirely
in Coleridge's handwriting, except for two brief passages written by
Dorothy' (*CL STC* I. 593). William contributes a note on the address sheet
with orders to 'being the printing immediately' (*CL STC* I. 592–593). The
other sheets submitted over the course of the summer switch between
Coleridge's hand and Dorothy's for the most part. Similarly, Butler and
Green note edits to the manuscript of William's poem 'Lines left upon a seat
in a yew tree' in the hand of Coleridge: 'In MS 1798/1800 STC writes …
'Now wild, to bend its dark arms to form a circling shade' please to print it
'With its dark arms to form a circling Bower" (*Cornell LB* 48). The full
passage is then written out by Dorothy. These kinds of editorial comments
can be read as part of an ongoing conversation about the best version of the
lines: a conversation not just between Samuel and William, but including
Dorothy, as a creative partner, not just a scribe.

Silent Co-partner

Finally, I want to consider the role of John Wordsworth in *Lyrical Ballads*
as another hidden body in the literary co-partnery. In 'Home at Grasmere'
William writes of the 'happy band' (Line 874, 94) that makes up his home
as including himself, Dorothy, and the 'brother of our hearts' (Line 870,
92) [Coleridge], but also 'a never-resting Pilgrim of the Sea' (Line 866, 92)
[John Wordsworth] and the 'Sisters of our hearts' (Line 869, 92) [Mary,
Joanna and Sara Hutchinson].[32] When Fay writes of Wordsworth's

'sibling companion', she clearly means Dorothy, who, if construed as a model for dwelling, can throw William into relief as incorrigible wanderer:

> the Poet who is completed by his sibling companion, the poet of pastoral lyric and vision, is always threatened by the spectre of the solitary poet who walks pastoral paths in spiritual crisis, but he is also always – through his ties to the sister-maiden – within safety. (8)

If the sibling companion were – or includes – John, this false dichotomy is collapsed. Dorothy famously described the Wordsworth siblings as 'squandered abroad' as John set sail for Barbados in 1789, and it was the siblings' intention that John would join them in Grasmere permanently, completing their home and the 'happy band' (*Letters EY* 16). Like Dorothy, John is an often-hidden companion at key moments in the poems and for the poems. Moreover, John is central both to William's increasingly maritime poetic imagination, and to his ability to live the creative life he and Dorothy are building. John was with William and Coleridge when they first saw the cottage to rent in Grasmere that became William and Dorothy's home, and that ongoing home was to be founded on the proceeds of John's overseas trades. More importantly, if we are to consider the collaborative aspect of *Lyrical Ballads* to be one of mutual conversation as part of daily domestic creativity, John's presence in Grasmere during the construction of the 1800 edition – a time eulogized by William and Dorothy after his death as those 'blessed months' – cannot be ignored (*Letters EY* 547).

Samuel Baker calls for an understanding of John and William as 'dynamically interrelated through . . . twin offices of world sailor and island poet', represented in Wordsworth's poetry as 'dual engines of mutual advancement'.[33] Baker presents Wordsworth's home as haunted by his circumnavigating brother's lack of home, and the 'parallelism between their projects' (112). In this reading William's poetic project, his 'world-making ambition for his project of a moralizing literary culture', both 'correlated with, and compensated for, his brother's navigation of the treacherous maritime sphere of circulation' (112). Richard Matlak similarly makes a strong case for the pervasiveness of the influence of John on his brother's writing.[34] William's interest in the sea and seafaring as poetic subject that infuses *Lyrical Ballads* was both personal and political, local and national, and steeped in dialogue with John.

Dorothy's letters show that John not only hoped to contribute to the home financially, but did so in practical ways during his visit, helping with building, gardening and general homemaking. If we are to follow Fay,

Wallace and others in considering the literary work of the Wordsworth household indivisible from the 'domestic' work, then in 1800 John was part of that literary co-partnery, and was intended to become even more intrinsic in the future. Indeed, Dorothy regularly refers to one of the beds in the house as 'John's Bed' long after his visit (*Letters EY* 361). 'John's Bed' is echoed in 'John's Grove', the name associated with the fifth of the 'Poems on the Naming of Places', 'When first I journey'd Hither'. This was not completed and not included with the set in *Lyrical Ballads*, but is often paired critically with 'The Brothers' for thematic reasons, and links William's pre-occupation with seafaring figures with his domestic circumstances. It describes a process wherein John, by pacing, inscribes one of his 'own deep paths' in a fir grove.[35] For this William dubs John a 'silent poet' (l.88, 566). It is his 'watchful heart' and 'eye practised like a blind man's touch' (echoing William's portrayals of Dorothy) as well as his habits formed from years at sea which enable him to make this poem-path (ll.9–10, 563).

Coleridge had noted these sensitive qualities, writing to Dorothy after he, William and John visited Grasmere together in 1799: 'Your Br. John is one of you: a man who hath solitary usings of his own Intellect, deep in feeling, with a subtle Tact, a swift instinct of Truth and Beauty' (*CL STC* I. 543). Later, as Wallace notes, Coleridge wrote of him in his notebooks as a 'loss to "*the concern*"': the Grasmere household to which John had intended to retire with his profits'.[36] I would suggest 'the concern' is more than the household, and more than even the sense of the creative household referred to here, but the whole project of the Wordsworthian Life with all it entails and all its promise. Although there may be an element of confirmation bias in all their assumptions about John, they certainly saw him as someone who would fit well into their 'corporate household'. Wallace sees 'Dorothy and Mary walking (an agent of composition for the Wordsworths)' in John's Grove in 1802 as epitomizing 'the encompassing of domestic and poetic labo[urs] in a single corporate household effort' (106).

While *Lyrical Ballads* has long been recognised as an important work of creative collaboration and co-authorship, indivisible into individual labour, the understanding of who was involved in that labour has been limited by cultural and critical pre-occupations. Perhaps it is time to stop trying to divide up the parts, but to recognise the full extent of the co-mingling of work that went into *Lyrical Ballads*, and the full cast of co-partners who made it.

Endnotes

1 Sebastian Domsch, 'William Wordsworth and Samuel Taylor Coleridge, *Lyrical Ballads* (1798, 1800)', in *Handbook of British Romanticism,* ed. Ralf Haekel (Berlin: De Gruyter, 2017), 344–359; 344.

2 Jack Stillinger, *Multiple Authorship and the Myth of Solitary Genius* (Oxford: Oxford University Press, 1991), 69.

3 William Wordsworth, 'The Prelude' (1805), in *The Thirteen-Book Prelude by William Wordsworth,* ed. Mark L. Reed, 2 vols. (Ithaca: Cornell, 1991), I. 6. 263.

4 Elizabeth A. Fay, *Becoming Wordsworthian: A Performative Aesthetic* (Amherst: University of Massachusetts Press, 1995), 3.

5 Nicola Healey, *Dorothy Wordsworth and Hartley Coleridge: The Poetics of Relationship* (London: Palgrave Macmillan, 2012), 145.

6 Lisa S. Ede and Andrea A. Lunsford, *Singular Texts/Plural Authors: Perspectives on Collaborative Writing* (Carbondale: Southern Illinois University Press, 1992), 14.

7 Ede and Lunsford, 'Collaborative Authorship and the Teaching of Writing', in *The Construction of Authorship: Textual Appropriation in Law and Literature,* ed. Martha Woodmansee and Peter Jaszi (Durham and London: Duke University Press, 1994), 417–438; 418.

8 'Note', *Lyrical Ballads 1798: William Wordsworth and Samuel Taylor Coleridge* (Menston: The Scholar Press, 1971), n.p. This copy was owned by Robert Southey and includes his notes about the cancellation.

9 William Wordsworth, *The Fenwick Notes of William Wordsworth,* ed. Jared Curtis (London: Bristol Classical Press, 1993), 2. Hereafter referred to as *FN.*

10 Gene Ruoff, *Wordsworth and Coleridge: The Making of the Major Lyrics, 1802–1804* (New Brunswick and Brighton: Rutgers University Press, 1989), 17.

11 Lucy Newlyn, *Coleridge, Wordsworth, and the Language of Allusion* (Oxford: Clarendon Press, 1986), 45–48; Paul Magnuson, *Coleridge and Wordsworth: A Lyrical Dialogue,* (Princeton: Princeton University Press, 1988), 136.

12 Daniel Robinson, *William Wordsworth's Poetry* (London and New York: Continuum International Publishing Group, 2010), 10.

13 Daniel Robinson, 'Wordsworth and Coleridge's *Lyrical Ballads',* in *The Oxford Handbook of William Wordsworth,* ed. Richard Gravil and Daniel Robinson (Oxford: Oxford University Press, 2015), 168–185; 169.

14 James Chandler, *Wordsworth's Second Nature: A Study of the Poetry and Politics* (Chicago: University of Chicago Press, 1984), 247.

15 Samuel Taylor Coleridge, *Biographia Literaria,* ed. Henry Nelson Coleridge, 2 vols. (London: William Pickering, 1847), II. 3.

16 Michael Gamer, *Romanticism, Self-Canonization, and the Business of Poetry* (Cambridge: Cambridge University Press, 2017), 121.

17 It should be noted that on 25 July 1800 STC wrote to Humphrey Davy that WW was 'a lazy fellow' in getting to work (*CL STC* I. 611).

18 Felicity James, 'Wordsworth and Literary Friendship', in *The Oxford Handbook of William Wordsworth,* 65–80; 74.

19 Sharon Ruston, *Creating Romanticism: Case Studies in the Literature, Science and Medicine of the 1790s* (Basingstoke: Palgrave, 2013), 20.

20 Stopford A. Brooke, *Dove Cottage: Wordsworth's Home from 1800–1808* (London: Macmillan and Co., 1890), 28.

21 William Knight, ed., *Journals of Dorothy Wordsworth*, 2 vols. (London: Macmillan and Co, 1904), I. xii.

22 Edmund Lee, *Dorothy Wordsworth: The Story of a Sister's Love* (London: James Clarke & Co, 1886), 21–22.

23 Catherine MacDonald Maclean, *Dorothy and William Wordsworth* (Cambridge: Cambridge University Press, 1927), 22.

24 Thomas De Quincey, 'Lake Reminiscences, from 1807–1830, by The English Opium-Eater, No.1', in *The Works of De Quincey*, ed. Grevel Lindop and others, 21 vols. (London: Pickering and Chatto, 2000–2003), vol. I, ed. Julian North (2003), 52.

25 Harriet Martineau, 'Lights of the English Lake District', *Atlantic Monthly*, 7 (1861): 541–558; 545.

26 Tilar J. Mazzeo, *Plagiarism and Literary Property in the Romantic Period* (Philadelphia: University of Pennsylvania Press, 2007), 69.

27 Newlyn, *All in Each Other* (Oxford: Oxford University Press, 2013), 11.

28 Alan Liu, 'On the Autobiographical Present: Dorothy Wordsworth's Grasmere Journals', *Criticism*, 26 (1984): 115–137; 117.

29 Anne Wallace, '"Inhabited Solitudes": Dorothy Wordsworth's Domesticating Walkers', *Nordlit*, 1 (1997): n.p.

30 For an example of composing versus altering, see 28 October 1800: 'Wm could not compose much fatigued himself with altering' (*DWJ* 29).

31 Sally Bushell, *Re-reading the Excursion: Narrative, Response and the Wordsworthian Dramatic Voice* (Aldershot: Ashgate, 2002), 120–121.

32 William Wordsworth, 'Home at Grasmere', in *Home at Grasmere, Part First, Book First, of the Recluse, by William Wordsworth*, ed. Beth Darlington (Ithaca: Cornell University Press, 1977), MSB, 38–106.

33 Samuel Baker, *Written on the Water: British Romanticism and the Maritime Empire of Culture* (Charlottesville: University of Virginia Press, 2010), 113.

34 Richard E. Matlak, *Deep Distresses: William Wordsworth, John Wordsworth, Sir George Beaumont: 1800–1808* (Cranberry, NJ: Associated University Presses, 2003), 18.

35 William Wordsworth, 'When first I journeyed hither', in *Poems, in Two Volumes, and Other Poems, 1800–1807, by William Wordsworth*, ed. Jared Curtis (Ithaca: Cornell University Press, 1983), Line 82, 566.

36 Anne D. Wallace, 'Home at Grasmere Again: Revising the Family in Dove Cottage', in *Literary Couplings: Writing Couples, Collaborators, and the Construction of Authorship*, ed. Marjorie Stone and Judith Thompson (Madison: University of Wisconsin Press, 2006), 103–123; 106. Emphasis in original. In an entry dated 8 April 1805, Coleridge writes, 'Now it was next to certain that you would in a few years settle in your native hills and be verily one of the *Concern!*' (*CN STC* II. 2529).

CHAPTER 3

Coleridgean Contributions

Tim Fulford

By 1802, Coleridge had begun to suspect what the next thirty years would confirm – that there was a 'radical Difference' between Wordsworth's conception of poetry and his own (*CL STC* II. 830). *Lyrical Ballads* was the outcome of a period of initial excitement when, at the start of a relationship, each man was able to suspend his difference and, for a while, be a version of himself that met the other's hopes and ideals. As such, it was a typical project for Coleridge, who had an intense need to be part of a literary circle in which friendship gave rise to, and was in turn intensified by, communal writing, reading and publishing. He had been co-writing or co-publishing poems with Southey since 1794; in 1797 his first verse collection included poems by his friends Charles Lloyd and Charles Lamb. Wordsworth, on the other hand, had never published collaboratively before and never would again. In a sense, then, *Lyrical Ballads* (1798) was a Coleridgean volume, one of many co-authored outlets for a practice of versifying that he shared with friends – a practice that was often self-reflexive: the poems were often about the shared experiences of the friends with whom they were written and/or to whom they were recited. A case in point was 'This Lime Tree Bower My Prison', the poem in which Coleridge first invoked William and Dorothy in the conversational voice that he and Wordsworth would develop during the next five years. The poem features Charles Lamb as well as the Wordsworths and was recited to them on the spot where it was composed. It was not, however, published in *Lyrical Ballads* but in Southey's *Annual Anthology* alongside contributions by other members of the circle – including Joseph Cottle, the Bristol bookseller who published both it and *Lyrical Ballads*. This pattern suggests that *Lyrical Ballads* was just one of many joint publications by which Coleridge sought to promote the innovatory poetic style of the West Country circle, and in so doing endorse their group language. Other poems went into the columns of *The Morning Post*, where verse by Southey and by Mary Robinson (a satellite member of the group) also appeared.

Seeing *Lyrical Ballads* as one of several reports from a Coleridge circle with a shifting membership and evolving language allows us to view it as a hastily assembled anthology of work in progress published to raise funds for a foreign trip. Once demystified in this way it can be seen not quite to fit the coherent experimental programme that Wordsworth announced in the 'Preface' to the remodelled second edition of 1800: Coleridge's contributions were manifestly different from Wordsworth's attempts to make poetry from the 'plainer and more emphatic language' that belonged to 'low and rustic life . . . because in that condition the passions of men are incorporated with the beautiful and permanent forms of nature' (*LB* 97). The baggier and less class-specific description of the 1798 'Advertisement' was nearer the mark: 'They were written chiefly with a view to ascertain how far the language of conversation in the middle and lower classes of society is adapted to the purposes of poetic pleasure' (*LB* 3). Coleridge's contributions were various: 'The Rime of the Ancyent Marinere' featured a lower-class narrator and used a form associated with lower-class locations – dockside, tavern and street; on the other hand, 'The Nightingale' and 'The Foster-Mother's Tale' fitted the middle-class side of the bill – neither was a ballad nor, in conventional terms, a lyric: they approximated to polite speech rather than song.

'The Nightingale' and 'The Foster-Mother's Tale'

'The Nightingale', which Coleridge labelled a 'conversation' poem, was a fine example of the effusive, blank verse pieces that he had begun writing in 1795 and had brought close to perfection, in interchange with William and Dorothy, in poems published outside *Lyrical Ballads* – 'This Lime Tree Bower' and 'Frost at Midnight'. Within the volume, it formed a dialogue with the Wordsworth poem that it had, in fact, helped inspire – 'Lines Composed a Few Miles . . . Tintern Abbey'. Both pieces were supposedly in-the-moment addresses to companions made while in the process of taking a leisurely country walk to nowhere in particular. As contemporary readers would at once have seen, there was a purpose in this apparent purposelessness: the solitary walker was Rousseauvian, purging himself of the false sophistication of urban civilisation by immersing himself in the non-human energies of a rural world taken to be simple, innocent and sincere. This immersion was a matter of form as well as content: 'The Nightingale' eschewed rhymes and stanzas; it rambled in step with its rambling narrator; its wandering progress was a way of liberating poetry from the dead weight of traditional form by basing it on the rhythms of the body in motion. It sounded natural too: diction and syntax were colloquial, and this approximation of speech was taken to be analogous to the unmotivated sound-stream of birdsong. The poem preached what it practised, thematising the liberation of perception from the prison of the inherited view. In an extended opening, Coleridge sets up various echoes from the past only to challenge and overturn them:

> "Most musical, most melancholy" Bird!
> A melancholy Bird? O idle thought!
> In nature there is nothing melancholy.
> – But some night-wandering Man, whose heart was pierc'd
> With the remembrance of a grievous wrong,
> Or slow distemper or neglected love,
> (And so, poor wretch! fill'd all things with himself,
> And made all gentle sounds tell back the tale
> Of his own sorrows) he and such as he
> First named these notes a melancholy strain;
> And many a poet echoes the conceit;
> Poet, who hath been building up the rhyme
> When he had better far have stretched his limbs
> Beside a brook in mossy forest-dell
> By sun or moon-light, to the influxes
> Of shapes and sounds and shifting elements
> Surrendering his whole spirit, of his song
> And of his fame forgetful! so his fame
> Should share in nature's immortality,
> A venerable thing! and so his song
> Should make all nature lovelier, and itself
> Be lov'd, like nature! – But 'twill not be so;
> And youths and maidens most poetical
> Who lose the deep'ning twilights of the spring
> In ball-rooms and hot theatres, they still
> Full of meek sympathy must heave their sighs
> O'er Philomela's pity-pleading strains.
>
> (*LB* Lines 13–39)

Coleridge opens with a direct quotation from Milton's poem 'Il Penseroso' but does so only to reject the traditional poetic interpretation of the nightingale as melancholy; likewise, the Ovidian myth of the bird as the metamorphosed incarnation of the raped nymph Philomel is cited only in order to be critiqued as the affectation of amorous 'youths and maidens' in the stuffy indoor venues of the civilised world. To be outdoors, where narrator and reader go to ground (lying down so as to feel nature's influxes through their bodies), is to be free of such confining views. The burden of the past is escaped by giving oneself to the rhythms of nature: it is not what the bird has meant in its prior literary incarnations but what it now does, that brings the poet to utterance.

There is, nevertheless, no purely new language; the lyrical balladeer cannot begin from scratch; all writing invokes a past. 'The Nightingale' may enact what it discusses – a rejection of the Miltonic syntax and Ovidian diction that had once attracted Coleridge – but it cannot simply mimic the nonverbal sonic sequence of the bird. And conversational speech is in itself no model for written poetry unless it is, as Wordsworth put it in the 'Preface', 'purified indeed from what appear to be its real defects' (*LB* 97). Coleridge attempts this purification by updating Elizabethan dramatic language: 'The Nightingale' turns from 'Il Pensoroso' to the forests of Illyria and Arden: its natural language is a development of Shakespeare's pastoral verse at the expense of Milton's (with William Cowper's subjectivisation of *Paradise Lost* – what Coleridge called his 'divine chit chat' – an intertext) (*CL STC* I. 197). Coleridge was, from summer to November 1797, writing his Shakespearian drama *Osorio*, while Wordsworth was working on his Shakespearian play *The Borderers*. 'The Nightingale' is informed by this effort to render speech in verse for the stage; 'That strain again', the poet says, interrupting himself to respond to the bird's renewed song, and so achieving an interplay between the stream of meditation and the spontaneous noticing of the external world. The phrase, however, invokes the Duke in *Twelfth Night* (WSCW; 1.1 p.693), a weary governor seeking escape from his role through the sound of music, as if Coleridge is paying homage to the poet from whom he has learnt the self-interruption device.

The Shakespeare lesson is also prosodic. The relationship between the speech rhythms of the colloquial phrases and the underlying iambic pentameter is supple: from the start, the phrases pause, delay, quicken and flow, longer and shorter, overriding metrical norms and overflowing line ends but never dissolving them altogether. Coleridge echoes Shakespeare in the degree to which he lets the irregularity of unplanned speech take liberties with the bracing order of iambic pentameter:

> Come, we will rest on this old mossy Bridge!
> You see the glimmer of the stream beneath,
> But hear no murmuring: it flows silently
> O'er its soft bed of verdure. All is still,
> A balmy night! And tho' the stars be dim,
> Yet let us think upon the vernal showers
> That gladden the green earth, and we shall find
> A pleasure in the dimness of the stars . . .
>
> (*LB* Lines 4–12)

'Yet let us think upon': Coleridge urges his readers to think with him, self-reflexively modelling the community he hopes to achieve via the poem. This exhortation is apparently spontaneous but in fact derives from Shakespeare: it updates the self-dramatising, exhortatory speech of Richard II: 'For God's sake, let us sit upon the ground, / And tell sad stories of the death of kings' (*WSCW*; *Richard* II 3.2, Lines 151–152, p. 382). Meanwhile, apart from 'verdure', the diction is entirely that of plain, middle-class conversation – as Richard's also is: Coleridge's diction is Shakespearian in its plainness.

Shakespeare and Rousseau also inform two excerpts from *Osorio* about the corrupting effect of jail and the ability of nature to convert wrongdoers to peaceful ways – 'The Dungeon' and 'The Foster-Mother's Tale'. Both imitate middle-class speech; thematically, both are linked to 'We Are Seven' and 'Anecdote for Fathers', suggesting that the natural innocence of the child is wiser than the educated knowledge of the adult. 'The Foster-Mother's Tale' is an allegory of the repression of radical intellectuals in Britain of the 1790s, showing that innocence is not just misunderstood but actively suppressed by adults. Its hero, a precocious boy, is imprisoned because church and state cannot tolerate his unorthodox learning, derived as it is from exploring wild nature and reading heretical books. He escapes, however, because his nature song, a song of liberty, moves a rural labourer to help him:

> My husband's father
> Sobbed like a child—it almost broke his heart:
> And once as he was working in the cellar,
> He heard a voice distinctly; 'twas the youth's,
> Who sung a doleful song about green fields,
> How sweet it were on lake or wild savannah,
> To hunt for food, and be a naked man,
> And wander up and down at liberty.
>
> (*LB* Lines 57–64)

It is significant that the song is received at third or fourth hand: the father-in-law, its auditor, has spoken of it to the foster-mother, who describes it here to Leoni, with the reader, standing in for the playgoer, eavesdropping. This displacement not only models the reader's emotional reaction on that of the father-in-law and foster-mother but also links it to action: the reader is at one end of a chain that begins with a man so moved by song that he liberates the singer from his bastille. The boy is freed into a Rousseauvian idyll of noble savagery, but liberation occurs by a Shakespearian device – as the allusion to Falstaff's death, summoning all the pathos of the famous speech from *Henry V*, signals:

> A made a finer end, and went away an it had been any christom child. A parted ev'n just between twelve and one, ev'n at the turning o' th' tide – for after I saw him fumble with the sheets, and play with flowers, and smile upon his finger's end, I knew there was but one way. For his nose was as sharp as a pen, and a babbled of green fields. (Act 2, Scene 2, p.576)

Here Coleridge alludes to a report: Shakespeare's audience does not witness Falstaff's dying words except as told by the hostess to his old companions. 'Green fields' – the affiliation to nature – are shown to be emotionally powerful and politically revolutionary as mediated and remediated by crafted narratives – plays, songs and poems. 'The Foster-Mother's Tale', in effect, is all in the telling; the volume of which it is part – *Lyrical Ballads* – is, it implies, less a return to nature than a deferral to pastoral as exemplified by Shakespeare. It is a telling comment on the ornamented couplet verse of the 1780s and 1790s that this development of Shakespearian blank verse should have seemed experimental.

'The Rime of the Ancyent Marinere'

Not all of Coleridge's contributions attempted to rehabilitate middle-class conversation, via Shakespearian blank verse, as a model for poetry. 'The Rime of the Ancyent Marinere' has a common sailor as its narrator. As a ballad, it is aligned with the oral poetry of the lower classes, whether the rural labourers of Elizabethan times or the pedlars, beggars and vagrants of eighteenth-century towns and villages. Despite this difference, it shares with 'The Foster-Mother's Tale' the determination to tell stories that show society's treatment of transgression as a sign of its political health – or disease. More successful than that tale, it is one of the most vivid portraits of shame, guilt, terror and alienation in the English language. To understand how Coleridge came to narrate these states of abjection in such extraordinary form – in a work more powerful than anything else he ever wrote – it is necessary to explore the poem's contexts. These include his writings about superstition, which he saw as a key to understanding the politics and society of post–French Revolution Britain; his reading of voyage narratives and reports about indigenous people; and his engagement with the revival of old folk ballads.

In 1799, Coleridge told William Hazlitt that he suspected 'Wordsworth was not prone enough to believe in the traditional superstitions of the place'.[1] He himself was fascinated by what we would now term the social psychology of superstition, viewing it as a communally maintained belief system designed to cope with vulnerability to things beyond the group's power to understand or control. It stemmed from 'having placed our summum bonum (what we think so, I mean,) in an absolute Dependence on Powers & Events over which we have no Controll' (*CN STC* II. 2060). It followed that those with the least power over their environment were most superstitious. These were primarily poorly educated, barely techno-logical groups, whether the semi-literate rustics of the English West Country, the 'primitive' Indians of the Canadian Arctic, or the enslaved Africans of the Caribbean. Sailors were also highly superstitious for this reason, as Coleridge implied when he wrote that superstition sprang from 'the consciousness of the vast disproportion of our knowledge to the terra incognita yet to be known' ('terra incognita' designated the unknown land after which voyagers searched).[2] Their credulity made these groups prone to dominance by those who knew how to exploit their fearful beliefs. In Britain, Coleridge complained in a 1794 sonnet, politicians used 'wizard spell[s]' to whip them into a mob to act against their own best interests ('Burke', Line 8; *PW STC* II. i. 206). He elaborated this complaint in 'France: An Ode' (1798). Britons had become a 'slavish band' who did the bidding of a cruel monarch who bound them with 'a wizard's wand' (Lines 27, 29; *PW STC* II. i. 588). Kept for generations in ignorance, they were mental slaves who were incapable of independence because they craved a master:

> The Sensual and the Dark rebel in vain,
> Slaves by their own compulsion! In mad game
> They burst their manacles and wear the name
> Of Freedom, graven on a heavier chain!
>
> (Lines 85–88)

Worshipping the gods their political masters chose for them, the sensual gods of avarice, ambition and absolutism, the people assisted in their own oppression. Politicians and priests, meanwhile, were the fiendish manipulators of popular superstition: Coleridge likened them to Mesmerists (hypnotists) as well as wizards. The repressive society of the 1790s, in which pro-democratic journalists were arrested and public meetings banned, and in which a government agent was sent to spy on Coleridge and Wordsworth as potential traitors even as they wrote *Lyrical Ballads* – all without widespread protest – was produced by the political magic of tyrants and the complicity of a superstitious people.

What is expressed in 'France: An Ode' in the form of political analysis appears in narrative form in 'The Rime'. This change resulted from Coleridge's reading of tales of adventure – explorers' narratives – and from his co-writing of tales of superstition – joint efforts with Wordsworth. He explained some of this process in the 'Preface' to 'The Three Graves', a Somerset-based ballad he and Wordsworth tried jointly to compose in November 1797. The ballad concerned rural villagers; it featured a young son-in-law who believed so strongly in the power of curses that, when cursed by his jealous mother-in-law, he became psychosomatically ill in mind and body. Coleridge took this idea from:

> Bryan Edwards's account of the effect of the *Oby* Witchraft on the Negroes in the West-Indies, and Hearne's deeply interesting Anecdotes of similar workings on the imagination of the Copper Indians ... and I conceived the design of shewing that instances of this kind are not peculiar to savage or barbarous tribes, and of illustrating the mode in which the mind is affected in these cases, and the progress and symptoms of the morbid action on the fancy from the beginning. (*PW STC* II. i. 466)

The Copper Mine Indians, according to Samuel Hearne's *A Journey from Prince of Wales's Fort in Hudson's Bay to the Northern Ocean*, let the curses of their shamans drive them to death:

> When these jugglers take a dislike to, and threaten a secret revenge on any person, it often proves fatal to that person; as ... he permits the very thoughts of it to prey on his spirits, till by degrees it brings on a disorder which puts an end to his existence: and sometimes a threat of this kind causes the death of a whole family.[3]

The slaves of the Caribbean, according to Bryan Edwards's *History of the West Indies*, presented a similar case of superstition internalising guilt, shame and terror, for they died when cursed by the obeah-man (or voodoo priest), who touched them with a fetish composed of the body parts of the dead.[4] Coleridge commented:

> the supposed exercise of magical power always involved some moral guilt, directly or indirectly, as in ... touching humours with the hand of an executed person &c. Rites of this sort and other practices of sorcery have always been regarded with trembling abhorrence by all nations, even the most ignorant, as by the Africans, the Hudson's Bay people and others.[5]

Edwards's African obeah-men and Hearne's Hudson's Bay shamans gained their supernatural power from their culture's superstitiousness: they manipulated this power by making believers complicit in their violation of taboos. Believing themselves claimed by the dead when touched by the obeah-man's fetish, Caribbean slaves, Edwards wrote, would almost never betray his identity even when dying under his curse. This complicity, Coleridge noted (in 'The Destiny of Nations'), was a covert form of resistance to enslavement. The British master's physical power over the slave was exceeded by the African obeah-man's 'magic'. Paradoxically, dying under the compulsion of an obeah-curse was a form of freedom: the superstitious soul would liberate the enslaved body in death.

'The Three Graves' was never finished, Wordsworth proving unable to write his part. What Coleridge drafted of it, however, reveals its significance to the development of 'The Rime'. Not only does it hinge upon the operation of curses and acceptance of guilt in a superstitious group, but it also dramatizes the resultant effects in ballad stanzas, in which rhyme enforces horror:

> His face was drawn back on itself,
> With horror and huge pain.
>
> Both groaned at once, for both knew well
> What thoughts were in his mind;
> When he waked up, and stared like one
> That hath been just struck blind.
> (Lines 305–310; PW STC II. i. 476)

Though they failed to write the Somerset ballad together, the two poets attempted to take up the theme of a pariah – a man cursed and cast out because he had transgressed against the beliefs of his society – in another form. They tried to cooperate on a three-canto poem, 'The Wanderings of Cain', about the ostracised murderer forced to become a vagrant. Coleridge produced his part, but Wordsworth could scarcely write a word: he was already turning out to be a different kind of poet, less interested in the socio-psychology of superstition than his friend. The poem then, in Coleridge's words, 'broke up in a laugh: and the Ancient Mariner was written instead' (*PW STC* II. i. 497). Wordsworth, who had been reading George Shelvocke's *A Voyage Round The World by Way of the Great South Sea* (1726), suggested the motif of a sailor punished for having shot an albatross.

Shelvocke's was not the only voyage narrative that enabled 'The Rime' to succeed when 'The Three Graves' and 'The Wanderings of Cain' failed. At school, Coleridge had been taught by William Wales, the astronomer who had, as recently as 1774, sailed on James Cook's second expedition through the Pacific and deep into Antarctic waters. He may have heard

tales of the voyage in his classroom – Cook had become a national hero –
and he later read the massively popular printed accounts, with their
staggering sights and sounds: 'long columns of a clear white light, shooting
up from the horizon to the eastward, almost to the zenith, and gradually
spreading on the whole southern part of the sky'; the sea 'luminous at
night'; 'a large island of ice, which . . . crumbled to pieces with a tremendous explosion'; 'the ice . . . often tinged, especially . . . with a most
beautiful sapphrine or rather beryline blue'; rigging covered in ice; shooting albatrosses.[6] These accounts did more than provide Coleridge with
scenery for his tale: they enabled an external narration – dramatic, visual,
topical – of the inward conditions that, in Coleridge's diagnosis, produced
superstition. It is towards the Terra Australis Incognita – the uncharted
southern continent sought by Cook – that the Ancient Mariner is sailing.
He journeys beyond the limits of geographic knowledge and finds himself
helpless before powers and events over which he has no control. The
further he penetrates into a physical terra incognita, a place of green ice,
fog-smoke white, and red ocean, the more he discovers his own powerless-
ness. Unsailed waters leave him in uncharted moral and social states – not
just guilt and alienation but also living death. On an ocean that is like 'a
Slave before his Lord' (*LB* Line 419; p. 17), he too is controlled by forces
he cannot resist. He is, in other words, a cousin of the British and French
people whom Coleridge described as a 'slavish band' in 'France: An Ode'.
He resembles them in his need to believe in the supernatural power of the
forces in authority over him. He is a figure who owes his being to
Coleridge's political disenchantment with both imperialist Britain and
revolutionary France.

What produces the mariner's abjection is his own subscription to the
belief system of a closed group. His voyage into isolation and terror begins,
as in 'The Three Graves', with a casting-out ritual. This results from the
retrospective interpretation of killing the albatross as a breach of the line
between the living and the dead. His shipmates, ignorantly superstitious,
strive to give his shooting of the albatross supernatural significance. First,
they blame him, then, when the weather on which their safety depends
improves, praise him. Then, as the winds drop, they blame him again.
They try to propitiate the god who controls the elements by making the
mariner bear and purge the blame for them. And so they ostracise and
curse him: making him what sailors' called a 'Jonah'. The mariner accepts
the role of scapegoat because he knows he has violated the crew's taboo.
And, because he tells his own story without correction from an

independent narrator, events bear out his superstitious view. Becoming a pariah, in his own eyes as well as the condemnatory eyes of the crew, he sees himself to be responsible for the ship's journey – like Odysseus's in Homer – into a world in which humans are subject to cruel and arbitrary punishment at the hands of a nature controlled by forces they have no means of understanding.

Arbitrariness is suggested by the poem's form, as well as by events such as the spectres of Death and her 'fleshless Pheere' (Line 180) playing dice for the shipmates. Coleridge developed the old border ballad-form that had been revived by Thomas Percy (*Reliques of Ancient English Poetry*, 1765), adapted by Gottfried August Bürger to tell stories of supernatural terror ('Leonore', 1774), and further developed by Bürger's translator William Taylor ('Ellenore', 1796). The form, with its short lines, spare stanzas, lack of narratorial commentary, and sudden changes from one unidentified speaker to another, and from speech to report, created a fast-paced tale in which the sequencing of events was often abrupt. There was little room for interpretation and explanation, and so the images of strangely coloured ice, snow and fog derived from the voyage narratives stood out starkly, acquiring a vividness so strong that they appeared surreal. This effect was enhanced by another typical ballad device – repetition, as in 'Whiles all the night thro' fog-smoke white / Glimmer'd the white moon-shine'; the 'white foam'; 'white as leprosy'; 'shining white' (Lines 75–76, 99, 188, 266). Indeed, skeins of colour imagery run through the poem, making its imagined world uncannily brighter than the familiar world: 'The water, like a witch's oils / Burnt green and blue and white'; 'Blue, glossy green, and velvet black / They coil'd and swam; and every track / Was a flash of golden fire' (Lines 125–126, 271–273). The reality effect is powerfully emphasised by the rapidly repeated rhymes and thumping rhythms of the ballad stanza while at the same time, the archaic diction distances the scenario from the everyday – allowing supernatural elements to be more believable. Moreover, by reputation, the ballad was the form of unlettered rural folk – exactly the traditional rustic communities in which superstition flourished. This made 'The Rime', by association, oral, rural and primitive, as if it authentically emerged from a culture that believed in ghosts and spirits. Nonetheless, the poem is not antiquarian. Its old-fashioned diction is mixed with common speech so that a combination of strangeness and familiarity is present at the verbal level. Uncanniness is also produced by parataxis – the rhetorical device in which causal links between phrases are omitted:

> The Marineres gave it biscuit-worms,
> And round and round it flew:
> The Ice did split with a Thunder-fit;
> The Helmsman steer'd us thro'.
>
> (Lines 65–68)

Does the ice split because the bird eats forbidden fruit? Or does one event just follow after another by chance? The reader is tantalised by the syntactic structure just as the mariner is by the structure of nature. Coleridge later said that 'The Rime' was 'incomprehensible, and without head or tail'.[7] It is his handling of ballad form and diction that makes us want to comprehend it, but prevents us from arriving at a logical construct from which redemptive meaning can be inferred in nature.

The poem provides a stronger logic for degeneration and abjection – but a psycho-social rather than moral one. The mariner, cast out, experiences the voyage as a nightmare in which guilt and shame are imaged by a tantalising mockery of companionship with crewmates:

> The body of my brother's son
> Stood by me knee to knee:
> The body and I pull'd at one rope,
> But he said nought to me –
> And I quak'd to think of my own voice
> How frightful it would be!
>
> (Lines 333–338)

Here, in one of the earliest uses of the zombie motif (derived from Southey's reading about Caribbean voodoo) alienation is brought home to the family and slavish obedience is written on the body.[8] The mariner's zombie crewmates are embodiments of the political plight of which Coleridge had complained, embodiments closer to home (because English sailors described in an English town) than the African slaves on which they are based.

Closer to home, but other-worldly too. In touching his nephew's living corpse, the mariner violates another taboo – that which separates the living from the dead. Later, Coleridge suggested that it is the mariner's violation of this taboo that makes him an object of terrified and superstitious awe. Like the shaman and the obeah-man, who are treated with 'trembling abhorrence' because they touch people with the hand of an 'executed person', the mariner becomes uncanny. His power, Coleridge noticed, resembled the power attributed to the dead body by superstitious people: 'Eldridge & his Warts cured by rubbing them with the hand of his Sister's dead Infant / knew a man who cured one on his Eye by rubbing it with the dead Hand of his Brother's – Comments on Ancient Mariner' (*CN STC* II. 2048). The fetish-wielding obeah-man, Coleridge had suggested, worked by complicity. The mariner works in this way too: as powerless as a slave, he acquires power over his fellows by making them touch his body, a living corpse that embodies his guilty violation of the boundary between life and death (the albatross, hung around his neck by the crew, is a symbol of this status). He is a foreign body come home, a cursed victim who passes on guilt by the curse of his hand, eye and voice:

> I mov'd my lips: the Pilot shriek'd
> And fell down in a fit.
> The Holy Hermit rais'd his eyes
> And pray'd where he did sit.
> (*LB* Lines 593–596)

He entrances those who come into contact with him. Held in the mariner's grip, fixed by his eye, 'The wedding-guest he beat his breast, / Yet he cannot chuse but hear' (Lines 41–42). To stay and listen is to replace the loving social union of the wedding with the guilty community of the living dead. It is to become a 'savage' or a 'slave' by our own compulsion – obedient, in fear and desire, to an obeah-man, or a Mesmerist – for Coleridge viewed the new pseudo-science of hypnotism as another means by which believers allowed men who ritualized power to enthrall and entrance them. At the end the wedding guest, spellbound, is, like Edward in 'The Three Graves', 'one that hath been stunn'd / And is of sense forlorn' (Lines 655–656). Sadder and wiser on the readers' behalf, he has endured a terrible lesson about the destructive power of superstitious belief and the abjection (mental and physical) to 'magicians' and 'wizards' that it involves. Coleridge, that is, had developed what he had read about superstition into his most incisive account of the nature and consequences of the dynamic that, he thought, ruled British culture.

It was a fine mess that Coleridge had got his mariner into. Getting him out proved difficult. 'The Rime' imagines degeneration more vividly than it imagines recovery. The terrible events that the mariner endures in the later parts of the poem may be 'penance' – and so part of a path towards forgiveness – but they are numerous. There is no simple road to redemption and certainly no chart: the ship's physical and the mariner's moral voyage are beyond his steering. It is by an unconscious, unknowing act that he begins to throw off the living death to which his imagination has led him:

> O happy living things! no tongue
> Their beauty might declare:
> A spring of love gusht from my heart,
> And I bless'd them unaware!
> Sure my kind saint took pity on me,
> And I bless'd them unaware.
>
> (Lines 274–279)

Coleridge makes an act of love into a saving grace, but, tantalisingly, leaves it unconscious. How to know what to do to gain forgiveness remains obscure. Continued suffering, including the especially cruel suffering produced by disappointed hope of relief, is followed by an unpredictable and sudden arrival back at the voyage's departure port. The poem then ends with a moral which endorses the power of love – 'He prayeth best, who loveth best / All things both great and small' (Lines 647–648). Coleridge came to feel that this moral appeared too openly in the poem and certainly it is too neat to allow an effective catharsis of the fear and guilt already explored. But it is not, in fact, the end. The mariner is compelled to repeat his tale again and again. Spellbound still by the journey he relives, he continues to spellbind others. The mental world of shared superstition is not to be put by with an easy generalisation.

'The Rime' was the strangest poem in *Lyrical Ballads*, and although it had some affinities with Wordsworth's own Bürger-influenced exploration of superstition, 'The Thorn', it stood alone – longer, more intense, more archaic, more visual than any of the other contributions. It began the volume, establishing Coleridge's as the leading voice in a collection composed in his neighbourhood and published by his friend Cottle while the two poets were in Germany. The German sojourn, however, separated the partnership: Coleridge went to university in Göttingen while the Wordsworths travelled to Goslar. When all three returned to England in 1799, the Wordsworths' political reputation prevented them from renewing their rental in Somerset and they resolved to live where they had grown up, the Lake District. Coleridge, keen to renew the partnership, followed in 1799, and the two poets set about preparing a second edition, Cottle having given up publishing and passed his list to Longmans. The new *Lyrical Ballads* was thus a very different beast – a Lake District publication rather than a West Country one. It was also less Coleridgean: now the leading partner, Wordsworth supplied more poems, and, feeling that the strangeness of 'The Rime' had prejudiced reviewers, relegated it to a position near the end, where it was stripped of its archaic diction, retitled 'The Ancient Mariner', and given the apologetic subtitle 'A Poet's Reverie'. Wordsworth even included a note drawing attention to the poem's 'defect', that the mariner 'does not act but is continually acted upon' (thus suggesting he had utterly failed to understand that the exploration of paralyzing abjection was the poem's achievement) (*LB* 346). Coleridge was now visibly a relegated junior contributor revising to placate Wordsworth's disapproval: the increasing difference between their conceptions of poetry was plain to see.

Admiring Wordsworth's new poems, Coleridge attempted to make more contributions of his own and so win the approval of his increasingly dominant friend. Although Southey repeatedly pressed him to publish 'Christabel' (his follow-up to 'The Rime') in an anthology of verse by the West Country circle, he reserved the poem for *Lyrical Ballads* and tried to finish it while living on Wordsworth's ground, in the Lake District. Like its predecessor, 'Christabel' explores the psychodynamics of entrancement within a closed world – on this occasion the medieval baronial hall, deep in the forest. Whereas 'The Rime' made the dead body the taboo through which belief is manipulated and abjection induced, 'Christabel' placed the sexual body in that role. Sex, in effect, becomes the discourse in which power is exercised and subjugation experienced as both desire and guilt. The incomer to the castle, Geraldine, imprisons the 'lovely' daughter, Christabel in her arms. The narrator, in a phrase that usually connotes male sexual seduction, declares that she has 'had [her] will' for an hour (Line 306; *PW STC* II. i. 635). Here again Coleridge develops his interest in hypnotism: a 'steady exertion of … Volition', transmitted through gazing and touching, was the Mesmerist's recipe for entrancing a patient.[9] Geraldine operates like a hypnotist when she instructs the suggestible Christabel what she will do while enchanted and what she will remember afterwards:

> 'In the touch of this bosom there worketh a spell,
> Which is lord of thy utterance, Christabel!
> Thou knowest to-night, and will know to-morrow
> This mark of my shame, this seal of my sorrow;
> >   But vainly thou warrest,
> >   For this is alone in
> >   Thy power to declare,
> >   That in the dim forest
> >   Thou heard'st a low moaning,
> And found'st a bright lady, surpassingly fair;
> And didst bring her home with thee in love and in charity,
> To shield her and shelter her from the damp air'.
>
>   (Lines 267–278)

Alternately guilty and delighted, Christabel is entranced by the exciting and forbidden bodily intimacy:

> The touch, the sight, had passed away,
> And in its stead that vision blest,
> Which comforted her after-rest,
> While in the lady's arms she lay,
> Had put a rapture in her breast,
> And on her lips and o'er her eyes
> Spread smiles like light!
>
> (Lines 463–469)

As in 'The Rime', Coleridge found it more difficult to conceive of redemption than fall: Christabel remains spellbound by Geraldine and is rejected by her father because her speech and her body now manifest her animality and sexuality: she no longer appears innocent.

Wordsworth was a main cause of Coleridge's failure to free Christabel from her subjugation. Whereas the closeness of the poets' partnership had initially enabled each to create new kinds of poems, an increasing distance now inhibited Coleridge. In autumn 1799, he wrote from the Lakes telling Southey he no longer thought 'Christabel' a fit opening poem for a proposed new volume of the *Annual Anthology*: 'those who dislike it w [ould] deem it extravagant ravings' (*CL STC* I. 545–546); it would make them averse to the volume as a whole and so, if included at all, should be placed last. This bleak view of a work that Southey much admired shows that Coleridge was influenced by Wordsworth's fear that its archaic diction and metrical experimentalism would be unpopular, as he thought 'The Rime' had been. In the face of this lack of enthusiasm, Coleridge, depressed, proved unable to finish the poem. It was then abruptly dropped from *Lyrical Ballads* (1800) although the printer had already set up the type: 'I found', Wordsworth declared, 'that the Style of the poem was so discordant from my own that it could not be printed along with my poems with any propriety' (*CL STC* I. 643).[10] *Lyrical Ballads* was now to be a Wordsworthian, rather than a joint, collection; Coleridge, edged out, never entirely recovered his self-belief and wrote no more verse of the calibre of his extraordinary seafarer's ballad and chivalric romance. It would take another sixteen years before their unique achievement was appreciated: 'The Rime' was a seminal influence on Byron's 'Cain' and 'Don Juan', and on Mary Shelley's *Frankenstein*, while 'Christabel' made possible Keats's 'Eve of St Agnes', 'Lamia' and 'La Belle Dame Sans Merci'.

Endnotes

1 William Hazlitt, 'My First Acquaintance with Poets', in *The Complete Works of William Hazlitt*, ed. P. P. Howe, 21 vols. (London: J. M. Dent and Sons, 1930–1934), XVII. 117.

2 *The Collected Marginalia of S. T. Coleridge*, ed. George Whalley and H. J. Jackson, 6 vols. (Princeton: Princeton University Press, 1980–2001), IV. 579.

3 Samuel Hearne, *A Journey from Prince of Wales's Fort in Hudson's Bay to the Northern Ocean in the Years 1769, 1770, 1771, and 1772* (London, 1795), 233. See also Bryan Edwards, *The History, Civil and Commercial of the British Colonies in the West Indies*, 2 vols. (London, 1793), II. 91–92.

4 See Alan Richardson, 'Romantic Voodoo: Obeah and British Culture, 1797–1807', *Studies in Romanticism*, 32 (1993): 3–28.

5 S. T. Coleridge, *Lectures on Literature, 1808–19*, ed. Reginald A. Foakes, 2 vols. *CW STC* vol. V. (Princeton: Princeton University Press, 1986), II. 211.

6 George Forster, *A Voyage Round the World in His Britannic Majesty's Sloop, Resolution, Commanded by Capt. James Cook, during the Years 1772, 3, 4, and 5*, 2 vols. (London, 1777), II. 68–77.

7 'To the Author of the Ancient Mariner', Lines 3–4; *PW STC* II. ii. 770.

8 Southey published his materials about zombie practices in his *History of Brazil*, 3 vols. (London, 1810–1819), III. 25–26.

9 John Boniot De Mainauduc, *The Lectures of J. B. de Mainauduc, M.D.* (London, 1798), 107.

10 In the 'Preface' to *Lyrical Ballads* Wordsworth's opposition to metrical experimentation is intertwined with his dislike of diction removed from the 'real language' of ordinary speech and plain prose: 'Our feelings are the same with respect to meter; for, as it may be proper to remind the Reader, the distinction of meter is regular and uniform, and not like that which is produced by what is usually called poetic diction, arbitrary, and subject to infinite caprices upon which no calculation whatever can be made' (*LB* 108).

CHAPTER 4

Lyric Voice and Ballad Voice

Pete Newbon

If the first readers of *Lyrical Ballads* were perplexed by the title of Wordsworth and Coleridge's anthology, this was not immediately clear in the
initial flurry of critical reviews. Where commentators were either pleased
or irritated by the collection as a whole, there was little to indicate that they
were at all flummoxed by the concept of 'lyrical ballads'. In his
'Advertisement' to *Lyrical Ballads* Wordsworth had informed his readers
that the poems contained therein should be considered 'experiments' (*LB*
3), and he was at pains in the 'Preface' to *Lyrical Ballads* to elucidate the
innovative poetics of the anthology. Yet neither he nor Coleridge felt it
necessary to clarify their unusual title. This was despite the fact that the
lyric tradition in the Western canon, and the ballad form, connoted very
different – sometimes seemingly incommensurate – histories, conventions,
and aesthetic and social connotations.

The 'lyric' component traces a lineage that stretches back to classical
antiquity. Resurgent in the European Renaissance, lyric poetry was later
widespread in the form of eighteenth-century loco-description. Such verses
espoused philosophical and spiritual meditation in an exalted, elite register.
Conversely, ballads had emerged in the medieval period, and were associated
with unadorned, humble language, rude plebeian culture and folklore. As
the poet Walter Savage Landor was to observe, this blending of classical and
medieval created potential dissonance: 'lyre and ballad belong not to the
same age or the same people'.[1] This chapter analyses the legacy of distinct lyric
and ballad voices that Wordsworth and Coleridge inherited. Moreover, it
explores why these two dynamics within poetry – often seemingly so disparate –
might have appealed to the two friends as especially apposite to combine.

The extent to which this anthology should be considered a radical break
with poetic tradition, or an idiosyncratic continuation of pre-established
conventions, has been an enduring point of debate among critical readers
of *Lyrical Ballads*. So, despite Wordsworth's eagerness to proclaim the
novelty of his 'experiment' in both the 'Advertisement' to *Lyrical Ballads*

and the more expansive 'Preface' to *Lyrical Ballads*, John E. Jordan cautions against exaggerating the novelty of the project (103–104, 7). Rather than perceiving these poems as radical experiments, William Keach, in his introduction to the Penguin edition of *Lyrical Ballads*, regards them as the gradual culmination of dynamics inherent in eighteenth-century balladic culture, which was already shifting towards a more lyrical register by the time it was taken up by Wordsworth and Coleridge. For both Mary Jacobus and Daniel Robinson, tradition and experiment are thoroughly interwoven in this collection: a fusion of radical contemporaneous innovation, tempered by a keen awareness of the burden of the past.[2]

In assessing the originality of *Lyrical Ballads*, bringing into alignment – or collision – such disparate poetic voices as the lyric and balladic, various critics and scholars have propounded complex and nuanced arguments about the meaning of the enigmatic title that was chosen for the collection. Stuart Curran exemplifies this tendency where he writes:

> When Wordsworth and Coleridge designated their original collection *Lyrical Ballads*, it was with an assured sense that throughout the volume they had endeavoured to reconcile opposing literary, and even philosophical, modes.[3]

Curran's assertion contains a series of claims: that Wordsworth and Coleridge were united in a common endeavour; that this shared mission had – from the outset – a coherent philosophy of poetry; and that *Lyrical Ballads* (and later *Lyrical Ballads* [1800]) somehow succeeded in reconciling elements of literature and philosophy deemed to be oppositional. However, there are numerous reasons for being circumspect about such confidence in this supposedly fully premeditated and cogent project.

As many commentators have observed, many stages in the composition and publication of *Lyrical Ballads* were marked by quite pronounced contingency. Although clearly inspired by certain fundamental artistic convictions, an irrefutable motivation for publishing their anthology in 1798 was that the Wordsworth siblings were in need of money. In part, this was due to their ongoing struggles to wrest their father's inheritance from Lord Lowther; but also, their need to finance a sojourn, accompanying Coleridge on his studies in Germany (Jordan 29). So many characteristics of their preparation for publication suggest, rather than a governing poetical philosophy, instead a series of somewhat last-minute and piecemeal choices. Seamus Perry opines that the speed with which Wordsworth, in particular, composed so many of the ballads within the volume intimated his desire to 'cash in' on the contemporary vogue for balladry to secure

money for their excursion.[4] Coleridge had entreated Joseph Cottle, their
Bristolian publisher, to release the anthology as an anonymous work,
under the rationale that Wordsworth's name at that time meant 'nothing'
to the reading audience, while his own, associated with West Country
radicalism *'stinks'* (*CL STC* I. 412). If this did not present the hapless
Cottle with enough challenges, Wordsworth then proposed to name the
collection with the minimalist appellation *Poems* – a request that Cottle
promptly vetoed. But had Cottle not so insisted, it is possible that literary
analysis of this singular anthology would not have revolved so much
around untangling the lyric and balladic voices of the collection, which
might not have been made so prominent.

What are 'lyrical ballads'? At no point in their career did Wordsworth or
Coleridge ever seek to explain this potentially oxymoronic coinage. One
problem with a heuristic answer to this question is that critics cannot even
be entirely sure which specific poems were to be considered as 'lyrical
ballads'. Clearly not all of the poems within the anthology can be termed
'lyrical ballads', for the simple reason that 'ballad' designates a formal
choice of poetry, and certain lyrical poems therein are demonstrably not
ballads. Works like 'Lines Written a Few Miles above Tintern Abbey',
'The Nightingale: A Conversation Poem' and 'The Brothers' are important
to analyse in order to understand innovations that Wordsworth and
Coleridge brought to the specifically 'lyric' voice of *Lyrical Ballads*. But
they cannot fall within the designation of 'lyrical ballads'. So, the title of
the volume indicates that the ballads contained within should be understood as different from normative ballads, due, in some sense, to an
infusion of qualities of lyricism. But this does not exclude the possibility –
neither confirmed nor denied by either of the friends – that some ballads
within the collection were deemed new, innovative 'lyrical ballads',
whereas others were not. And perhaps 'lyrical ballads' did not denote a
fixed, regular formula that would be operative throughout all of the poems
in the anthology considered under this rubric, but instead intimated a
broader set of novel ways of rethinking balladry.

A further complication worth considering when analysing the innovation of lyric and balladic voices in *Lyrical Ballads* is the extent to which
Wordsworth and Coleridge were always invested in the same project.
Lyrical Ballads is renowned not only as a turning point in the history of
British poetry, but also as a great work of collaboration. This is unsurpris-
ing given the exertions of both men to cement this impression with
retrospective evaluations in later years. Writing to Cottle at the time of
publication, Coleridge maintained that *Lyrical Ballads* was '*one work*, in

kind tho' not in degree' (*CL STC* I. 412). He would go on in subsequent epistles to claim that the 'Preface' to *Lyrical Ballads* (written solely by Wordsworth) was 'half a child of my own Brain', which expressed 'our joint opinions on poetry' (*CL STC* I. 627, II. 830). Furthermore, in his *Biographia Literaria* (1817), Coleridge would give a rather schematic account of the division of artistic labour within the project, as though conceived from the first. Coleridge was to address the supernatural, whereas Wordsworth was to represent 'ordinary life', although sometimes flavoured with hints of the seemingly supernatural (*BL* II. xiv). Wordsworth went some way to confirming this account in a note to Eliza Fenwick in his commentary upon his ballad 'We Are Seven' (Jordan 11). Yet James A. Butler questions the reliability of these *ex post facto* claims: it strains credulity that the anthology was always determined by the coherence later attributed to it by such different poets, with often quite radically disparate ideas about poetry.[5]

While it is true that Coleridge had previously worked with moderate success on earlier ventures with several other writers, this was Wordsworth's first collaborative venture in literature. As is illustrated by their abortive attempt to compose together the fragmentary *Wanderings of Cain* (1797), the two friends did not work directly together, and had quite different styles. This by no means undermines the extent to which Wordsworth and Coleridge had a profound influence upon each other's poetry in the *annus mirabilis* of 1797–1798 – an influence tangibly manifest in specific verses of some of their greatest writings. But none of the poems in *Lyrical Ballads* were co-authored (aside possibly from a few small but significant suggestions made by each party). Moreover, the division of labour was never equal. From the outset, Wordsworth composed the majority of the poetry for the volume; in 1800, only his name appeared as author; and with the revision of *Lyrical Ballads*, Wordsworth expanded his theoretical framework with the expansive – and contentious – 'Preface'. He also rearranged the order of poems within the collection in such a way that many critics have interpreted as a deliberate demotion of Coleridge's poetry (especially 'The Rime of the Ancyent Marinere').[6] So when considering an understanding of the fusion of 'lyric' and 'balladic' voices in *Lyrical Ballads*, it may be prudent to be receptive to ways in which Wordsworth and Coleridge understood their undertaking in different ways.

This chapter is divided into three sections. The first addresses the category of a distinct lyric tradition of poetry that Wordsworth and Coleridge inherited from rather elevated eighteenth-century precursors, predominantly in the field of loco-descriptive black verse. As part of their poetic evolution in the aesthetically and political turbulent 1790s, they experimented with various forms of lyrical expression, culminating in the 'conversational' mode characteristic of poems such as 'The Nightingale', 'Tintern Abbey' and later fragmentary pieces included in *Lyrical Ballads* (1800) that were offshoots from Wordsworth's larger project: *The Prelude* (1805). The second segment examines the nature of 'balladic' voice. Ballads represented a more plebeian strand, often associated with primitive and oral poetics, with roots in an anti-Enlightenment celebration of superstition and the supernatural. Finally, I conclude this chapter with an analysis of those poems designated the 'Lucy Poems', considered as 'lyrical ballads', and exploring the ways in which they fuse these poetic dualities of lyricism and balladry.

Lyric Voice

The term 'lyric' derives etymologically from ancient Greek and translates literally as 'a song to be sung to the lyre'. The 'lyric' does not designate a specific form of poetry, nor does it entirely circumscribe a precise genre of poetic subject matter. Rather, 'lyric' denotes a mode or voice of poetry. *The Princeton Encyclopedia of Poetry and Poetics* differentiates the 'lyric' within Greek poetry from two other dominant modes, the 'dramatic' – which presents contemporary action – and the 'narrative' – which mediates a series of events.[7] In contrast, the lyric articulates a distinct voice, generally taken to be the voice of the poet as speaker, either expressing a private, introspective meditation, or engaged in a public declaration. Because lyric does not describe a particular poetic form or genre, the lyrical mode is to be found across a range of different types of poetry. As such, lyrical expression has evolved to fit with the cultural and aesthetic requirements and imperatives of a series of Western European epochs.

In sixteenth-century Britain, the lyric emerged as a dominant mode in the elite circles of the Tudor court. By the seventeenth century, the iambic pentameter had emerged as the primary prosodic vehicle for lyrical expression. By the turn of the eighteenth century the most common character of lyricism was the acerbic public register of Augustan satire, arranged in strict heroic couplets, with their rigid end-stops.[8] Yet in the course of the century, with the rise of the genres of loco-description and the picturesque, and the apotheosis of the 'culture of sensibility', the restrictions of heroic couplets gave way to the comparative expressive freedom of post-Miltonic blank verse. Under the aegis of materialist philosophies that gave primacy to sensation and the malleability of the human mind, espoused variously by John Locke and David Hartley, new nature poetry voiced an optimistic confidence that the divinely created world was instrumental in the benign shaping of the human subject. Works such as James Thomson's *The Seasons* (1726), Joseph Warton's *The Enthusiast, or the Lover of Nature* (1744), William Collins' *Odes* (1746) and William Cowper's *The Task* (1785) presented an interplay between the external natural world of sensation and the subject's internal states of feeling. Yet another related offshoot of the culture of sensibility was the maudlin and pensive genre of lyrical poetry often described as 'graveyard poetry'. In such works as Edward Young's *Night Thoughts* (1742–1745) and Thomas Gray's 'Elegy Written in a Country Churchyard' (1751), elements of neoclassical stoicism are blended with gothic aesthetics. Such poems focus upon the individual's moral sentiments when confronting the existential reality of death, situated in proximity to a rural grave. These three strands – philosophical loco-description, sensibility and graveyard poetics – are integral to understanding the lyrical voicing of *Lyrical Ballads*.

From childhood, both Wordsworth and Coleridge were steeped in the classical, Renaissance and contemporary lyric traditions. Despite the parallel financial precariousness of their families, both men received remarkable educations. At school, they were made familiar with such classical writers as Homer, Democritus, Xenophon, Virgil, Horace, Ovid, Cicero and Tully. Indeed, under the stern tutelage of the stentorian James Boyer, Coleridge became the most impressive 'Grecian' in his year at Christ's Hospital school. He would go on to win prizes at Jesus College, Cambridge, for his imitation of the celebratory style of Pindar's odes.[9] In the 'Preface', Wordsworth would signal his resistance to the shibboleths of eighteenth-century 'poetic diction' (*LB* 100). Yet, as Andrew Bennett notes, Wordsworth's opposition to certain conventions of poetic language were intrinsically informed by his saturation in poetic tradition.[10] As Ben Ross Schneider demonstrates, Wordsworth was always eager to downplay the extent of his erudition in both classical and modern continental literature.[11] While at St. John's College, Cambridge, he became well versed in a range of French, Spanish and Italian poetry. From childhood, both men devoured contemporary sentimental literature. While still schoolboys they had already read such influential writers as Thomas Chatterton, James Beattie, Thomas Percy, Charlotte Smith, Joseph Warton, William Cowper and Robert Burns. The influence of such poets resonates within their juvenile and preliminary imitations of established lyrical modes.

In 1788, while still an undergraduate at St. John's, Wordsworth began composition of his *An Evening Walk*. With its heroic couplets, conventional loco-description and a panoply of eighteenth-century stock phrases, couched in the genre of florid sentimentalism, the poem sits unobtrusively in the tradition of eighteenth-century nature poetry. Wordsworth's notebook indicates that, contemporaneous to his composition of *An Evening Walk*, he had been translating Virgil's *Georgics*, with their celebration of bucolic virtue in the retreat from urban corruption.[12] Similarly, his *Descriptive Sketches* partially narrates a walking tour in revolutionary France, with scenes of nascent Republican politics intermingled with elements of the Alpine sublime, delivered in unexceptional iambic pentameter. Wordsworth published both poems in January 1793 through the radical publisher Joseph Johnson, in part to raise funds to support his French lover, Annette Vallon, and their daughter, Caroline. Wordsworth's correspondence suggests he was never satisfied with either poem, in 1801 sending them as proof to friends of how much his politics, and poetics, had evolved (*Letters EY* 120). A far greater achievement in his lyrical development came in 1797, when Wordsworth presented to Coleridge his *The Ruined Cottage* (1797). The poem – which would eventually become Book I of *The Excursion* (1814) – deploys Shakespearian, Spenserian and biblical allusion, blended with the elegiac pastoral of graveyard poetics, and an angrier vein of social protest, in its narration of the decline of a rural family.

By their meeting in the spring of 1797, Coleridge's experimentation with various forms of the lyric mode, put to both political and philosophical purposes, had been somewhat more advanced. In imitation of his beloved William Lisle Bowles, Coleridge began with a series of loco-descriptive paeans to the River Otter of his Devonshire childhood. Later, in the aftermath of the French Revolution he utilised the sonnet form in a series of political celebrations of British heroes of 'Liberty'. Amplifying his radical and political credo, Coleridge then turned to Milton – the great Republican poet – for his overly ambitious *Religious Musings* (1796). In contrast to the somewhat dense metaphysics and frequently cumbersome Miltonics of *Religious Musings*, at the same time Coleridge was discovering a new voice in poems like 'The Eolian Harp' (1795), 'Thoughts on Having Left a Place of Retirement' (1796) and 'Frost at Midnight' (1798). Here, Coleridge had germinated a new hybrid of philosophical lyric which would blossom into what are now classed as the 'conversation poems'.

The nomenclature 'conversation poems' was given to a collection of Coleridge's poems of the mid and late 1790s by twentieth-century critics.

But Coleridgean scholars have found a salient coherence to the term. These lyric 'conversations' are fluid, blank verse effusions, which blend loco-description, materialist metaphysics and a somewhat quietist political radicalism. They are situated in domestic surroundings, yet also in the heart of nature, and in the company of friends and family. This 'conversational' strain in Coleridge's poetry had a powerfully transformative influence over Wordsworth: both for his metaphysics and his poetic voice. This influence is redolent throughout many lyrics within *Lyrical Ballads* but is exemplary in 'Tintern Abbey'. 'Tintern Abbey' with its sense of a spirit working within and throughout nature to reconcile the disharmonies and antinomies of the human condition, deploys language very similar to Coleridge's materialist speculation in the 'Conversation Poems':

> And I have felt
> A presence that disturbs me with the joy
> Of elevated thoughts; a sense sublime
> Of something far more deeply interfused,
> Whose dwelling is the light of setting suns,
> And the round ocean and the living air,
> And the blue sky, and in the mind of man:
> A motion and a spirit, that impels
> All thinking things, all objects of all thought,
> And rolls through all things.
>
> (*LB* Lines 94–103)

Here, Wordsworth's sense of something 'far more deeply interfused' echoes Coleridge's 'plastic power, that interfused / Roll through the grosser and material mass / In organizing surge!' of 'Religious Musings' (*PW STC* I. i.; Lines 405–407). Yet beyond this, Wordsworth learns from Coleridge's model a paradigm for philosophical conviviality, in which the solipsist finds epiphany in reaching out to a beloved companion with whom to share the sublime experience. This is exemplified by the address to Dorothy, Wordsworth's sister, in the closing lines of 'Tintern Abbey':

> Nor perchance,
> If I were not thus taught, should I the more
> Suffer my genial spirits to decay:
> For thou art with me here upon the banks
> Of this fair river; thou my dearest Friend,
> My dear, dear Friend; and in thy voice I catch
> The language of my former heart, and read
> My former pleasures in the shooting lights
> Of thy wild eyes.
>
> (*LB*, 114–120)

Indeed, Wordsworth later turns to Dorothy in his childhood reminiscences from 'Nutting', included in *Lyrical Ballads*, inviting her to share in his psychodynamic experience. So, in this strain of philosophical poetry, Wordsworth and Coleridge mould the eighteenth-century lyric voice into a register that is simultaneously introspective and conversational.

Ballad Voice

The contrast between lyric and ballad traditions is quite stark. Inherent throughout traditions of lyric expression is the conviction that elevated poetry is morally and spiritually edifying. In contrast, ballads occupied a far less exalted situation. With their roots in illiterate rustic, plebeian culture, ballads were initially transmitted orally, and predominantly for the purposes of popular entertainment. Where lyric describes a *mode* of poetry, ballad is a quite clearly defined *form*. The term 'ballad' derives from the French 'ballad chanson' – 'dancing song' – intimating the tripping metrical regularity of balladic prosody.[13] The structure of a common ballad is a quatrain in iambic tetrameter, but the form is versatile, and lends itself to alternating tetrameters and trimeters, and to longer stanzaic constructions. While there is a danger of essentialising the language of ballads, they tend to be composed in either a demotic idiom with short syllabic utterances, or by deploying a self-consciously archaic lexicology. Ballads almost invariably rhyme, and the most common rhyme scheme is a simple alternating pattern, but varieties of couplets and chiasmic rhymes are not unusual. Traditionally ballads have been used for narrative purposes, relating folkloric subject matters, which are generally tragic in nature, and often dwell upon superstition and the supernatural.

The eighteenth-century 'ballad revival' formed from a confluence of complementary cultural dynamics. A core impetus for ballad revivalism was a counter-Enlightenment current that ran through mid-century philosophy and art. Enlightenment *philosophes* were increasingly interested in comparative cultural anthropology between Western civilisation, and supposedly 'primitive' peoples in pre-industrial and commercial societies. Advocates of a 'stadial' theory of human development viewed such societies as emblematic of earlier stages in the narrative of human development. But under the aegis of the counter-Enlightenment, thinkers in the vein of Jean-Jacques Rousseau argued that such cultures could potentially highlight corruptions in current European civilisation, and indeed, in more extreme terms, some believed they were more authentic and organic than contemporary Western civilisation. The cultural primitivism inspired by Rousseau (and others) directed the focus of the culture of sensibility towards primitive, uncultured peoples – including peasants – and their supposedly more authentic, unadorned feelings (Novak 461). Yet another tangent from Enlightenment primitivism was linguistic. For Enlightenment *philosophes* searching for an *ursprach* (originary language) underpinning all languages and human expressions, so-called primitive peoples and their oral cultures tantalised with the potential endurance of remnants of an antediluvian, or even Adamic language. With their interest in 'the language of ordinary men', Wordsworth and Coleridge were alive to the significance of these conjectures about pre-literary cultures, as part of what Alan Bewell terms their 'domestic anthropology'.[14]

Another impetus for self-conscious ballad revivalism was nationalistic. In choosing to compose in ballad form and metre, Wordsworth and Coleridge were deliberately taking a stance against established neoclassical codes of respectable poetry. But they did not arrive at this position independently of already emergent trends in British poetry. In the literary culture of the mid eighteenth century, with the emergence of new strands of nationalist sentiment, British critics and writers were seeking a narrative of national genius and poetic expression that was not dependent upon Greco-Roman classicism, nor the erudition and polish of Augustanism. Instead, they looked to sources of literature from the medieval and ancient Celtic eras. Wordsworth's allusions to the merits of the antiquarian ballad 'The Children in the Wood' in the 'Preface' aligned him with a tradition stretching back to Joseph Addison in *The Spectator* who had, despite its vulgarity, praised the unpolished sentiment of the tale.[15] A pivotal moment in the history of ballad revival came in 1765 when Bishop Thomas Percy published his *Reliques of Ancient English Poetry*, a collection of courtly ballads dating from the mid seventeenth century. In response, Joseph Ritson issued his accusation in 'Observations on the Ancient English Minstrels' (1783) that Percy had both fabricated many of his ballads and artificially gentrified others. While manuscript evidence shows that Percy did not falsify his poems, Ritson was substantially correct that Percy had amended the cruder elements of the original language to add polish to his anthology. At the heart of this controversy were questions about the value of authenticity, of the merits of elite versus demotic registers, and the role of the bardic minstrel in modern literary culture. The result of this contretemps was to generate a renewed interest in the ballad form, given testimony by such works as David Herd's *Ancient and Modern Scots Songs* (1769), Thomas Evans's *Old Ballads* (1777–1784) and

John Pinkerton's *Scottish Tragic Ballads* (1781). This culture of popular antiquarianism seeded further important works of revivalist and forged medieval and primitive manuscripts. Among these, the shade of the suicide Thomas Chatterton – whom Wordsworth later dubbed the 'marvellous boy' – and his innovative, forged 'Rowley' manuscripts, hangs heavy over *Lyrical Ballads*. Yet among the select number of early reviewers of *Lyrical Ballads*, Dr Charles Burney signalled his dissatisfaction with the volume, that while it indicated its adherence to antiquarian balladic tradition, this adherence had not been complete enough. Burney concluded that he could not:

> regard [the poems] as *poetry*, of a class to be cultivated at the expense of a higher species of versification, unknown in our language at the time when our elder writers, whom this author condescends to imitate wrote their ballads.[16]

Burney criticises Wordsworth and Coleridge for attempting to imitate the antique style of traditional ballads or revivalist composers of the previous generation, but not quite accomplishing the polish of a gentleman antiquarian like Percy.

In addition to nationalist and primitivist orientations, Wordsworth and Coleridge's interest in ballad revivalism was also entwined with their radical politics of the 1790s. Popular antiquarianism often manifested a blend of nostalgia with radical utopianism, embodied in mythical golden ages of medieval history, styled as repositories of ancient British liberty. Coupled with this was a counter-Enlightenment resistance to the class politics of the patrician elements of the Enlightenment, which frequently endeavoured to erase backward plebeian culture. As Olivia Smith observes, late eighteenth-century British culture was divided between a refined elite, and the supposedly crude, materialistic, semi-lettered masses.[17] And yet plebeian and working-class tastes were becoming increasingly culturally and economically amplified by the close of the century, with significant rates of functional literacy within the populace. This was expressed in the popularity of 'idiot savant' or peasant poets such as Stephen Duck and Ann Yeardsley, but also in the form of 'broadside ballads' – simple, topical and highly commercial poems, printed on cheap and disposable paper, often addressing contemporary political and social events. With the roots in the marketplace of popular plebeian culture, appealing to a lower class, and often semi-literate readership, street ballads could be a vehicle for disseminating political radicalism. Later, in Book VII of *The Prelude*, Wordsworth writes equivocally of seeing 'files of ballads dangl[ing]' for sale 'from dead walls' in London streets (1805 VII. 195). Yet *Lyrical Ballads* is replete with poems that address rural poverty, the economic costs of famine and war, and social injustice. Texts such as 'Goody Blake and Harry Gill', 'The Female Vagrant', 'Ruth', 'The Last of the Flock' and 'Simon Lee' pertain quite closely to the Broadsheet tradition of condensing issues of social concern into tightly arranged ballad metre.

A further class dimension to *Lyrical Ballads* was Wordsworth and Coleridge's enthusiasm for the supernatural – or the seeming supernatural – widely perceived as the predilection of the ignorant and credulous peasantry. Ballads, with their tales of folklore and witchcraft, appealed to eighteenth-century authors attracted to the dynamics of the counter-Enlightenment, and the ballad revival coincided closely with the fashionable aesthetics of the Gothic. From childhood, both Wordsworth and Coleridge were steeped in traditions of popular antiquarianism, balladry and folkloric superstition. Wordsworth's first extensive and extant poetic experiment was an ambitious piece of Gothic juvenilia, *The Vale of Esthwaite*, composed in balladic iambic tetrametric couplets, inspired by Helen Maria Williams and Charlotte Smith. This early piece of imaginative morbidity broods upon his self-recriminations for his father's early demise:

> At noon I hied to gloomy glades,
> Religious woods and midnight shades,
> Where brooding Superstition frowned
> A cold and awful horror round,
> While with black arm and bending head
> She wove a stole of sable thread.
>
> (Lines 25–30)[18]

That Wordsworth considered such peasant superstition integral to the progression of his moral and artistic being is given testimony by his inclusion of traditionary chapbook ballads and folkloric legends in the education of his semi-autobiographical 'The Pedlar' – later 'the Wanderer' of *The Excursion*:

> many a Legend
> Traditionary, round the mountains hung,
> And many a Legend, peopling the dark woods,
> Nourished Imagination in her growth,
> And gave the Mind that apprehensive power
> By which she is made quick to recognise
> The moral properties and scope of things.
>
> (*Excursion* I, 185–187)[19]

The Wanderer owns a 'straggling volume' of 'preternatural tale[s]' composed of chapbook 'wooden cuts / strange and uncouth' which, once seen 'Could never be forgotten!' (Excursion I, Lines 196–197; 199–200.)

This vein of plebeian Gothic folkloricism was reignited during the phase of Wordsworth's adherence to William Godwin's rational critique of political injustice, redolent in the lurid imagery of *The Salisbury Plain Poems*. These Gothic nightmare scenes, composed in archaic Spenserian stanzas, situate tragical stock figures of remorseful murderers and abandoned mothers, in proximity to primeval scenes of druidic human sacrifice and human barbarism, in rather crabbed and hackneyed verse. Indeed, as Simon Jarvis observes, the cumbersome prosody and labourer imagery of *The Salisbury Plain Poems* underscores Wordsworth's growing suspicion of easy resolutions in politics and poetry alike.[20] In contrast, Wordsworth's seeming-supernatural in ballads like 'Good Blake and Harry Gill' leave ambiguous whether the 'curse' in the poem is magical or psychological, but is also an exhaustive palliative for economic oppression. In contrast, Coleridge was always far more enthusiastic for the regional folkloric superstitions of his West Country childhood – even taking Wordsworth to task for his scepticism for such provincial beliefs. Whether or not the division of 'supernatural' and 'ordinary life' given by Coleridge in the *Biographia* predated composition, or was a *post facto* rationalisation, Coleridge's 'The Rime of the Ancyent Marinere' is a more overtly supernatural and pseudo-medieval ballad than any of Wordsworth's contributions to the anthology.

'Lyrical Ballads'?

Lyricism is a mode of poetic expression – a type of voice, or an attitude of a speaker, rather than a specific form. It might then be argued that there is no impediment to a ballad becoming a vehicle for lyricism. Yet an objection in the cultural context of *Lyrical Ballads* would have been that the conventional expectations evoked by using ballad form would be seen as antithetical to the very nature of the lyric. Ballads are demotic and plebeian, where lyrics are erudite and elevated in register. Ballads narrate sensational plots, while lyrics alternate between introspective reverie and patrician public address. And a probable reason that ballads had not hitherto been seen as an ideal form in which to express lofty, or profound, or powerful ideas and feelings was that the line length limited expression to minimalist concentration. Similarly, the rhythms common to metrical frames like tetrameter and trimeter felt too jaunty, trivial and coarse in comparison with the more paced and varied iambic pentameter.

Wordsworth and Coleridge were engaged in both ballad and lyric traditions, balancing the weight of the lyric as vessel of beauty, philosophic truth and profound emotional sentiment, against the stigma of ballads as popular titillation and trashy ephemera. If a 'lyrical ballad' was intended to synthesise this dialectic, the perceived limitations of the ballad had to be in some way surmounted. To some extent they found an instructive precursor in the form of the German poet Gottfried Bürger. Bürger's popular ballads 'Leonore' (1773) and 'Des Pfarrers Tochter von Taubenhain' (1782) exemplify the fashionable trend for sexually risqué sentimentality, combined with Gothic graveside excesses. Yet despite their mutual appreciation, Wordsworth was sceptical about the fundamental power of Bürger's poetry:

> Bürger is one of those poets whose book I like to have in my hand, but when I have laid the book down I do not think about him. I remember a hurry of pleasure, but I have few distinct forms that people my mind, nor any recollection of delicate or minute feelings which he has either communicated to me, or taught me to recognise. (*Letters EY* 234)

In Bürger, Wordsworth perceived the danger that his ballads might produce only a fleeting sensation, but leave no lasting impact upon the memory, and therefore the moral and imaginative senses. In the 'Preface' Wordsworth would later claim that, if conventional ballads engage interest by stimulating through narrating outrageous events, then in his 'lyrical ballads' 'the feeling therein developed gives importance to the action and situation, and not the action and situation to the feeling' (*LB* 99). As Curran observes, throughout *Lyrical Ballads*, the promise of some form of remarkable action is habitually hinted at, but at the last moment denied, and thus the drama of the situation is diffused, giving way to the psychological introspective characteristic of the lyric mode (182). In developing his idea of 'lyrical ballads', Wordsworth sought for balladic compositions that were both mnemonic and psychologically transformative. For Daniel Robinson, a lyric poem allows for greater tonal and technical sophistication than a standard folk ballad: 'A 'lyrical ballad', therefore, makes a greater demand on the reader, who must manage the lyrical, and thus interpretive, complexities and ambiguities that interrupt the usual course of storytelling' (Robinson 176–177). The lyric creates a mental space, whereas the ballad delineates a sequential line of dramatic narrative. As such, a 'lyrical ballad' becomes a nexus in which the Wordsworthian 'spot' and the balladic narrative tradition are brought into tense productivity.

The so-called Lucy Poems are exemplary 'lyrical ballads': varied in structure and character, but still characterised by shared themes and motifs, literary minimalism and emotional intensity. While the grouping of these poems as a distinct collection owes much to the caprices of Victorian anthologisation, Wordsworth's placement of these poems together in *Lyrical Ballads* intimates a more intentional connection (Butler 43). Composed alongside profoundly introspective lyric verses such as 'The Boy of Winander' and 'Nutting', the 'Lucy Poems' were penned during the winter of 1799, while Wordsworth and his sister Dorothy were confined to isolation in the small rural German town of Goslar (*Letters EY* 89). These striking poems have garnered numerous influential critical readings. Geoffrey Hartman interprets the 'Lucy Poems' in terms of 'ritual mourning and personal reminiscence' for a 'boundary being' who fluctuates somewhere between 'nature sprite and human', representing the 'intermediate modality' of the speaker's consciousness 'rather than an intermediate being'.[21] Similarly, Frances Ferguson analyses the verses in terms of the strange ontological absence of Lucy. David Bromwich reads Lucy in psychobiographic terms, while Paul H. Fry focuses on Wordsworth's metaphysics through his fluctuation between prosopopoeia and anti-prosopopoeia in his representation of Lucy. Alan Bewell and Kurt Fosso both approach the 'Lucy Poems' in terms of Wordsworth's attitudes towards communal rituals of mourning.[22]

The 'Lucy Poems' are also illuminating in considering the convergence of lyric and balladic voices, their generic origins and the way they are expressed in 'lyrical ballads'. In an insightful reading of 'We Are Seven', Philip Connell illustrates the ways in which plebeian strains of literary culture in Wordsworth's early oeuvre have often been effaced by processes of canonisation.[23] The roots of the 'Lucy Poems' demonstrate Wordsworth blending of literary sources and conventions from across the various lyric and balladic traditions. All of the 'Lucy Poems' pertain to Wordsworth's preoccupation with loss, grief and commemoration, a predilection referred to by critics as his 'epitaphic mode'.[24] As such, the 'Lucy Poems' are offshoots of the lyric tradition of pastoral elegy popularised by the mid-eighteenth-century graveyard poets like Gray and Young. Indeed, elements of these compact verses seem almost parodies of the conventional topoi of earlier loco-descriptive lyricism: in 'She dwelt among th' untrodden ways', the enigmatic Lucy is connected with the generic (and 'untrodden', and therefore presumably unseen) 'springs of Dove', likened to a 'Violet' that is almost entirely occluded: 'Half-hidden from the Eye!' (*LB* Lines 2, 5, 6). In 'A slumber did my spirit seal', the unnamed 'she' is, by the end of the poem, juxtaposed with inanimate nature 'rocks and stones and trees' (8) in an inversion of the classical *locus amoenus*. The lyric is a mode for grandiloquence. Yet in 'She dwelt among th' untrodden ways' Lucy is a being, a 'Maid whom there were none to praise', while still being a 'very few to love' (3, 4). So rather than complete solitude, this suggests Lucy inhabited a pre-linguistic, or per-haps rather a pre-poetic, community.

Yet communion with the phantasmal dead was also a prerogative of balladic tradition. The anonymous medieval ballad 'The Unquiet Grave' situates a bereaved lover by the graveside in disquieting dialogue:

> 'I'll do as much for my true-love
> As any young man may;
> I'll sit and mourn all at her grave
> For a twelvemonth and a day.'
>
> The twelvemonth and a day being up,
> The dead began to speak:
> 'Oh who sits weeping on my grave,
> And will not let me sleep?'[25]

In contrast, throughout the 'Lucy Poems' the female subject/object is rendered voiceless, her fate solely narrated by the presumably male speaker, whose maudlin meditations fluctuate between her ontological being and his psychological state. Indeed, where traditionary ballads were commonly dialogic, the 'Lucy Poems' cleave more to the lyrical in being monologic. Similarly, where ballads narrate a sequential series of exciting – even lurid – events, the 'Lucy Poems' narrate almost nothing, and are characterised by radical indeterminacy: a being referred to as 'Lucy' who was once alive is now – or may be – dead, and this excites some powerful, but often enigmatic emotions in the survivor. The reader feels that the speaker of 'Strange fits of passion' is indeed strange, as his paranoiac feelings lack an objective correlative. Similarly, in 'She dwelt among th' untrodden ways' the lines 'But she is in her grave, and oh / The difference to me!' only informs us that the speaker feels there to be a difference, but deliberately does not describe this changed state (*LB* 11–12). And the speaker of 'A slumber did my spirit seal' describes himself as initially cocooned from normal sensibilities. Feeling 'no human fears' he becomes increasingly like his nameless Lucy, who 'seemed a thing that could not feel / The touch of earthly years' (2, 3–4). Tantalising and thwarting with supernatural expect-ations, Lucy appears more spectral in life, whereas in death, she seems more concretely thing-like than ever:

No motion has she now, no force
She neither hears nor sees;
Roll'd round in earth's diurnal course
With rocks and stones and trees.

(Lines 5–8)

Conversely the poem 'Lucy Gray' does indeed appear to have a revenant, in the form of an eternally homeless wraith, blending the folkloric with the classical in its allusion to (and inversion of) Orpheus and Eurydice, from Ovid's *Metamorphoses* (Bewell 205–207). However, the poem conflates the classical and the folkloric, as the events of the plot retrace the tragic plot of 'The Children in the Wood' (204). The poem, narrating the disappearance of a small child into the natural realm, had a balladic revivalist precursor in Johann von Goethe's *Erlkönig* (1782) (The Alder King), which was itself inspired by Johann Gottfried Herder's translation of a medieval ballad *Erlkönigs Tochter* (1695) (The Alder-King's Daughter). These folkloric and supernatural events are naturalised by the rapacious spirit of Nature, anthropomorphised in 'Three Years She Grew in Sun and Shower' (Hartman 160–161). Yet of the 'Lucy Poems', the ghostly 'Lucy Gray' is curiously the closest to the more earthy genre of broadside ballads, relating as it does (albeit in etherealised form) a series of real events: in notes to the poem, Wordsworth acknowledges that he was inspired by a true story of a child who had drowned in a frozen canal near the Yorkshire town of Halifax (*LB* 352). With this indebtedness to a local tragedy in the newspaper press, converted into a Gothic ballad, Wordsworth seems to be deliberately complicating his criticism in the 'Preface' of the inundation of 'frantic novels, sickly and stupid German Tragedies, and deluges of idle and extravagant stories in verse' (*LB* 99). In contrast to the cliches of the Gothic, the 'Lucy Poems' render ghosts ambiguous, while making the living uncanny, and the departed unsettlingly material.

In *Lyrical Ballads* Wordsworth and Coleridge inherited traditions of lyricism and popular balladry. But rather than passive recipients, their engagement was active and innovative. From 1798 – and beyond – they had adapted the eighteenth-century lyric into a conversational form, capable of conveying nuanced philosophical and theological concepts, but in an idiom relatively denuded of the contortions so commonplace in conventional poetic language and convention. In parallel with this achievement, the concept of the 'lyrical ballad' catalysed the common ballad as a vehicle for compressed lyric expression, blending seeming rhetorical and metrical simplicity with emotional intensity. In his 'Lucy

Poems' especially, Wordsworth fused the maudlin meditations of grave-yard poetry, the heightened emotional excesses and self-reflection of the culture of sensibility, the expectations of the Gothic supernatural, and the ontological inquiries of metaphysical poetry, constrained by the most economic verse in *Lyrical Ballads*.

Endnotes

1 Walter Savage Landor, 'Archdeacon Hare and Walter Landor', in *Dialogues of Literary Men*, vol. IV of *Imaginary Conversations* (London: J. M. Dent and Sons, 1891). Qtd. in John E. Jordan, *Why the Lyrical Ballads? The Background, Writing, and Character of Wordsworth's 1798 Lyrical Ballads* (Berkeley and London: University of California Press, 1976), 174.

2 Wiliam Keach, ed., *William Wordsworth and Samuel Taylor Coleridge: Lyrical Ballads* (London: Penguin, 2006); Mary Jacobus, *Tradition and Experiment in Wordsworth's 'Lyrical Ballads' (1798)* (Oxford: Clarendon, 1976), 209; Daniel Robinson, 'Wordsworth and Coleridge's *Lyrical Ballad*, 1798', in *The Oxford Handbook of William Wordsworth*, ed. Richard Gravil and Daniel Robinson (Oxford: Oxford University Press, 2015), 168–185.

3 Stuart Curran, *Poetic Form and British Romanticism* (Oxford and London: Oxford University Press, 1986), 182.

4 Seamus Perry, 'Wordsworth and Coleridge', in *The Cambridge Companion to Wordsworth*, ed. Stephen Gill (Cambridge: Cambridge University Press, 2003), 161–179; 168.

5 James A. Butler, 'Poetry 1798–1807: *Lyrical Ballads* and *Poems in Two Volumes*', in *The Cambridge Companion to Wordsworth*, ed. Stephen Gill (Cambridge: Cambridge University Press, 2003), 38–54; 38–39.

6 Stephen Gill, *William Wordsworth: A Life* (Oxford: Oxford University Press, 1989), 185.

7 For definitions of 'Lyric' see Martin Gray, *A Dictionary of Literary Terms*, 2nd ed. (Harlow: Longman, 1992), 164; *The Princeton Encyclopedia to Poetry and Poetics*, ed. Alex Preminger and T. V. F. Brogan (Princeton: Princeton University Press, 1993), 826–824.

8 Susan Stewart, 'Romantic Meter and Form', in *The Cambridge Companion to British Romantic Poetry*, ed. James Chandler and Maureen N. McLane (Cambridge: Cambridge University Press, 2008), 53–75; 55–56.

9 Richard Holmes, *Coleridge: Early Visions* (London: HarperCollins, 1989), 31, 37.

10 Andrew Bennett, *Wordsworth Writing* (Cambridge: Cambridge University Press, 2007), 1–3.

11 Ben Ross Schneider Jr., *Wordsworth's Cambridge Education* (Cambridge: Cambridge University Press, 1957), 4, 64, 99.

12 Schneider, *Cambridge Education*, 166; Kenneth R. Johnston, *Wordsworth and the Recluse* (New Haven: Yale University Press, 1984), 13; Paul D. Sheats,

The Making of Wordsworth's Poetry, 1785–1798 (Cambridge, MA: Harvard University Press, 1973), 45.

13 For definitions see 'Ballad' in *The Princeton Encyclopedia to Poetry*; Maximillian Novak, 'Primitivism', in *The Eighteenth Century*, ed. H. B. Nisbet and Claude Rawson, vol. 4 of *The Cambridge History of Literary Criticism* (Cambridge: Cambridge University Press, 2005), 456–469; 461; Charles Mahoney, 'Wordsworth's Experiments with Form and Genre', in *The Oxford Handbook of William Wordsworth*, ed. Richard Gravil and Daniel Robinson (Oxford: Oxford University Press, 2015), 532–546; 535; Martin Gray, *A Dictionary of Literary Terms*, 2nd ed. (Harlow: Longman, 1992), 39.

14 Alan Bewell, *Wordsworth and the Enlightenment: Nature, Man, and Society in the Experimental Poetry* (New Haven: Yale University Press, 1989), 30–40.

15 Joseph Addison, 'On *The Two Children in the Wood*', *Spectator*, no. 85 (Thursday June 7th 1711), in *The Commerce of Everyday Life, Selections from The Tatler and The Spectator*, ed. Erin Mackie (London: Macmillan, 1997), 369.

16 Charles Burney, '*Lyrical Ballads* with a Few Other poems', *Monthly Review* (29 June 1799): 202–210.

17 Olivia Smith, *The Politics of Language 1791–1819* (Oxford: Clarendon, 1984), 3, 12–13.

18 *William Wordsworth: Poems,* vol. 1, ed. John O. Hayden (London: Penguin Books, 1977), 51.

19 *The Excursion by William Wordsworth*, ed. Sally Bushell, James A. Butler and Michael C. Jaye (Ithaca and London: Cornell University Press, 2007), 53.

20 Simon Jarvis, *Wordsworth's Philosophic Song* (Cambridge: Cambridge University Press, 2007), 42.

21 Geoffrey Hartman, *Wordsworth's Poetry, 1787–1814* (New Haven and London: Yale University Press, 1964), 157–158.

22 Frances Ferguson, 'The Lucy Poems: Wordsworth's Quest for a Poetic Object', *ELH* 40 (1973): 432–448; David Bromwich, *Disowned by Memory: Wordsworth's Poetry of the 1790s* (Chicago and London: Chicago University Press, 1998), 128–129; Paul H. Fry, *Wordsworth and the Poetry of What We Are* (New Haven and London: Yale University Press, 2008), 6–10; Alan Bewell, *Wordsworth and the Enlightenment*, 188; Kurt Fosso, *Buried Communities: Wordsworth and the Bonds of Mourning* (Albany: State University of New York Press, 2004), 141–163.

23 Philip Connell, 'How to Popularize Wordsworth', in *Romanticism and Popular Culture in Great Britain and Ireland*, ed. Philip Connell and Nigel Leask (Cambridge: Cambridge University Press, 2009), 262–282; 262–278.

24 Mark Sandy, *Romanticism, Memory, and Mourning* (London: Routledge, 2016), 33.

25 *The Oxford Book of Ballads*, ed. James Kinsley (Oxford: Oxford University Press, 1989), 96–97.

PART II

Subjects and Situations from Common Life

CHAPTER 5

Conversation in Lyrical Ballads

Frances Ferguson

When William Wordsworth published his 'Preface' to *Lyrical Ballads* in 1800, he disparaged many things that had come to seem the signal attributes of poetry: elevated diction, personifications of abstract ideas and 'phrases and figures of speech which from father to son have long been regarded as the common inheritance of Poets' (*LB* 101). His aim in his poems, he said, was to justify his conviction that poetry could do without such elegances, and to describe 'incidents and situations from common life. . . . In a selection of the language really used by men' (97). He wrote in the conviction that poetry needed to tap into the most fundamental sources of pleasure, rather than the most refined, and identified his own writing more with the perceptions of rustic people than with those of professional poets. In particular, he singled out 'the pleasure which the mind derives from the perception of similitude in dissimilitude', which he instanced as 'the life of our ordinary conversation' (111). Conversation itself – what one person might actually say to another in the process of exchanging remarks in their different voices – might provide an example and a standard for poetry. Comparing lines from the 'Babes in the Wood' with some that Samuel Johnson had written in order to mock poetry using 'language that closely resembles that of life and nature' (113), he implicitly drew a distinction. Dr Johnson's lines do not rise to the level of good poetry, because they do not rise to the level of conversation, something that one person might actually feel impelled to tell another. When Wordsworth considers the roles of the poet and the scientist, versions of that word 'conversation' appear again:

> the Poet, prompted by this feeling of pleasure which accompanies him through the whole course of his studies, converses with general nature with affections akin to those, which, through labour and length of time, the Man of Science has raised up in himself, by conversing with those particular parts of nature which are the objects of his studies. (106)

Poets, shepherds, and natural historians alike appear in the 'Preface' conversing with the things that they attend to, and they then report on that converse in their talk with other persons. In this chapter I aim to indicate some of the writing that forwarded Wordsworth's thinking about conversation, and to track the effect of his understanding of conversation on the development of *Lyrical Ballads*, and particularly on the changes that Wordsworth introduced into the 1800 edition.

'Conversation' and the 'conversable' were, as Kevis Goodman has observed, 'master word[s] of the period'.[1] Various poets in the eighteenth century – especially James Thomson, William Cowper and Anna Letitia Barbauld – had prepared the way for Wordsworth's attention to conversation. Even though Wordsworth regularly joined writers such as John Aikin in criticising Alexander Pope for drawing his language from that of other poets, Pope himself had participated in a conversational style when he addressed his epistles to specific named individuals like John Arbuthnot and his *Essay on Man* to Lord Bolingbroke. Both Goodman and Jon Mee, in his *Conversable Worlds: Literature, Contention, & Community 1762 to 1830*, have observed how extensively the notion of conversation circulated to embrace items that appeared in the latest instalments of newspapers delivered to William Cowper's rural retreat, as well as the conversational debating that various Dissenters adopted in turning ideas over with one another.[2]

One of the most influential and proximate models for a conversational poetry was William Cowper's *The Task* (1785), in which Cowper had gone so far as to take up a friend's challenge that he write a poem on a sofa. The poem that resulted was the product of a conversational dare – a description of a sofa as the subject matter for poetry, and an account of the sofa as a featured site for conversation among friends. Pope had enlisted his friends to represent a conversation that leagued him and them against sometimes anonymous and sometimes pseudonymous opponents, but Cowper drew the friends he addressed in his poem close. Together they could demonstrate how their retreat from the busy and contestatory world of the city made it possible for them to see the importance of subjects that had often seemed beneath the notice of poetry. Their rural existence made winter walks and manures and the movement of the flame of a fire the occasion for poetic conversation, and Cowper prized a poetry that came as close as possible to capturing the diction and rhythms of ordinary, conversational speech. His aim was to make the things of ordinary life that are governed by the natural cycles of the day and the year appear to be as significant – or more significant – for poetry than the concerns of 'the busy and the gay world'.[3] It was, he thought, a task both difficult and important 'to make sense speak the language of prose without being prosaic, to marshal the words of it in such order as they might naturally take in falling from the lips of an extemporary speaker, yet without meanness; harmoniously, elegantly, and without seeming to displace a syllable for the sake of the rhime' (Cowper, qtd. in Mee, 172–173). While Pope's conversational gestures linked him with allies in opposition to others, and while Dissenters such as Philip Doddridge were promoting conversation as interrogation and re-examination, Cowper's conversations were themselves tokens of friendship.

The ease with which Cowper could address a season like winter helped him to develop a mild form of personification. It is a conversable friend, whom he loves even when others do not:

> Oh Winter, ruler of th'inverted year,
> Thy scatter'd hair with sleet like ashes fill'd,
> . . . .
> I love thee, all unlovely as thou seem'st,
> And dreaded as thou art! (IV. 120–129)[4]

Reacting to the seasons and their weather relieved him, as it had Thomson, from having to devise a plot driven by strongly characterised humans or heroic actions. The reports on daily walks at different hours and the arrival of the post with news continually provided new material for conversation. *The Task* was in that sense an improvisational poem, absorbing and assimilating whatever might come to Cowper's attention. But the cost of that fluidity was high. The poem could seem (as Goodman has described it) 'a desperate attempt to keep up the conversation – any conversation' (87). Moreover, the poem was basically trapped in its poet's genial and convivial voice, ultimately yielding up a picture of a domestic circle that seemed bent on cutting itself off from a world not already companionable. The projected image of the poet and his audience made them seem to close ranks with one another against outsiders to such an extent that Leonore Davidoff and Catherine Hall identified the popularity of *The Task* in the Victorian age as a notable symptom of the limitations of Victorian society.[5]

Cowper was, in other words, an amiable host, but to a small circle, and portrayed England as a beneficent home to some, but not to all. Although he introduced Crazy Kate, gypsies and the South Sea Islander Omai into his poem, he addressed only Omai, and did not stay for an answer from him. While Cowper imagined that Omai, after his sojourn in England between Captain Cook's second and third voyages, had 'found again / Thy cocoas and bananas, palms and yams' (*The Task* IV. 639–640), he also pictured Omai longing for news of England and the sight of English ships. 'Sweet Nature' may please 'ev'ry sense' (I. 427), but it is a nature that extends itself to natives more than to others. Though *The Task* continually treats the landscape as inspiring both virtue and freedom, it also distinguishes between those who can see and those who recognise that mere sight is a kind of blindness: 'Admitted once to [God's] embrace, / Thou shalt perceive that thou wast blind before' (V. 780–781). Cowper depicted a natural world that spoke to all, but spoke *more* emphatically and feelingly to some than to others, and the various characters he mentioned, whether public figures or individuals whom he named almost by happenstance, were themselves objects of description. They were not, that is, interlocutors. The idea that the natural world conversed with humans tended to push writers such as Cowper away from dialogue and into description of nature and the humans who drew on it, and to sort the humans into more and less qualified conversationalists.

The problem that some essayists and writers set for poetry was the creation of an audience as extensive and inclusive as possible. Such a project involved natural observation as fully as James Thomson and Cowper imagined, but it relied on descriptions that emerged from direct contact with the natural world rather than routing natural description through paths already well-tracked in poetry. Thus, John Aikin, in his *Essay on the Application of Natural History to Poetry* (1777), criticised 'descriptive poetry [for having] degenerated into a kind of phraseology, consisting of combinations of words which have been so long coupled together, that, like the hero and his epithet in Homer, they are become inseparable companions'.[6] And he made a negative example of Pope, criticising him for having, in his first pastoral, represented the rose as flowering when the crocus and the violet do (20). In the process, Aikin was defending the importance of direct and attentive observation, but he was also noticing the way in which a poetic description like Pope's might needlessly divide an audience into segments, those who would accept the authority of poetry and poetic license and those who would object to importing a needless inaccuracy. Care and accuracy made poetry available to an audience that included everyone who could see, and not merely those who saw through eyes trained in poetic traditions or avowed religious belief.

But while Aikin prescribed natural observation as the most democratic of all subjects and accurate description as the most effective way of preserving its openness, his suggestions about the importance of nature poetry became particularly important when his sister, Anna Letitia Barbauld, began to consider how to authorise as many speakers as possible in the *Hymns in Prose for Children* that she wrote in 1780 and 1781.[7] The form of the hymn was one that Cowper, along with his collaborator John Newton, had used to engage voices other than his own in the *Olney Hymns* (published 1779). The insistently first personal stance of hymns such as Newton's 'Amazing Grace' with its testimony that 'I once was lost, but now am found; / Was blind, but now I see' used the occasion of congregational singing to make that first-person plural rather than merely singular.[8] The poetic voice was therefore no longer localised in the person of the poet. The singer of a hymn uttered its words equally with the author of the hymn. Any singer, every singer could testify about the two different states of their soul, the one that preceded full and confident sight, and the one in which sight was graced.

In *Hymns in Prose for Children* Barbauld aimed to 'impress devotional feelings as early as possible on the infant mind' so that a child would so 'feel the full force of the idea of God [as] never to remember the time when he had no such idea' (238). She stripped her hymns of poetry and delivered them in metrical prose that would be both accessible and memorable to her young audience. The creatures and plants of the natural world appeared almost as the illustrations in a child's picture book, so that children who remembered and recited the hymns were participating in acts of recognition. William Hazlitt was only one among the many who spoke of having carried the hymns in their heads for a lifetime, and saw them as evidence of the importance of memories of the natural world: 'It is', he wrote, 'because natural objects have been associated with the sports of our childhood' that the mind 'clings with the fondest interest to whatever strikes its attention'.[9] Moreover, a poetry on and about the natural world seems never to restrict its scope in the way that dramatic interchange does, because the 'interest we feel in external nature is common, and transferable from one object to another of the same class' (Hazlitt, V. 100). It is abstracted, in that it never need distinguish between one daisy and another, never need affirm the peculiarities of personality and situation.

The child's thinking becomes important, for Barbauld and for Hazlitt, not for children's innocence but rather for their confidence in their own knowledge, their feeling of never not having known the things that they know. And in a collection like *Evenings at Home; or, The Juvenile Budget Opened* (1796) by Barbauld and Aikin, conversations about the natural world – what an adult and his or her charges see and discuss on a walk –

become the occasion for exchanges that are reciprocal. When an adult describes the metal iron as 'the most tenacious or difficult to break, next to gold', a child 'properly [objects]' that he snapped his penknife and that his mother continually breaks needles.[10] Conversation is instructive less because it involves communicating an adult's knowledge to a child than because it illustrates the ways in which conversation can establish a platform of equality between persons who have different relations to the objects of their knowledge.

Barbauld and Aikin set an example for many with their attention to conversation about an immediately available natural world and by making the natural world the occasion of a conversation of and to the deity ('But now I can speak, and my tongue shall praise him', Barbauld, *Selected Poetry and Prose* 239). These literary models of conversation help us to begin to understand why it has long been difficult for readers to accept the aptness of the title *Lyrical Ballads* for the poems in the 1798 volume – and difficult for them to see why Wordsworth persisted with that title in 1800 and 1802. At least one contemporary reviewer noted that lyrics are meant to be accompanied by music, and Maureen McLane has approvingly noted the riddle that Bertrand Bronson posed: '*Question*: When is a ballad not a ballad? *Answer*: When it has no tune'.[11] Wordsworth's and Coleridge's poems in 1798 were, by contrast, as 'tuneless' as John Keats's numbers in his 'Ode to Psyche'. When John E. Jordan asked *Why the Lyrical Ballads?* he called attention to Wordsworth's statement in the 'Preface' to the *Poems* of 1815 that lyrical poems require 'for the production of their *full* effect, an accompaniment of music'.[12] Compiling various different statements of Wordsworth's on ballads and balladry, he finally concluded that 'impressive meter ... sets a ballad apart' (174) and that '*Lyrical Ballads*, then are finely crafted songs of popular feeling' (180). Metrical language was particularly important for creating a feeling that approximated congregational singing. It represented a tune in attenuated form.

On the one hand, the title of the 1798 volume of *Lyrical Ballads* makes sense of various decisions that Wordsworth announced in the 1798 'Advertisement' and particularly in the 1800 'Preface'. The ballad form epitomised a poetry that was not in need of professional poets and the specialised learning that they brought to their writing. The memorability that allowed a ballad to continue to be sung by a series of persons allowed it to dispense with elaborate poetic diction, stock images, and formulaic personifications. Yet, on the other hand, Jordan's analysis highlights the degree to which the title *Lyrical Ballads* raised as almost as many questions as answers, and provides a context for understanding Dorothy

Wordsworth's comment in a letter of 10 September 1800 that Wordsworth intended to publish the poems of the 1800 edition under the title of
Poems by W. Wordsworth. She wrote as if to steer clear both of a possible
confusion with Mrs. Robinson's 'volume of *Lyrical Tales*' (*Letters EY*
297–298), also being published by Longman, and of debates about the
fit between the title of the volume and its contents (Jordan 173).

By focussing on the volume as a volume, Anne Janowitz has effectively
charted a progression in *Lyrical Ballads* from ballads such as 'The Rime of
the Ancyent Marinere' that could express 'the pan-cultural possibility of a
democratic' and communitarian poetry that incorporated multiple voices
to 'Tintern Abbey' as a poem of lyric subjectivity.[13] She has, in other
words, stressed the variety of poems included in the volumes of *Lyrical
Ballads* so as to avoid suggesting that the poems all adopt the same solution
to the question of why readers might find the poems compelling. Janowitz
persuasively treats the *Lyrical Ballads* as a volume-long conversation, and in
that sense, honours the ongoing dialogue between Wordsworth and
Coleridge that sparked the volume and Coleridge's later description of
the distribution of labour that he and Wordsworth agreed to. Yet the
changes that Wordsworth introduced between the 1798 and the 1800 editions made the title *Lyrical Ballads* increasingly seem like a misnomer. For,
as Zachary Leader pointed out in an essay published in 2001, the number
of poems that are identifiably ballads remained constant, at twelve, even
when the number of poems in the entire collection increased from twenty-
three in 1798 to forty-one in 1800.[14] And while the number of recognis-
able ballads was unchanged, the new ordering that Wordsworth provided
in 1800, along with the 'Preface', altered the look of the ballads
themselves.

Jordan's observation that the 1798 poems are 'finely crafted songs of
popular feeling', which I quoted earlier, meshes well with the tension that
Janowitz has described in the ballad's importance 'to the founding of
romantic lyricism: simultaneously dated and fashionable, oral and written,
choric and monologic' (33). But Jordan notes a distinctive syntactic
anomaly that Wordsworth introduces into various poems that he provided:
the 'disjointed syntactic trick of repeating the subject of a sentence or an
objective complement in noun and pronoun form' (181). Jordan offers, as
'the archetypal example', the formulation 'The eye it cannot chuse but see'
from 'Expostulation and Reply', but he also instances 'The Last of the
Flock', 'Simon Lee', 'The Mad Mother' and 'The Idiot Boy' to demonstrate how thoroughly the trick became part of Wordsworth's standard
poetic procedure (181). Jordan's gloss – 'Apparently Wordsworth believed

that people in a state of strong feelings do not think their sentences out'
(181–182) – helps to explain how syntax amplified diction in marking the
simplicity of the poems of *Lyrical Ballads*. The recurrent syntactic trick
identified the poems as poems that aimed to preserve their conversational
immediacy, their participating in the thoughts of a moment rather than
the formulations that, corrected, might be seen as fit for print.

In the 1800 edition of *Lyrical Ballads*, then, Wordsworth was trying
to capture the dialogism of the ballad form, but to do so in the form of
a conversation that approached as nearly as possible that of ordinary
speech. Even as he feared that describing his poetic creed in the
'Preface' that he added in 1800 would appear 'the selfish and foolish
hope of *reasoning* [his reader] into an approbation of these particular
Poems' (*LB* 95), he intensified his concentration on conversations as if
they were the working definition of interchange without argumentation.
Coleridge's 'The Rime of the Ancyent Marinere' which had opened the
1798 volume, came to look more artificial, more an artefact of writing
than of speech, and more 'poetic' in the light of Wordsworth's
sharpened ear for conversation. And Wordsworth seemed to have registered the fact that he and Coleridge were already in 1800 moving in
different directions in their thinking about a poem like the 'Rime' – as
if anticipating that Coleridge would add marginal glosses to the poem
when he published it in *Sibylline Leaves* in 1817 and would thus present
it as an archaic text, written in another era and not spoken in their own.
In the later editions of *Lyrical Ballads*, Coleridge's poem appeared under
a more nearly contemporary-sounding title, 'The Ancient Mariner,
A Poet's Reverie', and with more nearly colloquial spellings and diction.
Yet we might also imagine that one of the main reasons for Wordsworth's demotion of Coleridge's poem from its initial prominence at
the beginning of the 1798 *Lyrical Ballads* to a position just before
'Tintern Abbey' in Volume I in 1800 and 1802 was the enormous
disparity between the situations of the mariner and the wedding guest,
the mariner's blasted and blasting knowledge of supernatural occur-
rences appearing less in the form of conversation, more in the form of
a directive: 'Listen, Stranger!' (*LB* Line 45).

Coleridge has been credited with having developed the conversation
poem as a distinct poetic category ever since George McLean Harper
applied the 1798 subtitle of 'The Nightingale: A Conversational Poem'
to eight of Coleridge's poems that Harper characterised as 'fluent and
easy'.[15] But George Watson's qualification is important for our understanding of the place of conversation in the 1800 *Lyrical Ballads*: 'the name

is both convenient and misleading. A conversation is an exchange; and these poems . . . are plainly monologues'.[16] Between the publication of the 1798 *Lyrical Ballads* and the 1800 edition, 'The Nightingale' lost the subtitle 'Conversational Poem' and acquired information about the time of its composition: 'written in April, 1798'.[17] The poem was topical in articulating the suspicion of rehearsing specific poetic associations that Wordsworth had expressed in the prose associated with the *Lyrical Ballads*. It quoted Milton's description of the nightingale as 'Most musical, most melancholy' only to proceed to object to the way 'many a poet echoes the conceit' when he would have done better to 'have stretch'd his limbs / Beside a brook in mossy forest-dell / by sun or moon-light' (Lines 13, 23, 25–27). While the poem did include addresses to 'My Friend, and my Friend's Sister' as well as to the nightingale and Coleridge's 'dear Babe', the dating of the poem and the apostrophes to the nightingale and various persons left 'The Nightingale' in a state of merely monologic fluency (40, 91). Coleridge was speaking to – and not with – other persons and nightingales.

For the 1800 edition, Wordsworth dropped his poem 'The Convict' as if to reject a poetry that imagined sympathy proceeding through direct address, and he opened the first volume with 'Expostulation and Reply' and 'The Tables Turned; An Evening Scene, on the same subject'. Both of these poems consist almost entirely of reported speech, conversational exchanges between the poet William and his friend Matthew. Each have their lines as interlocutors, but the first of the poems extends the reach of conversation, calling attention to 'this mighty sum / Of things forever speaking' and recruiting 'that old grey stone' with which 'thus, alone' the poet 'convers[es] as he may' (Gamer, Lines 25–26, 1, 3, 30; pp. 188–189). Together the poems make up a conversation on a conversation. 'The Tables Turned' directly reverses Matthew's injunction to William to con his books in 'Expostulation and Reply'; it makes the approach of darkness an occasion for seizing the moment and letting 'Nature be your teacher' (Line 16; p. 189).

These and other poems in *Lyrical Ballads* have often seemed to be stamped with Coleridge's doctrine of the 'One Life': a spirit and force within us and abroad.[18] But they also reflect a view that Barbauld expressed in her correspondence with her brother John Aikin – namely, that a poetry in and from nature possessed the singular virtue of never seeming to try to instruct anyone.[19] The reversibility of the advice that one speaker gives another – first, apply yourself to your books; then, leave off your studies and notice the natural world – captures an important feature

of conversation. It can take up topics and state positions without commit-
ting itself to the doctrines of 'all the sages' ('The Tables Turned' 24).

These poems that opened the 1800 *Lyrical Ballads* stood as examples of
human conversation about the converse between humans and nature,
almost as if Wordsworth were at the outset declaring loyalty to Thomson
and the praise his poetry won for giving 'a moral sense to nature' (Hazlitt
V. 90). They constituted something like a poetical 'Preface' and a statement of purpose for the various poems that would follow in the volumes –
particularly as 'Expostulation and Reply' moved from named speakers to
speakers in 'The Tables Turned' whose voices are indistinguishable and
unassignable to either of the interlocutors. Moreover, these poems prepared the way for notable additions in 1800 that represented conversation
among *natural* forces. 'The Waterfall and the Eglantine', for instance,
staged an interchange between the 'thundering Voice' of a waterfall 'swoln
with snows' and 'a poor Briar-rose' and made a political statement all the
stronger for the psychological shallowness of the poem's protagonists
(Gamer, Lines 2, 5, 6; p. 318). Most of the poem consists simply of the
eglantine's attempt to remind the waterfall of the amicable relationship
that they had maintained through various seasons and to hold out the
prospect of future amity, with the poet only entering in the final stanza to
say that there was no further conversation for him to overhear. He did not
hear 'aught else' (54).

This modest allegory of resistless force and helplessness was immediately
followed by 'The Oak and the Broom, A Pastoral' in which Andrew the
Shepherd related the story of two vegetable interlocutors who occupied
strongly contrasting positions and stood in widely different relationships to
the world around them. Predictably and wittily, the poem involved almost
nothing more than the shepherd's recognising that the preachy oak and the
lowly broom between them made up a comparison between great things
and small. The shepherd heard the oak hectoring the lowly broom on how
woefully misplaced it was. The shepherd recognised how fully the oak
encouraged the broom to see how tenuous was its hold on life, sheltered as
it was in a narrow cleft of rock that could be dislodged by the fall of other
rocks. The oak's speech was a memento mori. And the shepherd heard the
broom singing in response about the pleasures of home, of rootedness. It
claimed to feel 'a favor'd plant' in and around which yellow flowers and
verdant leaves gathered (Gamer, Line 74; p. 322). Butterflies, ewes, lambs,
and shepherd boys sought it out. The poem earned its pastoral subtitle
with its ending: a storm felled the oak,

> and whirl'd him far away;
> And in one hospitable Cleft
> The little careless Broom was left
> To live for many a day.
>
> (Lines 107–110)

The oak that had thought that it could merely convey the message that death occurs even in Arcadia finds that the message applies to him. But the poem extended past the narrative conclusion that ended the conversation between the oak and the broom. It was key to the force of the tale that it had a teller, Andrew, who was capable of registering the oak's reversal of fortune, and who saw the alteration in the landscape as a natural tale, a story to be read off from the landscape by someone who knew it well.

The waterfall, the eglantine, the oak, and the broom were personified enough to have speaking voices in these poems, but their characters differed from those of Thomson's or Cowper's seasons. In Thomson or Cowper, a personified season such as winter or spring is apparent through its effects, its dampening organic life or its bringing flowers into bloom, its sending chill or warming winds to subdue or revitalise a person's spirits. Wordsworth's allegories in these poems function differently. They do not dwell on what Hazlitt calls the 'abstractedness' of nature: the way that the natural cycle makes individual examples of an oak or a broom seem entirely replaceable. In these poems, by contrast, Wordsworth sets up his poems to draw a stark distinction between one situation – a before – and another – an after. The poems present a moralised nature only because of the presence of a human speaker, the poet in 'The Waterfall and the Eglantine' who can remember an earlier interaction between the two and can know of the eglantine's demise, the shepherd who knows the landscape so well as to be able to register changes in it.

That emphasis on distinct alterations in the natural landscape became particularly prominent in 'The Brothers' one of the most impressive of the conversational poems that Wordsworth added in 1800. Wordsworth noted that the 'Poem was intended to be the concluding poem of a series of pastorals, the scene of which was laid among the mountains of Cumberland and Westmoreland' (Gamer 301), and in the process suggested how thoroughly he was assigning a shepherd's role to the residents, making even the 'homely Priest of Ennerdale' (Line 16) closely observe the particular features of the landscape as if his unstudied attention were the purest natural history. The Priest, his wife and other residents know this place, and he tends it and talks about it much as if he were a custodian, or even a shepherd gathering its history and relating it to the human histories that have taken place in it. The graves of the rural churchyard, unmarked by plaques and tombstones, are for him and the other residents 'a pair of diaries, one serving ... / For the whole dale, and one for each fire-side' (161–162).

While 'The Oak and the Broom' revolved around a conversation in which the oak intoned its advice without realising that danger might apply to itself, the priest of 'The Brothers' mistakes his situation socially rather than existentially. Although Leonard recognises the priest 'at once', Leonard does not identify himself to the priest but carries on the conversation 'as to one / Unknown' (114, 116–117). The waterfall and the eglantine, on the one hand, and the oak and the broom, on the other, were bound together – and, in effect, speaking with one another – continuously by virtue of their proximity to one another. Leonard's departure at the age of thirteen and his absence of twenty years, by contrast, allow for the talk he and the priest have (about changes in the landscape and changes in the country churchyard) to take place as if Leonard were a stranger rather than someone who knew:

> every corner
> Among these rocks and every hollow place
> Where foot could come . . . .
> Was known as well as to the flowers that grew there.
> (Lines 269–272)

In the asymmetrical conversation that is the poem, the priest participates in what he thinks of as an exchange with a tourist, and a tourist he is eager to dismiss as a 'moping son of Idleness' (11) upon whose forehead 'the setting sun/ Write[s] Fool' (109). He sees Leonard as a stock type, someone merely interested in doing sketches of picturesque scenes and eager to observe natural catastrophes as if they were spectacles designed for the amusement of 'folks that wander up and down like you' (147).

By contrast with the proximity that aspects of the natural world such as the oak and the broom have with one another, or with the sociability and familiarity that Cowper describes in his rural retreat, the priest and Leonard interact at distinct cross-purposes. The narrator's description echoes the priest's half hour of observing Leonard with Leonard's 'full half hour' (82) of looking at the graves in the country churchyard, as if to use the recurrence of the detail to indicate how thoroughly the two men's understandings of their interchange differ. Moreover, the priest recounts Leonard's own history to him, even as Leonard seems caught between hurrying to request information about his brother and forestalling its reception, as he shows himself to be more observant of the landscape than a casual observer would be, and he describes the elder Walter Ewbank's grandsons, Leonard's brother James and Leonard himself, as 'orphans' even when the priest has not said anything that would identify them as such.

In one sense the story of the Ewbank family is central. The debt that Walter Ewbank inherited; the love that his two grandsons felt for him, one another and the mountains in which they lived; and Leonard's having gone to sea to earn money; all constitute events and eventfulness in the poem. They are the stuff of stories that local residents would tell one another. But the poem adds a new dimension to the story by delivering it in conversational form. Had the story been recounted to an actual stranger, it would have had the effect of suggesting that the stranger's being 'mov'd' (349) was a sign that sympathy for the suffering of others might bind together individuals who do not know one another. Wordsworth, however, sets up the conversation in almost novelistic fashion, so that the immediacy of Leonard's grief will be all the more apparent to readers. The priest is convinced that he is talking to an idler, and does not know what the narrator has told the readers of the poem – namely, that Leonard had been so much marked by his upbringing among the mountains that he had been 'half a Shepherd on the stormy seas' (43) and had seen mountains, sheep, and shepherds 'in the bosom of the deep' (58). The priest's speaking to Leonard with misplaced pity about Leonard's fate ('When last we heard of him / He was in slavery among the Moors' (Lines 312–313)) makes him particularly slow to arrive at the information that Leonard was in need of – how sleepwalking had led James to his death, in a lethal version of calenture in his native mountains that repeats the merely nostalgic calenture in which Leonard had renewed his sense of immediate connection with those distant mountains.

In a novel such as Jane Austen's *Emma*, conversations structured around a character's reluctance to declare their identity fully would ultimately be a cause for amusement. Emma Woodhouse's only slightly veiled hints to Frank Churchill about the possibly scandalous provenance of Jane Fairfax's piano would have been resolved when Frank disclosed his romantic relationship with Jane. The uneven distribution of information would have been sorted out as the characters arranged themselves into marriage pairs. In 'The Brothers', by contrast, Leonard discloses his identity to the priest in a letter, even as he treats the information he has received of his brother's death as life-altering. He had been a 'Shepherd-lad'; he had been 'half a Shepherd on the stormy seas'; but he became a different person, 'A Seaman, a grey headed Mariner' (430–431) under the pressure of his conversation with the priest. The man who returned 'With a determin'd purpose to resume / The life which he liv'd there' (66–67) hears all that the priest has to tell him:

> 'All press'd on him with such a weight, that now,
> This vale, where he had been so happy, seem'd
> A place in which he could not bear to live:
> So he relinquish'd all his purposes'.
>
> (Lines 420–423)

Wordsworth contrasts the voluble priest, who thinks he addresses a stranger, with the man bound to the place by his store of childhood memories and his love for his brother, and in the process, offers a clear example of how 'the feeling developed [in his poems] gives importance to the action and situation and not the action and situation to the feeling' ('Preface' *LB* 99). The man who had imagined that his interlocutor courted his sentiments lightly turns out to have the shallower engagement. The burden of the conversation falls on the man who has little to say, and who speaks largely to interrupt.

But if Wordsworth makes 'The Brothers' convey the feelings of an adult who relinquishes all the attachments of his childhood, he also includes in *Lyrical Ballads* poems that exactly situate speaking children by matching them with adult interlocutors who put leading questions to them. The poem 'We Are Seven' recounts a conversation between a 'little cottage girl' (Gamer Line 5; p. 213) and a pedestrian tourist – an actual stranger rather than an unrecognised past acquaintance like Leonard. The poem's adult speaker treats the girl as a native informant, in the way a tourist might, but also in the somewhat stilted manner of a grownup trying to find something to say: 'Sisters and brothers, little maid, / How many may you be?' (13–14). Yet that polite inquiry creates an opening in which the child turns the tables on the adult. She, 'wondering' (16), looked at him, as if she felt the answer to be so self-evident that it made the question somehow ridiculous. Her reply is that there are seven children in her family, including two who are in the churchyard. As the tourist repeatedly tries to explain to the child that she is mistaken ('If two are in the church-yard laid, / Then ye are only five' (35–36), she provides details about the deaths of her siblings even as she insists that 'we are seven' and thus makes it clear that she is fully in command of the knowledge that they have died. The tourist continually points out that only the living should be included in the count, but the girl persists in numbering her dead siblings with the living. She repeatedly corrects the adult, with the confidence of a child in the reality of their perceptions. But she also disputes his account as if she were illustrating the remarks of the priest in 'The Brothers': 'The thought of death sits easy on the man / Who has been born and dies among the mountains' (181–82). The evenness of her insistent refrain – its lack of argumentative vehemence – underscores the strength of her confidence that her relationship with her siblings continues, whether they be living or dead.

Many have found the tourist of 'We Are Seven' to be obtuse or inane or worse, but it is a striking fact about the conversational exchanges in Wordsworth's poetry that they do not call up fully developed characters and character traits. Most of the interlocutors – with the exception of Leonard in 'The Brothers', Matthew in 'The Two April Mornings' and 'The Fountain, A Conversation' or Edward in 'Anecdote for Fathers' – have only general outlines. They are no more – or scarcely more – than types. The tourist of 'We Are Seven' is a generic tourist asking generic questions of a local girl who is represented as talking as an eight-year-old girl in the mountains might talk. Her feelings derive directly from her sense of relationship between herself, her siblings, and the natural world.

'Anecdote for Fathers', the poem which immediately follows 'We Are Seven' in the 1800 and 1802 editions of *Lyrical Ballads*, takes on a subtitle – *'Shewing how the practice of Lying may be taught'* – shifting from a conversation between strangers to one between intimates. The subtitle virtually announces that the speaker, the father who quizzes his son about whether he prefers Kilve or Liswyn Farm, recounts the conversation as a generalisable lesson. Walking and talking at Liswyn, the father thinks of 'former pleasures' (Gamer, Line 9; p. 215) at Kilve even as he observes the young lambs frolicking and the morning sun shining. Even as he adds an appealing descriptor to Kilve all three times he mentions it, even as he repeats the bare refrain '"Or here at Liswyn farm"' (28, 32, 36) he does not stop to notice that he has preordained Edward's reply. Not content to catechise his son to retrace the preference that he has himself expressed clearly if not entirely directly, the father asks 'Why' five times. As the child seizes on the weathercock at Liswyn Farm as a reason to prefer Kilve, the father begins to see his own mild coerciveness. He has demanded a reason for a preference that he himself had steered his son to. Moreover, the very act of having a preference – especially a preference for 'former pleasures' over immediate ones – bespeaks an adult perspective. The father is requiring that experiences be compared, and that some be ranked higher than others, when the son ought to be able to feel satisfaction in what he sees around him, wherever he is. In the end, though, 'Anecdote for Fathers' takes the edge off the father's leading questions and demands for answers by having him effectively retract his earlier words and allow himself to be taught. The poem is ultimately shown to be rightly titled 'Anecdote for Fathers', not because it instructs other fathers but because it instructs this father in self-management.

While 'Anecdote' presents the consciousness of the difference in perspective of the son and the father in a fleeting and anodyne situation, poems such as 'The Two April Mornings' and 'The Fountain, A Conversation' foreground the difference between the poetic speaker and his older friend Matthew as ineliminable. Matthew, seeing '"Yon cloud with that long purple cleft"' (*LB* 'The Two April Mornings' Line 21), views it as a replica – '"the very brother"' (Line 28) – of the sky as it appeared when he was moved by the sight of his young daughter's grave. His sense of the rhyme in the look of the sky leads him both to remember what he felt that day – as if he had never loved his Emma more than he did at that moment – and how he had immediately rejoiced in the sight of a young girl who happened to appear before him, before realising how little he could imagine her as a substitute for the daughter he had lost. 'The Fountain, A Conversation' loosely continues the conversation from 'The Two April Mornings'. In response to Matthew's lamenting that '"many love me; but by none / Am I enough belov'd"' (*LB* 'The Fountain' Lines 55–56), the poet proffers the right/wrong response: '"And, Matthew, for thy children dead / I'll be a son to thee!"' (61–62). His words are right in that they express his deep affection for Matthew and his desire to cheer him; wrong in that they miss the depth of Matthew's consciousness of loss.

The awkwardness of conversation that Wordsworth represents in poems such as 'Anecdote for Fathers', 'The Two April Mornings' and 'The Fountain' helps us to see that he models conversational exchange as something other than social maladroitness, something other than lack of affection. Conversation in these poems appears in the form of mild, well-intentioned mistakenness. It honours the concern that speakers have for one another, and in the process of showing how little their words succeed in conveying that concern, it shifts the emotional register of the poetry. No longer does conversation simply report incidents or convey the affection of interlocutors in 'The Two April Mornings' and 'The Fountain'. Instead, it points to affections so deep that they cannot be addressed, even in talk between close friends. Poems such as these then prepare us to qualify various accounts of 'Lines Written a Few Miles above Tintern Abbey, on revisiting the banks of the Wye during a Tour, July 13, 1798'. Anne Janowitz, as mentioned earlier, has seen the poem as a fully lyric and first-person poem that caps a progression from ballad to lyric in the 1798 volume. Marjorie Levinson has influentially seen the poem's description as an erasure of the landscape before Wordsworth's eyes, while Margaret Homans has focused on its near-erasure of Dorothy Wordsworth's presence.[20] Yet the poems of awkward conversation may help us imagine that it might instead be a poem of perfected conversation. The poems of maladroit conversation continually depict common natural scenes in order to bring out how differently the interlocutors register them. 'Tintern Abbey', by contrast, is a poem in which the eyes so fully carry the affections for both the scene and Dorothy that no direct quotation enters to introduce an awkwardness or disrupt the conversation with a need for more speech.

Endnotes

1 Kevis Goodman, *Georgic Modernity and British Romanticism: Poetry and the Mediation of History* (Cambridge: Cambridge University Press, 2004), 86.

2 Jon Mee, *Conversable Worlds: Literature, Contention, & Community 1762 to 1830* (Oxford: Oxford University Press, 2011), 3–7, 121–124.

3 Cowper to William Unwin, quoted in Mee, *Conversable Worlds*, 172–173.

4 William Cowper, *The Task*, in *Cowper: Poetical Works*, ed. H. S. Milford (London: Oxford University Press, 1967).

5 Leonore Davidoff and Catherine Hall, *Family Fortunes: Men and Women of the English Middle Class, 1780–1850* (Chicago: University of Chicago Press, 1987), 165.

6 John Aikin, *An Essay on the Application of Natural History to Poetry* (Warrington, 1777), 5. *Eighteenth-Century Collections Online*, Gale, Doc. CW119020651.

7 *Anna Letitia Barbauld: Selected Poetry and Prose*, ed. William McCarthy and Elizabeth Kraft (Peterborough: Broadview Press, 2002), 234–260.

8 John Newton and [William Cowper], *Olney Hymns, in Three Books* (London: W. Oliver 1779), I. 53. *Eighteenth-Century Collections Online*, Gale, Doc. CW119020651.

9 William Hazlitt, *Lectures on the English Poets*, in vol. V, *The Complete Works of William Hazlitt*, ed. P. P. Howe (London: J.M. Dent and Sons, Ltd., 1930), 101.

10 John Aiken and [Anna Letitia Barbauld], *Evenings at Home; or, the Juvenile Budget Opened*, 6 vols. (London: [J. Johnson], 1792–1796), IV. 130. *Eighteenth Century Collections Online*, Gale, Doc. CW104230550.

11 Maureen N. McLane, *Balladeering, Minstrelsy, and the Making of British Romantic Poetry* (Cambridge: Cambridge University Press, 2008), 233;

Bertrand Harris Bronson, *The Traditional Tunes of the Child Ballads* (Princeton: Princeton University Press, 1972), I. ix.

12 John E. Jordan, *Why the Lyrical Ballads? The Background, Writing, and Character of Wordsworth's 1798 Lyrical Ballads* (Berkeley: University of California Press, 1976), 173.

13 Anne Janowitz, *Lyric and Labour in the Romantic Tradition* (Cambridge: Cambridge University Press, 1998), 33–37.

14 Zachary Leader, '*Lyrical Ballads*: The Title Revisited', in *1800: The New Lyrical Ballads*, ed. Nicola Trott and Seamus Perry (Houndmills: Palgrave, 2001), 23–43; 24.

15 George McLean Harper, *Spirit of Delight* (New York: Ayer Publishing, 1928), 3.

16 George Watson, *Coleridge the Poet* (New York: Barnes & Noble, 1966), 61.

17 For amendments made to the 1798 edition for the new edition of 1800, I use Michael Gamer and Dahlia Porter, eds., *Lyrical Ballads 1798 and 1800: Samuel Taylor Coleridge & William Wordsworth* (Peterborough: Broadview Press, 2008), 231. Hereafter referred to as Gamer.

18 Mary Jacobus, *Tradition and Experiment in Wordsworth's Lyrical Ballads 1798* (Oxford: Clarendon Press, 1976), 59.

19 Sharon Ruston, 'The Application of Natural History to Poetry', *Literature and Science Hub Online*, University of Liverpool.

20 Marjorie Levinson, *Wordsworth's Great Period Poems: Four Essays* (Cambridge: Cambridge University Press, 1986), 32; Margaret Homans, *Women Writers and Poetic Identity: Dorothy Wordsworth, Emily Bronte, and Emily Dickinson* (Princeton: Princeton University Press, 1980), 26–27, 76–78.

CHAPTER 6

The Power of Things in Lyrical Ballads

Paul H. Fry

> [To] hear no so[und]
> Which the heart does not make or else so fit[s]
> To its own temper that in external things
> No longer seems internal difference;
> All melts away, and things that are without
> Live in our minds as in their native homes.
> (*Cornell LB* 'Lines Composed a Few Miles above
> Tintern Abbey, Lines 4–9; p. 322)

It may be that this chapter will appear to make too much of the word 'things'. After all, in common usage 'things' and 'objects' are more or less synonymous, and with that understanding the chapter might as well have been called 'The Power of Objects in *Lyrical Ballads*'. What follows is written in the belief not only that there *is* a distinction between things and objects but that Wordsworth attends carefully to the distinction, and that it is helpful to think of *Lyrical Ballads* as an exploration, at certain moments, of the imagination's way of seeing objects primordially – of seeing them, that is, as *things*. Much of the time, to be sure, things and objects are as interchangeable in Wordsworth's vocabulary as they are for most of us. But sometimes there is a difference, an important difference that helps to explain the frequent vagueness of his language in his more ecstatic moments (in contrast, for example, with the precise niceties of Coleridge even in such moments), a vagueness disagreeable to his detractors, yet perhaps the very quality his admirers relish most when they find him most affecting. There will be no need here to pause over his vagueness, let alone subject it to stylistic analysis; rather, it will be taken for granted as his way of expressing the power of things, all things in their unity, including the senses in which humans too are things.

'Things' in the plural appear at two moments of heightened reflection, certainly vague enough, in 'Tintern Abbey':

> While with an eye made quiet by the power
> Of harmony, and the deep power of joy,
> We see into the life of things.
>
> (*LB* Lines 47–49)

> A motion and a spirit, that impels
> All thinking things, all objects of all thought,
> And rolls through all things.
>
> (Lines 101–103)

In both passages we come face to face with Wordsworth's pantheism, the supposition in the second passage that things 'think' carrying us even beyond the conscious enjoyments of the plant world in 'Lines Written in Early Spring'. If there is facetiousness in 'But then he is a horse that thinks' in 'The Idiot Boy' (Line 122), where all sentient things feel but rarely think – perhaps to their credit – and if there is merely mechanical concentration on the part of the old man who 'moves / With thought' in 'Old Man Travelling' (Lines 6–7), there is surely nothing facetious or mechanical about the thinking of nonhuman things in the second of these passages from 'Tintern Abbey'. Perhaps not *all* things think: the line 'rolls through all things' would be redundant if it did not add things that may *not* think to 'all thinking things'. Nonetheless, the threefold insistence on 'all' throughout the passage brings with it a continuum of oceanic inclusiveness.

But things in themselves are not objects, as the crucial line 102 surprisingly makes clear. Regardless whether someone might say that all things or just some things think, no one would ever consider 'objects' as cognitive subjects. An 'object', in any standard usage, is a designated thing *about which* a *subject* thinks. Things become objects as soon as they are reflected on as distinct entities by a thinker, but when we just gaze at things without reflection, they remain Wordsworth's 'all things'. This distinction is philosophically familiar from Kant's reminder that we cannot know things in themselves but require a cognitive scaffolding to make them objects. It is in the moment when we make things significant that those things become objects. It may be that for consciousness there is no moment when we see things prior to seeing them as objects. Rather, we may confront them from the very beginning with a hesitant conjecture, if not with a strong presupposition, about what they should be called.[1] In that case, as we shall see, for Wordsworth it becomes the role of the imagination to recover the thing-hood of objects, always with the intimation that there are states of mind, such as childhood, in which things, including human things, are not yet objectified.

The distinction between things and objects is not an obscure or unusual one, then. But what might well give pause, and sharpen one's understanding of 'Tintern Abbey' (the poem William Empson called a 'muddle'), is that Wordsworth makes this *same* distinction within the flow of his oceanic rhetoric, which seemingly overrides distinctions, in a lyric meditation.[2]

Because they cannot be known in themselves, and cease to be things as soon as they are identified as objects, things are intimated as uncanny and attract speculation such as the pantheism of Erasmus Darwin, Priestley, and other Wordsworthian sources, resulting in the 'One Life' that Wordsworth shared – at various times – with Coleridge. It is tempting to say that this charisma of the unknown is the power of things. But even in 1798, Wordsworth never speaks in so many words of 'the power of things' – despite our feeling somehow that he must have done so repeatedly. The first passage from 'Tintern Abbey' quoted above shows him again to be more precise than we expect him to be. In this passage, power belongs not directly to things but to the correspondent breeze of the poet's imagination, a power residing in 'harmony' and in the 'joy' that in the 'Prospectus to *The Recluse*' the poet hopes to 'spread' in 'widest commonalty' (i.e. everywhere, pervading the oceanic 'all').[3] It is this power that enables enthusiasts as visionaries, half perceiving and half creating, to 'see' that things may be alive.

Wordsworth does not authorize us to conclude, then, that the power of things is their sentience, however fully that sentience may remain an article of faith in 1798, and may contribute, indeed, to the claim – soon to embarrass him – that he is 'a worshipper of Nature' ('Tintern Abbey' 153). And even then, drawing on Milton's more transitory dalliance with false surmise in 'Lycidas', he knows that his belief is speculative: 'If this / Be but a vain belief' (Lines 51–52). By 1800 in any case, when the expression 'all living things' in the first 'Poem on the Naming of Places' ('It was an April morning', Line 7) would seem to suggest that some things are not living, Wordsworth's vitalism extends less predictably to the non-organic world. Nor, in addition, does the power of things have to do with any quality they acquire as objects, those *differentia specifica* that are each in turn unique (in contrast with things, inseparable because undifferentiated) except insofar as all objects without exception come into their own, as it were, through the medium of human thought ('all objects of all thought'). Interestingly, the unity of objects thus understood can accord with the diagnosis of narcissism to which Wordsworth is often subjected, but the unity of *things* cannot. He is one with things only as a thing himself, but he can never think himself as a thing, a thinking thing or otherwise. He is nevertheless fascinated by the thought of what it might be like to *be* a thing, hence his interest in the bodies of the dead; in the marginalization of human sentience – recognized as a tendency in *Lyrical Ballads* by readers both derisively and affirmatively from Hazlitt and Byron to Alan Bewell – and in the conjectural stationing of his own corpsehood with 'thoughts of more deep seclusion' (7).[4] One finds such thoughts even, and especially, at the beginning of 'Tintern Abbey': from his own place of 'repose' in dark shade (9–10) he views the 'plots' around him (11) – all harbingers of the grave that prepare for his striking last will and testament in conclusion, bequeathing life itself to his sister when he shall be where he no more can hear her voice (viz. Lines 148–149).

Yet we feel that things in Wordsworth, all things, do have power. I shall argue henceforth that this power acquires an even deeper interest for Wordsworth in some of the poems prepared for the second volume of *Lyrical Ballads* in 1800 than it had in the volume of 1798. There are anticipations apart from 'Tintern Abbey' in 1798, though. In 'The Tables Turned' one finds another of Wordsworth's tantalizing expressions: 'the light of things' (Line 15). It is as though the poet were exhorting his bookish acquaintance to emerge from Plato's cave into materialism rather than idealism, not to experience sunlight alone but rather the visionary gleam of all phenomena: 'Come forth into the light of things, / Let Nature be your teacher' (15–16). It has to be admitted, though, that in this poem what can hesitantly be called phenomena waver between things and objects. Whatever they are, they have the essential sameness that belongs to things prior to becoming the objects of thought that they are in the sorts of analytic treatise 'Matthew' reads (intellect 'misshapes' them, we 'murder to dissect' them [27–28]), but at the same time the aura of their presence has an aesthetic quality that can only belong to objects. They are the 'beauteous forms of things' (27) that we find recalled in the 'forms of beauty' of 'Tintern Abbey' (24), where again the Platonic absence of vision comes into play, with the assurance that such forms – again, decidedly not Platonic Forms – have been an influence that differs from the influence of 'a landscape to a blind man's eye' (25).

'The Thorn' is about the power of a particular object – not yet, or no longer, quite a thing – a power that Wordsworth forty-five years later recalls having hoped his reader would experience in the same way he had experienced it in a storm ('Fenwick Note', *Cornell LB* 10). And yet we first encounter it indexically, like the ancient mariner's ship or the boy of Winander: 'There is a thorn'.[5] It is 'a wretched thing forlorn', empty of vitality 'like rock or stone' (*LB* 9, 12). We shall learn soon that it has a certain size, shape and character, together with a narrative history as a site of suffering and perhaps even a gibbet; but prior to description the emphasis falls on indication, the fleeting insistence that something is just there giving way to the name that makes it an object, like the ship or the boy. There are moments, however, abetted by the mist of the storm Wordsworth had experienced and perhaps by the retired sea captain's weak eyesight, when the thorn cannot be seen at all, and an adjacent shape recovers the thorn's initial interchangeability with other things: what the speaker takes for 'a jutting crag' turns out to be the wretched Martha Ray herself (197–198). The narrator's very unreliability has its didactic side, as he fosters gothic melodrama in being uncertain about differences, hoping his sceptical interlocutor (quoted at the beginning of stanzas X and XIX) will decide the matter by going to see the spot, with its 'heap that's like an infant's grave' (93), for himself. Here it takes superstition and melodrama to make all these indiscriminate things significant; yet not wrongly, we suppose (as the gothic atmosphere is after all consistent enough with a probable event and its aftermath), an event that remains obscure to us only in leaving it an open question whether the infant was murdered. The other particulars are virtually certain despite being disclaimed as fact in the ''Tis said' mode of traditional storytelling. In the stormy world of 'The Thorn', things mystified by mist are made objects by inference.

Reducing the difference among objects to a zero degree that makes them things again – as 'The Thorn' stops short of effecting fully – is a gesture that Wordsworth would eventually link to the agency of the imagination. He reminds his readers in a prose discussion of that faculty, for example, that his leech gatherer in 'Resolution and Independence' had seemed in the heat of imagination to be at once a stone, a sea beast and a cloud.[6] Could it be the office of the imagination as Wordsworth conceives it to make objects things again? The idiot Johnny in 'The Idiot Boy', uttering the lines that inspired the writing of that poem, models for the reader the mode of imagination that refuses difference: 'The cocks did crow to-whoo, to-whoo, / And the sun did shine so cold' (*LB* Lines 460–461).

No one who tries to understand Wordsworth can stray far from the paradox at the heart of his accomplishment and reputation: the poet of the 'egotistical sublime' known to Keats and Keats's mentor Hazlitt (the 'Matthew' of 'Expostulation and Reply' and 'The Tables Turned'), the bard of 'the Mind of Man' ('Prospectus to *The Recluse*', Halmi 445) who is valued and devalued in turn, yet viewed from all standpoints as a psychological poet by the otherwise conflicting schools of modern Wordsworth commentary. This is also the poet, the 'nature poet', who put more emphasis on the nonhuman world than had any predecessor.[7] Undoubtedly this innovative emphasis remains an exploration of consciousness, but it is best understood as phenomenological rather than psychological. By the 'Preface' of 1800, or in any case by his amplifications of 1802, Wordsworth was clear about this drift in his proposed vocation for the poet when listing the topics that perforce engage the poet's attention: some topics are human-centred while some are of interest, not as resources for illustrating human behaviour (that would have been their purpose even in Cowper, not to mention Imlac in Johnson's *Rasselas*), but simply to register the community of human and nonhuman things as the 'all' of 'Tintern Abbey'. In addition to 'loss of friends and kindred ... injuries and resentments, gratitude and hope ... fear and sorrow', there are also 'the operations of the elements and the appearances of the visible universe ... storm and sunshine ... the revolutions of the seasons ... cold and heat' (*LB* 'Preface' p. 108). These phenomena may all affect 'our moral sentiments', to be sure, but they also affect the 'animal sensations' (*LB* 108) that have not been the focus of Enlightenment humanism.

Nonetheless, Wordsworth rightly understood that the focus of his own work was on 'character', which is to say, 'the moral sentiments'.[8] As he later told Lady Beaumont, all of his poems have a moral purpose ('a worthy *purpose*', he called it in the 'Preface' (98)), and certainly all of these poems do have one (*Letters MY* II. 178). This purpose in 1798 is presented with no special effort to conceal the traditional *moralisation* of the *paysage*, affording some lesson or other to be learned from things – 'should you think', as in 'Simon Lee' (Line 46). In that poem, the moral purpose of a stump is to call attention to the futile disproportion between gratitude for the well-meaning condescension of a helping hand (together, it is implied, with all other convention-bound tokens of good will) and the irreversible social and geriatric circumstances of the grateful, but perhaps also humiliated, old man. This didactic message, it may well be said in qualification, like that of 'The Old Cumberland Beggar', is at least as political as it is moral. Wordsworth's moral purpose never wavered after this, whatever became of his politics, and indeed he continued to write judgementally ambivalent 'Characters' (as of his Alpine and Snowdonian walking companion Robert Jones, or of the then unpublished 'Farmer of Tilsbury Vale', subtitled 'A Character'); but in the final two years of that most anthropocentric of all centuries, the eighteenth, he began to see how subtle, extensive and perhaps also obscure the overlap between the human and the nonhuman is, and to see this overlap in new ways. At this point, the word 'thing' plays a somewhat larger role in his vocabulary, and he begins to see the ways in which human beings themselves belong in, are most fully at home in, the universal community of things. The point is still a moral one, but it cannot so easily be attached to the Theophrastean notions of 'character', the evermore fine-grained but still typifying lessons about our all-too-human humanity that prevail, for example, in the bourgeois tragedy, the Hogarthian 'progress', or the rise of the novel.

Take, for example, Wordsworth's perfunctory treatment of, or refusal to treat, the Hogarthian progress of the boy Luke in *Michael*, considered in contrast with what a George Lillo might have done with it. In this leisurely narrative, offering plenty of opportunity to observe character in action, with the interesting evidence along the way that Michael has been more harsh towards the boy than he realises (with his 'looks / Of fond correction and reproof', the boy 'not always, I believe / Receiving from his Father hire of praise' (*LB* Lines 182–183, 200–201), the reader might well expect to hear something more of Luke's life in the city. Instead, with distaste – not so much for the sad details as for the narrative investment required to describe them, the poet gives us a minimal account and then hurries on, even stressing the 'length' he passes over so quickly to get to 'at last':

> Meantime Luke began
> To slacken in his duty; and at length,
> He in the dissolute city gave himself
> To evil courses: ignominy and shame
> Fell on him, so that he was driven at last
> To seek a hiding-place beyond the seas.
> (Lines 452–457)

What interests the poet, and Michael too, a great deal more about this boy, what truly endears him to them both, is his virtually nonhuman and speechless infancy. 'Never to living ear', says Michael, sharing the spontaneity of his love with all *things that live* to hear, not just with humans,

> came sweeter sounds
> Than when I heard thee by our own fire-side
> First uttering, without words, a natural tune,
> (Lines 355–357)

Yes, that ostensibly unnecessary word 'own' does keep before us the theme of property that interests most readers of this poem, but here the possessive

would seem to suggest that this experience belongs privately to Michael
and his helpmeet Isabel because of what they are: beings more attuned to
the continuity of consciousness with the nonhuman world, even in its
impulse to '[s]ing' (Line 359), than with humankind – which species
indeed obtrudes upon this fragile pastoral chiefly as an encroachment on
property. Michael is never interested in *meum* and *tuum* but only in the
vitality of belonging in a place, inseparable from the phenomena within its
horizon:

> these fields, these hills,
> Which were his living Being, even more
> Than his own Blood – what could they less? had laid
> Strong hold on his affections, were to him
> A pleasurable feeling of blind love,
> The pleasure which there is in life itself.
>
> (Lines 74–79)

Much that is described in the poem has the character of *objects* because
they can be enumerated and are often single: the unfinished sheepfold
(lacking the stones that Michael 'never lifted up' [476]), the lamp as
'EVENING STAR' (146), the two spinning wheels operated one at a
time, the Clipping Tree; but in the description of Michael quoted above
the presence of the fields and hills is diffused into a mode of being, and
takes on the power of things.

Michael's 'blind love' partakes in the promise of insight linked with the
bardic blindness of Homer and Milton for the ambitious Wordsworth. We
find it already in Simon Lee, who 'reeled and was stone blind' (Line 44
[1798 version]) when he was a huntsman merry, suddenly one with the
dizzying whirl of the world like the skating child in *The Prelude* for whom
all became tranquil as a dreamless sleep; and we find it again linked to
another huntsman in the inaugural poem of the new second volume in
1800, 'Hart-leap Well', but here the blindness is that of Sir Walter's dogs
dying along the chase: 'breath and eyesight fail, and, one by one, / The
Dogs are stretch'd among the mountain fern' (*LB* Lines 23–24).[9]
The 'Hart, stone-dead, / With breathless nostrils stretch'd above the
spring' (Lines 77–78), and eventually Sir Walter himself, whose 'bones
lie in his paternal vale' (Line 94), join the dogs in good time. What is
revealed in the second part of the poem is an uncanny place of death
amid nature, a place in which the absence of life, with the unwillingness
of living things to visit it (like the birds and bees that stay away from the
vale in 'The Danish Boy') discloses a more radical thing-hood than any
speculative 'active principle' could disclose.[10] Surprisingly, the 'moral'

does not finally adhere to the 'objects' left by nature 'to a slow decay' (Line 173), as we know those objects to have been what they are, *characterised* in fact. The moral, rather, stressing the word 'thing', recalls the 'All things both great and small' (Line 648) of Coleridge's moral: 'Never to blend our pleasure or our pride / With sorrow of the meanest thing that feels' ("Hart-Leap Well", *LB* Lines 179–180). To restore feeling to things here at the last, pointing ahead to 'the meanest flower that blows' in the 'Ode: Intimations to Immortality' four years later, is simply to restore things to human consciousness, where their power is, binding all together (Halmi, Line 205; p. 439).

'Poor Susan' in her plain russet gown seems to be the reddish-brown thrush she listens to, or wishes that she could be, estranged as she is in Luke's dissolute city. But the central exhibit for the deepening of Wordsworth's interest in things in advance of 1800 is the 'Lucy Poems', not just one but all of them. Something compels Wordsworth to call the elusive figure addressed in these poems a thing, or to compare her with things (violet and star in 'She dwelt among th' untrodden ways', the conventional stellification of the flower here mediated metonymically by the mossy stone adjacent to it), or to be incited by a thing (the moon dropping like a stone) to think of her as dead in 'Strange fits of passion I have known'. In 'Lucy Gray' she is 'The sweetest Thing that ever grew / Beside a human door' (7–8). The comparison suggests a foundation planting, although there is admittedly also a touch of the gendered 'sweet thing' of modern usage in the epithet as well.

These instances of almost devotional reification establish a pattern that at the least offers another means of arguing that the 'Lucy Poems' really do deserve to be clustered in a group even though Wordsworth saw fit to place only three of them together in the contents of his Volume 2 – the other two appear separately – and wrote two more later.[11] It is worth remembering that the 'Lucy Poems' written in Goslar seem at times to be expressions of homesickness, an emotion distilled finally in 1801, long after his return, in 'I travelled among unknown men', where Lucy becomes the genius of England itself, representative of all things earliest known and lost. The last poem to name Lucy, called 'The Glow-worm' in Dorothy Wordsworth's *Grasmere Journal* (1802), is not often grouped with the others because it is not elegiac and because we know Dorothy to be its object of affection, but it does nevertheless recapitulate Lucy's continuous merger with her environment in its first line: 'Among all lovely things my Love had been' (Halmi, Line 1; p. 392). Among all the critical conjectures about what or whom Lucy may stand for, there is much to be said for the 'celestial light', or lucency, that once appareled '[t]he things which I have seen' in the Intimations Ode (Halmi Lines 4, 9).

'Three years she grew in sun and shower' introduces another suggestive turn of phrase to the theme of 'things'. Nature decides to take this 'flower' unto herself, lending substance to the 'child of nature' topos by making herself the child's 'law and impulse' (*LB* Lines 2, 8). As the genius of Nature, the child will be a part of all levels of being, including the mineral: 'hers the silence and the calm / Of mute insensate things' (17–18). In this moment there is an order of things that does not think or feel ('insensate' drives the point home) and may not be alive, though 'mute' does not necessarily imply that. Regardless whether this means that things like flowers remain sensate in Wordsworth's mind, however, this insistence on difference among the classes of things actually reinforces their underlying sameness because Lucy glows in all of them. After she dies in adolescence, the speaker is left with all that she had inspired, reduced to its lowest common denominator registered in the word 'calm' (an echo suggesting *common* things): 'This heath, this calm and quiet scene' (40).

It is the mineral common denominator, I think, which shapes the miniature masterpiece, 'A slumber did my spirit seal':

> A slumber did my spirit seal,
> I had no human fears:
> She seem'd a thing that could not feel
> The touch of earthly years.
>
> No motion has she now, no force;
> She neither hears nor sees,
> Roll'd round in earth's diurnal course
> With rocks and stones and trees!
>
> (*LB* Lines 1–8)

Vast quantities of ingenious commentary have been unleashed by the poem's eloquent reticence and brevity. The poem then *could* mean simply this: (1) My ability to see beyond present appearances and remember that humans die was put to sleep by the apparent imperviousness of this girl to change. (2) But now to my sorrow I realize my mistake because she lies inert and senseless, orbiting daily with everything else that is inert and senseless. Two things even about this plodding paraphrase are shocking. First, you would expect sentiments so conventional at least to hint at some sort of consolation, probably Christian. After all, 'spirit', which in this paraphrase means only the ability to think clearly, surely also implies the ability to apprehend transcendence once spirit is unsealed. And second, in the absence of any consolation there is a surprising emphasis on the mineral aspect of the natural world, to which dead bodies are to be added, as if to a pile of stones. Perhaps even the trees are petrified, as in any case they show no sign of sentience, of an active principle or of participation in the 'One Life'. Two-thirds of the world at least is bedrock, insensate and then some – the world that for Coleridge, without the 'shaping spirit of Imagination', is 'fixed and dead'.[12]

That is the world of things, *not* objects – but things without charisma or power. How can we read Wordsworth here, with his intuition that attunement to things is power, if we assume that the paraphrase I have offered is insufficient? The premise of the paraphrase, like that of more imaginative but still conventional readings, is that this is a before-and-after poem, its two stanzas with the gap of death in between them compressing into the smallest possible compass the great meditations on loss and recompense (fortunate falls) like 'Tintern Abbey', the 'Intimations Ode', and *The Prelude*. I was blind, but now I see. The trouble with this premise is that in a great many ways the second quatrain repeats the first: Lucy seemed a thing, now she is a thing; she was untouched by the phenomenal world before, now she has no senses with which to experience that world; my spirit was asleep before, and now I find myself in a world without spirit. Hence if spirit *can* be unsealed this poem offers no assistance; the slumber of my spirit is now the slumber of Lucy's spirit, if she ever had one, so what I was then, she is now, meaning that even the before and after of life followed by death needs severe qualification. What is the difference between life and death? In the first stanza I was oblivious to reality, and Lucy at least seemed to be oblivious to reality; in the second stanza Lucy joins the reality to which she continues to be oblivious, while I stand apart from that reality only because I can name it, not at all because I can point to its limitations or to a reality beyond it. What Lucy participates in as a thing I can name as an object, and this fact is the only thin line of difference between us, between my life and her death.

This very depressing way of looking at the poem is what brings it closest to the major 'crisis' poems mentioned earlier, struggling to compensate for their perceived loss of poetic inspiration, or 'spirit'. Whereas all those poems have the leisure and scope to find their 'abundant recompense'('Tintern Abbey' 89), this taciturn poem with its grim mineral horizon seems bereft of such resources. The rhetoric of those poems, as in 'Tintern Abbey', 'rolls through all things' (103), and carries the day with grand cadences. After all, anyone immune to the sway of oratory can show that even such poems as these are burdened – or perhaps blessed – with returns of the same even while they plot the archetype of before and after. And in any case 'Slumber' too 'rolls though all things'. As an oratorical performance the first six lines communicate pathos, with its helplessness. But the last two lines are another matter, introducing a heightened and productive tension between logic and rhetoric: yes, Lucy is just a thing (and so therefore am I), but *what a thing!* (I am here alluding to the mark with which the poem ends: '!'). Everything that is dynamic in the universe inheres in things, even and especially in inanimate things. Gravity, governing the relations among those rocks and stones called moons and stars, invests things with extraordinary power, the dynamism of the unity that only things can reveal once imagined. Even the consolation of perdurability is entailed because, while objects have lifespans, things, some things at any one time, are always there.

'Slumber' too, then, discovers its abundant recompense in the form of an insight, towards which the argument of this chapter has tended. What is important about things, and what sets them apart from objects that have been classified, is their unity. This unity, which defines them, consists in the realization that in concert 'all' things cannot be known as objects. The unity of human beings imagined apart from things, their specifically human community, is a political idea devoted to the overcoming of difference, and Wordsworth's imagination in 1800 struggled perhaps increasingly to find a community of this kind viable or, in any case, sufficiently inclusive. There is one kind of community, however, that is indissoluble and unexceptionable, and that is the community of things, to which human beings can belong consciously and imaginatively when they recognize that they are things among all other things. In this widest commonalty the power of things resides and offers a saddened tranquillity – a notion that runs through the 'Lucy Poems'. 'Tintern Abbey', as many have argued, is grounded in the politically suspect paradox that the poet needs to estrange himself as far he possibly can from even the slightest of social relations in order to hear 'the still, sad music of humanity' (92). What, you desert the human sphere in order to hear its music? Yes, the music emerges as a confirmation of the most stable bond among humans there is, when consciousness is experienced not in the markets of human competition, with the still remembered acts of kindness and of love being the exceptional moments of self-forgetting, but rather as the levelling exhilaration of being a thing among things.

Endnotes

1 Martin Heidegger, *Being and Time*, trans. John Macquarrie and Edward Robinson (New York: Harper & Row, 1962), 192.
2 William Empson, *Seven Types of Ambiguity* (1931; rev. ed. London: Chatto & Windus, 1949), 153–154.

3 *'Prospectus* to *The Recluse,'* Line 18, in *Wordsworth's Poetry and Prose,* ed. Nicholas Halmi (New York: W. W. Norton, 2013), 445.

4 William Hazlitt, *Lectures on the English Poets,* in *Lectures on the English Poets and the Spirit of the Age* (1818, 1825; rpt. New York: Everyman, 1960), 163; Byron's 'all who view the 'idiot in his glory' / Conceive the Bard the hero of the story' is in *Lord Byron: The Major Works,* ed. Jerome McGann (Oxford: Oxford University Press, 1986), 'English Bards, and Scotch Reviewers', p. 7, lines 253–254. See also Alan Bewell, *Wordsworth and Enlightenment: Nature, Man and Society in the Experimental Poetry* (Yale, Yale University Press, 1989).

5 On indexical stationing, see the letter in which Wordsworth tries to convince Sara Hutchinson to like 'Resolution and Independence', speaking of '"a pond by which an old man was, far from all house or home"; not stood nor sat, but was' (*Letters EY* 306).

6 'Resolution and Independence', Lines 64–72, 82–84, quoted and discussed in the 'Preface' to *Poems,* 1815. See Halmi, *Wordsworth's Poetry and Prose,* 514.

7 For 'the egotistical sublime', see John Keats, Letter to Richard Woodhouse (27 Oct. 1818), 157.

8 Perhaps to counter stereotypes about Wordsworth's egoism, his partisans are pointedly conscientious in stressing Wordsworth's devotion to character and ethics. See, e.g., Butler and Green's 'Introduction', *Cornell LB* 20; and the insistence of Wordsworth's own 1798 'Advertisement' (*LB* 3–4).

9 See *Prelude* 1805, I. 489.

10 'There is an active principle alive in all things: / ... a power by which they make / Some other being conscious of their life' ('Fragment' composed in Germany probably between October and December 1798, *Cornell LB* 309).

11 On the advantages and pitfalls of grouping the Lucy poems, see Mark Jones's excerpt from his chapter *The Lucy Poems,* in Halmi 645.

12 Coleridge, 'Dejection', *The Complete Poems,* ed. William Keach (London: Penguin, 1977), Line 86 and *BL* 304.

CHAPTER 7

Marginal Figures

Philip Shaw

One winter evening in Somerset, in the early months of 1798, Dorothy Wordsworth observes 'the moon and two planets; sharp and frosty . . . The sea very black, and making a loud noise as we came through the wood, loud as if disturbed, and the wind was silent' (*DWJ* 147). In between these descriptions of natural phenomena she records, as if in parentheses: 'Met a razor-grinder with a soldier's jacket on, a Knapsack upon his back, and a boy to drag his wheel' (*DWJ* 147). Unlike the lyrically suggestive accounts of sea, wind and sky, this human encounter is pared to a sequence of bare facts and, while we may deduce that the man is an army veteran now making a living as an itinerant laborer, no attempt is made to derive any further significance from the incident. In the Alfoxden Journal this entry marks the only meeting with a stranger encountered on the roads. By contrast, in the 1800–1803 Grasmere Journal Dorothy records numerous meetings with men, women and children on the public highway and, more often than not, these meetings yield insights into the consequences for the rural poor of the British involvement in the war against revolutionary France, and of the Pitt government's relentless pursuit of socio-economic 'improvements' to support this involvement. Many of these meetings were subsequently developed in poems written by Wordsworth. But, whether written as poetry or in prose, the stories of these outcast and denuded figures, striking in their mundanity, were to cast a searching light on the iniquities of the times.

While Wordsworth and Coleridge would not have recognised the modern, sociological understanding of marginalisation, *Lyrical Ballads* is populated by characters whose experiences of loss, rejection and neglect may be traced directly to the effects of conflict, industrialisation, agricultural reform and economic expansion. Wordsworth offers a very precise diagnosis of the difficulties experienced by these characters in a letter written on 14 January, 1801 to the Whig opposition leader Charles James Fox, which accompanied a presentation copy of the recently published two-volume second edition of *Lyrical Ballads* ("Appendix 2," *LB* 306–309). In the letter, the poet writes of how 'the spreading of manufactures through every part of the country', along with the effects of high taxation, the invention of workhouses and 'Soup-shops', and the 'encreasing disproportion between the price of labour and that of the necessaries of life' contribute to 'the decay of the domestic affections among the lower orders of society' (307). Wordsworth directs Fox to 'The Brothers' and to 'Michael' as illustrations of how 'the bonds of domestic feeling among the poor ... have been weakened, and in innumerable instances entirely destroyed' (307) as a result of these effects. In these poems the bonds between siblings and between fathers and sons are broken as a result of economic hardship, resulting in exile, alienation and, in the case of 'Michael', a fall into moral depravity on the part of Luke. Repeatedly in the letter Wordsworth emphasises how it is the home that bears the brunt of the changes that have resulted from war, manufacturing and economic rationalism. As that *oikos* which, according to Aristotle, is situated at the margins of the political realm or *polis*, the home becomes not only a register of the vast changes that are sweeping society but also an indicator of the increasing indeterminacy of the boundaries separating domestic and political life. Those wanderers encountered on the public highway are thus symptomatic of the collapse of the domestic sphere that is an effect of what Dorothy describes as these 'hard times' (37).[1]

The focus of this chapter is, accordingly, on the representation of marginal figures in the *Lyrical Ballads*. It engages with poems printed in the 1798, 1800 and 1802 editions that highlight the plight of the rural poor during a period of economic hardship, political oppression and war. My particular interest is in how Wordsworth's marginal figures register and respond to the emergence of modern 'biopower', a concept introduced by the French social theorist and historian of ideas Michel Foucault and subsequently developed in the work of the Italian political philosophers Giorgio Agamben and Roberto Esposito.[2] Derived from the ancient Greek word *bios*, meaning the form or way of living proper to an individual or group, biopower is concerned with the use of disciplinary technologies and institutions to increase the productive force of the human body by means of, for example, control of labour power (the factory), economic accountability (taxation), regulation of health (the hospital), suppression of deviance (the workhouse and the prison), and the harnessing of violence (the military). Wordsworth's denunciation of the pernicious effects of manufacturing, taxation and the invention of the workhouse and the soup kitchen speaks directly of those techniques of power used by the nation state to monitor and control the poor.

In the letter to Fox, Wordsworth follows his prescient critique of modern biopower by mounting a spirited defence of the rites of the rural smallholder. As 'the proprietors of small estates, which have descended to them from their ancestors', this class of men demonstrate 'affections' of a 'power' that is 'inconceivable by those who have only had an opportunity of observing hired labourers, farmers and the manufacturing Poor'; their 'little tract of land serves as a kind of rallying point for their domestic feelings, as a tablet upon which they are written' and, in allusion to the origins of the pastoral tradition that has shaped the literary representation of rural lives, as a 'fountain fitted to the nature of social man from which supplies of affection ... are daily drawn' (*LB* 308). The echoes in this letter – of Edmund Burke's paternalistic conception of the relations between land ownership, the domestic affections and social cohesion – have long been used to qualify arguments for Wordsworth's political radicalism. However, such criticisms tend to overstate the poet's indebtedness to Burke and thus to miss the unique character of his critique of the dehumanising effects of industrial capitalism.[3] Two points should be noted here: first, as 'tract' or 'tablet' the smallholding represents a portion of land that is both inhabited and that is also written on. This alludes on the one hand to the notion of a simple, natural life (*zoē*) excluded from State control. On the other, it describes a form of life (*bios*) that – insofar as it is subject to language and therefore to law is at the same time included in the political realm – the 'little tract' of land thus signifies. In Giorgio Agamben's words, this is the 'state of exception' that constitutes 'the hidden foundation' of the *bios politikos*.[4] Second, the comparison of the land to a 'fountain' works also to conflate the boundary between nature and politics: as a symbol of purity, plenitude and renewal the fountain is set apart from the *polis*, yet this symbolic status is itself a product of the political milieu to which it is formally opposed. In Horace's Ode 3.13, for example, a verse alluded to in Wordsworth's 'An Evening Walk' and translated by the poet in 1794, the purity of the '*fons Bandusiae*', a sacred spring believed to be located in the grounds of Horace's Sabine estate, is tainted by the blood of a sacrificial kid. While the ode endeavours to resolve the conflation of love and war encoded in this image (*et venerem et proelia*) through incorporation within a larger structure of artistic harmony, the slaughtered goat serves as a reminder that pastoral innocence is forged, from the outset, on the basis of a violent act of exclusion.[5]

Dwelling and Dying on the Margins

An engagement with the political significance of the fountain is sustained throughout *Lyrical Ballads*, and serves as a reminder of the specific, geographical significance of the margin; that is, 'the ground immediately adjacent to a river or body of water; a river bank, a shore'.[6] Almost all of the marginal figures in *Lyrical Ballads* are born, live, work and die beside a river, lake or ocean: the two brothers are described as 'Springs which bubbled side by side' (Line 136); the female vagrant is nurtured alongside Derwent Water; Michael builds his shepherd fold beside the 'tumultous brook of Green-head Gill' (Line 2); the boy of Winander blows 'mimic hootings to the silent owls . . . / Across the watr'y vale' ('There was a boy', Line 12); while Lucy dwells 'Beside the springs of Dove' ('She dwelt among th' untrodden ways', Line 2). In all these cases, water dwelling entails that characters are exposed to some form of violence, be it the consequences of economic precarity ('The Brothers', 'Michael'), the exigencies of war ('The Female Vagrant', 'Old Man Travelling'), the effects of ageing ('The Fountain') or the brute facticity of untimely death (the 'Lucy Poems', 'There was a boy'). Throughout the collection, brooks, streams and rivulets blur categorical distinctions, reminding readers of the Heraclitean dictum that it is not possible to step into the same river twice: 'The little Brooks, that seem all pastime and play / When they are angry, roar like Lions for their prey' ('The Pet-Lamb', 55–56). Thus, while the poet 'murmurs near the running brooks', gathering inspiration from a 'fountain in a noonday grove' ('A Poet's Epitaph', Lines 39–42 passim), there are other waters that instil feelings of vulnerability and despair: the illimitable seas in 'The Rime of the Ancyent Marinere'; the 'dead' fountain in 'The Brothers' (142); the sacrificial fountain in 'Hart-Leap Well' (41–44); the 'thundering', destructive stream in 'The Waterfall and the Eglantine' (2).

To dwell on or near the water margins is to expose oneself to the inherent ambiguity of the pastoral fountain tradition. On the one hand those modest dwellings, built in harmony with the natural surroundings, are repositories of pacific calm: in 'Poems on the Naming of Places: I', the poet creates an 'out-of-doors abode' (41) in which 'The Shepherd's Dog, the Linnet and the Thrush' vie with 'this Waterfall' in the creation of song 'like some natural produce of the air / That could not cease to be' (Lines 25–30 passim); in 'Poems on the Naming of Places: V. To M.H.', he envisions a cottage, built beside 'a Well', in a 'calm' and sheltered 'recess . . . made by nature herself' (Lines 8–15 passim), while in 'Lines Written with a Pencil upon a stone in the wall of the House (an Out-house) on the

Island at Grasmere' he looks out from the shelter of a 'homely pile' (13) 'towards the lake' (26), attendant to 'stirring breezes ... Fair sights, and visions of romantic joy' (27–29). On the other, the extravagant follies of the wealthy are apt to fall into ruin. On one of the islands in Rydal Water a heap of 'misshapen stones' is all that remains of Sir William Fleming's projected pleasure 'Dome' ('Lines Written with a Slate-pencil, upon a Stone, the largest of a heap lying near a deserted Quarry, upon one of the Islands at Rydale', 1), while Sir Walter's 'Pleasure-house', a 'great Lodge' placed near a spring where a hunted deer met its death, is nothing but 'a forgotten dream' ('Hart-Leap Well', 132). Yet even those modest constructions succumb to the inexorable encroachment of the *polis*: in 'The Female Vagrant', a landowner's denial of the family's ancient fishing rites results in the loss of their 'dear-loved home' (1798; 63); in 'Michael' the sheepfold signifies a 'covenant' (425) between father and son, but Luke fails to return from the city, to which he has journeyed in order to restore his family's prosperity, and the sheepfold remains unfinished at the time of the old shepherd's death. That 'tract' which was intended to affirm the rites of the statesman against the claims of the State is read now through the lens of nostalgia; for as Wordsworth informs Fox, 'this class of men is rapidly disappearing' (*LB* 308).

A striking illustration of the socio-economic precariousness of lives lived on the water margin is displayed in 'Poems on the Naming of Places: IV'. Based on a real incident, the poem tracks the musings of three 'Friends' (William and Dorothy Wordsworth and Coleridge) as they wander along a 'narrow girdle of rough stones, and crags', a 'rude and natural causeway, interpos'd / Between the water and winding slope / Of copse and thicket' (1–4).[7] At leisure on the shore, the wanderers 'play' (11) with their time, observing 'in vacant mood' (16) passing shows of being: a 'Feather, or leaf, or weed, or wither'd bough' (14) tossed on the shore. Echoing Coleridge's conversation poems, the friends preoccupy themselves with images of transience, with toy-like forms that merge the divide between life and lifelessness, activity and inertia: the 'sportive wanderings' of a 'dandelion's seed or thistle's beard' making 'report of an invisible breeze' (Lines 18–25 passim). As the poem proceeds, a subtle, critical voice begins to emerge, qualifying the mood of indolence, which allows the friends to indulge a taste for the picturesque, the contemporary aesthetic category associated with the rise of leisure tourism towards the end of the eighteenth century. The change is subtle, but the lengthy catalogue of 'Fair Ferns and Flowers' (35), culminating in a comparison of the *Osmunda regalis* fern to a 'Naiad' 'by the side / Of Grecian brook, or Lady of the Mere / Sole-sitting by the shores of old Romance' (35–40) serves as a reminder of how the encounter with simple, natural beauty is shaped by knowledge gained from literature and the natural sciences. This mannerist dead end, redolent of the artificial and overly elaborate similes of the Della Cruscan poets, is countered by the 'busy mirth' of 'Reapers, Men and Women, Boys and Girls' (43) labouring in the nearby fields. At this point the reader might assume that pastoral romance has yielded to the bracing intrusion of georgic labour, but this mood is itself swiftly dispelled as, 'Through a thin veil of glittering haze' (Line 48), the wanderers see before them,

> on a point of jutting land
> The tall and upright figure of a Man
> Attir'd in peasant's garb, who stood alone
> Angling beside the margin of the lake.
>
> (Lines 49–52)

Oblivious to irony, the friends cry out 'with one and the same voice' (55) that the man must be an idler who could afford to lose a day's wages during the harvest season. But as they approach the man they encounter a figure 'worn down / By sickness, gaunt and lean, with sunken cheeks / And wasted limbs' (64–66), a man who, too weak to labour in the fields, must use his skill 'to gain / A pittance from the dead unfeeling lake' (70–71). Struck by the figure's ghastly appearance, the speaker is compelled to refocus his attention as, by means of slow, ponderous rhythms, he comes to detach his 'single self' (67) from his otiose companions, too consumed by fleeting images of beauty to apprehend the human suffering that constitutes the material foundation of their leisurely wanderings. As Lucy Newlyn has noted, 'the scene has a haunting quality, reminiscent of Hamlet's meeting with his father's ghost, or Achilles' encounter with Anchises in Virgil's underworld' (130). In sparse, unadorned language, the man is granted tragic status, a mode of radical isolation that georgic, for all its openness to harsh reality, is unable to accommodate but which the verse registers in the image of 'the dead unfeeling lake / That knew not of his wants' (71–72). The poem ends, nevertheless, with a restatement of collective purpose as, shifting their attention from 'lovely images' (Line 75) to 'serious musings and to self-reproach' (76), the friends draw a moral lesson from their encounter and recover a sense of self-command by renaming the foreland 'POINT RASH-JUDGEMENT' (85).

'Poems on the Naming of Places: IV' is one of several poems in *Lyrical Ballads* to upbraid the presuppositions of the leisure classes. Most notably, in 'Simon Lee: The Old Huntsman' (1798), a cultivated or 'gentle reader'

(Line 69; p. 46) is goaded by the speaker into revising their expectations of what constitutes a 'tale' (72), and, perhaps more importantly, to review their response to the subject of that tale, in this case an aged and ailing huntsman struggling to sever a tangled stump of rotten wood. Simon Lee lives 'near the waterfall' (31), but expectations of an account of Arcadian simplicity are dashed by implicit criticism of the shortcomings of rural patronage – Simon's master has died without providing for his servant – and by evidence of the ill-preparedness of the retired huntsman for agricultural labour: 'when he was young he little knew / Of husbandry or tillage' (37–38). Spurred along by the speaker's teasing, conspiratorial tone, and by the verse's artful variations on trimeter and tetrameter, as well as by the subtle use of bathetic or weak rhymes ('weighty ... eighty'; 'merry ... cherry'), the ballad propels the reader forward, encouraging the adoption of a condescending attitude towards the elderly man. The comedic mode is, however, subverted as, at the close of the poem, the 'gentle reader' is requested to 'make' something of the tale by entering into the emotional complexities of the 'incident' signalled in the poem's sub-title. Supplanting blithe loquacity with the gravity of 'silent thought' (74), reader and speaker unite in stunned response to a terminal act of kindness: 'I struck, and with a single blow / The tangled root I sever'd' (93–94). While signifying a radical break with the social forces that are responsible for Simon's condition, the act of severance speaks also of a nuanced and near un-paraphrasable cluster of feelings as the speaker, whose wielding of the mattock recalls the drawn sword of the angel of death, is left 'mourning' (104) at the fluvial outpouring of Simon's gratitude.[8] The 'tears' and 'thanks and praises' that 'run / So fast out of his heart' (97–99) provide another form of upbraiding, reminding speaker and reader of the family resemblance between the facile assurances of metre and rhyme, which for the greater part of the poem have worked to discourage reflec-tion, and the rapid flow of time that conspires to prevent us from apprehending everyday intimations of mortality, as signalled by the caesura that falls between 'I struck' and the connective that initiates the comple-tion of the speaker's act of kindness.

Simon's transformation into a sacred fount, a symbolic status born out of a sacrificial act, may be usefully compared and contrasted with the transformation that occurs in 'Old Man travelling; Animal Tranquillity and Decay, A Sketch' (1798). Regarded by Wordsworth as 'an overflowing from the Old Cumberland Beggar', a description that takes on literal force when observing how, across two facing pages of DCMS 13, the piece emerges in the margins of that poem, 'Old Man travelling' seems, at first, to offer a related lesson in the supplementary labour of the indigent other.[9] Neglected even by the 'hedge-row birds' (*LB* Line 1; p. 82) the old man 'travels on / . . . insensibly subdued / To settled quiet' (Lines 3–8 passim), enduring 'pain' with such 'patience / That patience now doth seem a thing, of which / He hath no need' (10–12). Abstracted from physical and mental care, the traveller becomes an emblem of stoical endurance, 'by nature led / To peace so perfect' that 'the young behold with envy, what the old man hardly feels' (13–14). As Sally Bushell has noted, the first fourteen lines of the poem work to 'naturalize' the old man by rendering him 'the passive object rather than the active subject of the sentence', a figure 'to *whom* things happen, himself dispossessed of agency'.[10] Were the poem to end at this point, the impression of passivity would be sustained, but Wordsworth chooses instead to limn the poem with a five-line coda, transforming what would otherwise be read as a thematically unified blank verse sonnet into a poetic 'sketch' of indeterminate significance:

> I asked him whither he was bound, and what
> The object of his journey; he replied
> 'Sir! I am going many miles to take
> A last leave of my son, a mariner,
> Who from a sea-fight has been brought to Falmouth,
> And there is dying in an hospital.'
>
> (Lines 15–20)

The impression of settled calm established by lines 1–14 is here abruptly qualified, in what amounts to a reversal of the narrative trajectory of 'Simon Lee', by the sharp turn from lyrical contemplation to prosaic reportage. The old man is given a voice, and what that voice conveys is the harsh dailiness of war, which makes a sudden entry at the close of the poem to remind readers of the violence implicit in literary attempts to transform ragged human lives into aesthetically perfected emblems of peace.

Enduring War: 'The Female Vagrant' and 'The Discharged Soldier'

Although the origins of modern biopolitics – which may loosely be defined as the State regularisation of human life and death – predates the 1790s, the various kinds of regularisation that Wordsworth identifies in his letter to Charles James Fox were to increase in number and to multiply in form following Britain's entry into the war against France in 1793.[11] The war necessitated not only the mobilisation of large numbers of men, deployed to fight on multiple fronts, but also the spread of disciplinary mechanisms, ranging from institutions, such as factories, workhouses, barracks, hospitals, asylums and prisons, to techniques of surveillance, statistics, inspections, bookkeeping and reports, which aimed to take control of life in support of the war. Wordsworth's marginal figures are all, to some extent, victims of biopolitics, but a poem that shares with 'Animal Tranquillity and Decay' an overt concern with the effects of war on ordinary human lives is 'The Female Vagrant'. Extracted from 'Salisbury Plain', a lengthy narrative poem begun in 1793, which was then revised as 'Adventures on Salisbury Plain' in 1795 before being abandoned, 'The Female Vagrant' (1798) charts the decline of a young woman following the loss of her lakeside home, her fall into poverty as a result of the collapse of the textile industry, and the devastation of her family during the war against America. The first 160 lines make clear the socio-economic consequences of war on the domestic sphere, laying stress on how military recruitment capitalises on the sufferings of the poor ('the noisy drum / Beat round, to sweep the streets of want and pain', *LB Lines* 93–94), condemning them, in an artful conflation of *Henry V* (WSCW. Prologue Lines 5–8 p.569) and *Julius Caesar* (WSCW 3.1. Line 276 p.614), to wade 'dog-like' at the 'heels of war', protracting 'a curst existence' with the 'brood / That lap ... their brother's blood' (124–126). Further, more subtle indicators of the transformative effects of war on the home front can be seen in the description of the voyage to America, a journey undertaken by the family following the husband's enlistment, as during a storm the woman observes how the 'deep / Ran mountains-high before the howling blast' (110–111) and of the 'harvest of affliction' (115) reaped by the waves. That nature itself should be subjected to violence is an indicator of how war saturates all aspects of life, including the non-human realm. The conflation of the distinctions between land and sea, echoing related episodes in 'The Rime of the Ancyent Marinere' and 'The Brothers', spills over into the description of the 'storming' (155–156) conflict that results in the death of her husband and children.

Waking 'as from a trance restored' (135) the young woman displays symptoms of the condition now commonly known as post-traumatic stress disorder but which in the long eighteenth century was described as 'nostalgia', a disease of the mind and body associated with the alienated young and, in particular, with soldiers and sailors longing for home. The woman's trauma is evident in her description of 'some mighty gulph of separation' and in her sense of having been 'transported to another world' (163–164), expressions of disjunction that arise from a deep-rooted feeling of homelessness:

And oft, robb'd of my perfect mind, I thought
At last my feet a resting-place had found:
Here will I weep in peace, (so fancy wrought,)
Roaming the illimitable waters round.

(Lines 172–175)

The blurring of the distinction between the circumscribed dwelling and the 'illimitable waters' is checked when the vessel reaches its 'bound' (178), but which nevertheless leaves the woman 'homeless near a thousand homes' (179). Destitute, starving and 'weak' (200) of mind, the woman is eventually admitted to a hospital from where, following her recovery, in what amounts to a deftly targeted jibe at the harsh inadequacies of biopolitical care, she is curtly 'Dismissed' (211). Joining a band of travellers, the woman finds some respite from her misery, but the sense of homelessness prevails, leaving her a wanderer on the edges of society. That the woman's story ends in broken, paratactic constructions, and that she weeps because she can no longer fashion words to contain her grief, gives a strong indication of trauma's capacity to exceed narrative sense, placing the sufferer, as it were, outside the linguistic order that defines their sense of self.

'The Discharged Soldier', a blank verse poem dating from January 1798, which, although not included in *Lyrical Ballads* was written in concert with poems prepared for this volume, may be read as a development of the focus of 'The Female Vagrant' on the human costs of war. The opening of the verse establishes a mood of meditative calm as, wandering alone at night, the speaker, 'disposed to sympathy / With an exhausted mind' (16–17), is lulled into a state of tranquillity on account of his receptiveness to the surrounding natural beauty.[12] The speaker's 'self-possession' (34) is checked, however, by the sight of an 'uncouth shape' (38), a 'ghastly' (51) vision of a 'long', 'lank' and 'lean' figure (43–51), 'clad in military garb' (54), resting by the wayside. Stepping back into 'the shade / Of a thick hawthorn' (39–41) the speaker is able to 'mark' (41) the man's 'wasted' (49) demeanour. Derived from an Indo-European root shared by the Latin word for 'margin' (*margo, marginis*), but also redolent of harming, staining and surveillance, the act of marking initiates the process through which the poet attempts to bring this disturbing figure to account. Like 'The Female Vagrant', the veteran appears 'Forlorn and desolate, a man cut off / From all his kind, and more than half detached / From his own nature' (58–60), with the line breaks enhancing the sense of the man's divided condition. Rooted to the spot, as it were, the veteran maintains a 'fearful steadiness' (71), jeopardising the poet's ability to 'scan'

(67), a word connoting close observation but that is associated also with the analysis of metre and, via its root in the Latin word *scandere* (to climb), with the raising and lowering of the foot when marking rhythm. To move the poem forward the man and his no less immovable observer must be made to move in step, in time, with the verse; yet while both remain 'Fixed' to their 'place' (77), the speaker hidden in silent contemplation and the veteran rapt in 'uneasy thought' (70), there appear to be limited opportunities for narrative progression. The tension is relieved when the observer, subduing his 'cowardice' (84), leaves his shelter to address the 'Stranger' (86), thus signalling a commitment to fellowship, which the soldier, rising from his resting place, returns with 'measured gesture' (87). The reintroduction of motion and 'measure' is coincident with the reintroduction of 'discourse' (90) as, released from incoherent 'murmuring' (69) and groans 'scarce audible' (79), the man responds to the speaker's questionings with a 'stately air of mild indifference' (97), relating the 'simple fact' (98) of his discharge from service in 'the tropic isles' (99) and of his long journey home.[13] Yet despite the return of narrative coherence, the soldier remains a 'ghostly figure' (124), his uncanniness amplified by the 'strange half-absence' (141) with which he responds to the speaker's questionings. Redolent, perhaps, of the desire for sensationalist accounts of war and battle, of the sort denounced explicitly by Coleridge in 'Fears in Solitude' (1798) and implicitly so by Wordsworth in the 1800 'Preface' to *Lyrical Ballads* (*LB* 99) the speaker's interrogations fail to elicit the expected response. Like the old man in 'Animal Tranquillity and Decay', the soldier seems no longer to feel the 'importance of his theme' (143), yet it is by virtue of this 'weakness and indifference' (142) that the sensitive listener and reader may gain a sense of that which language fails to capture: the refusal of traumatic experience to lend itself to story.

Unlike the female vagrant, the discharged soldier is led by the narrator to shelter, and is advised to 'demand the succour which his state required' (168), a reminder of the importance of those 'domestic affections' celebrated by Wordsworth in the letter to Fox and which underpin the charitable actions of the villagers in 'The Old Cumberland Beggar'. Yet unlike *that* vagrant figure, the soldier's nostalgic condition appears, at times, to present a threat to the home. For while the Cumberland beggar's indigence is accommodated by the community and is, indeed, presented as a sign of that community's capacity to acknowledge and incorporate the marginal other, the speaker's entreaty that the soldier 'not linger in the public ways' (156) seems, if anything, to suggest that the speaker perceives the soldier as an unwelcome presence, and that the cottage to which he is returned is less a home and more a place of containment. The earlier description of the soldier as 'uncouth' (38), which in Old English has connotations of being wild and out of place, as well as unknowable (from the past participle of *cunnan*: to know) thus persists, and is echoed in the return of that look of 'ghastly mildness' (161) and in his admonition that relief from suffering is afforded not within the domestic sphere but by 'the God of Heaven' (162). The veteran thus retains his status as a fundamentally homeless presence, at odds with the pacific values of the rural community. That the 'gaunt and lean' figure, with 'sunken cheeks / And wasted limbs', encountered in 'Poems on the Naming of Place: IV' (Lines 65–66; p. 279), should resemble the discharged soldier is perhaps no accident. Encountered at the margins between the water and the land, his recurrence confirms the sense in which certain figures exceed not only the disciplinary reach of the state but also the tranquillising influences of nature and the home.

Nature beyond the Polis: 'Nutting', 'Hart-Leap Well' and 'She dwelt among th' untrodden ways'

Suggestions of the latent violence of the pastoral mode are threaded throughout *Lyrical Ballads* but are most evident in two poems from the second volume of the 1802 edition: 'Nutting' and 'Hart-Leap Well'. While the poems discussed thus far use natural settings as a context for broader observations on the politicisation of marginal figures, both 'Nutting' and 'Hart-Leap Well' show how human violence transforms nature itself into a war-like *polis*. Thus, the youthful subject of 'Nutting', having 'forc'd' his way through 'the woods / And o'er the pathless rocks' (12–13), comes across a bower of 'milk-white' hazels, which he then proceeds to decimate.[14] Like many of the significant locations in *Lyrical Ballads* the bower is presented as pure and 'Unvisited' (15), 'a virgin scene' (18–19) beyond the reach of the *polis*. In the highly eroticised lines that follow, the youth takes 'Voluptuous' delight at the prospect of his forthcoming 'banquet' (22–24), and plays with the surrounding flowers – the violets 'unseen by any human eye' (30) echoing the beloved *sans pareil* of 'She dwelt among th' untrodden ways' – while the murmurs of 'fairy water-breaks' (31) lull him into a state of oneiric repose. The mood of dream-like suspension, framed by long, suspended clauses with a present or past participle postponed towards the end, is curtailed by the sudden intrusion of the emphatic 'Then up I rose / And dragg'd to earth both branch and bough'

(41–42). The act of violation marks the moment at which the 'quiet being' (46) of nature is sullied by human desire, but it can also be understood as an act of political deformation, an emblem of how the accrual of riches 'beyond the wealth of kings' (49) is founded in the destruction of simple, natural life. The poem's coda, addressed to a hitherto unmentioned female companion, shifts the attention away from the 'ravage' of nature to affirm an attitude of chastened respect, with the enjambment, intransitive verb and prolonged caesura creating an impression of delicate suspension:[15]

> Then, dearest Maiden! Move along these shades
> In gentleness of heart; with gentle hand
> Touch, — for there is a Spirit in the woods.
>   (Lines 32–34)

In one of the early manuscript versions of 'Nutting', the 'gentle' maiden is depicted as progenitor of the young man's violence, her description as a 'houseless being in a human shape, / An enemy of nature', underlining the sense in which the demands of the *polis* corrupt the primacy of *zoē* and *oikos*, thereby threatening, as foregrounded in another manuscript version of the poem, the association between dwelling in harmony with nature and the liberation of poetic creativity.[16] While the coda to the published poem ensures that the distinction between ravishment and respect is marked by a clear division between heedless masculinity and respectful femininity, the manuscript version suggests that the impulse to engage in 'rude inter-course' (Line 14; *Cornell LB* 302) is shared by men and women alike and that release from the de-creative effects of environmental destruction is achieved only by aligning a domesticated, desexualised femininity with the unsullied margins.

The eco-critical undertones of 'Nutting' are deepened in 'Hart-Leap Well', a poem of two parts that tells the story of a 'remarkable Chace' (*LB* 203), culminating in the death of a 'poor Hart' (Line 29) by the side of a small spring of water. The first half of the poem proceeds in a matter-of-fact way to evoke the delight of the hunter, conspicuously avoiding 'mention' (31) of how the deer died; we are told merely that the beast is found beside a fountain and that 'with the last deep groan his breath had fetch'd / The waters of the spring were trembling still' (41–42). With the briefest of hints at the sullied or mixed nature of the sacred fount, the verse goes on to describe how the huntsman commemorates his success by building a 'Pleasure-house' and a 'small Arbour, made for rural joy' (57–58), creating a 'bason' (62) for the fountain and bestowing on it a name: 'HART-LEAP WELL' (64). With a glance towards 'Kubla Khan' the first part concludes with an evocation of the 'merriment within that pleasant Bower' (92) and with a seemingly un-ironic endorsement of the violent effects of human making.[17] In the second part, however, the focus turns to the decline of the pleasure-house and to the doleful aftermath of the bower, as related by a shepherd who informs the narrator that the 'jolly place' of old is no more: 'something ails it now; the spot is curs'd' (123–124). Like the old sea captain in 'The Thorn', the shepherd hints darkly at the local superstitions that seek to account for the area's absence of life and for the 'dolorous groan' (136) issued by the spring. But rather than relaying a sensationalist tale to 'freeze the blood' (98), he speculates instead on the innocent life of the Hart and the sentiments that prompted him to 'make his death-bed near the well' (148).[18] In what amounts to a synthesis of the opposing perspectives on the knight's tale (merry vs. gloomy; comedic vs. Gothic), the poem culminates with the narrator's affirming that the animal is 'mourn'd by sympathy divine' (164) and that nature will, in course of time, restore the land to 'bloom' and 'beauty' (172).

The promise of fluvial renewal takes on further significance when the poem's relationship with 'The Brothers' is noted. In later life Wordsworth recalled that the 'first eight stanzas were composed extempore ... after having tired and disgusted myself with labouring at an awkward passage in "The Brothers"' (*LB* 347). It may be that Wordsworth had in mind the symbolic significance of the desolated spring, which, 'now dead and gone' (142), prefigures the poem's stark, uncompromising conclusion. Where suffering in 'Hart-Leap Well' is relieved through dialogue, sympathy and recollection, in 'The Brothers' it is intensified by silence, alienation and cultural amnesia, as manifested in Leonard's failure to recognise the unmarked grave of his younger brother. Paul Magnuson concludes that 'The Brothers' 'challenges the assurance of "Hart-Leap Well" that intelligible signs and memorials can create a community of sympathetic hearts', but it serves also as a reminder of how *Lyrical Ballads* eschews the myth of a pure, pastoral margin, untainted by violence and unmarked by loss.[19]

Still, Lucy *dwells* 'among th' untrodden ways' (1). Written into that self-cancelling phrase – can 'ways' be 'untrodden'? – is a marginal space that, although unrealisable, is not unimaginable. Like the pedlars, veterans and beggars encountered on the wayside, Lucy introduces a disturbance into the world that jolts us out of complacency, forcing us to recall that the realms of language, sense and law are founded on an act of exclusion. 'Beside the springs' of the pacific river Dove (2) Lucy appears protected from violence, yet in her comparison to a 'Violet by a mossy stone', 'a star, when only one / Is shining in the sky' (Lines 5–8 passim), we see that she is already touched by death. Lucy's singularity is thus made dependent on a relationship with loss, a tarrying with negation – 'She liv'd unknown, and few could know' (9) – that suspends, for a moment, the 'difference' (12) between being and non-being.

Endnotes

1 Aristotle, *The Politics and the Constitution of Athens*, ed. Steven Everson (Cambridge: Cambridge University Press, 1996), 11–29.

2 See Michel Foucault, *The History of Sexuality*, vol. 1, *The Will to Knowledge*, trans. Robert Hurley (London: Penguin, 1989), 139, and *'Society Must Be Defended': Lectures at the Collège de France, 1975–76*, trans. David Macey (London: Penguin, 2004), 243–245. See also Giorgio Agamben, *Homo Sacer: Sovereign Power and Bare Life*, trans. Daniel Heller-Roazen (Stanford: Stanford University Press, 1998) and Roberto Esposito, *Bios: Biopolitics and Philosophy*, trans. Timothy Campbell (Minneapolis: University of Minnesota Press, 2008). The readings developed in this chapter draw in particular on Agamben's work.

3 See Stuart Allen's nuanced commentary on Wordsworth's reworking of Burkean paternalism in *Wordsworth and the Passions of Critical Poetics* (Houndmills: Palgrave Macmillan, 2010), 76–78.

4 For further discussion of this idea, see Agamben 4–9.

5 Horace, *The Odes*, ed. Kenneth Quinn (Houndmills: Macmillan, 1980), 75.

6 'margin, n.', *OED*.

7 For discussion of the background to this poem, see Lucy Newlyn, *William and Dorothy Wordsworth: 'All in Each Other'* (Oxford: Oxford University Press, 2013), 129–131.

8 See 1 Chronicles 21:15–16.

9 See the photographic reproduction and transcription of 'Old Man travelling' in *Cornell LB* 482–487.

10 Sally Bushell, 'Composition and Revision', in *William Wordsworth in Context*, ed. Andrew Bennett (Cambridge: Cambridge University Press, 2015), 27–37, (33–34).

11 For related discussion, see *Romanticism and Biopolitics*, *Romantic Circles Praxis Series*, ed. Alastair Hunt and Matthias Rudolf, December 2012, www.rc.umd.edu/praxis/biopolitics (accessed 12 September 2017).

12 Quotations are taken from the version of the poem published in the *Cornell LB* 277–282.

13 Kenneth Johnston notes that British military interventions in the West Indies, mounted in support of the lucrative sugar industry, led to the deaths of an estimated 'forty thousand soldiers since the plantations were first established'. Kenneth R. Johnston, *The Hidden Wordsworth: Poet, Lover, Rebel, Spy* (New York and London: W. W. Norton, 1998), 145.

14 For commentary on the complicated textual history of this poem see Newlyn 95–97.

15 Kenneth Johnston suggests that the 'Lucy Poems' and 'Nutting' 'are, in varying degrees, evidence of his effort to deny Dorothy a love she wanted' (*The Hidden Wordsworth*, 651).

16 'Nutting', *DCMS* 15. Lines 14–15; *Cornell LB* 302.

17 As David Chandler points out, Sir Walter is based on Sir Walter de Barden, a veteran of the Scottish wars of the thirteenth century. See 'The Politics of "Hart-Leap Well"', *Charles Lamb Bulletin*, 111 (2000): 109–119.

18 Here Wordsworth signals a departure from the poem's origins in Gottfried August Bürger's sensationalist ballad 'The Wild Horseman'.

19 Paul Magnuson, *Coleridge and Wordsworth: A Lyrical Dialogue* (Princeton: Princeton University Press, 1988), 262.

PART III

Feeling and Thought

CHAPTER 8

Silence and Sympathy in Lyrical Ballads

Andrew Bennett

It is no exaggeration to say that sympathy is the founding principle of the poems collected in both the first and second editions of the *Lyrical Ballads*. Together with the associated and overlapping affective impulses of compassion, pity, identification, and what we tend now to call 'empathy', sympathy, or its absence, is a central organising impulse of almost every poem in the collection. Sympathy – a feeling for or feeling with – is expressed and explored in various ways and with, or towards, different kinds of individuals or objects (including animals and inanimate objects), but is consistently the focus of poem after poem. As Wordsworth comments in the final poem in the 1800, two-volume edition of *Lyrical Ballads*, the 'power / Of Nature' has led him to 'feel / For passions that were not my own' and thereby to think 'On man, the heart of man, and human life' (*LB* 'Michael', 28–31).

Yet, more often than not, sympathy is presented as a question or conundrum, a limit-case – as an ethic or affect that raises difficult and often imponderable questions and that leads even to a series of conceptual and ethical crises. Rather than simply a principle that may be said to give the rule to human behaviour and relationship – a principle that 'worked its miracles' as the 'effectual mother of all virtues' in a prominent strand of late eighteenth-century thinking – for Wordsworth and Coleridge the question of sympathy also unmoors behaviour, ethics and even indeed emotion from 'pre-established codes of decision'.[1] And I will suggest that it is through silence – through the ideal of 'silent sympathy' and through its disruption – that the poems often work out their conflicted dynamics of sympathetic identification.

* * *

In *Lyrical Ballads*, the principle of sympathy is not only *thematic* but also *formal* or *poetic*, and may indeed be said to underpin Wordsworth's theory

of poetic composition. Sympathy, in fact, is the very basis for Wordsworth's definition of the poet in the 1802 version of the 'Preface' to the
collection. Introducing a lengthy passage on poetic identity ('What is a
Poet?', he asks, baldly), he describes such a person as 'a man speaking to
men' who is, however, at the same time 'endued with more lively sensibility' and has 'a greater knowledge of human nature' than is commonly the
case (*LB* 103). But Wordsworth also argues that the poet has a greater
'disposition' than other people to be 'affected . . . by absent things as if they
were present' and wishes 'to bring his feelings near to those of the persons
whose feelings he describes' (104). Although a poem can only represent
passions as 'shadows' of the real thing, he argues, in order to transcend a
'slavish and mechanical' reproduction or representation, the poet should
'for short spaces of time' be able to 'slip into an entire delusion, and even
confound and identify his own feelings' with those of other people (104).

   Wordsworth's theory of poetic identity, and his model of poetic composition as structured around sympathetic identification, do not, of course,
emerge out of thin air. The principles can be traced to the philosophical
discussions of sympathy that had come to dominate both theory of mind
and philosophical debates on ethics in the eighteenth century. Despite an
underlying antagonism towards the writings of David Hume and Adam
Smith, in his talk of a delusional identification and of confounding his
feelings with those of others, Wordsworth slips seamlessly into the rhetoric
of sympathy that is worked through philosophically in Hume's *A Treatise
of Human Nature* (1739–1740) and in Smith's *The Theory of Moral
Sentiments* (1759). Addressing the question of sympathy within the context of his analysis of human understanding, for example, Hume argues
that 'No quality of human nature is more remarkable' and insists that
when an 'affection' is 'infus'd by sympathy' it is soon 'converted into an
impression' that 'acquires such a degree of force and vivacity, as to *become
the very passion itself*', such that it produces an emotion that is 'equal' to
the original.[2] The conceptual model of sympathy whereby the object or
individual that is perceived, thought or imagined is transformed into the
actual experience *of* that object or individual itself, suffuses – and indeed
underpins – dominant strands of eighteenth-century thinking: 'the ideas of
the affections of others are converted into the very impressions they
represent' (*Treatise* 208). Hume goes on: 'When I see the *effects* of passion
in the voice and gesture of any person my mind immediately passes from
these effects to their causes, and forms such a lively idea of the passion, as is
presently converted into the passion itself' (368). Wordsworth's sense that
a poem does not simply or 'slavishly' represent the object, feeling or

individual described but allows the poet to 'confound his identity' with those of his subjects, is a direct descendent of Hume's thinking.

Writing two decades later, and building on Hume's conception of the importance of imagination in sympathy in the opening pages of *The Theory of Moral Sentiments*, Adam Smith addresses the philosophical question of theory of mind by arguing that we can have 'no immediate experience of what other men feel' and can therefore only perceive how they are 'affected' by 'conceiving what we ourselves should feel in the like situation'.[3] Since we can have no direct knowledge of other minds, Smith contends, it is through the imagination that we can 'form any conception' of the experience of another person (11). Offering the limit-case of a man being tortured on the rack, Smith analyses the mechanism of sympathetic identification:

> By the imagination we place ourselves in his situation, we conceive our-selves enduring all the same torments, we enter as it were into his body, and become in some measure the same person with him, and thence form some idea of his sensations, and even feel something which, though weaker in degree, is not altogether unlike them. His agonies, when they are thus brought home to ourselves ... begin at last to affect us, and we then tremble and shudder at the thought of what he feels. (12)

Although Smith takes extreme physical suffering as his example, he is also quick to generalise such a case and indeed to remark that the mechanism that produces sympathy is not limited to 'those circumstances only, which create pain or sorrow' (13). And like Hume before him and Wordsworth later, Smith presents a notably hallucinatory account of the working of sympathy whereby one somehow experiences the same cognitive, affective and even physiological symptoms as the person observed. 'Whatever is the passion which arises from any object' in any particular individual, he maintains, 'an analogous emotion springs up, at the thought of his situation, in the breast of every attentive spectator' (13).[4]

* * *

Concerned to argue that the poet is particularly gifted with the ability to make absent things be, or appear to be, as if they were present, Words-worth's poetics can be securely located within assumptions governing the eighteenth-century principle of sympathy. And there is no question that the poems collected in *Lyrical Ballads* do indeed allow for or provoke our sympathy: with a traumatised, conscience-wracked sailor; a female vagrant whose 'spirit' is burdened by a 'perpetual weight' ('The Female Vagrant',

Line 270); a desperate young mother who may or may not have murdered her own child, or another driven mad by grief; an ailing Indian woman left to die by her tribe; an old man who is hardly moving and yet travelling to see his dying son; with other forsaken or abandoned individuals or even indeed with a sensitive, seemingly humane but peculiarly self-involved poet as he contemplates his surroundings in the context of his past experiences of them. Sympathy, in each case, is invited, expressed or performed. And yet sympathy is hardly ever straightforward in these poems, and a provocative and often decidedly destabilising questioning of the limits of the principle is apparent in many of the more prominent poems, especially in the first, shorter version of *Lyrical Ballads* (a book in which 'nothing is quite as it seems', as Fiona Stafford remarks (*LB* xix)). Does the Ancient Mariner generate the wedding guest's sympathy, and indirectly ours, in his demand for an audience, we might ask, or is he a figure of warning, alienating fear and isolation? Should the young girl in 'We Are Seven' provoke our sympathy for the loss of her siblings and on account of the speaker's tactlessly querulous objections to her world-view, or do we in fact share *his* frustration at the girl's stubbornly unrealistic refusal accurately to compute her loss? What are we to make of Simon Lee's tears when the speaker helps him to chop down a tree, or of the unnervingly uncanny, settled quiet and animalistic tranquillity of an old man who is travelling to be with his son, who is in turn dying in a hospital in Falmouth? How much sympathy might we allow ourselves to feel for the self-absorbed and interiorly focused speaker in 'Tintern Abbey'? As David Simpson comments, there is a curiously disturbing effect in Wordsworth's representation of our appeal to sympathy whereby his poems 'ask questions even as they seem to be answering them' (27). And this may be because, as Wordsworth himself avers in a slightly defensive letter from 1802, he does not 'delineate merely such feelings as all men *do* sympathize with' but also 'such as all men *may* sympathize with' (*LB* 320).

Almost every poem in *Lyrical Ballads*, then, can be read as in some way generating rather than settling such questions in what is, in effect, a rigorous and unrelenting testing-ground for sympathy as the governing principle of eighteenth-century political and ethical action: the ethical and political principle of sympathy is questioned or undone as it comes up against challenges to its coherence and viability. We might consider this question in relation to the fact that sympathy in Wordsworth's poems is often articulated in, or directed by, various forms of silence. Silence in different manifestations features prominently in many of the poems in *Lyrical Ballads* and is often specifically linked to sympathy since, in

principle, sympathy is that which transcends or evades the communi-
cative meaning-making potential that is intrinsic to information-bearing
sound (most prominently and concentratedly, of course, in speech).
Sympathy should in principle – in its ideal state – transcend the vicissi-
tudes of language-based communication. The working of sympathy, in
this sense, is implicitly based on a silent or wordless identificatory ethic,
on a reaching out to embrace, and even in an imaginative sense to
become the person or object that one is not, but with whom or with
which one might feel. And yet, as this might already suggest, there is
something about this transgression of the boundaries and categories of
personal identity that is implicitly disruptive of sympathy itself. Silence
as both an evocation of and a disturbance to sympathy is undoubtedly an
uncannily notable feature in *Lyrical Ballads*, from the cataclysmic aural
vacancies that operate in and around the Ancient Mariner as he sails the
silent seas alone, to imagined moments of eerie and sometimes apocalyptic pausation in the environmental sounds that feature in several other
poems. A notable example is 'Three years she grew', one of the so-called
Lucy Poems, in which a personified, masculine Nature promises that
he will 'take' a three year's child to himself so that she will never 'fail
to see' a certain spiritual 'Grace' even in 'the motions of the Storm' (*LB*
Lines 4, 21–23). Observing such nature-driven grace, Lucy will herself be
moulded, Nature affirms, by her 'silent sympathy' with it (24). And yet,
as this might suggest, there is a darker side to the sympathy that the poem
evokes, since it is, disturbingly, if euphemistically, a silent sympathy that
will eventuate in the girl's death. Even while silence can be taken as a
critical signifier of the production of sympathy, in other words, it is also
markedly disquieting, and in this case, indeed, deadly. In this sense, the
eighteenth-century category of sympathy – a kind of cultural, philosophical, ethical, and political prerequisite, in effect – is intrinsic to the poems
gathered in the *Lyrical Ballads* but at the same time often eerily
disruptive. Sympathy in its ideal formation is articulated in and as the
'pauses of deep silence' that – just in the kinds of uncanny breaks in
communication that Wordsworth's 'There was a Boy' and Coleridge's
'The Nightingale' record – have the power to disturb the sympathetic
principle through which poems are nevertheless generated.[5]

In 'Lines written at a small distance from my House', the affective
production of sympathy, now in the 'hour of feeling' (Line 24), is again
presented as a function of the wordless linking of individuals in an implicit
assertion of communitarian association. The speaker in the poem sends a
message (the poem *is* the message, indeed) to his sister to put down her

books and join him outside on this, the 'first mild day of March' (1). Love, he declares, is 'stealing' from 'heart to heart' as well as from 'earth to man' and from 'man to earth' (21–23). The pantheistic associative linkage of person to person and from person to 'earth' and back again seems to be induced by 'silent laws' that 'our hearts ... make' with each other (29).

But there is a paradox even here, in this celebratory poem of nature-based sympathetic affirmation, just in the fact that it exists. By writing to his sister and insisting on the wordless connection with her, the poet undoes his own argument as he makes it, *in* making it. If love steals from heart to heart according to these 'silent laws', then the speech-act and the mediating technology of writing and transmission by which it is communicated and that announces this affective-cognitive or telepathic transmission is effectively redundant, and the whole procedure announced in the poem's title (the note-poem is written, given to the 'little boy' who is to take it to the poet's sister who will read and act on it) is unnecessary. In the light of John Bugg's reading of the politics of Wordsworthian silences in the context of the 1795 'gagging acts', it is difficult not to interpret the technics of 'silent' communication (whether telepathic or epistolary, indeed) as aligned with self-protectively secretive (because politically radical and even subversive) discourses and practices.[6] And yet the poem is so naturalistically affirmative, so siblingly solicitous, that it is also hard not to read it as driven by its own affective epistemology in which silent sympathetic communication is insisted on but also undermined just on account of that verbal insistence.

The correspondence of silence and sympathy in Wordsworth can be singularly and paradoxically performative, as in a key moment from 'Simon Lee' in which readers are encouraged to draw on the kind of 'stores' that 'silent thought can bring' in their acts of interpretation (Line 74). In this poem, the speaker encounters an elderly retired huntsman who is half blind and whose body is described as 'lean', 'sick', and 'half awry', with ankles 'swoln and thick' and legs 'thin and dry' (33–36). Weakened by extreme old-age, and by the exertions of his youth, the man is vainly attempting to chop out the root of an old tree.[7] After sixty-eight lines that describe the man's history and current condition, the speaker breaks off to mildly admonish his implied reader for presuming to look for a story:

> My gentle reader, I perceive
> How patiently you've waited,
> And I'm afraid that you expect
> Some tale will be related.

> O reader! had you in your mind
> Such stores as silent thought can bring,
> O gentle reader! you would find
> A tale in every thing.
> What more I have to say is short,
> I hope you'll kindly take it;
> It is no tale; but should you think,
> Perhaps a tale you'll make it.
>
>   (Lines 69–80)

The reader-focused interpolation is followed by three stanzas (twenty-four lines) in which the speaker describes helping the old man to cut out the root with 'a single blow', after which tears come into the elderly man's eyes as he thanks and praises his youthful helper (93). The poem ends with an enigmatic comment on benevolence (on 'kind deeds' and gratitude for them):

> – I've heard of hearts unkind, kind deeds
> With coldness still returning.
> Alas! the gratitude of men
> Has oftner left me mourning.
>   (Lines 101–104)

The lines present a sympathy-puzzle that the reader needs to work through in 'silent thought'. We have to ask ourselves why it is gratitude that has left the speaker mourning rather than *in*gratitude. What is the mourning *for*? What is the loss? The standard assumption – but this is an extrapolation, a reading *into* or beyond the words, which are effectively opaque, or silent, on the matter – is in fact really quite shocking: the speaker has been left mourning when he has encountered gratitude because such gratitude is understood to be an indirect result, and indeed a marker, of the suffering that the poor, weak, sick, aged, poverty-stricken, destitute or abandoned have endured.

Whether or not we accept this interpretative extrapolation, however, the point is that the poem does not just describe but inscribes and indeed produces an inscrutable *performance* of sympathy that, precisely in perplexing our sympathetic response, marks the limits of the empathetic operation that supposedly underlies all ethical action. If 'Simon Lee' evokes the strange workings of sympathy, in other words, the ending throws us back to the one-and-a-half parenthetical stanzas that have earlier instructed us to think, in a way that inculcates a 'silent' sympathetic imaginative ethic in its readers by informing us that it will withhold the tale that it thereby in fact presents. The emphasis on silence in this readerly directive is, perhaps, curious (what is 'silent thought', after all, and is there any other kind?). But what is implied most strongly is that the kind of thought that can allow for understanding and sympathy is the kind that is best (or only) achieved in the absence of language, of words, and of speech – and perhaps also of logic, reason and understanding. Against the ideological chatter, the incessant murmur of hegemonic capitalist-individualist models of benevolence, we might think, the poem silently asserts an unbridgeable or abyssal divide between donor and recipient, one that undoes or at least challenges the idea of economic or charitable 'gratitude'. It is a poetic manoeuvre that may in turn be understood to raise questions about the underlying assumptions of humanitarian benevolence that the poem also at the same time wordily promulgates. The poem, in other words, works quietly to reveal and indeed to undo its own contingencies of sympathy.

* * *

The very meanings and impulses by which sympathy is produced and operates, then, are quietly and disquietingly contested in *Lyrical Ballads*, not least by the linguistic and rhetorical resources that are deployed to generate or express it. But Geoffrey Hartman has noted what he calls a 'sympathy paradox' in Wordsworth that, he proposes, is foundational to the condition of modernity, with its ever-increasing access to visual and narrative reports of suffering, both local and global.[8] As Wordsworth himself acknowledges in the 'Preface' to *Lyrical Ballads*, he is responding to a new media age – an age that acts to 'blunt the discriminating powers of the mind' and reduce it to 'a state of almost savage torpor' (*LB* 99). For an increasingly industrialised society and urbanised population, Wordsworth contends, the 'great national events' that are 'daily taking place' serve to generate a 'craving for extraordinary incident' that is 'hourly gratified' by the 'rapid communication of intelligence' (*LB* 99).[9] Hartman argues that the media-saturated modernity that Wordsworth identifies leads to the paradox that the more an individual responds with sympathy or 'sensibility' to scenes of suffering the more she tends to become aware of the limits of and limitations on even her own capacity for sympathy.[10] It is partly on account of his realisation of and response to modernity, we might surmise, that Wordsworth's poems challenge sympathy and sympathetic identification so prominently and so consistently. And it may be that Wordsworth's cultural critique is symptomatic of a poet who was, as his friend and co-author later opined, 'always a spectator *ab*

extra of nature and society' (*CW STC* 14, I. 306). Coleridge is reported
to have commented rather sourly in the 1830s that Wordsworth 'felt
for, but never sympathized with, any man or event' and indeed
possessed 'a quality of non-sympathy with the subjects' of his poetry
(*CW STC* 14, I. 306, 342).[11]

One way to read Wordsworth's poems in the light of such comments
would be to pathologise the poet (as Coleridge hints that we might) as
uniquely un-sympathetic or as peculiarly resistant to the affective conditions and responses of others: we might then say that Wordsworth's
individual psychology, his character, is itself reflected in the way that the
poems regularly involve individuals who resist sympathy or present situations in which our humanitarian, sympathetic response is challenged or
turned back on itself. But another way to think about Wordsworthian
sympathy (or its absence or undoing) would be to read his poems as
making particular demands on, and asking difficult but pertinent questions
of, sympathy in general as well as sympathy within the cultural-economic
conditions of modernity, and to see the poems as thereby asking about
sympathy's epistemological, ethical or affective limits, and its social and
political efficacy.

The poems in *Lyrical Ballads* seem intent on examining the implications
of the eighteenth-century conception of sympathy, then, in order to push
the idea towards – and indeed beyond – the limits of thought. Silence can,
of course, act as a form of resistance by the relatively powerless to those in
power and is figured in some poems in the collection as a way of challenging or subverting situations in which sympathy is evidently lacking. In
this sense, silence is articulated in, or as, a certain verbal reticence or refusal
of speech by various men, women and children – people who are encountered or described, or who speak directly or indirectly in the poems, or who
refuse or fail to do so, often from an abjected, objectified position that is
powerless, disenfranchised and effectively silenced. Silence in such cases is
imaged and imagined phenomenologically in *Lyrical Ballads* in terms of a
material absence of sound that allows a space for empathy and identification while at the same time challenging sense-making itself. For this
reason, perhaps, silence is often configured as a form of restraint on speech
that both reflects deep emotion and expresses a kind of noncommittal
hesitation, withdrawal or interpersonal reticence – as well as, indeed, in
terms of a refusal or disavowal of compensatory or remedial praxis, of any
act that might seem to promise alleviation from suffering.[12] Rather than
responding verbally to the adult's coercive demand to choose between
Kilve and Liswyn farms, for example, the five-year-old boy in 'Anecdote

for Fathers' hangs his head and makes no reply (Lines 45–46). Such incompatible conversational perspectives in poems seem to express what the philosopher Jean-François Lyotard analyses as the *différend* – an unbridgeable difference in discourse, a fundamental gap in ways of speaking – constituting the other of sympathy, the limits of its possibility.[13] In this respect, the poem might be compared with 'We Are Seven', which presents another instance of a coercive conversation that records a *différend* or discursive impasse: in this poem, the adult attempts to persuade the child that she is wrong but ends up declaring that '"Twas throwing words away' to argue with her because whatever he says (however much he repeats his version of the truth) 'the little Maid would have her will', repeating her mantra 'we are seven!' regardless (Lines 67–69). The silence here is the enforced silence of a disagreement that cannot be resolved but can only end.

As an analysis of a rural sympathy deficit, however, 'Lines left upon a seat in a yew-tree' is more complex and opaque than many of the poems in *Lyrical Ballads*. And the poem is particularly resistant, indeed, to the sympathy that it also seems to evoke. The poem concerns a young man – a poet *manqué* often seen as a young William Wordsworth – who is 'pure in his heart' and of 'No common soul' (Lines 15, 13).[14] The young man sets out into the world 'big with lofty views' (14), but is soon rebuffed and ends up 'a captive of sterile self-regard' – oppressed, as David Bromwich wryly puts it, by 'his own resentment of the world's failure to serve him'.[15] He therefore retires, with 'rash disdain' and yet with 'his spirit damped', into a hermit-like solitude where he ventures to 'sustain . . . his soul' with 'the food of pride' (18–20). The poem can be read as a warning against personal pride and against a tendency in some to turn away from sympathy with others: we are warned that pride is 'littleness' (48) and instructed that 'True dignity abides with him alone' who can, in 'the silent hour of inward thought, / . . . still suspect, and still revere himself, / In lowliness of heart' (56–60). It is pedagogical, edifying, moralistic, even: the poem commends humility and sympathy with others. And yet it is also conceptually complex and seems uncertain even about its own sympathy towards its protagonist. The precise formulation of the warning that the poem issues is particularly nuanced, troubling and ambiguous – as if Wordsworth is testing the rhetorical and conceptual limits of didactic or moralistic poetry. The poem's key line in this respect refers to people who are able properly to regard the 'loveliness' of both the world and other people because they are 'Warm from the labours of benevolence' (36).

By contrast with such people, the poem's protagonist is figured as someone who is unable to experience or express 'benevolence' and who instead grieves with 'mournful joy' when he thinks that 'others felt / What he must never feel' (39–40). Wordsworth seems to be concerned with what, in a very different context, Keats calls 'the feel of not to feel it'– with a striking affectlessness that is also prominent in 'Old Man Travelling', where the old man is notable, and envied, for what he himself 'hardly feels' (14).[16] The unnamed protagonist in 'Lines Left Upon a Yew-Tree' takes a certain negative pleasure, in other words, precisely by way of his sense that his own sympathetic capacities are limited. It is clearly presented as a perverse 'joy' (Line 44), and one that we are supposed to critique and reject. But the very fact that such resistance to the sympathetic principle exists – and the fact that Wordsworth dwells on it prominently in the first of his own poems in the 1798 edition of *Lyrical Ballads* – confronts us with the limits of sympathy, and with the possibility that sympathy is by no means a universal human attribute. The poem prompts its readers to ask whether they can have sympathy for an individual whose pride prevents him from sympathising with others – and with someone, indeed, who takes pride precisely in *not* sympathising.

* * *

I want to end with a consideration of a poem that raises questions about the legitimacy of the object of one's sympathy and that involves a markedly different form of silence. 'The Convict' was included in the 1798 version of *Lyrical Ballads* but was dropped in 1800 (and its place taken in the second edition by Coleridge's 'Love' – a mock-medieval ballad that tells of how the speaker 'won my Genevieve, / My bright and beauteous Bride!' (Lines 95–96) in a way that seems relatively untroubled by the problem of sympathy or by sympathy *as* a problem). 'The Convict' was effectively silenced by Wordsworth himself, in other words, and we might speculate that he never reprinted it precisely on account of the difficulties that it introduces with regard to the representation or performance of sympathy.

The poem tells of a visit by the speaker to a dungeon-like prison where a convict – an 'outcast of pity' (12) – is incarcerated, apparently punished for heinous but unnamed crimes and apparently facing the death penalty (the 'fetters' that constrain him in the cell also 'link him with death' (15)). It works particularly hard to articulate two considerations. In the first place, the poem emphasises the emotional suffering signified by the convict's demeanour: his head is 'black matted' and is 'bent' despairingly on his shoulder (13); the 'sigh of his breath' is 'deep' (14); his eyes are 'intent' with 'steadfast dejection' (15); and the speaker can telepathically see through the convict's body into his 'heart' and therefore knows that his 'bones are consumed', that his 'life-blood is dried', and that the thought of his crimes 'blackens and grows on his view' (21–24), while also having the empathetic insight to know of the 'thousand sharp punctures of cold-sweating pain, / And terror' that 'leap' at the convict's heart (39–40). In this sense, the poem moves towards a paronomastic assurance that the perpetrator of a crime by which he is himself tormented is both con*vict* and 'Poor *vict*im!' (45), in a move that seeks to dislodge the oppositional logic of criminality and punishment on the one side and victimhood and pity on the other. And it is this duality that generates the second focus of the poem, its insistence on the speaker's logically impossible sympathy for an 'outcast of pity' – sympathy generated just *because* it cannot be. There is certainly a great deal of sympathy: the speaker turns towards the jail 'with a deep sadness' (7) and feels intense 'sorrow' on seeing the convict in this state (17). But the poem culminates in the speaker's defensive assertion that he is no 'idle' prison-tourist, and his belief that his visit and his sympathy are unequivocally purposeful rather than frivolous or self-serving. His 'first wish' is 'to be good', he declares, in a rather limp rhyme with 'has stood', and he 'comes as a brother' to 'share' the convict's 'sorrows' (47–48). The final stanza seems almost to collapse under the weight of its acknowlededgment of the sympathy paradox that the one who most demands sympathy cannot, or should not, be afforded it:

> 'At thy name though compassion her nature resign,
> Though in virtue's proud mouth thy report be a stain,
> My care, if the arm of the mighty were mine,
> Would plant thee where yet thou might'st blossom again'.
>
> (Lines 49–52)

There can be no sympathy for this 'outcast of pity' (12) because compassion 'resigns' at his very name. And yet it is this resistance to compassion that itself *generates* compassion: precisely because we cannot feel sympathy with the criminal, we feel sympathy for him. While the speaker wishes 'to be good' (47) – partly by speaking to the convict and by writing the poem – virtue itself is 'stained' by the very 'report' of the criminal, by speaking to or writing of him; and the Godwinian condemnation of incarceration (and the death penalty) together with an argument for deportation as an alternative (figured, disconcertingly, not as transportation of a convict but as a literal transplantation) remains only an unfulfilled wish.[17] The 'arm of the mighty' is *not* 'mine', the speaker affirms, implying (against his earlier assertion of benevolence) that he is indeed as idle, ineffectual and self-serving as any other prison-tourist.

As the only poem from the first edition that was not included in the second edition of *Lyrical Ballads*, it was, we might speculate, excised as a result of a shift in Wordsworth's views on incarceration and capital punishment between the time of its first publication in 1797 and 1800, or, indeed, Charles Burney's prominent castigation of the poem for sympathising with the wrong person in his review of the volume in *The Monthly Review* was critical in the decision.[18] We might alternatively ask whether it is the poem's moments of verbal and rhetorical rawness that impelled Wordsworth to self-censor, to silence himself.[19] But a third possibility worth pondering is, as I have suggested, whether the poem may have been dropped on account of its explicit exposure of the intrinsic paradoxicality embedded and generally hidden within the poetry and poetics of sympathy. The problem that the poem addresses but cannot overcome is that the metrical representation of those silent others with whom we are invited to sympathise (the indigent, the oppressed, the neglected, dying, or lonely, those that suffer, and the victim who is also here the criminal outcast) can always, just in its very gesture of sympathy, be regarded as a demeaning or debasing of the objectified and aestheticised victim while thereby exalting or elevating the subject who owns such a refined sensibility and taste – so refined, indeed, that he and he alone can properly experience and express sympathy. It is not just that sympathy – that outward-facing, humanitarian, benevolent and selfless ethical principle – is also presented as directed nowhere else but inward, to the sympathiser's proprietorial sense of his own ethical self, but that the poem is unable decisively to disentangle the idle touristic gaze from the idle poetic perspective.

In an earlier version, published in the *Morning Post* in December 1797, the poem ended with an additional stanza (possibly written by Coleridge) that is not included in the *Lyrical Ballads* but that offers an alternative and practical assurance of displaced benevolence in which sympathy is unproblematic because it is directed towards the unambiguously innocent – not towards the convict-victim himself but towards his posthumously surviving family in the future:

> Vain wish! Yet misdeem not that vainly I grieve –
> When vengeance has quitted her grasp on thy frame,
> My pity thy children and wife shall reprieve
> From the dangers that wait round the dwellings of shame.
> (*Cornell LB* 115)

The fact that this stanza was dropped on its brief appearance in the *Lyrical Ballads* is telling. The displacement of sympathy onto the unequivocally innocent wife and children manages to sidestep the convict/victim dilemma. But this sidestepping may precisely be the problem, with regard to the way that it allows a troublingly untroubled (a quietist or even complacent) ethics of sympathy to operate. By deleting the stanza in 1798, Wordsworth refuses to circumvent the final recognition that poems, like tourists, are powerless – however much sympathy might be experienced, expressed and exhorted – to effect any redemptive praxis, to perform any action that will undo the paradox whereby (in this case) the rightfully incarcerated convict is himself thereby the victim. Sympathy remains paradoxical, ineffectual, resisting its own efficacy, and continuing to raise questions about subject and object, viewer and victim, victim and perpetrator, that Wordsworth finds that he cannot resolve, to be sure, but also as time goes on increasingly finds that he cannot fully and finally encounter and address.

Endnotes

1 Wordsworth, 'Advertisement' (1798) (*LB* 3).
2 David Hume, *A Treatise of Human Nature*, ed. David Fate Norton and Mary J. Norton (Oxford: Oxford University Press, 2000), 206 (italics added).
3 Adam Smith, *The Theory of Moral Sentiments*, ed. Knud Haakonssen (Cambridge: Cambridge University Press, 2002), 11.
4 Smith is careful also to discriminate sympathetic emotion from the real thing: what the observer feels, he comments, 'will, indeed, always be, in some respects, different' from what the principle subject himself feels, and 'compassion can never be exactly the same with original sorrow' because the observer has a 'secret consciousness' that the affect he feels is in fact 'imaginary' (27).
5 See Wordsworth's 'There was a boy', Line 17; p. 208 ('pauses of deep silence') and Coleridge's 'The Nightingale', Line 77; p. 31 ('a pause of silence').
6 John Bugg, *Five Long Winters: The Trials of British Romanticism* (Stanford: Stanford University Press, 2014): see especially ch. 5.
7 He seems to be between seventy and eighty (Lines 7–8) at a time when average life expectancy for men was about forty.
8 Geoffrey H. Hartman, *The Fateful Question of Culture* (New York: Columbia University Press, 1997), ch. 5.
9 For Simpson, Wordsworth presents 'the first comprehensively modern formulation of the aporias of human interaction in a society of dispersed populations governed by the operations of commodity form' and the first in which the 'rhetoric of resolution is so fully withheld'. *Wordsworth, Commodification, and Social Concern: The Poetics of Sympathy* (Cambridge: Cambridge University Press), 27.

10 Hartman comments that 'the more successful an expanding sensibility becomes, the more evidence we find of actual of insensibility', and that it is a problem of 'whether we can deal with suffering that is not only local but general' (144, 143).

11 See James Chandler, *An Archaeology of Sympathy: The Sentimental Mode in Literature and Cinema* (Cambridge: Cambridge University Press), 185–187, for other examples of contemporary assessments (particularly Hazlitt's) of Wordsworth's egotism and a signal absence of sympathy.

12 See Simpson's comment that in Wordsworth's poems sympathy is often 'impeded or ineffective' and that dialogue is 'often stillborn', particularly in relation to those desperate and despairing individuals whose 'intransigent silence' or 'baffling withholding of expressivity' itself resists sympathetic identification on the part of the observer (*Wordsworth, Commodification, and Social Concern*, 28, 35).

13 Jean-François Lyotard, *The Différend: Phrases in Dispute*, trans. George Van Den Abbeele (Minneapolis: University of Minnesota Press, 1988).

14 See, for example, Paul Fry's conclusion to his brief analysis of the poem that 'in making his embittered young man a seeker of emblems, a cultivator of loco-descriptive conventions, Wordsworth dismisses the eighteenth-century poet in himself (*Wordsworth and the Poetry of What We Are* [New Haven: Yale University Press, 2008], 90).

15 David Bromwich, *Disowned by Memory: Wordsworth's Poetry of the 1790s* (Chicago: University of Chicago Press, 1998), 118.

16 See John Keats, 'In drear-nighted December', Line 21, *John Keats: The Major Works*, ed. Elizabeth Cook (Oxford: Oxford University Press, 1990. Rpt. 2008).

17 In *Enquiry Concerning Political Justice* (1793), William Godwin argues for the ultimate abolition of *all* punishment, but concedes that under currently existing circumstances, and with certain safeguards, transportation must be considered the most humane (Harmondsworth: Penguin, 1985), 677–680. See Mary Moorman's comment on the poem as 'a pure exercise in Godwinism', *William Wordsworth, a Biography: The Early Years, 1770–1803* (London: Oxford University Press, 1957), 352.

18 Burney laments the 'misplaced commiseration' and declares that he fails to understand 'the drift of lavishing ... tenderness and compassion on a criminal' (Charles Burney, unsigned review of *Lyrical Ballads* in *The Monthly Review*, 29 (1799): 209–210).

19 Moorman comments that the appearance of this poem in print at a time when Wordsworth was 'already the author of other and very superior poetry, is curious' (352); Duncan Wu characterises the poem as having a 'crude energy' that is 'equivalent' to 'political caricature or agitprop' (*Wordsworth: An Inner Life* [Oxford: Blackwell, 2002], 78).

CHAPTER 9

Domestic Affections and Home

Susan J. Wolfson

Home Is Where the Heart Is

That the language of 'domestic affections' and 'home' has a much wider register, and ideological reverberation, than a reference to any immediate domicile and family is reflected everywhere in *Lyrical Ballads*, localised in rural districts though its poetry and prefaces may be. In 1790, Edmund Burke excoriated the French Revolution's degradation of home and domestic affections in historical and national terms. He celebrated the antithesis to new France in traditional England, where 'conservation', 'transmission' and 'inheritance' of 'property' operate on one 'principle', founded on the 'method' and 'pattern of nature'. The Burkean state endures as a family settlement, 'a permanent body composed of transitory parts', a home for national domestic affection beating 'in a just correspondence and symmetry with the order of the world'. The pace and pathos of individual events of 'decay, fall, renovation, and progression' dissolve into one 'great mysterious incorporation':

> we have given to our frame of polity the image of a relation in blood; binding up the constitution of our country with our dearest domestic ties; adopting our fundamental laws into the bosom of our family affections; keeping inseparable, and cherishing with the warmth of all their combined and mutually reflected charities, our state, our hearts, our sepulchres, and our altars.

Burke's superstructure, naturalised and sacralised for 'family affections', bonds a quasi-divine alliance of the institutions of monarchy, aristocracy, Church, and parliament: ideology mystified in 'nature' and 'blood'.[1]

Wordsworth's project in *Lyrical Ballads* was to reflect dearest domestic ties in rural life and humble lives. Referring to two new poems in 1800, 'The Brothers' and 'Michael', he wrote to Whig statesman Charles James Fox of his intent 'to draw a picture of the domestic affections as I know they exist amongst a class of men who are now almost confined to the North of England' (*Letters EY* 314).[2] He would make his mark, make his claim, as the poet who could draw these affections, and would draw his

152

readers, across class differences, into sympathy on a 'common' ground with 'low and rustic life': intimate with 'nature' not as a method to rationalise social inequality but as a place of manners uncorrupted by 'social vanity' – so a new 'Preface' put it (*LB* 96–98). Wordsworth advanced a counter-Burkean picture on a Burkean framework of home and affection.

When in 1812 Felicia Browne (later Hemans) titled her second volume *The Domestic Affections*, it was to weave the several strands of her keywords into mutual reinforcements of hearth and home and the patriotic heart of England, especially in a long war with France that was pretty much synonymous with her life so far. Wordsworth was a durable anchor. Writing in 1826 to fellow Wordsworthian Maria Jane Jewsbury, Hemans likened him to Schiller's *William Tell* (1804), 'a calm single-hearted herdsman of the hills, breaking forth into fiery and indignant eloquence, when the sanctity of his hearth is invaded'.[3] She virtually nominated him as the Poet Laureate of 'Home' and 'Domestic Affections', a reverence inflected by a daughterly longing (her own father gone from her childhood, her husband a lost presence to her family):

> There is hardly any scene of a happy, though serious, domestic life, or any mood of a reflective mind, with the spirit of which some one or other of them does not beautifully harmonize. The author is the true <u>Poet of Home</u>, and of all the lofty feelings which have their root in the soil of home affections. (*FH* 492)

With this letter she included her poem 'To Wordsworth', casting a glow of homely sites for cherishing his poetry, to be 'read among the hills' (I) or in 'Garden's bowers' (II),

> Or by some hearth where happy faces meet,
> When night hath hushed the woods with all their birds,
> *There*, from some gentle voice, that lay were sweet
> As antique music, linked with household words.
>
> (III)

To Wordsworth himself she praised his 'enjoyment of . . . a domestic life, encircling you with yet nearer and deeper sources of happiness' than poetic fame and influence (*FH* 517). His 'gentle and affectionate playfulness in the intercourse with all the members of his family', she told another friend, 'would of itself sufficiently refute Moore's theory in the Life of Byron, with regard to the unfitness of genius for domestic happiness' (24 June 1830; 504). Thomas Moore's *Life* confirmed 'Byron' as the brand of a broken home, lost forever to wife, daughter, and England itself.

Hemans's Homebody-Wordsworth tells another tale from the prevailing one of the iconic Solitary: 'He lives in the busy solitude of his own heart; in the deep silence of thought' was Hazlitt's verdict after he read *The Excursion*.[4] Keats crafted a memorable eponym, 'the wordsworthian or egotistical sublime; which is a thing per se and stands alone'.[5] It is a 'sublime' to rival Wordsworth's 'sublime conviction of the blessings of independent domestic life' (*Letters EY* 314). Although Wordsworth meant 'independent of financial burden', Keats was not wrong about the character. Coleridge, friend and collaborator on *Lyrical Ballads*, had to coin the word *Self-involution* for his complaint.[6] Wordsworth recognised the logic in the third of his *Poems of the Naming of Places* (*LB*, 1800–1805), when a dear home-mate marks a high lonesome 'Eminence' for him:

> And She who dwells with me, whom I have lov'd
> With such communion, that no place on earth
> Can ever be a solitude to me,
> Hath said, this lonesome Peak shall bear my Name.
>
> (Lines 14–17)

This 'And', instead of an expected pivot ('But', for instance), is nicely accommodating. While the chime of 'She' and 'me', the lettering of 'we' at the very heart of 'dwells', and a trail of plurals ('we', 'us', 'our' (3, 6, 8)) issue soft objection, even ironising her so having said, it is candid of Wordsworth to stage a poet who doth protest too much. He knows 'She' is not wrong. She was with him when he revisited the Wye a few miles above Tintern Abbey, but 'dear, dear' as she is (117–122), she abides unmarked for almost three-quarters of his poem on the occasion.

In the years leading up to *Lyrical Ballads*, moreover, home was more of a question than a security for William Wordsworth. From 1793 to 1795, he was no domestic genius; he was errant across England, threading through a series of doubles on the fringes of human society. In late 1795 he and his sister, long separated from the diaspora of their childhood home, shared at last a series of residences – in Racedown, Dorset, in Alfoxden by 1797, miserably in Germany, 1798–1799. By late 1799, they were settled hopefully at Dove Cottage, Grasmere. While Wordsworth's affection was for 'this our little domestic slip of mountain' (*Letters EY* 274), *Lyrical Ballads* presents no timeless pastoral. It is an archive of material vulnerabilities: erosions and dispossessions, 'burthens ... buffeted with bond, / Interest and mortgages', lands yielding little to daily toil – so we hear a typical history in 'The Brothers' (210–213). Families suffer and fray, domestic affections strain into rupture, and homes are lost. Though not overtly political, such an affecting panorama could stir Francis Jeffrey, in the inaugural issue of

The Edinburgh Review (1802), to complain of agitations to political 'discontent'.[7] For this Whig advocate of reform on a middle-class consensus, populism was a problem, and its prompts in poetry amounted to counter-cultural activism in serial stories of homes fragile, lost, and an out-of-doors world on the moors and roads of wanderers, beggars, outcasts, homesick and half alive, with only a prayer of domestic affection in everyday, modern England. Even the un-Whig *Anti-Jacobin Review* regarded an 'attachment to *home*' as 'the source of much individual comfort and of infinite social good', not least in a tendency 'to connect more firmly the links of the social chain'.[8] The stress on these links was not any import from France, but home-grown historical displacements.

No Place Like Homelessness

The two most famous poems of the 1798 *Lyrical Ballads* are haunted by homelessness.[9] Coleridge's 'The Rime of the Ancyent Marinere' led off, claiming a quarter of the pages with a nightmare of eternal wandering. The Mariner's return to 'mine own countrée' (*LB* 1798, line 603) proves a delusion of hospitality. The concluding poem to the collection seems of an opposite temper, its inscribed date keyed, eight years to the day, to Wordsworth's first step into revolutionary France, and its brotherhood of man:

LINES

WRITTEN A FEW MILES ABOVE

TINTERN ABBEY,

ON REVISITING THE BANKS OF THE WYE DURING

A TOUR,

July 13, 1798.

Yet this revisit to Wye valley was to no home, and Tintern Abbey was a site of gothic abjection.

Here is another view of touring:

> These Tourists, Heaven preserve us! needs must live
> A profitable life: some glance along,
> Rapid and gay, as if the earth were air,
> And they were butterflies to wheel about
> Long as their summer lasted … (1–5)

So opens 'The Brothers' in *1800*. 'Tourist' was a fairly new word – not in Johnson's mid-century *Dictionary*.[10] The Wordsworth tour of 1798, on 'the tether of a slender income' as Dorothy wrote on 13 June (*Letters EY* 221), had no gay rapid carriage; it was on foot. Their course was uncertain. Having lost the lease on their happy Alfoxden home and, said William, 'utterly unable to say where we shall be' (6 March; *EY* 211), they were in effect homeless. Their departure on 25 June was the poet's latest of 'many wanderings' (*Tintern Abbey* 157) – the sole instance of this noun in *LB* 1798. The sylvan Wye, that 'wanderer through the woods' (57), was less a pattern than an extravagant fancy – one shaded, moreover, by the homeless wanderers and abject travellers across all the preceding pages.

There is a quiet urgency in Wordsworth's footnote, not even four full lines into the poem: 'The river is not affected by the tides a few miles above Tintern' (*LB* 87). Seeming to explain the description of its 'inland murmur', the wording is more deeply inflected, Nicholas Roe proposes, by a sense of safety from the wider world, within which this poet has to discipline his own 'murmur' of grievance (87).[11] William Gilpin's guide to the 'picturesque' promised that in this green world, 'Every thing around breathes an air so calm, and tranquil; so sequestered from the commerce of life'.[12] It is a binary romance, for just a few miles downriver is the world that the poet 'dreads' (line 72). The Wordsworths had Gilpin's guide with them and had stayed in Tintern on 12 July.[13] Up close, the town's famed Abbey-ruin disclosed a dwelling-place for the homeless, begging alms from tourists. Gilpin was stunned by 'the poverty and wretchedness' in this 'scene of desolation':

> They occupy little huts, raised among the ruins of the monastery; and seem to have no employment but begging . . . we found the whole hamlet at the gate, either openly soliciting alms; or covertly, under the pretence of carrying us to some part of the ruins, which each could shew and which was far superior to any thing which could be shewn by any one else. . . . One poor woman . . . engaged to shew us the monk's library. She could scarce crawl; shuffling along her palsied limbs, and meagre, contracted body, by the help of two sticks. (Gilpin 35–36)

This poor woman has poignantly nominated this her 'own mansion', but the 'shattered cloister' is a study in misery. Her only story 'was the story of her own wretchedness; and all she had to shew us, was her own miserable habitation. . . . I never saw so loathsome a human dwelling' (36). The lexicon of 'wretchedness', 'miserable', 'loathsome' in implicit antithesis to 'human' is bereft of domestic affection, with only a horrified sympathy:

It was a cavity, loftily vaulted, between two ruined walls; which streamed with . . . unwholesome dews. The floor was earth . . . not the merest utensil, or furniture of any kind, appeared, but a wretched bedstead, spread with a few rags. . . . At one end was an aperture; which served just to let in light enough to discover the wretchedness within. — When we stood in the midst of this cell of misery; and felt the chilling damps, which struck us in every direction, we were rather surprised, that the wretched inhabitant was still alive. (Gilpin 36–37)

Three more times 'wretched' is sounded, for the dweller and the dwelling, at the far end of the spectrum where human being declines into an old crawling animal.

As poet Wordsworth surveys the Wye's green pastoral, he is so haunted by what he has seen at Tintern (where on 14 July he actually started the poem) that a sight of 'wreathes of smoke / Sent up, in silence, from among the trees' (8–19) eludes picturesque capture. He wonders 'Of vagrant dwellers in the houseless woods, / Or of some hermit's cave' (lines 21–22). Lone hermit is the happiest surmise: a volunteer in resolution and independence. 'From the sweet thoughts of home, / And from all hope I was for ever hurled' is the record of the Female Vagrant in this same volume (132–33); even a company of 'wild houseless Wanderers' in happy mobility and cheerful thievery cannot sustain her. These last words were not in the 1798 poem, but drafted in 1800 and first printed in 1802 edition (line 218), I think, to tighten the relay with the darker surmise of *Tintern Abbey*. But it was in the poet's mind as early as 1794.[14] Drawn from Wordsworth's trek across Salisbury Plain in summer 1793, just before the pause named 'when first / I came among these hills' (*Tintern Abbey* 67–68), 'The Female Vagrant' is a record of loss, probably fatal, of all 'home delight' (260).

> Poor naked wretches, whereso'er you are,
> That bide the pelting of this pitiless storm,
> How shall your houseless heads and unfed sides,
> Your loop'd and window'd raggedness, defend you
> From seasons such as these?

This is deposed Lear's shock at the population scarcely alive outside his castle walls, taking physic from his sudden fall into their circumstance (*King Lear* 3.4.30–32). It amounts to a tacit allusion for both Gilpin's report and Wordsworth's vagrants.

Keats knew *Lear*, and was thinking about 'Tintern Abbey' when he compared the course of human life to a home whose delight darkens in realisation of pain and misery: 'We feel the "burden of the Mystery," To this Point was Wordsworth come, as far as I can conceive when he wrote

"Tintern Abbey" and it seems to me that his Genius is explorative of those dark Passages' (3 May 1818; *JK* 129–130). Wordsworth's dominant syntax has darkness 'lighten'd', with brief relief, by the gift of a 'blessed mood' (*Tintern Abbey* 38–42). Keats strips this to the dark passages.

While Hemans cherished the Genius of Home, she, too, knew, on the pulse of her own life, that the force of Wordsworth's poetry was in weighing the burdens of life in the world as it offered

> places of refuge ... in many an hour when
> ——————————"The fretful stir
> Unprofitable, and the fever of the world
> Have hung upon the beatings of my heart" (*FH* 517)

Inhabiting *Tintern Abbey* 53–55, Hemans can't help but speak the fever of the world.[15]

The Ends of Hearts and Homes

Revisiting the Wye in July 1798, Wordsworth went upriver to another ruin, Goodrich Castle, where five years past, he had conversed with a hospitable cottage girl. Just before he lost and left Alfoxden, in spring 1798, he wrote 'We Are Seven', so titled for her memorable metaphysical maths of domestic affections. Her immediate family consists only of herself and her mother; her six siblings are experiential apparitions: two gone to sea, two to the coastal town of Conway, and two in a graveyard nearby. Her interlocutor is a tourist who bullies her with his calculus: only 'five' are 'alive' (his rhyme abets), while she insists, 'Nay, we are seven' (line 69). Like a good Wordsworthian poet, she is 'affected ... by absent things as if they were present' (*LB* 1800 'Preface' p. 104):[16]

> 'Two of us in the church-yard lie,
> My sister and my brother,
> And in the church-yard cottage, I
> Dwell near them with my mother'. (21–24)

Her parallels of 'in the church-yard' and 'in the church-yard cottage' array one extended dwelling-place – 'near' and 'with' merely incidental modulations in the domestic corporation 'of us' and 'We'. John and Jane, the only ones she names, are in the churchyard, her daily company:

> 'My stockings there I often knit,
> My 'kerchief there I hem;
> And there upon the ground I sit –
> I sit and sing to them.' (41–44)

The present tenses, the ritual repetitions of work and song: all make it seem as if this dwelling, and the affections that bind it, could go on forever. 'We are' is immutable. Yet as charming as she is, she is eight years old, at the end of childhood and home in the rustic classes: 'a daughter sent to service' is a commonplace report ('The Brothers', line 157).[17]

'Poor Susan' (*LB* 1800) contemplates an older girl's exile in London. Susan's brief relief is a dawn-vision that might evoke comparison to 'Composed Upon Westminster Bridge' (1802), where London at a distance and at dawn, shimmering in vast natural splendor, halts a traveller in reverential awe.[18] Susan is a labouring resident in London's unlovely commercial district. Travel is not her life. But a bird's song in the mornings can enchant her into a counterfactual present:

> Green pastures she views in the midst of the dale,
> Down which she so often has tripp'd with her pail,
> And a single small cottage, a nest like a dove's,
> The only one dwelling on earth that she loves. – (9–12)

This sounds like Dove Cottage (the Wordsworths' home by December 1799). Susan's 'view' brings a beloved home to her with such phenomenological presence that when it does 'fade' (13) she seems to fade, too: 'the colours have all pass'd away from her eyes'. The poem tells two stories, however. Against the fatal tinge of *pass'd away*, the present perfect verbs of stanza one–Susan "has pass'd by" the spot where a thrush "has sung for three years," which she "has heard" every morning (1–4)–imply brief daily renewals. In *LB* 1800 a final stanza had the speaker call to this 'Poor Outcast' to 'return': 'to receive thee once more / The house of thy Father will open its door' (17–18) – a scriptural diction intoning some archetypal restoration of loss. Deleting this stanza in *LB* 1802 (2: 88), Wordsworth pared the poem to its morning apparition and evanishment. In the 1815 *Poems*, the title is *The Reverie of Poor Susan* (1:330), a fragile daydream (for her and the poet). The spare title in *Lyrical Ballads* is less decisive about home and the heart.[19]

That's one story. A darker one is the Female Vagrant's, for whom a memory of home is the deepest pain. Her father's beloved 'old hereditary nook' (44) was wrest from them by the greed of a wealthy new neighbour, who sees to it, moreover, that 'all [their] substance fell into decay' (50), forcing them into vagrancy. Social inequality sharpens her lonely misfortune: 'homeless near a thousand homes I stood' – this sigh, in the same volumes in 1800 and after (line 179), in which a poet can claim and name a chance-espied 'single mountain Cottage' as 'my other home, / My dwelling, and my out-of-doors abode', and who set this the first of *Poems on the Naming of Places* in his domestic world (lines 36, 40–41). The Female Vagrant has no home at all, and is barely alive without affection, without community, and only a proto-poet to hear her tale.

In Wordsworth's home-region is the managed vagrancy of 'The Old Cumberland Beggar', about which his headnote is matter-of-fact:

> The class of Beggars to which the old man here described belongs . . . consisted of poor, and, mostly, old and infirm persons, who confined themselves to a stated round in their neighbourhood, and had certain fixed days, on which, at different houses, they regularly received, sometimes in money, but mostly in provisions. (*LB* 1800 2:151)

What that word, 'belongs', does not embrace is a family or home. Wordsworth's speaker voices a romance of alms-giving, in passionate contempt of legislated captivity in a 'House, misnamed of industry' (line 172). Yet there is a begged romance in the alternative of life among 'wild unpeopled hills' (14), into which the old Beggar, to the end of his days, 'travels on, a solitary man' (24). Wordsworth does not resolve these conflicting indices, but plays them to extremes, so that the question of what it means to know, but not to house, an entire class of beggars is set beside itself to the point of unresolvable discord. As Charles Lamb commented to Wordsworth, 'the mind knowingly' indulges 'a fiction' (the romance of charity versus the cold comfort of a workhouse) and, 'detecting the fallacy, will not part with the wish'.[20]

Even homes in Cumberland fall into impossibility, if affections are defeated. 'The Brothers' opens with the Priest of Ennerdale at home-tasks with his wife and youngest child, observing a Stranger who (we slowly gather) turns out to be a local, too, absent for twenty years. A conversation unfolds the history of (this stranger) Leonard Ewbank and his younger brother James, their childhood in Ennerdale radiating from their grandfather's home, to the hills, rocks, and hollows they roved. With the grandfather's death, 'The Estate and House were sold, and all their Sheep', the toil of generations 'for a thousand years'; 'all was gone, and they were destitute' (lines 297–300). Although Leonard's 'soul is knit to . . . his native soil' (294), he left home 'to try his fortune on the seas' (302). Meanwhile the dale adopted lone James in surplus: 'If he had one, the Lad had twenty homes' (383). In the poem's present, Leonard has to 'this paternal home . . . return'd' (65) with financial means and a determination to resume

> The life which he liv'd there, both for the sake
> Of many darling pleasures, and the love
> Which to an only brother he has borne

> In all his hardships, since that happy time
> When, whether it blew foul or fair, they two
> Were brother Shepherds in their native hills. (67–73)

Yet it is the intensity of domestic affection that betrays a loss. As Leonard 'approach'd his home, his heart / Fail'd in him' (74–75). The first line joins home and heart; the next turns both to failure.

'The Brothers' is a long unwinding from its initial intimations of mortality.[21] Already disturbed by an unmarked grave that seems added since he left, Leonard notices a new dark cleft among the rocks. The Priest (still not recognising him) tells a story in painful symbols:

> There were two Springs which bubbled side by side,
> As if they had been made that they might be
> Companions for each other: ten years back,
> Close to those brother fountains, the huge crag
> Was rent with lightning – one is dead and gone,
> The other, left behind, is slowing still.— (138–143)

It is sheer redundancy to learn that James was given to sleepwalking, a 'habit [from] disquietude and grief' (391), as if – notwithstanding twenty homes in the dale – he was homeless without his brother, his search for him leading to his death and into that grave. There Leonard stands alone, to utter what readers already know: 'My Brother' (407).

> And thoughts which had been his an hour before,
> All press'd on him with such a weight, that now,
> This vale, where he had been so happy, seem'd
> A place in which he could not bear to live. (419–422)

The economic 'burthens' on generations of Ewbanks (210) could be borne by Leonard's hopes and hardships. The weight on his heart is more than he can bear. Wordsworth drops the impending epitaph of home and the domestic affections into this stark, final stanza:

> This done, he went on shipboard, and is now
> A Seaman, a grey headed Mariner. (430–431)

The *now* that was the dramatic present of return has become the *now* of a long, lonely life, bereft of all affection.

Not to, but from, home, in the pull of domestic affection felt in a lyrical ballad extracted from a draft of 'The Old Cumberland Beggar'. A sonnet-like poem in two acts, the affect of 'Old Man Travelling', brief and understated, is a devastating irony against its subtitle in 1798: ANIMAL TRANQUILLITY AND DECAY / A SKETCH. An octave sketches the old

man's pace, so slow and 'insensibly subdued / To settled quiet' (7–8), so
near to dissolving into nature, that even hedgerow birds are unflapped.
A sestet (9–14) weaves a romance of one 'by nature led / To peace so
perfect' that patience is hardly needed for this course. Then a second sestet,
in which the sketcher turns interviewer, reverses it all:

> —I asked whither he was bound, and what
> The object of his journey; he replied
> 'Sir! I am going many miles to take
> A last leave of my son, a mariner,
> Who from a sea-fight has been brought to Falmouth,
> And there is dying in an hospital.'
>
> (17–20)

There is no 'tranquillity' in this race of two goings, the long travelling and
imminent dying: 'is dying' is unique in the 1798 text. The texts of 1800,
1802 and 1805 have 'was dying'–a slight temporal haze over the emergency,
in the poet's report not the Old Man's, and in this mode a nearly closed
event. Some 130 miles from Cumberland at the tip of Cornwall's south
coast, Falmouth is the first port for returning ships, site of a hospital for
seamen. The irony against the speaker is extreme, the romance of 'peace so
perfect' undone by what Wordsworth could name as 'the calamities of war as
they affect individuals' (20 November 1795; *Letters EY* 159). In 1800, he
stripped the title to 'Animal Tranquillity and Decay', as if to stabilise a
harmony of pathos, no irony impending. How telling that in 1799, when
the recruitment of young men into military service was becoming urgent
(sometimes by impressment), Charles Burney, in *The Monthly Review*, could
wish that the son 'might have died of disease' instead (209). The shock of it
all is epitomised by John Jones: the final stanza does 'violence' to the delicate
sketch, and is such a 'mistake' that Wordsworth's decision in *Poems* 1815 to
delete it actually 'saved the poem'.[22] Poetic violence and poetic saving prevail
over the wartime violence and little saving.

'the parental affection, and the love of property'

A son is family investment for affections and hope. What happens when
domestic affections conflict with love of property that feels like family?
Another interview, 'The Last of the Flock,' is prompted by the spectacle
of a healthy man weeping in the public roads – alone, save a lamb cradled in
his arms (line 10). He tells the story of wild youth settled down with the
purchase of a ewe, from whom he bred enough 'other sheep' that he had the
means to marry, 'And every year increased my store' (30) – to fifty sheep and

ten children. But 'evil' times throw these 'dear' children (*endeared* and *costly*) into competition with the 'precious flock' (81–82), which must be divested in order to receive parish relief.[23] The ballad stops short of the full strain to domestic affections already admitted – 'yet every day I thought / I loved my children less' (87–88) – when the last of the flock is sold.

In his letter to Charles James Fox, Wordsworth takes pains to describe a Burkean order of strong 'domestic affections' in 'small independent *proprietors* of land here called statesmen, men of respectable education who daily labour on their own little properties'. If, moreover, they are

> proprietors of small estates, which have descended to them from their ancestors, the power which these affections will acquire amongst such men is inconceivable by those who have only had an opportunity and the manufacturing Poor. Their little tract of land serves as a kind of permanent rallying point for their domestic feelings, as a tablet upon which they are written which makes them object of memory ... a fountain fitted to the nature of social man from which supplies of affection, as pure as his heart was intended for, are daily drawn. (*Letters EY* 314–315)

Writing to Thomas Poole three months later, he explains on the template of *tract* and *tablet* his design for 'Michael':

> to give a picture of a man, of strong mind and lively sensibility, agitated by two of the most powerful affections of the human heart; the parental affection, and the love of property, *landed* property, including the feelings of inheritance, home, and personal and family independence. (*Letters EY* 322)

These sentences, shorn of specific modern developments and rendered almost as timeless folk history, are routinely cited or displayed in editions of this pastoral tale, often as immediate paratexts.[24]

Yet only one current is marked at the inception of Michael's story:

> these fields, these hills,
> Which were his living Being, even more
> Than his own Blood – what could they less? – had laid
> Strong hold on his Affections, were to him
> A pleasurable feeling of blind love,
> The pleasure which there is in life itself.
>   (*LB* 1800, lines 73–79)

This is more than a Burkean 'relation in blood'; it is Michael's own life– Being, Blood, Affections capitalized into more than personal categories. It's not just that his land is his living; "his patrimonial fields" (234) are continuous with his "living Being" in the world. It is the poem's sole instance of the word *affections*. In the 'picture' Wordsworth gives to Poole, the heart's two affections harmonise as one, in family, home, and inheritance. In tune, 'Michael' introduces a 'history' of shepherds, whose 'fields and hills' are 'their occupation and abode' (25–26); its very idiom is 'Homely' (35), a term infused with senses of household, way of life, humble class, and unornamented appeal to affection. The family's cottage draws all these senses into a rural mythology. Their 'endless industry' made them 'as a proverb in the vale' (96–97), and by 'chance' of its high location, their night-lit house was a landmark, place-named by the vale's 'dwellers' with reverence: The Evening Star (138–145). With 'forward-looking thoughts' (155), Michael invests in Luke (the name means 'light') as the bearer of his patrilineage; by age ten, he is the 'dearest object that he knew on earth ... His Heart and his Heart's joy' (160–162). The poet feels nearly redundant in his gloss:

> why should I relate
> That objects which the Shepherd lov'd before
> Were dearer now ?.....................
> And that the Old Man's heart seem'd born again.
>   (Lines 208–210, 213)

Wordsworth was distressed that the first printing of 1800 lost the run of these and nearby lines, 'absolutely necessary to the connection of the poem' (*Letters EY* 323).[25] It was more than textual necessity; the connection was inheritance, and in the capitals for Shepherd, Boy, Man (allied with Father and Son), symbolic.

The crisis comes in 'Distressful tidings', on tides of material obligation. Years before, Michael had been 'bound / In surety' for a loan to 'his Brother's Son'. By unspecified misfortune, the debt defaulted, and Michael is 'summon'd to discharge the forfeiture', almost 'half his substance'. In the prospect of selling a 'portion of his patrimonial fields', his site of toil for 'more than seventy years' and only freely held late in life (219–238), the two heart-affections that Wordsworth names to Poole become Michael's awful choice: between Luke in his 'heart', and Luke as an 'object' with a labor-value to save the lands. Michael does concede that other proprietors might yield some land with 'no sorrow' (250). But not he; in pained reluctance, he decides to send Luke to work for a prosperous 'Kinsman', to 'repair this loss' (257–262) and secure his patrimony:

> Our Luke shall leave us, Isabel; the land
> Shall not go from us, and it shall be free;
> He shall possess it, free as is the wind.
> (254–256)

In tones of scriptural authority, with the anaphora-symmetry of 'shall leave us', 'Shall not go from us', 'shall be free', 'shall possess it', Michael at once gives the grid of providential hope and exposes all that is risked.[26] Unworldly Luke is 'bound' to them 'Only by links of love', and he fears the break: 'when thou art gone / What will be left to us!' (411–413).

Michael anchors his son with a ritual, setting the cornerstone for a sheep-fold (410), a 'covenant' with 'the life thy Fathers liv'd' (421–425) – 'Fathers' here is plural and has symbolic capital. The crisis is the grammar of this ritual, but its syntax, a gathering of stones, reports its rupture. As in 'The Brothers', Wordsworth has set his readers to know the end here from the verbal markers in the prologue to the pastoral poem – 'straggling heap of unhewn stones' (17), arrested rather than built. Luke's default is dispatched with astonishing brevity: reports of diligence, frequent letters home (441–444), then a novel's-worth of failure in less than six lines. In a 'wond'rous' and 'dissolute city', unbonded from home and domestic affections, the son slackened,

> gave himself
> To evil courses: ignominy and shame
> Fell on him, so that he was driven at last
> To seek a hiding-place beyond the seas
> (453–456)

The remaining thirty-five lines are postscript and epitaph: Michael lives on for seven years, sometimes working at the sheepfold, sometimes, achingly, unable to lift up a single stone (476). Isabel survives a few more, then the lands of the Fathers pass – in Michael's worst nightmare – 'into a Stranger's hand' and agrarian modernity: The Evening Star / Is gone – the ploughshare has been through the ground' (485–486). All that's left are 'the remains / Of the unfinished Sheep-fold', which 'may be seen / Beside the boisterous brook of Green-head Gill' (489–491). In this grave of patrimony, the lost *boy* is cruelly echoed in its *boisterous* nature, eroding what only 'may be seen' but not read in disappearing local knowledge.

'It appears to me that the most calamitous effect, which has followed the measures which have lately been pursued in this country, is a rapid decay of the domestic affections among the lower orders of society', Wordsworth proposed to Fox (*EY* 313–314). The decay is another name for modernity, wrought 'by the spreading of manufactures through every part of the country, by the heavy taxes upon postage, by workhouses, Houses of Industry, and the Soup-shops &c. &c. superadded to the increasing disproportion between the price of labour and that of the necessaries of life' (*EY* 313–314). Homes and 'bonds of domestic feeling among the poor ... have been weakened, and in innumerable instances entirely destroyed ... parents are separated from their children, and children from their parents' (*EY* 313–314). 'Michael' is housed in this last archive. In her journal for 11 October, 1800, Dorothy Wordsworth notes that the sheep-fold on Greenhead Gill, 'falling away' in their day, seems to have been 'built nearly in the form of a heart unequally divided' (*DWJ* 26).[27] If this is too patently patterned for the heartache of Michael, the poet of *Michael* could state the case directly to Fox in what amounts to an 'Anecdote for Statesmen': the poem is about some neighbours, an elderly couple in increasing infirmity who fear 'they must both be boarded out among some other Poor of the parish'; the wife 'was sure that 'it would burst her heart'' (*EY* 314).

Men's Hearts, Women's Homes, Poetry's One Human Heart

In the expanded Preface of 1802, Wordsworth defines the Poet as "a man speaking to men" (xxviii). Gendered as well as general, the course of its poetry does not pause long in the female sphere of home and its cares, drudgery and melancholy. By 1817, *Blackwood's Edinburgh Magazine* could honor Wordsworth for a 'patriarchal simplicity of feeling'.[28] 'Michael' accomplishes this, movingly, as it tunes Burke's high argument to a humble 'Son and a Father' (99), the dearest of bonds, 'patrimonial fields' (234) and the life of 'Forefathers' (378). In the lament for lost ways of life that Wordsworth renders to Fox, woman is subordinate: 'the wife no longer prepares with her own hands a meal for her husband, the produce of his labour; there is little doing in his house in which his affections can be interested, and but little left in it which he can love' (*Letters EY* 314).

  While this isn't the narrative of 'Michael', the scattered lines of a Housewife's Tale can be assembled.[29] Isabel, a spinster or a childless widow in her early forties, has accepted a proposal of marriage from a solitary shepherd in his late sixties, at last able to support a family and an heir. (His inherited lands were burdened with debt, by age forty only half his own.) At the time of the poem she is around sixty-four, Michael is eighty-four and Luke, 'more dear' than 'his Help-mate' (149–150), is eighteen. Isabel's 'heart was in her house', its daily labour: skimming milk, making pottage, oaten cakes and cheese, and her perpetual industry at two spinning wheels, one for wool and one for flax (lines 84–87, 102–104). There is no mention of company or community for her, while, from Luke's early boyhood, father and son spend long days together in the hills and valleys – a bond from Luke's infancy, when Michael performed 'female service' (164). In the charge to Isabel to prepare 'Things needful' for Luke's stint in London, it is beyond poignant that she welcomed the Sunday relief from five-day's work, 'morn and night, and all day long', wrought 'with her best fingers' (presumably not all) (289–299). She has no voice in Michael's mandate, and her misgivings about the scheme are all for his sake. Her three years of life after his death can only be imagined in its solitude, poverty and hardship.

The poetry of women at home and the trials of their domestic affections would be left to Hemans and others. For her part, 'Mrs. Hemans' – self-styled icon of 'the domestic affections' – lived a contradiction: a daughter abandoned by her father, a diligent professional abandoned by her husband after the birth of their fifth son, left to manage their sons' care, education and fortunes. By 1833, just before writing of the refuge Wordsworth's poetry afforded from the fever of the world, she could murmur to Reverend Samuel Butler, 'I may say to you in confidence . . . that I have to struggle against much domestic Wrong of a kind the most crushing to a Woman's health and Mind' (*FH* 517). Unknown to her, what Wordsworth had left behind in France in 1792 was a domestic prospect with his lover Annette Vallon, pregnant with their daughter. His relation to his French family (largely mediated through his sister, always formal and dutiful) may well haunt *Lyrical Ballad*'s archive of abandoned, forlorn, crazed, homeless women.[30] Displaced to a world away, both in geography and culture, 'The Complaint of a Forsaken Indian Woman' is Wordsworth's experiment in imagining what it must be like for a mother, too weak to continue with a migration, to be abandoned (with minimal comforts) and see her baby given to another woman. Her last sight of her boy is his becoming a stranger and estranged: 'on me how strangely did he look' (34). In a headnote to the poem, he comments on the tribal practice, with a pause to note that females are 'equally or still more, exposed to the same fate' (*LB* 230).

On English ground, Wordsworth could solicit imaginative sympathy for homes and lives vulnerable to historically immediate depletions and ravages. He meant to move readers unprepared to discover 'delicate and refined feelings ascribed to men in low conditions of society, because their vanity and self-love tell them that these belong only to themselves and men like themselves in dress, station, and way of life' (7 June 1802; *Letters EY* 354).

He was gratified that 'Michael' had drawn tears from 'persons who never wept, in reading verse, before' (*EY* 322). For his part, Keats had by heart a line from 'The Old Cumberland Beggar': 'as Wordsworth says "we have all one human heart"' (*JK* 243). If the reviewer for the *British Critic* wondered if Wordsworth's subtle poetic procedures taxed readers with 'a persevering effort toward attention' to details 'wrought up gradually' in 'preparatory circumstances' and 'local descriptions', this reviewer could also appreciate the reward of patient reading in 'feelings' that grow 'by subsequent perusal'.[31] Wordsworth claimed such feelings as 'the common property of all Poets', and in *Lyrical Ballads* tested poetry itself as a 'little tract' for readers (and re-readers), a kind of home, or 'permanent rallying point for ... domestic feelings', a 'tablet upon which they are written' (*EY* 312, 314–315). Some critiques propose that Wordsworth capitalises on stories of ruined lives to build his modern profession.[32] I think this ungenerous. In imagining poetry as a home for domestic affection, beyond any contingency of property or circumstance, Wordsworth did not live to be a fool to his family of poems, but worked his materials through the social fabric that both grounded and traced the contradictions for his venture.

Endnotes

1 All quotations in this paragraph and inset are from Edmund Burke, *Reflections on the Revolution in France* (London: J. Dodsley, 1790), 48–49.

2 It was Coleridge's idea to send the 1800 *Lyrical Ballads* to 'persons of eminence', including Fox, Whig hostess and patron, the Duchess of Devonshire, abolitionist William Wilberforce, and republican-abolitionist woman of letters Anna Letitia Barbauld. Dorothy Wordsworth wrote to them all over William Wordsworth's signature, from Coleridge's dictation (Mary Moorman, *William Wordsworth, A Biography: The Early Years, 1770–1803* [Oxford: Clarendon Press, 1957], 502–4).

3 *Felicia Hemans: Selected Poems, Letters, &c*, ed. Susan J. Wolfson (Princeton: Princeton University Press, 2000), 491–493, 492. Hereafter *FH*. Wordsworth may have read this letter in H. F. Chorley's *Memorials of Mrs. Hemans, with ... her Private Correspondence*, 2 vols. (London: Saunders & Otley, 1836), I. 173–177.

4 'Character of Mr Wordsworth's New Poem, *The Excursion*', *The Examiner*, 21 (August 1814): 542.

5 To Richard Woodhouse, 27 October 1817; *John Keats: A Longman Cultural Edition*, ed. Susan J. Wolfson (New York: Pearson, 2006), 214. Hereafter *JK*. It is indicative of this durable 'Wordsworth' that the indexing of 'major concepts' in *The Oxford Handbook of William Wordsworth*, ed. Richard Gravil and Daniel Robinson (Oxford: Oxford University Press, 2015) does not include 'domestic affections' or 'home' (861).

6 To Thomas Poole, 14 October 1803; *Unpublished Letters*, ed. Earl Leslie Griggs (London: Constable, 1933), 1. 291.

7 'Art. VIII. Our modern school of poetry', *The Edinburgh Review*, 1 (October 1802), 63–83; comments relevant to *Lyrical Ballads*, 63–68, 71–72.

8 'Art. XXII', *Anti-Jacobin Review and Magazine*, 3 (August 1799): 457–459; 458–459.

9 For these bookend poems I use *1798*.

10 *OED*'s first entry is from 1780 in Wordsworthland, the front matter of *Ode to the Genius of the Lakes in the North of England* (London: [William Cockin], 1780), 3.

11 Roe, 'The Early Life of William Wordsworth, 1770–1800', in *Oxford Handbook of William Wordsworth*, 35–50; 49.

12 Gilpin, *Observations on the River Wye . . . relative chiefly to Picturesque Beauty* (London: R. Blamire, 1782), 32. Mirroring Gilpin's binary, Charles Burney thought Wordsworth's 'Lines' 'somewhat tinctured with . . . unsociable ideas of seclusion from the commerce of the world' ('Art. XIX [unsd]', *The Monthly Review*, 29 (June 1799): 202–210; 210).

13 Mary Moorman, *William Wordsworth, A Biography: The Early Years 1770–1803* (Oxford: Clarendon Press, 1957), 402. I appreciate Marjorie Levinson's sharp reading of the 'fragile affair' of this revisit, but I would stress *fragile*, rather than a deliberated 'project . . . artfully assembled by acts of exclusion' and studious 'suppression' (*Wordsworth's Great Period Poems* (Cambridge: Cambridge University Press, 1986) 32, 15).

14 A draft of 'Inscription for a Seat by a Roadside' asks able travelers on a steep footpath to ponder the relief for 'The houseless, homeless, vagrants of the earth' (*William Wordsworth: Early Poems and Fragments, 1785–1797*, ed. Carol Landon and Jared R. Curtis [Ithaca: Cornell University Press, 1997], 755).

15 Hemans hoped to publish these remarks in a dedication to *Scenes and Hymns of Life* (1834), but Wordsworth was embarrassed, and asked for something simple and minimal.

16 Frances Ferguson marks this affinity in *Wordsworth: Language as Counter-Spirit* (New Haven: Yale University Press, 1977), 24.

17 Michael Mason's edition glosses a cognitive marker: 'the age of conscious curiosity about her origins' with a knowledge of 'immortality' (*Lyrical Ballads* [New York: Longman, 1992], 129n), but a speculation of theological consciousness does not displace normal social fate for girls of eight.

18 Wordsworth did not put this sonnet in *Lyrical Ballads* but saved it for the 1807 *Poems* (1. 118).

19 In an incisive chapter in *Reading Romantics* (New York: Oxford University Press, 1990), 300–319, Peter Manning reads the shifting tenses and the flux of Wordsworth's revisions as nodal points 'of a historically specifiable conflict' (317) about how to read exiles from home, material and spiritual.

20 30 January 1801; *Letters of Charles and Mary Lamb*, 3 vols., ed. Edwin W. Marrs, Jr (Ithaca: Cornell University Press, 1975), 1. 265. For careful attention to these tensions and divisions (though I'd attribute these to a

speaker and not to Wordsworth himself), see Heather Glen, *Vision & Disenchantment* (Cambridge: Cambridge University Press, 1983), 82–84.

21 Attentive to the lodging of *The Brothers* in the section *Poems Founded on the Affections* in the 1815 *Poems*, Ferguson subtly reads the delicate links of affection to native home, and the painful instability that afflicts Leonard's return (42–53).

22 *The Egotistical Sublime* (London: Chatto & Windus, 1954), 63. Arthur Beatty thinks the excision was due to a close echo of Southey's *The Sailor's Mother*: 'Sir, I am going / To see my son at Plymouth, sadly hurt / In the late action, and in the hospital dying / I fear me now' (*Wordsworth: Representative Poems* (New York: Odyssey Press, 1937), 644). But the poems are rather differently tuned. Southey's interlocutors are a complacent patriot and a mother herself near to dying. Heather Glen has a fine ear for these polarized tonal extremes (*Vision & Disenchantment*, 225–226).

23 E. W. Bovill details such plights in *English Country Life, 1780–1830*, 2nd ed. (Oxford: Oxford University Press, 1962), 17 (excerpted, *Cornell LB* 353).

24 In 1882, William Knight excerpted the letter to Fox from *The Correspondence of Sir Thomas Hammer* (1838) as an appendix-note to *The Brothers* and *Michael* (*The Poetical Works of William Wordsworth* [London: Macmillan], 2. 396). Wordsworth protested the 1838 publication (without his permission), not for the sentiments but for violating a privacy essential to free correspondence (*Letters LY* III. 624–625). After Knight, excerpts became routine in back-matter appendices and notes. Classroom anthologies tend to move this material into closer proximity as virtual paratexts, either headnotes or immediately following postscripts.

25 See *1800* 2:210, discussed in *Cornell LB* 125–27; J. Dykes Campbell remarked that the omission made it seem that Michael would send his 'only child, at the tender age of five, alone and afoot, to seek his fortune in London' (127).

26 Not for nothing do these scenes evoke primary biblical typologies of paternal sacrifice (Peter Manning *Reading Romantics*, 41).

27 The working title was 'the Sheep-fold' (*DWJ* 27–28).

28 'On the Cockney School of Poetry, No. I', *Blackwood's Edinburgh Magazine*, 2 (October 1817): 38–41: 41.

29 It is telling that in her finely detailed discussion of the home economics of *Michael* (*Wordsworth's Great Period Poems* 58–79), Marjorie Levinson still compounds 'Michael's wife' into a corporate, one-flesh 'Michael's life' of 'unalienated labor' (64).

30 In such a line Manning reads Margaret and the Pedlar (*The Ruined Cottage*); *Reading Romantics*, 11–15.

31 Unsigned, 'Art VI. Lyrical Ballads, with other Poems: in Two Vols. By W. Wordsworth. Second Edition', *The British Critic*, 17 (February 1801): 125–131; 128.

32 James Buzard represents this argument in *The Beaten Track; European Tourism, Literature, and the Ways to 'Culture', 1800–1918* (New York: Oxford University Press, 1993), 24.

PART IV

Language and the Human Mind

CHAPTER 10

A 'Radical Difference'
Wordsworth's Experiments in Language and Metre

Brennan O'Donnell

The 'Advertisement' to the 1798 *Lyrical Ballads* anticipates a common theme in early responses to the volume: the poems are extraordinarily challenging. Reviewers were quick to agree that the poems frequently – and for some too frequently – required them 'to struggle with feelings of strangeness and aukwardness' and especially that they 'sometimes [descend] too low' stylistically, employing language that is 'too familiar, and not of sufficient dignity' (*LB* 3). One reviewer for the *New London Review*, reacting to Wordsworth's statement that a 'majority of the poems' are to be considered 'experiments' intended to 'ascertain how far the language of conversation in the middle and lower classes of society is adapted to the purposes of poetic pleasure' (*LB* 3), bluntly declares that such language 'can never be considered as the language of *poetry*'.[1] As discourse intended to 'affect the imagination', the commentator argues, poetic language must 'at least address itself to the imagination', which has its own 'peculiar style' (33). Quoting Wordsworth's advice to readers not to 'suffer the solitary word Poetry, a word of very disputed meaning, to stand in the way of their gratification', but instead to be pleased 'in spite of that most dreadful enemy to our pleasures, our own pre-established codes of decision', the reviewer comments: 'Nothing can be more ludicrous than this ingenious request of our author' (33). The experiments of *Lyrical Ballads* stem from an 'indecision of taste' traceable to the lamentable influence of Percy's *Reliques* on 'a numerous and meager race of *stanza-enditers*' who 'seem to have thought, that rudeness was synonimous [*sic*] to simplicity' (33).

Coleridge's major contribution, 'The Rime of the Ancyent Marinere', was found needlessly strange for other reasons. Writing in the *Critical Review* of October 1798, Robert Southey contradicts the claim of the 'Advertisement' that the 'Rime' is 'written in imitation of the *style* as well as of the spirit of the elder poets', claiming that he 'can discover no resemblance whatever ... except in antiquated spelling and a few obsolete words'.[2] Far from being a successful recovery of the style and spirit of early English poetry, the 'Rime' is 'perfectly original in style as well as in story'(200), writes Southey, as he condemns that originality as 'of little merit' and beneath the 'Genius' of its author (201). It is, he says, in a famously dismissive phrase: 'a Dutch attempt at German sublimity' (201). For Dr Charles Burney, the 'experiments' as a whole are part and parcel of a 'retrogradation' of poetic style, perversely 'cultivated at the expense of a higher species of versification', and the 'Rime', 'while containing 'poetical touches of an exquisite kind', is 'a rhapsody of unintelligible wildness and incoherence'.[3]

By the time Wordsworth wrote the 'Preface' to the 1800 second edition, Wordsworth and Coleridge themselves were beginning to realise that they shared some of their detractors' opinions, at least insofar as each poet saw some cause for correction of the other. Through word and action, in published texts and in letters and recorded conversations, it was becoming evident to both men that the tremendous creative burst of the early days of their friendship had masked serious disagreements in their understanding of the nature, style and purpose of poetry. For Wordsworth, Coleridge's 'Ancyent Marinere' was indeed passing strange, and he told Joseph Cottle that he believed it 'has upon the whole been an injury to the volume [of 1798], I mean that the old words and the strangeness of it have deterred readers from going on' (*Letters EY* 264). That assessment was no doubt behind his decision, in reorganising the contents of the 1798 volume for the 1800 two-volume publication, effectively to bury the poem, moving it from the first to the penultimate position in the first volume of the new edition. Moreover, in a note included in 1800 (removed in 1802), Wordsworth pointed out in some detail the 'great defects' of the 'Poem of [his] Friend', among them the fact that the mariner 'has no distinct character', that he 'does not act, but is continually acted upon', and that the poem's imagery 'is somewhat too laboriously accumulated' (*LB* 346). Anticipating the important rift that would eventually develop between the two on the subject of metre and diction, Wordsworth praises the versification of the poem as 'exhibiting the utmost powers' of the ballad metre that it employs, while simultaneously noting that the 'metre is itself unfit for long poems' (*LB* 346).

For Coleridge, no amount of critical justification by Wordsworth in prefaces, notes or appendices redeemed what he saw as his co-author's unaccountable unevenness or 'inconstancy' of style, his strange intermingling of what he would later call the 'impassioned, lofty, and sustained diction' found in poems, mostly in blank verse, such as 'Tintern Abbey' and attempts, usually in rhyme, to employ a variety of voices in a range of less 'lofty' styles (*BL* II. 8). As early as 1802, he was tracing connections between what he considered this odd defect in Wordsworth's practice and his arguments about poetic language in the 'Preface'. In a letter of July 1802 to Southey, Coleridge writes that 'altho' Wordsworth's Preface is half a child of my own Brain & arose out of Conversations, so frequent, that with few exceptions we could scarcely either of us perhaps positively say, which first started any particular Thought . . . yet I am far from going all lengths with Wordsworth' (*CL STC* II. 830). Noting that he has recently been 'startled' by 'daring Humbleness of Language & Versification, and a strict adherence to matter of fact, even to prolixity' among his friend's otherwise 'very excellent' recent compositions, he tells Southey that 'I rather suspect that some where or other there is a radical Difference in our theoretical opinions respecting Poetry' (*CL STC* II. 830). This theme would only become amplified in the coming years as Coleridge endeavoured to keep Wordsworth's attention focused on the great blank-verse philosophical poem that he believed Wordsworth was uniquely endowed to write.

The Coleridgean Critique

Coleridge's relentless pursuit of the sources of that 'radical Difference' eventually produced the influential critique, published in *Biographia Literaria*, of Wordsworth's theory and practice with regard to poetic metre and the language of poetry. The arguments on both sides are long, complex, ingenious, passionate – and not always clear and consistent. (Then, as now, writing about matters of language, metre and versification often led even the best thinkers into dark thickets of logical and terminological confusion.) For present purposes, what most needs to be appreciated is that Coleridge did indeed discover and elaborate a 'radical Difference', one that for many decades shaped – and misshaped – critical reception to Wordsworth's art, especially on questions of the intent, effect and purpose of his stylistic range and variety.

At the heart of the matter is Coleridge's grounding of his assessment of poems in an *ideal* conception of poetry and the Poet. For him, the Poet, 'described in *ideal* perfection', is one possessed to an extraordinary degree of 'that synthetic and magical power, to which we have exclusively appropriated the name of imagination' (*BL* II. 15–16). As it is the nature of that power to '[reveal] itself in the balance or reconciliation of opposite or discordant qualities', it follows that a poem ought to be a self-contained 'unity' in which '*all* of the parts . . . must be assimilated to the more *important* and *essential* parts' (*BL* II. 16, 72). Poetry is imaginative expression and poems are works that express the poet's power to 'reconcile discordant elements' in a work governed by the aesthetic ideal of 'unity in multeity'.[4] Within such a view, the relationship of metre and diction is ideally one of *balance* and *unity* of effect. Metre, originating in 'the balance in the mind effected by that spontaneous effort which strives to hold in check the workings of passion' signals and promises language that shares in this passion or 'excitement' (*BL* II. 64).

With regard specifically to Wordsworth's attempt to justify his use of language from '[l]ow and rustic life', Coleridge cuts to a fundamental disagreement with his friend, again firmly grounded in his adoption 'with full faith[of] the principle of Aristotle, that poetry as poetry is essentially *ideal*' (*BL* II. 45). In the 'Preface', Wordsworth discusses his choice of language in the context of his 'principal object': to 'chuse incidents and situations from common life, and to relate or describe them, throughout, as far as was possible, in a selection of language really used by men' and:

> at the same time, to throw over them a certain colouring of imagination, whereby ordinary things should be presented to the mind in an unusual way; and further, and above all, to make these incidents and situations interesting by tracing in them, truly though not ostentatiously, the primary laws of our nature: chiefly, as far as regards the manner in which we associate ideas in a state of excitement. (*LB* 96–97)

'Low and rustic life was generally chosen', he continues: 'Because in that condition, the essential passions of the heart find a better soil in which they can attain their maturity, are less under restraint, and speak a plainer and more emphatic language' (*LB* 97). In elaborating what he means by the conditions provided by rural life, Wordsworth emphasises a 'state of greater simplicity', allowing more accurate contemplation and more forcible communication of 'elementary feelings' (*LB* 97). Continuing the metaphor of rural life as a fertile seedbed, he describes the characteristic habits of social interaction or 'manners' of rural life as 'germinat[ing]' from these feelings, in a context in which the 'necessity of rural occupations' make them 'more easily comprehended and more durable' (*LB* 97). Finally, those in rural life, removed from the 'influence of social vanity', benefit from 'hourly' communication 'with the best objects from which the best part of language is originally derived' (*LB* 97).

Responding to this last point, Coleridge makes a key distinction with wide-ranging implications. 'The best part of human language, properly so called', he writes, is not derived from 'objects' but from 'reflections on the acts of the mind itself':

> It is formed by a voluntary appropriation of fixed symbols to internal acts, to processes and results of imagination, *the greater part of which have no place in the consciousness of uneducated man.* (*BL* II. 54; emphasis added)

In other words, Coleridge links properly poetic language to the kind of higher abstract thought that only a highly educated mind would be capable of and argues that such language cannot be present in a poem employing the persona and language of uneducated men. While Coleridge goes on to concede that 'in civilized society' even the 'most uneducated' speech may contain elements of language formed by mental and imaginative 'reflections', such speech arises from 'imitation and passive remembrance of what they hear from their religious instructors and other superiors' (*BL* II. 54). What Wordsworth would argue is a language founded on daily communion with nature, regular social interactions and the habits of rural work, Coleridge regards as a passive echo of sermons and the English Bible, a 'share in the harvest which [these uneducated speakers] neither sowed or reaped' (*BL* II. 54).

In short, the language worthy of a poet is the language of the active and synthesising mind; that is, the imaginative mind as elaborately defined and defended by Coleridge throughout his critical prose. Successful poems are those representing and expressing – through the ultimately harmonious, unifying and unified interplay of metre and diction, passion and restraint, spontaneity and structure – the poet's extraordinary powers of thought and feeling, while symbolising in their formal unity the reconciling power of imagination. If characters are to be employed, they are to be represented not as individuals, but as '*representative* of a class'. Such '*persons* of poetry must be clothed with *generic* attributes, with the *common* attributes of the class; not with such as one gifted individual might possibly possess, but such as from his situation it is most probable before-hand, that he *would* possess' (*BL* II. 46).

The ideal poet that Coleridge describes is, of course, Wordsworth himself, when Wordsworth is writing poems that Coleridge deems worthy of his genius – the kinds of poems that originally inspired Coleridge to discover the nature and sources of the 'magical power' of imagination (*BL* II. 16). It is confounding to Coleridge, then, that the poet who has taught him so much about how great poetry works also writes (and defends) poems that descend so often into an unbefitting humbleness of style and that allow for '*persons* of poetry' whose language is not conditioned by the distinctive marks and attributes – the clothing – of their appropriate class.

Moreover, in defending that work, Wordsworth had advanced a view of the function of metre that was just as wayward as his views on diction, as well as seriously at odds with what Coleridge would say is Wordsworth's own practice (again, at its best). In place of ideas of unity-in-multeity and harmonious balance of poetic elements sprung from the same source, Wordsworth speaks of 'similitude in dissimilitude', and describes metre and diction as seemingly distinct, and even at times oppositional forces or 'passions' (*LB* 110). Acknowledging Coleridge's view of metre as holding 'in check the workings of passion', Wordsworth also asserts that it can – and even more frequently does – play an opposite role, supplying 'feelings of pleasure which the Reader has been accustomed to connect with metre in general', feelings that 'greatly contribute to impart passion to the words' when the Poet's words 'should be incommensurate with the passion' (*LB* 110). Wordsworth's use of the metaphor of 'fitting' diction to metre underscores the differences, as does his description of the effects of metre as providing an 'intertexture' of 'feeling' which is 'not strictly and necessarily connected with the passion' of the speaker (*LB* 110). Maybe worst of all (from Coleridge's perspective), Wordsworth goes so far as to describe at least one kind of acceptable 'fitting' as an endeavour to 'super add' the 'charm' of metre to language that is not essentially different from the language of good prose (*LB* 109).

The Effect of the Coleridgean Critique

Coleridge's powerful analysis of his friend's inconsistency in theory and practice held great sway well into the twentieth century, helping to create a view of Wordsworth as something of a naïve genius – a sometimes great poet who, not quite understanding his own power or art, produces work marked by a befuddling alternation of the sublime and ridiculous. In J. K. Stephen's memorable parody, Wordsworth has 'Two voices'; one is 'of the deep'; the other of 'an old half-witted sheep' ('A Sonnet', Lines 1, 5).[5] While Wordsworth's 'experimental' poems did from the beginning have their champions, by the mid-twentieth century, the great majority of commentators largely accepted a Coleridgean distinction between 'high' and 'low' Wordsworth. The Wordsworth of the 'greater Romantic lyric' and of the posthumously published *Prelude* (the 'Poem to Coleridge') plays a major role in shaping understanding of Romanticism, the Romantic Poet and the Romantic Imagination, while the poet of the 'minor', 'experimental' poems receives relatively little serious attention. Writing in 1960, John Danby laments that, for all of the attention paid to Wordsworth in the century after his death, 'one feels Wordsworth himself still remains aloof. ... What he rated high his best supporters have tended to rate low. The poems he especially prized, his readers have smiled at as forgivable aberrations.'[6]

More recently, thanks in large part to the rise of approaches to late eighteenth- and early nineteenth-century verse that focus on the work of art in detail *as art*, a great deal of verse that had previously not fitted the mould of the 'Romantic' has received careful attention, whether it be the work of neglected poets – including women poets of the period – or poems of a 'canonical' poet previously regarded as anomalous or, more simply, as failures. This shift, which Stuart Curran describes in his groundbreaking work, *Poetic Form and British Romanticism*, involves paying attention to poetry, not exclusively as 'a center of psychological stresses or of historical and philosophical forces', but by paying attention as well to what 'is crucial to any poet as practitioner of a craft'. The result has been something of a renaissance of critical attention to the art – and the craft – of poetry, a re-engagement with questions of the power and purpose of poetry that has challenged notions of what makes for a successful poem, and broadened our sense of which (and whose) poetry matters and why.[7]

With respect to Wordsworth, this shift has certainly re-energised discussion of the 'minor' or 'experimental' poems throughout the corpus, including and especially those that appear in the *Lyrical Ballads*. Danby's *The Simple Wordsworth* was a trailblazer in this work, in that it took the marked strangeness and stylistic variety of Wordsworth as starting points in a project of uncovering the complexity of Wordsworth's actual poems, for too long obscured under a blanket of 'Wordsworthianism'. Among the many important insights of Danby's work is his recognition that Wordsworth in his 'experiments' was keenly aware that he was making 'unprecedented demands on the reader' not merely because he saw himself as providing a corrective to contemporary practice, but because he sought to create something genuinely new: a poetry capable of giving voice to a very broad range of '*persons* of poetry', including many who would otherwise be voiceless (25). What emerges from such attention is a clear sense of the limits of the high Romantic ideal of Wordsworth (the solitary genius described by Keats as the master of the 'egotistical sublime')– and renewed appreciation of the other-directed, sympathetic and communal elements of his poetry.[8]

Wordsworth's Experiments with Language

A key text for understanding this dimension of Wordsworth, for Danby and others, is a passage in a poem begun in 1800 as one of the poems 'On the Naming of Places' but not published until 1815, in which Wordsworth refers to his brother John as a '*silent* Poet' ('When, to the Attractions of the Busy World'; *Cornell LB* 570). John Wordsworth, the captain of a trading vessel who would die in a shipwreck in 1805, was for his brother a poet in all but words, possessed of 'a watchful heart', 'an inevitable ear', and 'an eye practiced like a blind man's touch' (Lines 89–91). He was, in a word, a man whose senses and sympathies were fully attentive to what Danby calls 'the real and the desirable' (16) a man very like those Cumberland 'Statesmen', the shepherds and farmers and tradesmen who had so impressed the young Wordsworth from his childhood, and whose virtues he had newly discovered upon his arrival at Grasmere, in the wake of the collapse of his revolutionary ideals and sympathies.

In Book 12 of the *Prelude* (1805), Wordsworth speaks of these men in ways that suggest that they, too, may be regarded as silent poets. While they are 'Shy, and unpractised in the strife of phrase':

> Theirs is the language of the heavens, the power,
> The thought, the image, and the silent joy;
> Words are but under-agents in their souls –
> When they are grasping in their greatest strength
> They do not breathe among them.
>
> (Lines 270–274)

These are, of course, the very people whom Wordsworth would boldly attempt to call to the attention of political elites, writing to Charles James Fox in January 1801 that the poems are presented in the hope that they 'may excite profitable sympathies in many kind and good hearts':

> And may in some small degree enlarge our feelings of reverence for our species, and our knowledge of human nature, by shewing that our best qualities are possessed by men whom we are too apt to consider, not with reference to the points in which they resemble us, but to those in which they manifestly differ from us. (*LB* 308)

With reference specifically to 'The Brothers' and 'Michael', he claims that they 'were written with a view to shew that men who do not wear fine cloaths can feel deeply' (*LB* 308).

Such a task, involving as it did a use of language to effect an 'enlarge [ment] of our feeling', connecting readers with those who by definition do not speak the kind of language that might produce (or reinforce) such connection, obviously puts enormous stress on the poet's resources and art. As Danby notes, such a goal required Wordsworth to insist upon and create the conditions for a 'new nakedness of relation' with his reader (25). Wordsworth's simplicity, his refusal to employ diction, metre, and all of the craft of poetry in ways that conform to 'pre-established codes of decision', then, is not merely a reactive or corrective strategy; it is a genuinely new kind of project, entailing a 'new intimacy, a new discipline, and a new complexity' (Danby 25–26).

Among the most important innovative techniques that Wordsworth develops to accomplish his goal, particularly in the 'experimental' poems, is what Danby calls 'dramatic self-projection' (35). Recalling that Wordsworth's largest work preceding *Lyrical Ballads* is not the loco-descriptive poetry of *An Evening Walk* and *Descriptive Sketches*, but a play, *The Borderers*, Danby points to the genre-bending nature of many of the *Lyrical Ballads*, identifying the use of a 'dramatic-narrative' technique – in 'Simon Lee', 'The Thorn', and 'The Reverie of Poor Susan' – as 'the peculiarly Wordsworthian innovation' (35). The experiments are neither straightforward narrative nor dramatic monologues. They do not focus primarily on story, conveyed through a narrator who 'must not be felt as interfering', nor is their central concern directly the character and psychology of a speaker (Danby 36). Rather, they are a mixed mode allowing for attention to both dramatic and narrative elements, thereby permitting 'a range of voices, and each voice for an ironic shift in point of view' (38). By 'irony', Danby means something that he presents as peculiar to these poems. 'It is unfortunate that Wordsworth's irony has not been much remarked', he writes:

> If irony, however, can mean the perspective and the co-presence of alternatives, the refusal to impose on the reader a predigested life-view, the insistence on the contrary that the reader should enter, himself, as full partner in the final judgement on the facts set before him, then Wordsworth is a superb ironist in *Lyrical Ballads*. (37–38; emphasis added)

For Danby, the experimental poem is less an art object and more a locus for active interaction between reader and poem, with the poet playing the role of the 'finally responsible assembler' (38). This insight allows for an important shift in understanding of the role of the poet that will become increasingly important in reception of the *Lyrical Ballads* – from maker of things (poems) to orchestrator of activity (speeches). And the poem is remarkable less for what it *is* than for what it *does*, engaging the reader in potentially multiple interactions created by the point of view and voice of a narrator, the characters and even upon occasion the poet 'assembler' himself. This freedom to move among three levels – characters, narrator, poet – shifting voice and stepping 'from one frame to another and back again' creates at least the fiction of stepping 'out of the frame of mere "literature" altogether and into the reader's own reality' (38).

Danby's 'exhibit A' for this kind of dynamic framing employed in the interest of establishing a 'new nakedness of relation' (and thereby new possibilities for response) is 'Simon Lee'. For Danby, the first hundred lines of the poem exist as a complex and elaborate means for preparing the reader to receive the last four lines, with the 'weight, the depth, the soberness, the measured seriousness and overflowing tenderness' that they deserve and that Wordsworth intended (38):

> – I've heard of hearts unkind, kind deeds
> With coldness still returning.
> Alas! The gratitude of men
> Has oftner left me mourning.
> (*LB* Lines 100–104)

Conscious that he is engaging readers unaccustomed to interacting with an 'Old Huntsman' and with no experience of discerning in such men's thoughts and emotions depths of fellow feeling, Wordsworth diligently creates the conditions in which the encounter can occur. He meets the reader where he is, so to speak, by offering 'ambiguities of tone' and narrative 'poses' that raise alternative possibilities of response. The first four lines illustrate this well, especially compared directly with the final lines just quoted:

> In the sweet shire of Cardigan,
> Not far from pleasant Ivor-hall,
> An Old Man dwells, a little man,
> I've heard he once was tall.
> (Lines 1–4)

The first two lines evoke the 'mannered revivalism' of Percy's *Reliques* and the conventional expectations with regard to characterisation and narrative distance, including a presumption of anonymous reliability on the part of the narrator (Danby 39). They take an immediate turn towards something different, however, as they identify the narrator as inhabiting a particular point of view, signaled by his dependency on local lore ('I've heard') and his capacity for risking the ludicrous, with the jaunty juxtaposition of the little man who once was tall. 'Though the ballads are in mind', Danby comments, 'there are no mechanical ballad-metrics' (40).[9] Danby's analysis continues in this vein with many telling observations of the ways in which the poem plays with such alternative frames and tones, subtly insisting on a developing relationship, traced in the temporal arc of a reading, among speaker, character and reader. For Danby, crucial to the art of these poems is the poet's subtle presentation of particularities of speech in a style that constantly suggests how that speech might have been presented otherwise.

Noting Wordsworth's frequent use of repetition-with-difference of common words as a means for effecting and marking these shifts, Danby focuses, for example, on the often repeated and variously combined words 'old' and 'poor'. In one sequence, we hear that, while the '*old* man' Simon wears a 'fair' livery-coat, (the remnant of his service as huntsman of Ivor Hall) yet, 'meet him where you will, you see / At once that he is *poor*' (Lines 9, 11–12, emphasis added). This is immediately followed by a description of the 'hunting feats' that have left him bereft of one eye, prompting the epithet: '*poor old* Simon Lee' (Lines 41, 46). In the next sequence, Simon's wife is identified as '*Old* Ruth', who helps Simon tend their 'scrap of land' (49). Together they are the '*poorest* of the *poor*' (60). This repeated sequence culminates in the combination of 'poor and old' in what is among the most 'homely' moments of description (and uses of diction) in the collection:

> Few months of life has he in store,
> As he to you will tell,
> For still, the more he works, the more
> His *poor old ancles* swell.
> (Lines 65–68, emphasis added)

The movement in both sequences is from the 'matter-of-fact' to the 'indulgently sympathetic', participating in the larger movement towards sympathy in the poem as a whole. To this I would add that, through such subtle repetition with difference, the phrase 'poor old ancles' is redeemed from banality (or bathos) and is able to bear the emotional weight of sympathy that Wordsworth needs it to bear, even as it risks being taken out of context as an instance of diction at too low a register for serious poetry. It is to such moments that Wordsworth calls attention when, in one of the most radical shifts of tone and 'frame' anywhere in his poems, his speaker turns directly to the 'gentle reader', anticipating his indulgent unease with being led on so unfamiliar and shifting a path, and challenging him to participate by thinking in the work of making the poem:

O Reader! had you in your mind
Such stores as silent thought can bring,
O gentle Reader! You would find
A tale in every thing.

(Lines 73–76)

By the time that the speaker relates, 80 lines into a 104-line poem, the 'incident' cited in the title, speaker and reader have been engaged in a relationship that has revealed, through indirection and consideration of alternate treatments of similar incidents and personages, that there is much more than might be anticipated in the relation of speaker and subject. In telling the tale of his thoughtlessly thoughtful act – quickly cutting through the roots of a tree stump that Simon had been vainly labouring to remove – the speaker seals his relationship with the reader, admitting that his own understanding of the 'tale' of Simon Lee has been substantially shaped by his own failure at one point to fully comprehend Simon's reality. It is this ability to shift frames, which Danby sees as a means for 'confronting the reader with the need to be aware of what he is judging *with* as well as *what he is judging*', that is 'above all, the Wordsworthian trick in *Lyrical Ballads*' (38).

A Poetics of Speech

The Simple Wordsworth marks an important step in moving beyond the 'inconstancy' or 'unevenness' arguments, providing a framework in which stylistic unevenness, or shifts and variations in conventional stylistic registers, may be read not as defects, but as, in fact, key elements of Wordsworth's art and of his understanding of himself as a poet. A major contribution to this continuing effort is the work of Don Bialostosky, most notably for our purposes here, in *Making Tales*. Bialostosky cites Danby, as well as Robert Langbaum's seminal work on dramatic monologue, as recognising the importance of 'a distinction between the poet and his represented speakers that had previously been thought inappropriate'.[10] Instead of taking Wordsworth's definition of the poet as 'Man speaking' at face value, identifying poet and speaker as one, these critics see Wordsworth as 'an artful maker of poems representing speaking persons' (Bialostosky 20).

Bialostosky, however, aims to go well beyond such observations to construct a theoretical framework comprehensive enough to provide an authentically Wordsworthian answer to the Coleridgean strictures that continue to shadow commentary on Wordsworth. For Bialostosky, the differences between the two friends and co-authors stem from a divide no less ancient and deep than that between Aristotle and Plato, and he argues that the dominance of Aristotle's poetics in the Western tradition has obscured the very different understanding of poetry that lies at the root not only of Wordsworth's experiments, but also of his poetics as a whole. Drawing on the work of Barbara Herrnstein Smith, Mikhail Bakhtin and others, Bialostosky's argument is grounded in a key distinction between the poet conceived as 'maker in language' (Aristotle) and as 'representor of speech' (Plato). The former regards poetry as an imitation of something other than language itself *in the medium* of words; in the latter, the poet represents not action *in* words, but words themselves in represented speeches.

The distinction provides a provocative basis for a fresh understanding of Wordsworth's approach (and Coleridge's struggle with it), especially as it relates to questions of diction and metre and the propriety of represented persons. If poetry is 'fictive speech' and not an imitation of something other than language 'in words', then the whole notion of 'Poetic diction' becomes for Bialostosky a 'special problem':

> [F]or, if poetry represents something other than speech, its language may be considered as a medium for the representation of that thing, but if poetry represents speech, its language is the object of representation itself and no distinct medium of representation is apparent. (5)[11]

The implications for assessing and judging poems and their makers are many and significant. If there is no medium, then there is 'no criterion of artistic excellence specific to mastery of a medium':

> The poem's words are not that material in which an action is artificially and skillfully embodied but the artfully represented body of someone's thought. While a critic who thinks in terms of medium looks to the diction of the poem for evidence of the poet's skill and genius as a synthesizer of language, one without that category considers the poet's capacity to represent speech expressive of a speaker's attitudes toward himself, his subjects, and his auditors. (Bialostosky 15)

Similarly, with respect to persons represented in poetry, the Coleridgean limitation of the poet to generic representatives of a class becomes beside the point. Once one sets aside the idea of the poem as a medium, there is no pressure to reconcile some appropriate level of character or diction with other aspects of the composition, all 'idealized and unified' by the power of imagination.

Here, Bialostosky notes an extraordinarily important implication of the radical difference between Wordsworth and Coleridge, one that illuminates the poetic principles underlying the tremendous range and variety of Wordsworth's experiments in voice in the *Lyrical Ballads*. With no compelling reason to respect 'class' as an aesthetic imperative, and employing a poetics that makes the experience of speech itself the centre of concern, Wordsworth is free to use his art primarily as a vehicle for establishing relationships, not representing distinctions. Poet, speakers and reader participate in an activity that enables a kind of communication that recognises no 'essential differences' among them. Thus, Wordsworth's larger democratic principles may be seen as embodied even at the most subtle levels of linguistic communication. The poet is free to explore the widest possible range of speeches, whether the poet's own or those of others, limited only by his ability to capture in his fictive utterances the 'fluxes and refluxes' of minds 'in a state of excitement' (*LB* 98, 97). It is this interaction that Wordsworth's speaker in 'Simon Lee' points to in his frame-breaking turn to the reader, encouraging that reader to 'think': 'It is no tale, but should you think, / Perhaps a tale you'll make it' (Lines 79–80).

The approach allows for appreciation of a remarkable and remarkably complex dynamism in Wordsworth's presentation of speakers both within poems and across the poems of the collection – including first-person 'lyrical', narrative and quoted or paraphrased speech of narrative characters or interlocutors. The narrative voice of 'Goody Blake and Harry Gill', for example, has traditionally been taken as among the most 'straightforward' or 'neutral' narrators in the collection.[12] Readers have read the closing lines, 'Now think, ye farmers all, I pray, / Of Goody Blake and Harry Gill' (*LB* Lines 127–128), as a moralising wrap up to a 'True Story' written (as Wordsworth claimed in the 'Preface') to 'draw attention to the truth that the power of the human imagination is sufficient to produce such changes even in our physical nature as might almost appear miraculous' (*LB* p. 112). As Bialostosky notes, however, the actual lines call for the reader *to think* while saying nothing about *what* to think. And, while they might 'sound like a packaged lesson' (and while Wordsworth's prose comments may in fact tempt us to simplify the 'what'), they are in fact an 'open invitation', leaving 'the task of making meaning unfinished' (70). Accepting that invitation entails attending closely to any and all indications in the speech of the narrator of his attitude towards both his characters (called the 'heroes' by Bialostosky) and his listener/reader. At any point, these attitudes and these relationships may satisfy or disrupt expectations, and the work of reading is the tracing of these often-subtle shifts and swerves in these relationships as they develop in the course of the represented speech.

The difference that such an approach can make is apparent in Bialostosky's discussion of aspects of the narrator's diction that seem to gesture towards a representation of Harry's thoughts and feelings, for example, in the italicised words in this stanza:

> Now Harry he had long suspected
> This *trespass* of old Goody Blake;
> And *vow'd* that she should be *detected*,
> And how on her would *vengeance* take.
> (Lines 65–68)

Whereas a more traditional approach reads these words as 'comic inflation', producing 'emotions heighted beyond their true importance', a poetics of speech is free to see them not simply as 'manipulations of a listener's responses' but as 'indicative of his hero's thoughts and feelings' (Bialostosky 72). For Bialostosky, the narrator is represented as genuinely 'caught up' in Harry's thought and feeling, especially at this moment:

> He hears a noise – he's all awake –
> Again? – on tip-toe down the hill
> He softly creeps – 'tis Goody Blake,
> She's at the hedge of Harry Gill.
> (Lines 77–80)

The distance and inequality of narrator and 'hero' implicit in a reading of this as 'comic deflation' is supplanted by the recognition that here the narrator actually captures in his speech Harry's deep and long-standing obsession ('Again?') with Goody Blake. Instead of condescension we have an example of a kind of extraordinary moment of identification described by Wordsworth in the 'Preface': that is, when it is 'the wish of the poet to bring his feelings near to those of the persons whose feelings he describes, nay, for short spaces of time perhaps, to let himself slip into an entire delusion, and even confound and identify his own feelings with theirs' (*LB* p. 104). And the reader is put in a position, by participating in the act of expression itself, to understand through the feel of the verse that Harry had been plagued by a diseased imagination long before he caught Goody Blake in the act and heard her prayer that he be cursed.

The implications of this approach with respect to the poet's uses of metre are similarly radical, and help to explain a great deal that has perplexed commentators about Wordsworth's theory and practice from Coleridge to the present day. Wordsworth's odd comments about metre as 'intertexture' or 'superaddition', as already noted, make little sense within a *Coleridgean* poetics. If the aim of a poem, however, is to present 'fictive speech' and not language shaped through its selection and arrangement of diction as the medium for displaying the representational power of its maker, then metre need not require any necessary relationship to a particular kind or register of diction. The poem, conceived of as a 'metrical performance of an utterance' (Bialostosky 19), is free to explore a range of 'fittings', the subtleties of which will be among the chief means through which the poet expresses the power of speech itself to embody thought and feeling.

This complex relationship between metre and other elements of the poem is, I believe, one of the most important and radical aspects not only of Wordsworth's experiments in *Lyrical Ballads*, but in his work as a whole. In an essay calling attention to the depth and complexity of Wordsworth's 'thinking about thinking in verse', Simon Jarvis notes Wordsworth's 'astonishing fearlessness' in the face of 'still powerful preconceptions about the connection of metre and register'.[13] Wordsworth's decisive 'step', writes Jarvis, was 'to imagine the possibility of detaching diction from metre entirely, to see that metre need not in any a-prioristically necessary way carry any implications whatever for the poet's lexicon' (111). Wordsworth arrives at this way of thinking about verse because he tends to regard metre and verse rhythm themselves not as 'symbolic', as does Coleridge, but as 'cognitive'. Metre and rhythm, then, are not the means for representing thinking but are part and parcel of the act of thinking itself. The 'experience of the materiality of language' – or the fact that words are not only tokens and symbols, but 'things' with 'sounding bodies' – allows for a kind of interplay through which Wordsworth is able to explore a broad range of 'powers of the human mind', including (but not limited to) the 'most fundamental and least understood' of such powers (Jarvis 111).

As I show in detail in *The Passion of Metre*, Wordsworth's approach to versification as a whole is grounded in an understanding of verse as requiring attention to and prompting this kind of experience of materiality.[14] For Wordsworth, metre brings to the poem a 'passion' of its own that may be, but is not necessarily, entirely consonant with the 'passion of the sense'. The interaction of the two 'passions', each with its own demands on the selection and organisation of language, manifests itself in everything from the choice of stanza forms, to management of line endings and pauses in blank verse, to the precision of rhymes, and even to the management of individual syllable stress or the use (or not) of typographical elision as a means for reconciling normal pronunciation with metrical expectation.

In such a view, the poem becomes a locus of dynamic interaction, as the poet 'fits' diction and metre in ways that evoke and variously satisfy (or not) the reader's expectations at every turn, depending on the particular character and circumstances of the represented speaker, not on conventional notions of 'harmony', or 'balance', as indicators of the poet's mastery and control. One obvious manifestation of this approach in *Lyrical Ballads* is the extraordinary range that it allows, both of divergent speakers and of the 'fluxes and refluxes' of individual speakers, across the collection and even within poems. Nothing in Wordsworth's view precludes his fitting of the passion of metre and the passion of the sense in ways that fulfil Coleridgean expectations. In 'Lines Composed a Few Miles above Tintern Abbey' for example, the speech represented is clearly expressive of the synthesising imagination. And much of the blank verse aspires to and achieves the kind of 'balance and reconciliation of opposite or discordant qualities' that is the appropriate expression of imagination (*BL* II. 16).

At the same time, Wordsworth's refusal to acknowledge any a priori constraint on his art allows him tremendous liberty to expand the community of speakers and voices, enabling exploration of varieties of thinking and feeling – through the 'fictive speech' of 'bards' and shepherds, an 'idiot boy' and his fond mother, or a forsaken 'Indian woman', a 'Youth from Georgia's shore', or a garrulous Sea Captain prone to superstition. A capacious aesthetic, it does not preclude even the presence of oddities such as the Ancient Mariner, whatever that mesmerising speaker's author may have thought of the principles on which his poem was written (or however successful Wordsworth may have thought the poem was as an instance of fictive speech inviting thought). All voices are presented as worthwhile to be engaged with not only in and of themselves, but also as they may be placed in significant relationship with each other, participating in their author's overarching effort to 'look at the world in the spirit of love [and pay] homage ... to the naked dignity of man' (*LB* 105).

Endnotes

1 'Unsigned Review', *New London Review*, 1 (January 1799): 33–35; 33.
2 Robert Southey, '*Lyrical Ballads* with a Few Other Poems', *The Critical Review*, 24 (October 1798): 197–204; 200.
3 Charles Burney, '*Lyrical Ballads* with a Few Other Poems', *The Monthly Review*, 2nd Series, 29 (June 1799): 207–208; 204.

4 Samuel Taylor Coleridge, 'On Poesy or Art', in *Biographia Literaria ... with his Aesthetical Essays*, ed. J. Shawcross, 2 vols. (Oxford: Clarendon Press, 1907), 2. 262.

5 J. K. Stephen, *Lapsus Calami and Other Verses* (Cambridge: Macmillan and Bowes, 1898).

6 John Danby, *The Simple Wordsworth* (London: Routledge & Kegan Paul, 1960), 1.

7 Stuart Curran, *Poetic Form and British Romanticism* (Oxford: Oxford University Press, 1986), vii.

8 Keats to Richard Woodhouse (27 October 1818), *Letters of John Keats*, ed. Robert Gittings (New York: Oxford University Press, 1970), 157.

9 It is telling that, in *Biographia Literaria*, Coleridge includes 'Simon Lee' among the poems in Wordsworth's corpus that would have been 'more delightful to me in prose, told and managed ... in a moral essay, or pedestrian tour' (2. 69).

10 Don H. Bialostosky, *Making Tales: The Poetics of Wordsworth's Narrative Experiments* (Chicago: University of Chicago Press, 1984), 20.

11 For the 'fictive speech' distinction, see Barbara Herrnstein Smith, *On the Margins of Discourse* (Chicago: University of Chicago Press, 1978), 25.

12 Bialostosky 69–70; citing Danby on the speaker as 'neutral'; Sheats on 'straightforwardness; and Jacobus on 'Wordsworth's humanitarian lesson' in the last stanza.

13 Simon Jarvis, 'Thinking in Verse', in *The Cambridge Companion to British Romantic Poetry*, ed. James Chandler and Maureen N. McClane (Cambridge: Cambridge University Press, 2008), 111. For Wordsworth on 'words as *things*, active and efficient, which are of themselves part of the passion', see his note to 'The Thorn' (*LB* 200).

14 Brennan O'Donnell, *The Passion of Metre* (Kent, OH: Kent State University Press, 1995).

CHAPTER 11

Awkward Relations: Poetry and Philosophy in Lyrical Ballads

Alexander Regier

Philosophy, like politics or ecology, is a constant presence in the poems of *Lyrical Ballads*. As Wordsworth and Coleridge openly state in the 'Advertisement', some of the poems are written in direct reaction to their contemporaries' engagement with philosophical thought: 'the lines entitled Expostulation and Reply, and those which follow, arose out of conversation with a friend who was somewhat unreasonably attached to modern books of moral philosophy' (*LB* 4). Other poems that position themselves in direct reference to questions of epistemology, ontology or the status of truth are 'We Are Seven' or 'Anecdote for Fathers, Shewing how the practice of Lying may be taught,' to mention two of the most obvious examples. In both cases the question revolves around what Andrew Bennett has termed the 'poetics of ignorance' of the collection.[1] Throughout, *Lyrical Ballads* has some form of conceptual ambition. Yet that ambition is not clear at all, and that is where the story (or, for others, the trouble) of poetry and philosophy begins in the text.

Adding to this complexity is the fact that the poems in *Lyrical Ballads* have become one of the prime test cases for the writers, poets, critics and philosophers whose work explores the relations of philosophy, poetry, Romanticism, Enlightenment and modernity. Some turn to *Lyrical Ballads* for answers about the relationship between poetry and philosophy. What that means is that all the terms in this equation – poetry, philosophy, Lyric, Ballad – not only are extremely difficult to figure out in relation to one another, but also do not even add up to what the image of the word 'equation' suggests. There is no mathematically balanced way to view their relationship. There is not really a way to settle their score. What students of Wordsworth and Coleridge's volume, especially the ones who are invested in categories such as 'poetry' or 'philosophy', have come to realise is that there is no satisfying answer. It is problematic to understand the relation between these terms in a comprehensive or traditionally systematic way. That is because the word 'systematic' in the context of *Lyrical Ballads* is almost as charged as 'philosophical', since the two sometimes seem to be, and sometimes are, equated by Wordsworth, Coleridge and their readers, though not in equal fashion, which makes this mess even more difficult to disentangle. What, then, are readers to do? We need to take advantage of, and not be paralysed by, the impossible plethora of options, the suppleness of descriptions that these discussions and readings have engendered.

What this chapter sets out to show is that this relation – the relation between poetry and philosophy – in *Lyrical Ballads* is, above all, *awkward*. By revealing the reasons why this awkwardness matters, the chapter fleshes out an aspect of the collection that is understudied, even though it is commonly cited. In itself, the claim that poetry and philosophy have a rather uncomfortable relation does not seem contentious, maybe not even very significant. Any student of the texts will know that there are moments when the two spheres or categories do not sit happily side by side. My argument, however, puts a little more pressure on the word 'awkward', a word that, as I will show, is of considerable significance if we want to understand *Lyrical Ballads*. When the 'Advertisement' states that the readers of the volume will 'frequently have to struggle with feelings of strangeness and aukwardness' (*LB* 3), it describes a central characteristic of the poetics at stake, not just an overhaul of Augustan standards of decorum. What is so intriguing is that *Lyrical Ballads* itself sets up the difficulty of the relationship as part of its internal structure. It does that with great success, holding its readers in thrall ever since its first publication. This awkward entanglement is part of the setup that *Lyrical Ballads* creates for itself. Some of this dynamic is conscious, but some of it is perhaps not. In both cases, it is deeply awkward, messy and inelegant. But that is, I will show, part of its point, both poetically and philosophically. It means that what is at stake here is a *way of reading*: the collection activates a problem of poetry and philosophy – an awkward problem. And the fact that we still wrestle with it as if it was something to be resolved is an ironic but often misguided misreading of the collection itself. However, before we turn to a detailed reading of awkwardness as an aesthetic and philo-sophically significant category in *Lyrical Ballads*, it is useful to provide a background for these claims through the wider context of a literary-historical debate on philosophy and poetry in the collection. It will allow us to appreciate how very awkward this focus on awkwardness really is.

Broadly speaking, there are two opposing positions when it comes to poetry and philosophy in *Lyrical Ballads*. The first position claims that philosophy has little relevance to the poetry of the collection; the second claims that philosophy is integral to the volume. (Of course, it all depends on what we mean by 'poetry' and 'philosophy', but let's try and keep matters relatively simple, at least for the moment.) Matthew Arnold and Leslie Stephen are the two authors who best illustrate each of these two positions. Arnold apodictically claims about Wordsworth that we 'cannot do him justice until we dismiss his formal philosophy' and dismisses critics who lay 'far too much stress upon what they call his philosophy'.[2] Crudely speaking, Wordsworth's philosophical attempts are a misguided and thankfully short-lived way of trying to live up to Coleridge's fantasy of the poet as a particular kind of philosophical synthesizer. Eventually, as Seamus Perry has written eloquently, the peculiar forms of Coleridge's disappointment led him to 'see his future less in poetry, and more in philosophy, especially when he compared himself with his one-time collaborator'.[3] On the other hand, there is Leslie Stephen, who endorses the poetry of Wordsworth because it 'has expounded his ethical and philosophical views so explicitly' in a manner that inextricably binds the two spheres together.[4]

Arnold and Stephen represent the poles on, or between, which most critics position themselves. This includes, of course, Wordsworth and Coleridge themselves because, as Perry's comment makes clear, the conversation around the relation between poetry and philosophy in *Lyrical Ballads* begins with its first readers, the authors themselves. There is a history of these conversations that can be told in many different ways; parsing views between Arnold and Stephen is merely one of them. Other influential approaches have included making the *Lyrical Ballads*, particularly the 'Preface', a privileged site for testing larger arguments, not just about the authors but also about more general critical categories, such as prosody, epistemology, ethics or the intersections between these large fields. The vastly different, even antagonistic, work of Marjorie Levinson, Simon Jarvis or Adam Potkay stands out in this regard. Levinson allows us to see a *Lyrical Ballads* whose Spinozean monism envelops philosophy and poetry, making their distinction obsolete. Her masterful reading of the 'philosophical ambition' displayed in Wordsworth's 'A Slumber Did My Spirit Seal' is a powerful illustration of how to connect such large-scale claims with the line of the lyric.[5] In Jarvis's case, Wordsworth's attempt to create a 'philosophic song' is a suggestive way of arguing that a 'different kind of thinking happens in verse – that ... verse is itself a kind of cognition'.[6] For Potkay, there is a sense that the *Lyrical Ballads* are part of a fundamentally ethical approach to writing and thus have to engage with the philosophical character of such thought. The sheer depth and variety of these responses suggests that there is something structural going on about the collection and that its presentation of the relation between poetry and philosophy is part of any discussion of the work that considers its theoretical dimensions seriously. For all its importance, however, it also becomes clear pretty quickly that this is one of these impossible problems in and for the study of Romanticism – and for the study of Wordsworth in particular. When we encounter such a problem, it is as common as it is correct to go back to the primary material: not so much in the hope that we will untie the Gordian knot, but rather that it will allow us to see strands of rope that we might loosen in a way that has not been done before.

Is Philosophy Philosophical?

Wordsworth's use of the term, idea or concept of 'philosophy' is not systematic throughout his work, not even in *Lyrical Ballads*. That is not to say that he did not take care in its use. He uses the word and its many variations deliberately, there is no doubt about that, and we have to attend to some of the differences. For instance, in *Lyrical Ballads* there is a distinction between 'philosophy' and the 'philosophical' and it is poetry that allows Wordsworth to make this conceptually important distinction.

I sympathise with the weariness that shines through Stephen Gill's tone when he states that the question of whether or not Wordsworth is a philosophical poet 'invariably' is 'the prelude to pointless manoeuvres aimed at redefining the word "philosophical" to ensure that the answer is Yes.' And yet, as Gill himself shows, there is merit in asking the question of philosophy and poetry when he proposes, contra Arnold, that instead of a 'wedge between philosophy and poetry ... what is needed in Words-worth's case is a bridge'.[7] It is interesting to note that what Gill and the 'pointless manoeuvres' have in common is the idea of harmonising the relation between those spheres. The bridge between philosophy and poetry supposedly *connects*, makes passage possible and allows for the carrying of metaphor and weight from one sphere to another. It is undoubtedly something that is productive and that we need to explore. However, do we really need a bridge? Or can we think of the relation between the two spheres as something different, less fitting, maybe even back to front? This alternative is not the same as the claim that the relationship between them is dialectical or produces a critical distance. Their awkwardness does not produce a new insight; it is an affective response that deserves a lot more attention.

The first time that 'philosophy' appears in *Lyrical Ballads* is as the last word of the 'Advertisement'. It sits, therefore, at a liminal space between poetry and philosophy. "'[P]hilosophy" comes before the poems, though it comes as a warning: "The lines entitled Expostulation and Reply, and those which follow, arose out of conversation with a friend who was somewhat unreasonably attached to modern books of moral philosophy'" (*LB* 4). The friend whom Wordsworth mentions is William Hazlitt. His attachment to philosophy is criticised for being unreasonable, a mildly humorous rebuke. Hazlitt is cast as a Don Quixote who has lost himself too deeply in the books of moral philosophy and, as a result, forgets the practical and moral dimensions that these works supposedly enlighten. Wordsworth invokes here a negative version of philosophy, that is, a rigid form of thought that is deeply oppositional to both the experience of the natural world and of poetry.

The poems Wordsworth mentions ('Expostulation and Reply' and 'The Tables Turned') invoke philosophy as a systematic, theoretical endeavour whose reading and bookishness distances the human subject from practical life rather than bringing deeper insight into it. The philosopher in 'Expostulation' believes that the dichotomy lies between attentively reading books and 'dream[ing]' one's time away. In the poem, a 'good friend' admonishes the speaker who is sitting, supposedly idly, on a stone for lacking a sense of purpose and direction:

> Where are your books?
> . . . .
> Up! Up! and drink the spirit breath'd
> From dead men to their kind.
> (Lines 5–8)

According to this friend, we should develop a sense of history and have a responsibility to understand the world in a particular way, not live:

> As if she for no purpose bore you;
> As if you were her first-born birth,
> And none had lived before you!
> (Lines 10–12)

The objection is an ethical one: we owe it to our existence to be active, not idle, and discover its purpose in the wider world. We can neither pretend that there is no purpose to our existence nor act as if we are Adam, the first-born of history. Because there plainly are people who have loved before us, we need to engage with the 'spirit' that these 'dead men' breathe down to us through history.

The problem with this accusation and its assumptions lies in the contrast they draw to begin with. The speaker was, contrary to the friend's assumption, not wasting time at all – as the poem goes on to make clear. Instead, he was dreaming, a deeply philosophical activity. He knows that it is not through rational thought or free will that we produce an understanding of existence, citing the same way that we have little control over our own bodily organs: 'The eye it cannot chuse but see, / We cannot bid the ear be still' (Lines 17–18), suggesting that our intentions and thoughts are subject to forces beyond ourselves. In fact, even the ways in which we collect the impressions around us are themselves powerful forces that are not under our control: 'Nor less I deem that there are powers / Which of themselves our minds impress' (21–22). As a result, the reliance on books, just as it was for Hazlitt, is unreasonable.

In 'The Tables Turned', Wordsworth gives himself the chance to present his case positively. The poem opens by admonishing the imagined adversary, ironically echoing his language from the previous poem: 'Up! up! my friend, and clear your looks ... Up! up! my friend, and quit your books' (1, 3). The case is made that the unreasonable attachment to a certain kind of knowledge or philosophy is damaging. The poem seems straightforward in its commitment to a book-free philosophy: the 'barren leaves' of volumes on art and science contrast with the 'heart / That watches and receives' the leaves of nature (30–31). It positions Wordsworth against a particular kind of philosophy that is portrayed as a dead end, both conceptually and affectively, and which comes to be associated with bookishness and detachment from the human spirit. Against that model, Wordsworth posits nature and education from and through it. The central line, situated in the middle of the poem, puts it as a programmatic cry: 'Let Nature be your teacher' (16), instead of the books that represent a more conventional schooling. This sort of reading would align poetry and nature as opposed to philosophy and books, a rather neat and suspiciously un-awkward symmetry, especially when we consider where and how we are accessing these ideas.

Some students might think that because Wordsworth rejects philosophy in its systematic and academic form for giving such an inadequate response to the world, this also means he rejects philosophical or theoretical thought. However, this is where the different categories of description (philosophy, philosophical, etc.) and their separate valences become powerful distinctions. In the very same *Lyrical Ballads* that rejects *philosophy* as bookish and alienating, Wordsworth states that he agrees with Aristotle that '[p]oetry is the most philosophic of all writing' (*LB* 105). If poetry, not philosophy, is the most philosophic form of all writing, then the experiments of this writing will be *philosophical* in ways we might not foresee. The philosophical dimension of poetry lies in *not* looking as much like philosophy as possible. We need to figure out different ways in which the poetry that Coleridge and Wordsworth produce is philosophical. One of the ways in which to understand this claim is by turning to the discussion Wordsworth provides about the qualities of his poetry in *Lyrical Ballads*.

Famously, the 'Advertisement' announces that at least some of the poems that follow will be unexpected: 'The majority of the following poems are to be considered as experiments' (*LB* 3). The experimental character is poetical and conceptual; what Coleridge and Wordsworth present is a new way of doing poetry that breaks not only with certain stylistic rules but also with forms of thinking. The poems themselves present different forms of how this relationship gets reimagined. They warn readers that they might encounter poems that will not look or feel like poems. Such works may not conform to the current style or taste or to what has been defined as poetry: 'such readers ... should not suffer the solitary word Poetry, a word of very disputed meaning, to stand in the way of their gratification' (*LB* 3). If we readily overlook how serious these warnings are, then it is because it is difficult for many readers today to appreciate and imagine just how jarring some of these lyrics and ballads would have been – a historical and theoretical dimension that bears repeating.

In the most concentrated version of the warnings about the uniquely different status of *Lyrical Ballads* among contemporaries, Wordsworth states that '[r]eaders accustomed to the gaudiness and inane phraseology of many modern writers, if they persist in reading this book to its conclusion, will perhaps frequently have to struggle with feelings of strangeness and aukwardness: they will look round for poetry and will be induced to enquire by what species of courtesy these attempts can be permitted to assume that title' (*LB* 3). This is one of Wordsworth's most important discursive statements in *Lyrical Ballads*, which is why he retains that sentence from the initial 'Advertisement' when he expands the theoretical text he puts before the poems into the 'Preface'. What is so important about *Lyrical Ballads* is the way it recognises poetry *as* philosophical writing *and* as poetry, and enables us to do so.

A key aspect of this complicated claim about by 'what courtesy' (*LB* 3) we can call the *Lyrical Ballads* poems, concerns the theoretical and aesthetic issues of what is generally called the standard of taste. 'Taste' questions under what aesthetic standard an aesthetic object (such as these poems or, say, art) can and would be considered such an object (or poem, or art). Very often, this philosophical problem is formulated in the British empiricist tradition of David Hume or Adam Smith. In the terms of this tradition, the central point is whether or not the aesthetic standards of the times are ready for this poetry. If not, then the question becomes whether, given enough attention and time, things will change and the poems will be recognised *as* poems (and maybe even become canonical). In this version of the argument, history has borne out Wordsworth's implicit fantasy, since Romantic poetry and *Lyrical Ballads* have become central touchstones for literary history and taste.

However, there is another reading of that passage that conveys a slightly different meaning. It suggests that the 'strangeness and aukwardness' are constitutive parts of what it is to be a poem. They produce a feeling of unease, but that is part and parcel of what it means to be reading poetry, at least of a particular style. In this reading, the 'strangeness and aukwardness' is not a problem that, primarily, needs to be historically overcome. Rather, it is a difficulty that the reader will face – whatever she thinks is a poem, and even if she has accepted *Lyrical Ballads* to be poetry. The awkwardness becomes, in this reading, a structural or essential part of what it is to be a poem, at least as envisaged by Wordsworth. It becomes part of poetry as a philosophical form of writing.

This structural claim makes it important to trace not just moments of deep defamiliarisation that have historically been absorbed (using antiquated terms, for instance). The deeper claim about multidimensionality and defamiliarisation is that they are structural and integral to poetry itself, so that, for instance, the title *Lyrical Ballads* is by definition awkward. 'Lyrical' and 'Ballad' are two genres that are very different and at odds with one another. To claim that a ballad is lyrical is to make a destabilising and awkward claim. The standard of taste about the acceptable topics in lyrics and ballads might change, and the diction of the poems in the volume might not be as unfamiliar to us as they would have been to an eighteenth-century reader. What does not change, as Peter de Bolla puts it in his answer to the question 'What Is a Lyrical Ballad?', is the fact that 'something . . . fundamental is at stake' in the cross-generic character of the poems.[8]

Feelings of Awkwardness

The philosophical significance of the claim that poetry is structurally strange and awkward is both historical and conceptual. Wordsworth's exact formulation of poetry as producing 'aukwardness' can help us understand both of those aspects of his argument. We can learn from developing both of these readings – the importance of the standard of taste as well as the structural argument about poetry – side by side.

When something is 'awk', it is 'in the wrong direction' or 'perverse', hence the sense and feeling of awkwardness as something that is '[u]pside down' or 'hindside foremost'.[9] When something is 'awkward' it is '[t]urned the wrong way' and thus gives the impression that it is untoward and clumsy.[10] It expresses a feeling that we are all familiar with, a category that is hard to translate and difficult to pin down analytically. People can be awkward, and so can furniture arrangements, situations, sentences or smiles. And poems can be awkward, too. It is just not very common that an author both warns the reader that the poems will be awkward and even suggests that this might be a good thing. In an important sense, the feeling of what is awkward changes with the standard of taste. This is why awkwardness, so intangible but felt so keenly, is a preferred indicator for this aesthetic and social standard. Wordsworth's use of the word is, therefore, deliberate, intentional and meaningful.

We find the term 'awkwardness' across the literature of the later eighteenth century. Samuel Johnson's *Dictionary* includes not only 'awkward' ('[i]nelegant . . . clumsy . . . [p]erverse') but also 'awkwardly' ('[c]lumsily . . . inelegantly; ungainly') and 'awkwardness' ('[i]nelegance . . . oddness').[11] 'Awkward' also appears in a variety of contexts, such as medical handbooks, theological writings, literary texts. The early eighteenth-century novelist Eliza Haywood is fond of it and uses it in *Memoirs of a Certain Island*: 'there was so much awkward Extasy in her Behaviour at the Condescensions he had made her, that he presently saw that there would be no great occasion for farther Courtship'.[12] 'Awkward' is especially prevalent in manuals, such as *The Art of Speaking* or *Beauties of Eminent Writers; Selected and Arranged for the Instruction of Youth* and others that cover social behaviour (dancing, for instance), which would be a reliable indicator of the standard of taste.[13] It is also used as an aesthetic category in the theorisation of art. Philip Dormer Stanhope, Fourth Earl of Chesterfield, was one of the main theoreticians of the social dimensions of 'awkwardness'. In his popular and standard *Letters* to his son, which was

used widely as a reference book about societal norms, he gives a stern
warning when he reports that 'I have known many a man, from his
awkwardness, give people such a dislike of him at first, that all his merit
could not get the better of it afterwards'.[14] There are also figures who
discuss its literary dimensions in prominent places, such as James Beattie
and his *Dissertations Moral and Critical*.[15] In more recent criticism, the
term has gone mostly unexamined. Mina Gorji has written about the
relevance of the term in John Clare's works, but the claims she makes for
it narrowly relate to his diction.[16] In other contexts, the term is used
frequently, especially in US coming-of-age culture. In all of these cases,
there is a sense that awkwardness is understood to be a thing that is to be
overcome, either by the person being awkward or by standards of taste that
must change in order for our sense of what is awkward to change. As we will
see, this is a dimension that is important already in Wordsworth's time,
though *Lyrical Ballads* will extend it to a more fundamental significance.

One of the most interesting and relevant discussions of 'awkwardness' in
the eighteenth century is provided in Adam Smith's *Theory of Moral
Sentiments*, quite possibly one of the books of moral philosophy that
Wordsworth criticised Hazlitt for being 'unreasonably' attached to. In part
V, section I – 'Of the INFLUENCE of CUSTOM and FASHION upon the
sentiments of moral approbation and disapprobation' – Smith argues that
there is a direct correlation between custom and 'our notions of beauty and
deformity'.[17] Cultural convention and habit mean that the imagination
associates two independent objects and conceives of them as almost
inseparable: 'Tho' independent of custom, there should be no real beauty
in their union, yet when custom has thus connected them together, we feel
an impropriety in their separation. The one we think is aukward when it
appears without its usual companion.' As a result, '[t]hose who have been
accustomed to see things in a good taste are more disgusted by whatever is
clumsy or aukward' (372). For Smith, a central philosopher of the time,
awkwardness becomes an aesthetic indicator or test of whether something
has been socially accepted. This development is important because it also
includes the relation between poetry and philosophy. Awkwardness
becomes a marker for the standard of taste, which, in turn, is also the site
for the relation between poetry and philosophy. It becomes an aesthetic
category – or, conversely, it falls out of fashion. For instance, when
something is dropped by those who provide the standard of taste, 'it loses
all the grace, which it had appeared to possess before, and being now used
only by the inferior ranks of people, seems to have something of their

meanness and aukwardness' (Smith 373). The implication in relation to class and language will be important for Wordsworth's interest in and defence of rustic language, which is so central to *Lyrical Ballads*.

The standard of taste is not only, of course, a matter of dances, social graces and sartorial fashion. It also involves painting, poetry and other arts. The principle of the standard of taste as a socially constructed norm 'extends itself to whatever is in any respect the object of taste[,] to music, to poetry, to architecture' (Smith 373–374). Although we might not admit it as easily, Smith suggests, these seemingly more important categories are subject to the same structural social dynamics as are other fashions. A direct and concrete sign of this is what becomes acceptable or unacceptable in conversation or poetic diction, such as the rustic language of the lower classes. It was precisely this language that *Lyrical Ballads* would champion as fit for poetry.

Wordsworth was familiar with Smith's struggles in *Theory of Moral Sentiments* to understand the circularity of the standard of taste. He might even have been inspired by the philosopher's conjecture that '[a]fter the praise of refining the taste of a nation, the highest eulogy, perhaps, which can be bestowed upon any author is to say, that he corrupted it' (231). That is exactly what Wordsworth tries to do. As a cornerstone of this 'corrupt[ion]', Wordsworth introduces a turn to 'language really used by men' (*LB* p.97) as part of poetry. In practice it means that 'low and rustic life was generally chosen' (*LB* 97), representing members of society that will be awkward, not polite. The rusticity of the language, and the people associated with it, would no doubt have been considered awkward, according to Smith's description.

Historically, awkwardness and rustic speech are associated with each other. They are uncomfortable and uncouth, and are a prime indicator for the lack of social grace. Plenty of handbooks and moral guides in the eighteenth century make a direct link between the perceived lack of urbanity and what Wordsworth terms the 'real language' (*LB* 95) in terms of awkwardness: 'an Age of refined and polished manners will be little disposed to esteem the Person ... remarkable for Rusticity, Awkwardness ... and Ignorance'.[18] The challenge for readers of *Lyrical Ballads* is whether they can change this attitude. It is a matter of whether, in Wordsworth's terms, the reader not only can delineate feelings 'as all men *do* sympathise with, but also ... to add to these others, such as men *may* sympathize with' (*LB* 320–321). One way to sound this '*may*' out is by sounding out how we handle our feelings of awkwardness.

Famously, the differences for Wordsworth are that he thinks of rusticity as positive and that poetry and our thinking about poetry need to value this insight over the social norms disassociating a description of 'common life' (*LB* 96) and poetry. With Romanticism, such an attitude becomes much more familiar. There are other sources contemporary to *Lyrical Ballads* that are part of this change, such as Curate John Bennett's *Letters to a Young Lady*, which states that he 'prefer[s] the plain, honest awkwardness of a mere, country girl to over-acted refinement'.[19] There is little question, however, that Wordsworth emerges as the most radical defender of awkwardness precisely because of his conviction that it is in rustic life and language where 'men hourly communicate with the best objects from which the best part of language is originally derived'. He continues, noting that 'because, from their rank in society and the sameness and narrow circle of their intercourse, being less under the influence of social vanity . . . such a language . . . is more permanent, and a far more philosophical language, than that which is frequently substituted for it by Poets' (*LB* 97). What we discover in *Lyrical Ballads* is that such a negative association between rusticity and awkwardness is mistaken not just in terms of poetic taste or standard, but also philosophically, in regard to moral philosophy in particular. We make a mistake when we think that awkwardness and rusticity are signs not just of a stylistic but also of an ethical shortcoming. And that is, importantly, a philosophical argument.

Philosophically Awkward

It emerges that there are two different levels of awkwardness, and that both of them are at play here. One concerns a standard of taste normally understood – that is, the historically and culturally specific norms that govern sociality and aesthetics. Here awkwardness is either used as a negative litmus test or presented as a new, positive break with the aesthetic norms that have to be changed. The second form of awkwardness is more fundamental and resides in the structure of the poetry itself. In those cases, the awkwardness is part of why poetry is the most philosophical of all writing.

A powerful example for this second, deeper sense of awkwardness comes from the last stanza of Wordsworth's best-known verse, 'She dwelt among th'untrodden ways'. It is a lyric so familiar to us that there should not be any feeling of strangeness at all. And yet, at least for me, whenever I read the last stanza, I cannot help but feel precisely that, an 'awkwardness':

> She liv'd unknown, and few could know
> When Lucy ceas'd to be;
> But she is in her Grave, and Oh!
> The difference to me.
>
> (*LB* Lines 9–12)

It is the metrical awkwardness of the word 'difference' that throws the reader off course and makes the poem feel unfamiliar. This difficulty is not primarily about shocking the reader by articulating a fear (or is it a fantasy?) that one's loved one is dead. The more powerful question is how the verbal articulation of that feeling is philosophically significant. The fact that Lucy is dead makes a difference, for sure. But what kind of a difference does it make? In this case, it is a difference that does not fit, that is awkward. We cannot read the word without either emphasising the difference ('dif-ference') or actively hiding it. It is a conceptual and poetical marker that slows the reader down, interrupting a metrical and conceptual flow in an uncomfortable way: the number of syllables might be the same, but the way that they are pronounced calls attention to the construction of the poem.

The awkwardness in this case is not historically specific – it is not even a question of rustic language – but rather part of the poem's structural quality. The impression of awkwardness is the result of the order of words and syllables. Their intentional placement not only makes them incidental passages but also emphasises their wider importance, even suggesting an aesthetic principle. What is at stake here is not awkwardness *contra* a standard of taste but rather awkwardness *as* a standard of poetry. It is this turn that allows us to read poetry as the most philosophical form of all writing in a new light.

It is relevant that the 'Lucy Poems', a particularly strong and important cluster in Wordsworth's writing, are all rather awkward. There is a metrical and conceptual 'dif-ference' that runs through all of them. The opening stanza of 'Strange fits of passion' is an example that illustrates this claim:

> Strange fits of passion I have known:
> And I will dare to tell,
> But in the Lover's ear alone,
> What once to me befel.
>
> (*LB* Lines 1–4)

It is a Wordsworthian moment of inversion that plays with stereotypical ideas about emotions and knowledge. To claim that 'I have known strange fits of passion' would be strange enough. Positioning the adjective 'strange' at the beginning of the poem leaves much room for poetical and philosophical doubt. It suggests that the formulation of 'strange fits' is as odd as it is important and that the lyric is, as Adela Pinch appropriately says, 'a poem of misfittings'.[20] Some of these 'misfittings' are, not surprisingly, rather awkward.

The most common reading of this line understands the fit as an attack, a paroxysm or a seizure – a moment that disrupts our normal order of life. It is an awkward moment both for the person who is experiencing it as well as for the observer. In this 'Lucy Poem', the fit is an idea that has entered the speaker's mind unintentionally: 'What fond and wayward thoughts will slide / Into a Lover's head' (Lines 25–26). What bothers the speaker is not just that we are not in control of our thoughts or their order, but also that we cannot really modulate their content. In this case, the worry and fantasy are what the world would look like and feel like "If Lucy should be dead!" (28). The thought enters the speaker's mind without much control. It results in a strange fit of passion that can never be quite accommodated or resolved.

But this paroxysm of thought also is a fit of a very different kind. It is the plural description of a passion that fits, that is suitable, that conforms to the shape in front of it. In this sense, the '[s]trange fit' is almost oxymoronic in character. There is something that fits and therefore should not feel awkward at all, and yet it is '[s]trange'. The lack of fit here is, of course, also between word and meaning, as Geoffrey H. Hartman points out: 'Every "passion" of words ... is under the shadow of being a "strange fit" – or not fit at all, because the correspondence (the expected harmony) between word and wish has been disturbed'.[21] This disappointment produces a feeling of unfamiliarity, strangeness and, ultimately, awkwardness. Whatever way we turn the strange 'fits of passion', they are awkward.

There is no doubt that lyrics like those of the 'Lucy Poems' produce 'feelings of strangeness and aukwardness' as Wordsworth predicts in the 'Advertisement' and repeats in the 'Preface'. There is a link between the feelings and judgements such lyrics elicit and their peculiar status as the 'most philosophic of all writing' (LB, 'Preface', p. 105). To see how these two characteristics are related, let us return to 'Expostulation and Reply', the poem that Wordsworth initially designates as a response to the 'unreasonable' attachment to 'modern books of moral philosophy' (LB 4). After listening to the friend's chastisement for idling his time away, the speaker reacts with a general observation of his own:

> The eye it cannot chuse but see,
> We cannot bid the ear be still;
> Our bodies feel where'er they be,
> Against, or with our will.
>
> (Lines 17–20)

The speaker's reply is remarkably philosophical in character. It argues for what he calls 'a wise passiveness' (24). Such a response presents a version of being in the world that accepts that the supposed control over projects such as history or philosophy is far less powerful than we normally admit. This includes the senses themselves that we use to interact with the world, the speaker says, for "[t]he eye it cannot chuse but see, / We cannot bid the ear be still" (17–18). Control, choice and volition are revealed to be far from reliable for our understanding of the world. Intentionality is not fully under our control.

The awkwardness of the expressions at play, though, makes us pause and reread those lines. The idea that our eye has no choice but to see and our ears no choice but to hear – and, in this odd formulation, to reproduce – the sounds around us is at the heart of the odd mixture between apodictic statement about lack of control and non-committal formulations. This is not just an awkwardness of expression but also an awkwardness of thinking. It is about having it back-to-front, and intentionally so, since that awkwardness has meaning. It reveals not only the power of defamiliarisation but also that Wordsworth's defamiliarisation begins to articulate a poetics that relies on the awkward relation between thought and word, and, more broadly, between philosophy and poetry.

One of the things that is so instructive about this poem is its representation of argument and dialectics. Together with the more one-sided 'Tables Turned', it represents a pair: two different approaches to the world. Even in itself the poem shows two contrary positions side by side. The prominence of this pair, and the two positions it represents, gains even higher visibility in the 1802 edition of the book, which not only opens with the 'Preface', but also positions these two poems as an opposing pair at the beginning, thus making the first three texts of the book explicitly about the relation between poetry and philosophy. There is little doubt that the speaker of the 'Expostulation and Reply' presents a more successful argument than his 'good friend' (15) who wants us to turn to books. It is a philosophical position, but one that is not unreasonably attached to the books of moral philosophy. The key thing is that the more successful position is also the more awkward argument. The poem and argument are not only awkward in their expression; they are also awkward in their commitment to awkwardness. It suggests that there is more behind the unusual, 'awk' positioning of words and thoughts than first meets the eye.

Good poetry is awkward, never inane. And this awkwardness mirrors the often back-to-front relation between poetry and philosophy in *Lyrical Ballads*. The awkwardness is not a sign of a failed relation between custom and innovation. On the contrary, it is actually a sign for a deeper understanding, a philosophical understanding of poetry. It is a relation that is itself awkward. The strange fit between philosophy and poetry is not so much a dialectical opposition, or a harmonious equivalence, but a quality that *Lyrical Ballads* presents as altogether different. It is a celebration of awkwardness as a philosophically meaningful relation that allows poetry to attain a more problematic, but also deeper, dimension that never quite fits.

Conclusion

Awkwardness emerges as a rich, helpful category with which to understand how *Lyrical Ballads* negotiates the close relation between poetry and philosophy. These two spheres live off each other in close but productive tension because they are not exactly opposite but rather askew. Their relation is what Wordsworth, in a different context, calls 'a finer connection than that of contrast' (*Prose* II. 53).[22] The structural awkwardness of poetry helps us understand what Wordsworth means when he positions poetry as the most philosophical of all writing. What is clear is that *Lyrical Ballads* leaves behind the traditional positioning of these two spheres. There are still plenty of ways in which to understand the precise way the collection of poetry relates the one to the other. As the opening of this chapter suggests, there are various forms in which we can do this, some of which emphasise either poetry or philosophy. What we have come to appreciate, though, is that *Lyrical Ballads* is not completely clear-cut on these relations. When Wordsworth in the 'Advertisement' and the 'Preface' repeats that these experimental poems will produce 'feelings of strangeness and aukwardness', he taps into a general discourse of the term and also makes the poems show that he is pushing the term further than is commonly assumed. In *Lyrical Ballads* the 'struggle with feelings of strangeness and aukwardness' emerges as not just a warning but also a promise. It becomes one of the ways in which poetry can be 'the most philosophic of all writing'. It is not a dialectical promise that there will be a resolution or progress after the awkwardness has subsided. Rather, it is a promise that these poems will make us feel strange and awkward for many years to come.

Endnotes

1 Andrew Bennett, 'Wordsworth's Poetic Ignorance', in *Wordsworth's Poetic Theory: Knowledge, Language, Experience*, ed. Alexander Regier and Stefan H. Uhlig (Basingstoke: Palgrave Macmillan, 2010), 19–35; 27.

2 Matthew Arnold, preface to *Poems of Wordsworth*, ed. Arnold (London: Macmillan and Co., 1879), v–xxvi; xviii–xix.

3 Seamus Perry, 'Wordsworth and Coleridge', in *The Cambridge Companion to Wordsworth*, ed. Stephen Gill (Cambridge: Cambridge University Press, 2003), 161–179; 172.

4 Leslie Stephen, 'Wordsworth's Ethics', *The Eclectic Magazine*, 24.87 (October 1876): 447–462; 450.

5 Marjorie Levinson, 'A Motion and a Spirit: Romancing Spinoza', *Essays in Romanticism*, 46.4 (Winter 2007): 367–408; 392.

6 Simon Jarvis, *Wordsworth's Philosophic Song* (Cambridge: Cambridge University Press, 2007), 4.

7 Stephen Gill, 'The Philosophic Poet', in *Cambridge Companion to Wordsworth*, 142–160; 143 and 149.

8 Peter de Bolla, 'What Is a Lyrical Ballad? Wordsworth's Experimental Epistemologies', in *Wordsworth's Poetic Theory*, 43–60; 46.

9 *OED* (2nd ed.), s.v. 'awk, *adj., adv.* and *n.*', A1–A2; and *OED* (2nd ed.), s.v. 'awkward, *adj.* and *adv.*', A[1]b.

10 *OED* (2nd ed.), s.v. 'awkward, *adj.* and *adv.*', B1.

11 Samuel Johnson, *A Dictionary of the English Language* (London: W. Strahan, 1755), 2 vols., 1. 188, s.v. 'awkward', 'awkwardly', and 'awkwardness'.

12 Eliza Fowler Haywood, *Memoirs of a Certain Island*, 2 vols. (London, 1726), 2. 166.

13 See James Burgh, *The Art of Speaking* (London: Longman, 1761) and William Scott, *Beauties of Eminent Writers; Selected and Arranged for the Instruction of Youth*, 2nd ed., 2 vols. (Edinburgh: Peter Hill, 1794).

14 Philip Dormer Stanhope to Philip Stanhope (25 July 1741), in *Letters Written by the Late Right Honourable Philip Dormer Stanhope, Earl of Chesterfield, to His Son, Philip Stanhope, Esq.*, 4 vols. (Edinburgh: C. Macfarquhar, 1775), 1. 199–203; 199–200.

15 See James Beattie, *Dissertations Moral and Critical*, 2 vols. (Dublin, 1783).

16 Mina Gorji, 'Clare's Awkwardness', *Essays in Criticism*, 54.3 (July 2004): 216–239.

17 Adam Smith, *The Theory of Moral Sentiments* (London: A. Millar, 1759), 371.

18 George Stinton, *A Sermon Preached in Lambeth-Chapel* (London: J. Hughs, 1769), 19.

19 John Bennett, *Letters to a Young Lady*, 2 vols. (Warrington: W. Eyres, 1789), 2. 68. Also see John Abernethy, *Sermons on Various Subjects*, 2 vols. (London: Printed for D. Brown, C. Davis, and A. Millar, 1748).

20 Adela Pinch, *Strange Fits of Passion: Epistemologies of Emotion, Hume to Austen* (Stanford: Stanford University Press, 1996), 106.

21 Geoffrey H. Hartman, 'Words, Wish, Worth: Wordsworth', in Harold Bloom, Paul de Man, Jacques Derrida, Geoffrey Hartman, and J. Hillis Miller, *Deconstruction and Criticism* (London: Continuum, 2004), 143–176; 162.

22 On the context of this formulation, see Alexander Regier in *Wordsworth's Poetic Theory*, 61–80.

PART V

A Global Lyrical Ballads

CHAPTER 12

Ecocritical Approaches to Lyrical Ballads

James C. McKusick

In recent years a new approach to the study of British Romantic literature has fundamentally altered the kinds of questions posed by literary criticism. This new approach, known as ecocriticism, first emerged into prominence during the 1990s, a period of increasing environmental concern throughout the industrialised world. Jonathan Bate's influential study *Romantic Ecology: Wordsworth and the Environmental Tradition* was among the first to examine the ecological elements of British Romanticism, arguing that Wordsworth articulated a powerful and enduring vision of human integration with nature.[1] Ecological critics have pondered fundamental questions about the purpose of literary criticism, and of imaginative literature itself, in a time of ever-increasing environmental crisis. In an era of impending threats to the global environment, the emerging discipline of ecocriticism is engaged in a vital re-vision of the fundamental task of poetry. Greg Garrard explains: 'Environmental problems require analysis in cultural as well as scientific terms, because they are the outcome of an interaction between ecological knowledge of nature and its cultural inflection'.[2] Because it often seeks to address perennial questions concerning the relationship between humankind and the natural world, British Romantic poetry has become one of the most important terrains for the development of ecocriticism. Moreover, the canon of British Romantic literature has been broadened and reshaped by the consideration of what constitutes an environmental text.[3]

William Wordsworth and Samuel Taylor Coleridge collaboratively pioneered new ways of seeing and responding to the natural world. Throughout the nineteenth century, Wordsworth was known to readers on both sides of the Atlantic as the most prominent of the Lake Poets, and the deep-rooted affiliation of his writing with a particular scenic locale in the north of England was further confirmed by the publication of his *Guide to the Lakes*, a guidebook that was the best known and most frequently republished of Wordsworth's writings during his lifetime.[4] More than just itinerant observers of picturesque beauty, Wordsworth and Coleridge were long-time inhabitants of the Lake District, and the poetry that they composed in that region often adopts the persona of a speaker whose voice is inflected by the local and personal history of the place he inhabits. Such a perspective may legitimately be termed an ecological view of the natural world, since their poetry consistently expresses a deep and abiding interest in the Earth as a dwelling-place for all living things. The word 'ecology' (first recorded in the English language in 1873, according to the *OED*) is derived from the Greek word *oikos*, meaning 'house' or 'dwelling-place', and the poetry of Wordsworth and Coleridge clearly foreshadows the modern science of ecology in its holistic conception of the Earth as a household, a dwelling-place for an interdependent biological and human community.

In his 'Preface' to *Lyrical Ballads*, first published in the second edition of 1800, Wordsworth justifies his preference for the language of 'low and rustic life ... because in that condition the passions of men are incorporated with the beautiful and permanent forms of nature' (*LB* p. 97). Wordsworth's advocacy of simple vernacular diction is predicated on his view that human passion *incorporates* the forms of nature. His metaphor of incorporation, or embodiment, is essentially ecological since it suggests that all language, and therefore all human consciousness, is affected by the 'forms of nature' that surround it. The natural world is a birthplace and vital habitat for language, feeling and thought. Although Coleridge did not fully concur with Wordsworth's theory of poetic language, he certainly shared the view that linguistic form must emerge from a distinctly local set of conditions; this is the main premise of his poetic style in 'The Nightingale: A Conversational Poem' (*LB* 29), and it is more explicitly developed in his early informal prose. In a notebook passage of 1799, for example, Coleridge affirms his conviction that the naming practices of the Lake District are related to the inhabitants' sense of political independence and their proximity to wild natural phenomena: 'In the North every Brook, every Crag, almost every Field has a name – a proof of greater Independence & a society more approaching in their Laws & Habits to Nature' (*CN STC* I. 569). Like Wordsworth, Coleridge was fascinated by the naming of places, and he often compiled lists of local place-names during his wanderings in the Lake District (*CN STC* I. 1207). Language, most evidently in the case of place-names, is the result of an ongoing conversation between the land and the people who dwell upon it.

The Shadow of the Ship

Coleridge's engagement with the integrity of the natural world, and his concern for its preservation, is apparent throughout his contributions to *Lyrical Ballads*, a volume that is constructed with thoughtful attention to the situation of poems in a larger discursive context. 'The Rime of the Ancyent Marinere', a deliberately archaic narrative poem in ballad stanza, appears as the very first poem in the 1798 edition of *Lyrical Ballads*. Its placement at the head of the collection serves to emphasise its role as a stark and compelling statement of themes that will receive more varied expression later in the volume. Regarded in this way, 'The Rime of the Ancyent Marinere' may be read as a parable of ecological transgression. The mariner, an Everyman figure on a voyage of exploration in 'the cold Country towards the South Pole' (*LB* 5), encounters a frigid realm that is apparently devoid of life: 'Ne shapes of men ne beasts we ken – / The Ice was all between' (Lines 55–56). The word 'ken' suggests that the mariner's plight is fundamentally a crisis in Western ways of *knowing*: an epistemic gap that separates him from the hidden creatures of the Antarctic. The mariner embarks on this voyage as a Cartesian dualist, a detached observer who is cut off from any feeling of empathy or participation in the vast world of life that surrounds him.

The Albatross appears out of the epistemic 'fog' as an emissary from the Antarctic wilderness. In a spontaneous act of identification, the mariners hail it as 'a Christian soul', as if it were a human being like themselves:

> At length did cross an Albatross,
> Thorough the Fog it came,
> And an it were a Christian Soul,
> We hail'd it in God's name.
>
> (Lines 61–64)

The Albatross crosses from the wild ice to the world of men, and its act of 'crossing' the boundary between nature and civilisation indicates a possible resolution of the mariner's epistemic solitude. The Albatross brings companionship to the lonely mariners, it guides them through the pathless ice, and returns 'every day for food or play' (71). The 1798 version of the poem specifies that 'The Marineres gave it biscuit-worms' (65), a homely detail that concretely renders the symbiotic exchange between man and beast: the mariners provide nourishment for the Albatross, while the bird provides them with more intangible benefits of companionship, guidance and play. These biscuit-worms are more than mere vermin; they play an essential role in the web of life, and they suggest that what we regard as ugly or obnoxious may nonetheless be appealing when considered from another (nonhuman) perspective.

The mariner kills the Albatross with his 'cross bow' (79), a weapon that embodies the relentlessly destructive tendency of European technology at the same time that it invokes, with some irony, the traditional Christian imagery of sacrifice and atonement. If the Albatross is regarded as an innocent emissary from the unspoiled natural realm of the Antarctic, then the mariner's deed represents an unmotivated act of aggression against all the creatures of that realm. But the Antarctic, through the agency of the Polar Spirit, wreaks a terrible vengeance upon the mariner, who must witness the death of his shipmates and the decay of the entire living world around him, as if the destruction of a single creature had disrupted the whole economy of nature:

> The very deeps did rot: O Christ!
> That ever this should be!
> Yea, slimy things did crawl with legs
> Upon the slimy Sea.
>
> (Lines 119–122)

These slimy creatures with legs, unknown in any textbook of natural history, represent with apocalyptic intensity the death of nature as a result of destructive human acts. On a concrete geographic level, the voyage of the mariner is modelled upon Captain Cook's second voyage, which mapped the Antarctic region, described the incredible abundance of its fauna, and thereby ushered in an era of wholesale destruction of seals, whales, birds and other marine life.[5]

Any wooden sailing ship in tropical waters will gradually accumulate a host of fellow travellers, ranging from barnacles and seaweed to schools of fish that shelter within her shadow. As the mariner's vessel 'made her course to the tropical Latitude of the Great Pacific Ocean' (*LB* 5), a community of living things is gathered around her. The ship comes to resemble a floating reef, and the teeming flora and fauna offer both perils and opportunities to those aboard her. As Coleridge could have learned from several narrative accounts of maritime exploration in tropical latitudes, the fouling of a ship's bottom and the rapid rotting of her timbers can lead to her destruction, but the abundance and variety of marine life surrounding the ship was the cause of wonder and amazement for many British explorers. John Livingston Lowes cites a typical passage from Cook's third voyage:

During a calm ... some parts of the sea seemed covered with a kind of slime; and some small sea animals were swimming about. ... When they began to swim about, which they did, with equal ease, upon their back, sides, or belly, they emitted the brightest colours of the most precious gems.[6]

The slimy creatures found in the vicinity of Cook's ship display unexpected flashes of beauty to the scientific observer, just as the water-snakes in Coleridge's poem are revealed to be vital participants in the ship's local ecosystem. Their repulsive aspect is eventually shown to have been the result of the mariner's flawed perception, not their intrinsic nature. The mariner's act of blessing the water-snakes enables him to see them, with a striking intensity of vision, as creatures that inhabit 'the shadow of the ship', an *ecotone* (or boundary region) that provides rich habitat for an abundance of marine life:

> Within the shadow of the ship
> I watch'd their rich attire:
> Blue, glossy green, and velvet black
> They coil'd and swam; and every track
> Was a flash of golden fire.
> (Lines 269–273)

Finding the hidden beauty in such slimy creatures, the mariner discovers that all life forms, even microscopic ones, play a vital role in the natural world. By blessing the water-snakes, the mariner is released from his state of alienation from nature, and the Albatross sinks 'like lead into the sea' (283), crossing back from civilisation into the untamed ocean. The mariner has learned what the Albatross came to teach him: that he must cross the boundaries that divide him from the natural world, through unmotivated acts of compassion between 'man and bird and beast' (*LB* 646).

'The Rime of the Ancyent Marinere' ponders the ethical significance of dwelling on boundaries between different realms. In the poem's initial episode, an Albatross crosses from the inhuman world of ice 'as green as Emerauld' (52) into the human community of the mariners. At the poem's climax, the 'shadow of the ship' (264) delineates a rich tropical ecotone inhabited by sea-snakes that the mariner must 'bless' in order to survive. At the end of the poem, the mariner returns from sea to land, drifting across the 'Harbour-bar' (473) and rowing ashore with the help of a Hermit who inhabits yet another ecotone, 'that wood / Which slopes down to the Sea' (547–548). All of these boundary regions serve as points of departure and arrival for the poem's profound meditation upon the green world of nature and the destructive tendencies of human civilisation. The wedding-guest is transformed by the mariner's tale into 'a sadder and a wiser man' (657), having learned that the deliberate destruction of any wild creature may bring unforeseen consequences. Written explicitly in defense of 'all things both great and small' (658), this poem exemplifies the environmental advocacy that is integral to Coleridge's ecological vision.

Coleridge's use of language in 'The Rime of the Ancyent Marinere' provides crucial evidence of his endeavour to construct a new way of speaking in harmony with the surrounding world of living things – an *ecolect*. As Lowes points out in *The Road to Xanadu* (296–310), the 1798 version of the poem is more than just a fake antique ballad on the model of Percy's *Reliques* and Chatterton's 'Rowley' poems. Lowes demonstrates that Coleridge combines three fairly distinct types of archaic usage: first, the traditional ballad lexicon ('pheere', 'eldritch', 'before', 'I ween', 'sterte', 'een', 'countrée', 'withouten', 'cauld'); second, the diction of Chaucer and Spenser ('ne', 'uprist', 'I wist', 'yspread', 'yeven', 'n'old', 'eftsones', 'lavrock', 'jargoning', 'minstralsy'); and third, seafaring terminology ('swound', 'weft', 'clifts', 'biscuit-worms', 'fire-flags'). All three types of archaic usage were severely curtailed in the 1800 edition of the poem, perhaps in response to a reviewer in the *British Critic* (October 1799) who denounced the poem's 'antiquated words', citing 'weft' and 'swound' as flagrant examples of nonsensical diction.[7] Coleridge omitted the vivid seafaring term 'weft' in 1800, along with most of the other archaic words listed here. Yet the accessibility and stylistic coherence of the 1800 version are accomplished at the expense of the multifaceted syncretic quality of the original version, which bespeaks the author's desire to reassemble the surviving fragments of archaic language into a richly textured and deeply expressive mode of poetic discourse. Coleridge's essential purpose in cultivating such lexical variety is to construct a uniquely expressive idiolect for the mariner. The adjacence of modern and archaic words enables the poem to characterise the mariner as a wanderer through space and time and to situate his discourse at the intersection of literary modernity and picturesque nostalgia.

Things Forever Speaking

In their collaborative composition of *Lyrical Ballads*, Wordsworth and Coleridge shared a common perception of the natural world as a dynamic ecosystem and a passionate commitment to the preservation of wild creatures and scenic areas. Their 1798 volume was designed as a habitat that would provide a nurturing environment for the diversity of poems contained within it. Coleridge's unique contribution to this collaborative endeavour was his conception of language as a living thing, an integral organic system that can be cultivated by the poet for maximum diversity, either through the coinage of new words or the recovery of archaic ones. This holistic conception of language was clearly indebted to the new understanding of the organism that had emerged from eighteenth-century biology.[8] For Coleridge, the historical development of language is deeply conditioned by its relation to the natural environment, and his aesthetic principle of organicism likewise entails reference to the linguistic habitat of a poem as an essential determinant of its meaning. Coleridge's poetic energies were devoted to the development of a distinctive ecolect that might express the proper role of humankind in the economy of nature.

Wordsworth's poetic voice likewise dramatises the involvement of the speaker with the places and events that he describes. Throughout the *Lyrical Ballads*, Wordsworth achieves a sense of participation that enables the reader to become vicariously invested in the world of the poem. His contributions to *Lyrical Ballads* are not 'nature poems', if that term is taken to denote the precise and detailed description of natural objects. Wordsworth's most distinctive poems are neither descriptive nor minutely detailed. Rather, they evoke a dynamic awareness of the natural world through the vivid sensory imagery of its beholding by an engaged participant.

A telling manifesto for this new kind of poetry is 'Expostulation and Reply', undoubtedly one of the most familiar poems in *Lyrical Ballads*. Its very familiarity, however, makes it difficult for a modern reader to notice the radical nature of its departure from prevailing cultural norms. The first stanzas are spoken in the voice of a schoolmaster, 'Matthew', chiding a wayward student:

> 'Why William, on that old grey stone,
> Thus for the length of half a day,
> Why William, sit you thus alone
> And dream your time away?'
>
> (Lines 1–4)

Although this question seems intended to be merely rhetorical, a way of rebuking the lazy student for his alleged waste of time, 'William' responds as if it were seriously intended to evoke a response. This response is telling, in part, for what it does *not* say. It does not engage the schoolmaster in a debate concerning the relative merits of books written by 'dead men', nor does it defend the value of 'looking round' on Mother Earth. To engage the question in those terms would be to concede the validity of the worldview they entail, in which books are the main repositories of knowledge, and sight is the primary modality of perception.

Instead, the speaker 'William' proposes that there are other ways of knowing, and various non-visual modalities of perception:

> 'The eye it cannot chuse but see,
> We cannot bid the ear be still;
> Our bodies feel, where'er they be,
> Against, or with our will'.
>
> (Lines 17–20)

In many ways, this stanza is a non sequitur. It bluntly declares that the senses affect us directly and immediately, without the intervention of our conscious will. Such a declaration should not be regarded as merely an assertion of empirical reality, however, since the content of sensory perception may be other than what 'science' teaches us. If science is the accumulated knowledge of humankind, as conveyed by books, then the repudiation of book-learning may also connote the rejection of secular humanism as a way of knowing. Since the advent of Renaissance humanism, book-learning (and the fetishisation of the printed book as an object of acquisition, textual analysis and marginal commentary) has impeded our contact with other ways of knowing, ways that precede humanism in the order of history and of experience. Humanism impedes our coming to know ourselves as participants in a living world, a world that we inhabit not only as knowing subjects but also as organic beings, mere animals engaged in the daily tasks of eating, breathing, sleeping and dreaming.

The poem's protagonist develops some of these implications in the following stanza:

> 'Nor less I deem that there are powers,
> Which of themselves our minds impress,
> That we can feed this mind of ours,
> In a wise passiveness'.
>
> (Lines 21–24)

What are these 'powers' that impress the mind, regardless of our conscious volition? The poem does not say. Indeed, it leaves the nature of these 'powers' deliberately imprecise, and the reader is left to ponder whether these 'powers' are meant to be the sort of intangible presences that Immanuel Kant calls the *Ding an sich* – the unknowable object that stands at the source of our perceptions – or whether Wordsworth intends something even more uncanny, such as the pagan nature-spirits that inhabit the world of the mariner. By its very imprecision, this stanza implies a critique of more precise ways of knowing, including those embodied in the 'books' that allegedly contain all that is known, and worth knowing. The student's dreamlike states of awareness, by contrast, are utterly inscrutable, and perhaps finally inexplicable by means of the rational method of scientific inquiry. Such uncanny 'powers' can be approached only indirectly and experientially, by a 'wise passiveness'.

'William' addresses his interlocutor with a further question concerning this state of 'wise passiveness':

> 'Think you, mid all this mighty sum
> Of things forever speaking,
> That nothing of itself will come,
> But we must still be seeking?'
>
> (Lines 25–28)

The answer to this rhetorical question is rather less evident than most readers would suppose. It both echoes and gently caricatures the Protestant work ethic of the schoolmaster, who evidently is in the habit of encouraging his students to engage in an active 'seeking' of knowledge. The student inquires whether such active 'seeking' is really the best way to attain knowledge, especially if the natural world is conceived as a 'mighty sum / Of things forever speaking'. If things speak directly to us, then we need not seek them out. Yet the tone of this question is hardly self-assured; it implies an openness to experience without predicating what the actual content of that experience may be. It is a meditation on the possibility of conversational exchange with the things that surround us, not a prescription for the results of rational inquiry.

'Expostulation and Reply' is a remarkably successful poem because it allows both sides of the argument to be heard. If the schoolteacher is made to appear a stern taskmaster, the student is also presented as somewhat defensive and dogmatic in his rejection of book-learning. The poem enables the reader to ponder the limitations of both positions while allowing each to speak for itself. The next poem in *Lyrical Ballads*, 'The Tables Turned', addresses some of the same themes, and is even more radically experimental in form. It explores whether a 'conversation' is possible between the human mind and the objects of the natural world, and it calls into question the objectivity of our conventional ways of knowing.

The poem's first stanza is addressed to a 'friend' who is stubbornly attached to book-learning; this addressee is presumably the schoolteacher 'Matthew' of the previous poem. The most significant interlocutors of this poem, however, are the personified presences of the sun, who casts 'his first sweet evening yellow' upon the surrounding fields, and the 'woodland linnet', whose sweet music conveys more wisdom than is found in any book. The transforming light of the sunset enables the poet to perceive something other than the cold, hard objects of Newtonian science, and the songs of the woodland birds similarly convey something more worthwhile and engaging than mere determinate knowledge. The critique of book-learning is most explicitly conveyed in the poem's penultimate stanza:

> Sweet is the lore which nature brings;
> Our meddling intellect
> Mishapes the beauteous forms of things;
> – We murder to dissect.
>
> (Lines 25–28)

The 'lore' of nature is something other than the factual knowledge obtained by the 'meddling intellect', and this poem is vehement in its rejection of such knowledge, especially if it is procured through the death-dealing methods of eighteenth-century natural history, a science that was mainly concerned with the dissection and anatomical description of individual specimens, not with the study of living creatures in their native habitat.

The final stanza of 'The Tables Turned' dismisses both 'science' and 'art', exhorting the reader to engage in a very different kind of seeing and knowing:

> Enough of science and of art;
> Close up these barren leaves;
> Come forth, and bring with you a heart
> That watches and receives.
>
> (Lines 29–32)

The 'barren leaves' of books are implicitly contrasted with the more fecund leaves of the 'long green fields'. The outrageously mixed metaphor of a 'heart / That watches' provides another indication of just how far beyond conventional epistemology this poem is prepared to go. As a radical credo of ecological awareness, this poem may seem preachy and even dogmatic in some of its pronouncements; yet its brash assertiveness bespeaks a willingness to run stylistic risks in the service of a larger and more comprehensive vision of human possibility. This poem 'turns the tables' upon the entire

Western tradition of scientific knowledge, and it proposes a new role for humankind among the speaking presences of the natural world. The place of poetry, and the task of the poet, is thus inherently dialogical; the poet must seek to engage those inhuman voices in conversation, at some risk to his own sense of identity, self-confidence and stylistic decorum. To judge by the early reviews, *Lyrical Ballads* broke many rules of good taste, and transgressed against numerous tenets of conventional wisdom.

Departure and Return

Many of the poems in *Lyrical Ballads* are shaped by an underlying narrative of departure and return. This form is decisively established by 'The Rime of the Ancyent Marinere', whose protagonist sets forth from his native land on a voyage of exploration, returning home after many adventures a changed man. This narrative pattern, whose literary analogues go at least as far back as *The Odyssey*, repeats itself in Wordsworth's poem 'The Female Vagrant', which describes how its protagonist lived happily in her rural cottage until she was thrown out into the wider world and carried off to America aboard a British naval vessel. She finally returns home to England, bereft of her family and broken in spirit. A more light-hearted instance of this pattern of departure and return occurs in 'The Idiot Boy', which tells how Betty Foy sends her son, Johnny, on horseback into the night to fetch a doctor for her sick neighbour, Susan Gale. Instead of carrying out his appointed mission, however, Johnny wanders aimlessly in the dark forest until, by good luck, the horse brings him safely home. Once again, the wanderer returns home deeply changed by his experience but, in Johnny's case, these changes are entirely beneficial, and even cathartic for the local village community. Susan Gale is miraculously cured of her illness, Betty Foy discovers how deeply she loves her son, and Johnny brings home vivid memories of a strange moonlit forest lurking just beyond the boundaries of the known and familiar world.

In all three of these poems, the resonances of 'home' are developed through a series of contrasts with the wild, remote and often terrifying places encountered on the outward journey. In 'The Rime of the Ancyent Marinere', the safe, comfortable setting of the mariner's hometown, with its kirk, lighthouse and festive wedding ceremony, is implicitly contrasted with the grotesque imagery of towering icebergs, luminous water-snakes and an ominous game of dice between Death and Life-in-Death for possession of the mariner's soul. It is only after he has departed from his homeland that the mariner comes to realise the value of everything he has left behind.

So too, in 'The Female Vagrant' the protagonist recollects her childhood in a cottage by the river Derwent in terms that evidently idealise that experience, presumably as a result of the misery she has suffered since her departure:

> Can I forget what charms did once adorn
> My garden, stored with pease, and mint, and thyme,
> And rose and lilly for the sabbath morn?
> The sabbath bells, and their delightful chime;
> The gambols and wild freaks at shearing time;
> My hen's rich nest through long grass scarce espied;
> The cowslip-gathering at May's dewy prime;
> The swans, that, when I sought the water-side,
> From far to meet me came, spreading their snowy pride.
>
> (Lines 19–26)

This catalogue of remembered sensations, olfactory and auditory as well as visual, reveals how the concept of 'home' is typically constructed after one has left it behind; notably absent are any jarring or discordant elements that would lend this imagery the facticity of an actual experience. The concept of 'home' tends toward the merely nostalgic in this poem, and the archaic metrical form of the Spenserian stanza also gives this passage a remote, dreamlike quality. Composed in 1793, this poem is among the earliest works ever published by Wordsworth, and it lacks the precision of imagery and the direct vernacular mode of expression that characterise most of his other contributions to *Lyrical Ballads*. Yet there is good reason to scrutinise the depiction of 'home' in 'The Female Vagrant', because it reveals a great deal about Wordsworth's fundamental attitudes and beliefs about the best way of life in a rural community.

The stanza just cited describes a broad range of domesticated plants in the speaker's garden, including edible peas, aromatic herbs and ornamental flowers. She is surrounded by a great variety of tame and wild animals, including the frolicking sheep whose fleece provides a commodity for the local market, the free-ranging hen whose eggs provide daily sustenance, and the wild swans who provide nothing more tangible than friendly companionship. Subsequent stanzas describe how she is accompanied to market by her faithful dog, while her father remains at home to tend their bee-hives, and a 'red-breast known for years' (Line 36) conveys a friendly greeting by pecking at her casement window. Their basic subsistence is further eked out by her father's catching fish in a nearby lake; in a note to the poem, Wordsworth describes how 'Several of the Lakes in the north of England are let out to different Fishermen, in parcels marked out by imaginary lines drawn from rock to rock' (*LB* p. 33n). These 'imaginary lines' define an individual's right to take fish from a lake that is the common property of the local village. The most notable feature of the lifestyle depicted in this poem is its reliance on multiple modes of subsistence – vegetable gardening, poultry-farming, sheep-raising, bee-keeping and fishing – which all contribute to the foodstuffs and market commodities produced by this father-and-daughter family unit.

The subsistence mode of agriculture described in 'The Female Vagrant' is entirely sustainable in the long term, and in fact such a mode of production, based on a widely varied set of crops rotated annually, eked out by fishing and livestock grazing and the seasonal gathering of nuts, berries and firewood from village common areas, had persisted relatively intact throughout rural England since the Middle Ages.[9] To be sure, such a mode of existence was far from being the relaxed and idyllic way of life depicted in 'The Female Vagrant', particularly in years of drought, pestilence or crop failure; there is certainly an idealised pastoral quality in the way Wordsworth describes it. Nevertheless, because it was based on a widely variable set of foodstuffs and commodities, such a subsistence lifestyle was intrinsically more sustainable and resilient than more modern methods of agriculture, which typically rely upon the intensive cultivation of a single crop, year after year, and provide very little recourse in the event of crop failure. As a mode of subsistence, polyculture is inherently more sustainable than monoculture, and it certainly provides a more varied and interesting way of life for the individual farmer. However idealised such a lifestyle may appear to the modern reader, we may safely assume that it is, on the whole, accurately drawn from Wordsworth's own memories of rural life as he observed it during his childhood on the banks of the river Derwent. Further instances of Wordsworth's personal knowledge of traditional modes of rural subsistence may be adduced from his poem 'Nutting' (*LB* 256), which portrays the guilty pleasures of nut-gathering in the woods, and *The Prelude*, which describes how the young Wordsworth clambered out on cliffs to gather eggs from birds' nests.

During the eighteenth century, the traditional methods of subsistence agriculture were gradually being supplanted by more capital-intensive modes of production, and the common areas upon which the local farmers relied for their seasonal grazing and gathering activities were increasingly being withdrawn for exclusive private use by the process of enclosure. These modernising tendencies in rural areas were greatly accelerated

during the 1790s with the advent of the Napoleonic Wars, which drove up
the prices of agricultural commodities and made the intensive production
of market crops a highly profitable endeavour. In 'The Female Vagrant',
Wordsworth describes how the incursion of a wealthy landowner, who
purchases and encloses all of the surrounding properties, eventually drives
out the poem's protagonist and her father from their hereditary lands. This
wealthy intruder erects 'a mansion proud our woods among' (39), and by
denying access to these local woods, while also withdrawing the right to fish
in local waters, he ultimately succeeds in evicting the father and daughter
from their humble cottage. Evidently their traditional rights of access to the
lake, woods and other common areas were not respected by the wealthy
intruder, who took 'no joy ... [to] stray / Through pastures not his own'
(41–42). Since these common rights are generally matters of local oral
tradition rather than law, the father and daughter have no legal recourse
when their rights are usurped by their wealthy neighbour. They are thrown
out of their ancestral home and into a wider world of suffering and death.[10]

'The Female Vagrant' is the most overtly political of any of the poems
published in *Lyrical Ballads*, and its harsh criticism of wealthy landowners
is integral to a larger set of political concerns, which also include a critique
of British military adventurism and a deep solicitude for the plight of
homeless wanderers. Although these political views could be regarded as a
fairly typical articulation of the ideology of the French Revolution and the
ideology of 'The Rights of Man', they might also be understood as
emerging from a deeper set of beliefs and concerns that remained crucially
important to Wordsworth throughout his entire career, even after his
youthful enthusiasm for revolutionary politics had waned. Throughout
his lifetime, Wordsworth remained consistent in his opposition to what we
might term the military-industrial complex, especially as it affected the
traditional ways of life in rural England. Wordsworth consistently opposed
the 'development' and 'improvement' of rural landscapes, and he remained
a staunch defender of sustainable agricultural methods, traditional rural
architecture and all of England's open, scenic and wild areas, especially in
the Lake District. Wordsworth was truly ahead of his time, and radically
innovative in his concern for the preservation of traditional rural folkways
and in his defense of the poor, the homeless and all the wild creatures that
dwell beyond the pale, outside the conventional boundaries of human
civilisation. In his persistent engagement with these issues, Wordsworth
foreshadows some of the most vital concerns of the modern environmental
movement.

Several of these environmental issues are addressed in 'The Idiot Boy', a poem whose protagonist, like the Ancient Mariner, crosses over the boundary between civilisation and wilderness and returns to tell his tale. Unlike the mariner, however, Johnny is virtually inarticulate, and his narrative account of his journey through the dark forest provides only a brief glimpse into the actual sensory basis of that experience:

> 'The Cocks did crow to-whoo, to-whoo,
> And the Sun did shine so cold'.
> – Thus answered Johnny in his glory,
> And that was all his travel's story.
>
> (Lines 460–463)

Johnny refers here to the hooting of the owls and the cold light of the moon, both of which are so far outside the realm of his normal experience that he has no proper words for them, and can only describe them metaphorically, in terms of things he does know: domestic farm animals and the ordinary light of the sun. Yet by the very act of assimilating the unknown to the known, Johnny bears witness to the uncanny otherness of those wild creatures of the night; the moonlit forest is a realm that truly exists beyond the pale of ordinary experience. Even in his brief description of this encounter with the wild, Johnny conveys the sensory intensity of that realm, using imagery that is auditory and tactile as well as visual. The cries of the owls, also mentioned in the poem's opening stanza, echo in the reader's mind with an enigmatic significance: although these voices are not intelligible, they nevertheless serve to remind us that there is another world out there, outside the boundaries of civilisation, human language and normal perception.

Johnny's return to his native village proves to be cathartic for the entire community. His neighbour, Susan Gale, recovers from an illness that may have been merely psychosomatic in the first place – a call for attention from her heedless neighbours. As soon as she learns how much Betty Foy cares about her, to the extent that she is willing to hazard her only son on a perilous mission to fetch the doctor, Susan finds herself miraculously cured. Betty, in turn, after contemplating the possible death of her son, discovers just how much she loves him, and she greets his return with an ecstatic display of affection, not only for Johnny but also for the faithful steed that brought him back alive. And even Johnny, though seemingly oblivious to the human drama surrounding him, nevertheless brings home vivid memories of his journey through the moonlit forest, and, like the

Ancient Mariner, finds within himself 'strange power of speech' (Line 620) to convey to his auditors the uncanny intensity of that experience. As a result of Johnny's encounter with the wild, the entire village finds itself healed of its sickness, purged of its indifference to others, and transformed into a more integral and caring human community.

The Wild Green Landscape

The transformation of human awareness through contact with the wild is the main theme of 'Lines Written a Few Miles above Tintern Abbey', the last poem published in the 1798 edition of *Lyrical Ballads*. In this poem, Wordsworth describes how he returned to the banks of the River Wye in 1798, after a five-year absence. Located in the southwest part of England, the River Wye was not a pristine wilderness; by the 1790s it had become the site of small-scale industry, such as tanning, charcoal-burning and iron-smelting and its waters were heavily polluted by the toxic by-products of these industries. Wordsworth mentions the 'wreathes of smoke, / Sent up, in silence, from among the trees' (18–19), evidence of itinerant charcoal-burners engaged in converting wood into charcoal for use in local iron foundries. Wordsworth does not dwell upon such unpleasant changes in the land; he focuses instead upon those aspects of the landscape that have retained their wildness, presenting the appearance of a 'wild secluded scene' (6) even in the midst of human habitation:

> The day is come when I again repose
> Here, under this dark sycamore, and view
> These plots of cottage-ground, these orchard-tufts,
> Which, at this season, with their unripe fruits,
> Among the woods and copses lose themselves,
> Nor, with their green and simple hue, disturb
> The wild green landscape.
>
> (Lines 9–15)

These lines stress the fecundity, greenery and wildness of the landscape on the banks of the Wye, even though it is densely inhabited by people engaged in farming, livestock raising and cottage industries. It retains its wild character, yet it is not a wilderness.

'Tintern Abbey' evokes the peaceful coexistence of human habitation and wildness in the same landscape, especially by describing the appearance of hedgerows that have reverted to a semi-wild condition:

> Once again I see
> These hedge-rows, hardly hedge-rows, little lines
> Of sportive wood run wild; these pastoral farms
> Green to the very door.
>
> (Lines 15–18)

Although these hedgerows were originally constructed to serve as fences for livestock, they have become so overgrown that they are now essentially wild, displaying the diversity of flora and fauna that are typically found in woodland. By preserving the biodiversity that once pervaded this region, the hedgerows now function as a remnant habitat, providing refuge for many kinds of wildlife and preserving some vital features of southwest England's primordial ecosystem. Wordsworth depicts the 'pastoral farms' of this region as existing in complete harmony with the wild habitat that surrounds them.

Like several other poems in *Lyrical Ballads*, 'Tintern Abbey' is centrally concerned with themes of departure and return. Wordsworth is returning to a place that he first visited five years earlier, and his initial response is one of sheer delight in the evidently unchanged appearance of the landscape. He celebrates the endurance of wild natural beauty, even in the midst of intensive human occupation. The act of returning to a known and familiar landscape, and finding it still essentially intact, provides him with an opportunity to meditate upon the changes that have occurred in his own way of responding to the natural world. Wordsworth describes his response to the landscape during his previous visit as if he were a wild creature running through it:

> when like a roe
> I bounded o'er the mountains, by the sides
> Of the deep rivers, and the lonely streams,
> Wherever nature led; more like a man
> Flying from something that he dreads, than one
> Who sought the thing he loved.
>
> (Lines 68–73)

Love and fear were inextricably mingled in the poet's initial response to this wild terrain, which he experienced with an intensity that he can barely find words to describe in his later adulthood. The poet goes on to describe the 'abundant recompense' that has followed from his loss of those 'dizzy raptures' (89, 86): having reached greater maturity, he has discovered 'a sense sublime / Of something far more deeply interfused' (96–97), perhaps another instance of the mysterious 'powers' of nature that we previously encountered in 'Expostulation and Reply'. Even such heightened sensitivity, however, leaves the poet with a sense of regret for the youthful intensity that he has lost. In the closing section of the poem, he turns to his sister Dorothy, who has evidently been standing silently by his side the whole time. He notices 'the shooting lights / Of thy wild eyes' (119–120) and exhorts her to sustain the immediacy of her response to the natural world. The word 'wild' occurs three times in this final verse paragraph, always in connection with Dorothy's 'wild eyes' and 'wild ecstacies' (139) in the presence of Nature. Although the poet himself can no longer feel such 'ecstacies', the poem clearly places great value upon such a fierce and passionate response to the natural world.

From an ecocritical point of view, 'Tintern Abbey' poses several important questions about the right relationship between humankind and the natural world. The opening lines of the poem depict a human community dwelling in harmonious coexistence with nature; the local farmsteads are 'green to the very door', and the local farmers have acted to preserve a remnant of the region's primordial ecosystem by allowing their hedgerows to run wild. Considering the increasingly destructive activities of the nearby charcoal-burners, however, it remains an open question whether such an environmentally benign mode of agriculture can be sustained in the long run.

The question of whether wildness can be preserved is also crucial to the central meditative development of the poem, in which Wordsworth depicts his younger self as if he were a wild beast, bounding over the mountains, and he later exhorts Dorothy to preserve her own inner wildness. This poem urgently raises the question of whether such wildness can be sustained in any human relationship with nature. Will Dorothy eventually succumb, as her brother already has done, to the civilising process by which 'these wild ecstacies shall be matured / Into a sober pleasure' (139–140)? Looking at *Lyrical Ballads* as a whole, it does appear unlikely that such a state of 'wild' awareness can be sustained for long by any individual; only the Idiot Boy emerges at the end of his poem with his appreciation for wild nature entirely intact. The prevailing tone of the collection is tragic; many of the characters in *Lyrical Ballads* are eventually broken, or at least tamed, by their circumstances.

The poems collected in *Lyrical Ballads* were intended as experiments in a new kind of literature, so it is not surprising that they raise more questions than they answer. However, these poems were deeply influential upon all subsequent developments in environmental awareness, both in Britain and America. Their profound questions concerning the possibility of sustainable development remain significant, and hotly debated, right up to the present day. Wordsworth was deeply concerned about the future development of the Lake District, particularly as its environmental integrity became threatened by the encroachment of wealth, industry and tourism, and his writings evince a growing understanding of the complex ecological relationships between people and the places they inhabit.

Endnotes

1 Jonathan Bate, *Romantic Ecology: Wordsworth and the Environmental Tradition* (London: Routledge, 1991).

2 Greg Garrard, *Ecocriticism*, 2nd ed. (London: Routledge, 2012), 16.

3 For a synoptic overview of the development of Romantic ecocriticism, see *Wordsworth and the Green Romantics: Affect and Ecology in the Nineteenth Century*, ed. Lisa Ottum and Seth T. Reno (Durham: University of New Hampshire Press, 2016), 3–7.

4 William Wordsworth, *Guide to the Lakes*, 5th ed., ed. Ernest de Selincourt (Oxford: Oxford University Press, 1906). First published anonymously in 1810 as an introduction to a collection of engravings, the *Guide* was later published as a separate volume, going through five editions by 1835.

5 Bernard Smith, 'Coleridge's Ancient Mariner and Cook's Second Voyage', *Journal of the Warburg and Courtauld Institutes*, 19 (1956): 117–154; 117.

6 John Livingston Lowes, *The Road to Xanadu: A Study in the Ways of the Imagination*, 2nd ed. (Boston: Houghton Mifflin, 1930), 42.

7 'Unsigned Review', *The British Critic*, 14 (October 1799): 364–369; 364–365.

8 James C. McKusick, *Green Writing: Romanticism and Ecology*, 2nd ed. (New York: Palgrave Macmillan, 2010), 37–41.

9 Kenneth MacLean, *Agrarian Age: A Background for Wordsworth* (New Haven: Yale University Press, 1950), 83. MacLean provides contextual information on Wordsworth's opposition to the enclosure of common lands in Grasmere, citing a local informant: 'It was all along of him [Wordsworth] that Grasmere folks have their Common open. Ye may ga now reet up to sky over Grisedale, wi'out laying leg to fence, and all through him' (21).

10 A similar act of usurpation occurs in 'Goody Blake, and Harry Gill', another poem from *LB* (1798).

CHAPTER 13

Rhyming Revolutionaries: Lyrical Ballads *in America*

Joel Pace

This chapter focuses on James Humphreys, the publisher of the 1802 Philadelphia edition of *Lyrical Ballads*, and examines many aspects of the text itself, such as the book's material form, price, date and place of issue. It considers how Humphreys' involvement in the American Revolution affected the political charge of the poems and how he used the *Ballads* and other works published by his press to critique and alter the course of the new nation. Humphreys was as concerned with people being disenfranchised during Jefferson's tenure as president as Wordsworth and Coleridge were with people being disenfranchised during George III's reign as king.

The questions *Lyrical Ballads* raises about the voices of everyday people also pertain pressingly to the present day. This chapter is thus framed by the continuing relevance of the *Ballads* to America, particularly regarding the ability of poetics to shape politics. The connection between artistic forms of representation and the construction of American national identity extends from the eighteenth century right through to the twenty-first. We can see this in Lin-Manuel Miranda's *Hamilton: An American Musical* which – like Humphreys' edition of the *Lyrical Ballads* – draws on the power of rhyming songs to raise questions about diversity and representation in the United States. Miranda and Humphreys alike drew on Alexander Hamilton's legacy not only as one of the founding fathers of the American Constitution and a member of Washington's cabinet, but also as an opponent of later presidents and the direction in which they were taking America. Miranda's musical then extends this critique of later presidents all the way up to the present administration.

When Vice-President-elect, Mike Pence, attended a November 2016 performance of *Hamilton*, Miranda and the cast seized the opportunity to push aside the veil of history and directly share concerns, choosing not to leave it to chance that he gleaned the message from the content of the musical and the story of its eponymous hero. At the end of the performance, as Pence rose from his seat in New York City's Richard Rodgers Theatre, he was asked to stop in the name of love by Brandon Victor Dixon, who plays Aaron Burr, 'I see you're walking out, but I hope you will hear us just a few more moments. There's nothing to boo here,' he continued, breaking from the prepared speech to address the audience's response to Pence; 'we're all here sharing a story of love':

> We, sir, we are the diverse America who are alarmed and anxious that your new administration will not protect us – our planet, our children, our parents – or defend us and uphold our inalienable rights, sir. But we truly hope that this show has inspired you to uphold our American values and to work on behalf of all of us. All of us. Again, we truly thank you for sharing this show. This wonderful American story told by a diverse group of men [and] women of different colors, creeds, and orientations.[1]

At the heart of this statement as well as of the musical itself – a hip hop rendering of Alexander Hamilton's life, featuring a multicultural cast portraying the founding fathers and mothers – is a question that the eponymous hero himself raised about the new government he was helping to frame: to what extent are the best interests of all Americans represented by the president and vice president? Hamilton was as anxious about Thomas Jefferson and Aaron Burr's administration as Dixon is about Donald Trump and Mike Pence's.

Dixon's address implies that *Hamilton* is a microcosm of what America should be: diverse voices functioning harmoniously as one through successful representation. The musical features not only an ethnically diverse cast portraying Burr, Jefferson, Washington and other male European American leaders, but also women in prominent roles with powerful voices, such as the Schuyler sisters:

ANGELICA   I've been reading *Common Sense* by Thomas Paine
              So men say that I'm intense or I'm insane
              You want a revolution? I want a revelation
              So listen to my declaration
ELIZA/ANGELICA/PEGGY   'We hold these truths to be self-evident
              That all men are created equal'
ANGELICA   And when I meet Thomas Jefferson
COMPANY   Unh!
ANGELICA   I'm 'a compel him to include women in the sequel!'[2]

Hamilton critiques the failure of representation by the Constitution in enshrining slavery and only giving authority and protection to property-owning white males. Not only does the diversity of the cast represent the (trans)nation(al) writ small, but so, too, does the diverse collective of writers led by Lin-Manuel Miranda, who identifies LatinX, black and white. For Miranda, the problematic elements of the 'America First' agenda are underscored by the Trump administration's devoting greater and more timely humanitarian aid to remedy hurricane damage in Texas and Florida than in Puerto Rico, the US territory where Miranda's parents were born: 'if the response of the American government were commensurate to the response of the American people, we'd be on the road to recovery so much faster'.[3] Miranda turns to music to comment on the ambiguity of Puerto Rico's status as neither a state nor a colony: in *Hamilton*'s hip hop, the measures count the voices of those on the island whose voices still are not counted or measured as votes. Miranda remixes syncopation, call and response, contrapuntal melodies with classical music to bring about harmony by providing a counterpoint to colonialism's constructs of race, rights, revolutions, religion, (taxation without) representation, reform, reflexivity and Romanticism.

Poetry of and for the People

Like Lin-Manuel Miranda and Brandon Victor Dixon, William Wordsworth and Samuel Taylor Coleridge sought to use rhyming verses in the language of everyday people to effect poetical and political change through a diverse array of speakers. The 'Preface' to *Lyrical Ballads* contains a poetical manifesto that is very similar to the words penned by Jefferson and sampled by Miranda:

> When in the course of human events, it becomes necessary ... to assume among the Powers of the Earth, the separate and equal station to which the laws of *Nature and Nature's God* entitle them, a decent respect to the Opinions of Mankind requires that they should declare the causes which impel them to the separation.
>   We hold these truths to be self-evident, that all Men are created equal, that *they are endowed by their Creator with certain unalienable rights*.[4]

The 'Preface' to *Lyrical Ballads* was also written to buttress its own revolution, in which there is a break with the poetry of aristocratic predecessors, and a democratic focus on the common woman and man, who are also entitled to unalienable rights. In the 1800 'Preface', Wordsworth declares the causes that impel him to separate himself from the poetical traditions of the past. He tells his readers that:

> to treat the subject with ... clearness and coherence ... it would be necessary ... to give a full account of the present state of public taste ... which again could not be determined ... without retracing the revolutions, not of literature alone, but likewise of society itself. (*LB* p. 96)

Wordsworth continues:

> I should be oppressed with no dishonorable melancholy, had I not a deep
> impression of certain *inherent and indestructible qualities of the human
> mind* ... and did I not further add to this impression a belief, that the
> time is approaching, when ... evil will be systematically opposed by men of
> greater powers, and with far more distinguished success. (*LB* p. 100)

Wordsworth's 'Preface' makes clear that he views *poetical* and *political*
revolutions as inextricably linked attempts to make outwardly manifest
the divine qualities of human minds. The 'Preface' is the declaration of
equality for the citizens of the *Ballads*: a Native American woman, an old
huntsman, a child with Downs syndrome and many others who were
marginalized in the Atlantic world. The *Ballads* themselves seek to be
voices of these characters, Wordsworth's and Coleridge's attempt to represent the under-represented.

Wordsworth and Coleridge were not the only ones to harness the power
of poetry to represent the nation in microcosm and critique its shortcomings. James Humphreys published the 1802 American edition of *Lyrical
Ballads* (which presented the complete contents of the 1798 and 1800
editions in one binding) as a means of entering into political debate and
articulating a middle ground between two divergent visions of America:
Alexander Hamilton's strong federal government, on the one hand, and
President Jefferson's agrarian republic that proclaimed to represent power
to the people, on the other. As Humphreys' publications during this time
show, he did not believe the Jefferson administration provided adequate
protection of the rights of African Americans, Native Americans, women
and other disenfranchised groups.

In addition to being a military battle, the American Revolution was also
a war of words. The politics of printing is illustrated by the American
typefounder Abel Buell, who led a mob that destroyed the lead statue of
George III on New York City's Bowling Green. When the statue was
found in Buell's home, he commented that 'as bullets or type, his Majesty
should be turned to a useful purpose, and make an impression'.[5] Among
the primary battle rappers, so to speak, of the American Revolution is
Thomas Paine, whose political pamphlet spread rapidly through the
colonies, selling over 500,000 copies in only three months. It was printed
by William Bradford, the patriot-publisher, who had taught Humphreys
the trade. Just as Hamilton opposed Jefferson but eventually came to
support him, so, too, did James Humphreys oppose American independence before he put the might of his press behind publications that would
hold the new nation accountable to its revolutionary promise(s).

Therefore, he did not side with his mentor Bradford but sought to press-gang the colonists into his Majesty's service by issuing a rejoinder called *Strictures on Paine's Common Sense* (1776), which argued that the action that Paine would have America take against England 'would resemble the conduct of a rash ... stripling, who should call his mother a d_mn-d b___ch, swear he had no relation to her, and *attempt* to knock her down'.[6] It was a risky manoeuvre on his part to publish it, as nearly all copies of the New York printing were seized and burned by advocates of the Revolution.

Humphreys' edition, however, was purchased by thousands of his fellow Philadelphians. Charles Inglis, the clergyman who wrote the pamphlet, was forced from New York where his church lay in ashes. In Philadelphia, Humphreys continued to raise the ire of the patriots by printing other Loyalist manifestos such as *The Political Family* (1776) by Isaac Hunt (father of Leigh). Isaac Hunt, *The Political Family: or a Discourse ... American Colonies*. (Philadelphia: James Humphreys, 1775). This publication was sold at an affordable price and dedicated 'to the worthy merchants, farmers, and mechanics of the province of Pennsylvania'; it voiced a concern that Hamilton would later echo over the economic consequences of severing ties with England. Originally a thesis written for what is now the University of Pennsylvania, the work was rejected because of its Loyalist politics. Isaac Hunt was dragged through the streets by the Patriots and, only because of his extraordinary eloquence, narrowly escaped being tarred and feathered.

Both Loyalists and Patriots used political symbols in printed texts to reinforce their causes. The most commonly reprinted plate by the latter was Paul Revere's engraving of the Boston Massacre. Humphreys swore his allegiance to the Crown in print by publishing a newspaper that displayed his own name and the King's Arms on its front page. As a compositor, he sometimes would place a political image on a random page of text, such as marking his *Works of Laurence Stern* with a Loyalist symbol (V. 93). The political markings he employed were not only typographic but also textual. The works by Inglis and Hunt hinge upon the metaphor of family: America as the disobedient and thus disrespectful son of England, a reversal of Paine's depiction of England as the abusive, neglectful parent country. Among the arsenal of Loyalist metaphors were not just the familial, but also theological and ecological symbols, such as the title of Humphreys' edition of William Smith's *The American Vine, a Sermon, Preached in Christ-Church, Philadelphia, Before the Honourable Continental Congress, July 20th, 1775. Being the Day Recommended by Them for a General Fast throughout the United English Colonies of America*. He published several other sermons that delineated a divine unity between Britain

THE

POLITICAL FAMILY:

OR A

DISCOURSE,

POINTING OUT THE

RECIPROCAL ADVANTAGES,

Which flow from an uninterrupted Union between
GREAT-BRITAIN and her AMERICAN COLONIES.

By ISAAC HUNT, ESQUIRE.

NUMB. I.

IF WE STRIKE, WE BREAK.

PHILADELPHIA:
PRINTED, BY JAMES HUMPHREYS, JUNIOR,

M DCC LXXV.

Figure 1   Title page of Isaac Hunt's *Political Family*, from the collections of the American
Antiquarian Society.

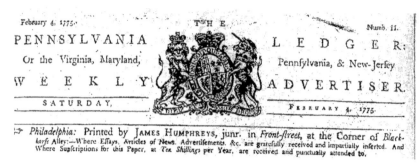

Figure 2   Front page of the *Pennsylvania Ledger*, from the collections of the American
Antiquarian Society.

and America. The fact that Humphreys stood for freedom, but not war,
was made clear by his 1774 edition of Joseph Priestley's *Address to
Protestant Dissenters on Public Liberty*, which upbraided the violent measures to which the American Colonies resorted. Thus, it was only a matter
of time until his opinions were attacked and, when they were, the blow was
swift and devastating. The *Pennsylvania Evening Post* issued an article that
rebuked Humphreys' Tory views and asked that his press be silenced. The
article makes the point that:

> amongst other implements of war, the *pen* and *printing-press* are not the
> least important. It is true they break no bones and shed no blood, but they
> can instigate others to do both; and, by influencing the minds of the
> multitude, can perhaps do more towards gaining a point than the best rifle
> gun or the sharpest bayonet. (Pennsylvania Evening Post, Front Page, 16.
> November 1776)

The article continues:

> The printer of the *Pennsylvania Ledger* must be . . . a well-wisher to the enemies
> of his country, commonly called a *Tory* . . . [W]ould not the Council of Safety
> of this state be very justifiable in silencing a press whose weekly labors
> manifestly tend to dishearten our troops [and] . . . throw disgust on the friends
> of America . . . [T]he public ought at least to shew their resentment against such
> an insidious enemy, by refusing to take a newspaper fraught with mischief, and
> continually aiming at the demolition of their peace. (*Evening Post*, Front Page)

Humphreys and his wife were forced to leave Philadelphia, narrowly
escaping the fifty armed men who surrounded his house and arrested both
his brother and father. Notwithstanding this, once the British troops
occupied the city, he returned and was made 'Printer to the King', and
under this title resumed the publication of his Loyalist paper. When these

troops retreated, Humphreys accompanied them. His press had been confiscated, and he was found guilty of high treason.

Lyrical Ballads in Philadelphia: Joseph Dennie, James Humphreys and the Politics of the (Printing) Press

During the remainder of the war, Humphreys removed to a Loyalist stronghold in Nova Scotia, where he became the publisher of the *Nova-Scotia Packet: and General Advertiser.* After the war, he returned to Philadelphia and attempted to re-establish his connections in the publishing trade by starting a newspaper; however, the memory of his Loyalist *Pennsylvania Ledger* was still fresh in his readers' minds and the project failed. Searching for a way to reconnect with the printing community, he found a friend in Joseph Dennie, editor of the successful newspaper the *Port Folio.* Humphreys relied on Dennie not only for his political reintegration into Philadelphia but also for creating a demand for the poetry of Wordsworth and Coleridge among readers in the new Republic. Therefore, before we discuss Humphreys' 1802 edition of *Lyrical Ballads*, it is necessary to examine how Dennie managed to create a taste for these poems in Philadelphia.

Dennie's strategy worked well: he de-emphasized the Englishness of the poets and poetry and underlined the similarities among their views and those held by two of the city's most powerful populations: American revolutionaries and Quakers. In the proposal for *Port Folio*, he aligns the newspaper with the principles of the Society of Friends through reference to the kind of paper used in its printing:

> No sonorous promises are made, and no magnificence of style attempted. The paper is neither to be wire-woven, nor hot pressed, and it certainly, in more senses than one, shall not be cream-coloured; but, in a plain dress of Quaker simplicity.[7]

He printed his newspaper on inexpensive laid paper that was beige-coloured and of a rough texture. It is vital to note that Humphreys' *Lyrical Ballads* was printed on almost identical paper that was more than likely made at the mill of the Gilpin brothers, sons of a Philadelphia Quaker merchant.[8] The typography of Humphreys' edition indicates that Wordsworth's and Coleridge's poems were presented to the American public in a 'plain state of Quaker simplicity' that would have corresponded to the unadorned style and language of the poems. The paper also intimates that, like the *Port Folio*, the edition was subtly marketed to Quaker readership.

Wordsworth and Coleridge could not have had a better introduction to Pennsylvania, a state named after its Quaker founder. William Penn himself was against the reading of romances, as he considered them morally reprehensible, and for this very reason the Society of Friends avoided drama as well as music. It is, however, due to the politics of its poetics that the *Ballads* was popular among them. Poems such as 'The Convict' and 'The Dungeon' were certainly in line with the political activism of the Philadelphia Quakers. The group not only succeeded in getting the legislature of Pennsylvania to reform the criminal code in 1786, but also formed a society for 'alleviating the miseries of public prisoners'.[9] By 1803, Wordsworth had become a poet whose unornamented poetic style and American publications embodied the austerity of the meeting places and dress of the Society of Friends. He was also a moral guide to the religious group. Dennie's editorial comments, which precede the reprinting of 'A Whirl Blast from behind the Hill', note that Wordsworth has:

> a rare talent of remarking many of the minuter operations of Nature, and of describing them at once in the simplest, and yet most interesting manner. The use that he derives from his observation of a rural circumstance, is a good lesson to those who walk in the forest.[10]

Dennie's assessment hints at the connection between Wordsworth's deriving divine truths from the natural world and the Quaker practice of revelation through 'inner light'. This concept was conceived by the founder of the Society of Friends, George Fox, who spent much time fasting, reading his Bible and receiving visions or revelations in nature. 'A Whirl Blast from behind the Hill' realises this concept in its final four lines:

> Oh! grant me, Heaven, a heart at ease,
> That I may never cease to find,
> Even in appearances like these
> Enough to nourish and to stir my mind!
> (Lines 24–27)

It is also worth noting that because the American edition was published as two volumes in one, it was not only more portable than its English equivalent, but it was also compact enough to be taken into nature and read.[11] This type of diction was also present in other Humphreys' publications such as Robert Bloomfield's *The Farmer's Boy*, which is praised in an advertisement for its 'true pastoral imagery and simplicity'.[12] *The Farmer's Boy* also contained views on nature that were similar to Wordsworth's and Fox's, particularly in the character Giles whose book of learning was nature. This idea of connecting the *Ballads* to the revelations of the natural world as well as to social justice begins with the Quakers in Pennsylvania, but extends to Massachusetts, where the Transcendentalists were inspired by Wordsworth and Coleridge to see nature as a text of divine truths, the preservation of the environment and civil liberties as chief among them.

Dennie did not, of course, single-handedly create the penchant for Wordsworth among Quakers, but he worked hard to increase what was already a transatlantic audience. In London, for instance, Thomas Clarkson's *Portraiture of Quakerism* features 'Expostulation and Reply' and notes that:

> William Wordsworth, in his instructive Poems, has described this teaching by external objects in consequence of his impressions from a higher power ... in so beautiful and simple a manner, that I cannot do otherwise than make an extract from them in this place.[13]

Politically, the Quakers were levellers and, as William Hazlitt notes of Wordsworth in *Spirit of the Age*, 'his muse ... is a levelling one'.[14] In this capacity the ideas expressed in his 'Preface' as well as Jefferson's Declaration would have appealed to them. The aesthetic of simplicity was not only realised by the material form of the *Ballads*. It is also laid out in the 'Preface' where Wordsworth notes that he chooses the language of labourers because 'they convey their feelings and notions in simple and unelaborated expressions' (*LB* 97). Wordsworth's ideas on language are very similar to those of Fox who, as Clarkson points out, thought that the expressions then in use had 'many censurable defects' which made them 'false representatives of the ideas they were intended to convey' (*Portraiture of Quakerism* I. 298). It is worth noting that Jefferson also held similar beliefs on language. In his *Notes on the State of Virginia* Jefferson claimed that the natural and pure emotions and simplicity of a speech by Logan (a Native American chief) to his people made it one of the best speeches in history. Wordsworth's 'Preface' reinforces the authority of every individual, for according to the 'Preface,' feelings are a person's 'stay and support, and if he sets them aside in one instance he may be induced to repeat this act until his mind shall lose all confidence in itself and becomes utterly debilitated' (*LB* p. 113). In this passage Wordsworth echoes concepts similar to Fox's 'inner light' and Jefferson's Declaration. He advocates universal suffrage for the internal government of the individual. For Coleridge, Hamilton, Humphreys and Wordsworth the question is not only whether words are accurate representations of thoughts, but also whether democracy's and monarchy's rulers are truly representatives of the people and their rights.

An example of the lasting effect of Wordsworth's poetry on Quakers is given full testimony in a letter written to him by Henry Reed, whose Philadelphia edition of Wordsworth (1837) sold thousands of copies nationwide. The missive, sent on 29 November 1841, recalls an American farmer,

> a very plain man—well nigh eighty years old—a kind hearted Quaker, little acquainted with books. One day at dinner, much to our surprise he recited with perfect accuracy several stanzas of '*The Pet Lamb*', which seemed to have taken quite a hold on his feelings and his fancy, uncultivated as the latter certainly was ...[15]

Dennie's *Port Folio* aligned itself with a Quaker readership and served as a mouthpiece for Alexander Hamilton's politics and Wordsworth's poetics, a combination he had tried with success in an earlier publication. Dennie began his career editing the *Farmer's Museum*, which became the Federalist newspaper of New Hampshire. Indeed, Wordsworth's first appearance in print in America (by an American press) is in a 1799 issue of the *Museum* that reprints 'Goody Blake and Harry Gill'. Dennie's move from New Hampshire to Philadelphia was political: it was prompted by a Federalist appointment. He became personal secretary to Timothy Pickering, President Adam's secretary of state. Moreover, his connections in the publishing trade were also linked to this party, as he later took an editorial position on the Federalist *United States Gazette*. With Dennie's help, then, Humphreys found a way not only for the patriots to accept him, but also to make his own peace with, and way into, the new Republic. Dennie's support of Alexander Hamilton was key, for Hamilton recommended that the US government retain a connection to England through trade in order to underpin economic prosperity. Concern over losing this connection is one of the reasons Humphreys was against the Revolution and published Isaac Hunt's book, which anticipated Hamilton's stance. President Jefferson, on the other hand, sought to support the French by declaring war on England, which Humphreys felt would have disastrous consequences for America.

It is of the utmost significance that one of the key texts Humphreys published to re-enter American politics and continue his dissent was his 1802 edition of *Lyrical Ballads*, a British text that contained similar tenets to the revolutionary ideals of America. Like Dennie, Humphreys used typography to convey messages both religious and political. Humphreys subtly declared his allegiance by printing *Lyrical Ballads* on paper that was watermarked with the US Federalist eagle, an endorsement of the new country, but a critique of its current president.[16] This paper would certainly have had a political charge as Americans started making their own in defiance of the tax the king had placed on imported stock. The very books that Humphreys sells also reflect both his allegiance to, as well as his concerns about, the new American government, particularly his edition of the *Debates and Other Proceedings of the Virginia Convention on the Adoption of the Federal Constitution.*

Dennie also introduced Humphreys to Joseph Groff, a Federalist who was able to help him set the type for an American edition of the *Ballads.* Although Dennie and Groff saw the poems as espousing their Federalist views, they also read sentiments in the poems that both aligned with and critiqued Jeffersonian Republicanism. It is, then, no mystery why a little more than a month after the American edition was issued, the newspaper informed its readers that the:

> popularity of Wordsworth's Ballads increases every hour. We are confident that Messrs. Humphreys and Groff . . . will be amply remunerated for their care and expense in publishing a complete and neat edition of verses, which *will outlive their century.*[17]

Figure 3   The watermark in Wordsworth's copy of the 1802 Philadelphia *Lyrical Ballads,* from the collection of the Wordsworth Library, Grasmere.

The poems were written by men who, in the not too distant past, had harboured Republican or 'democratic' ideals. Coleridge gave vent to these views in his 1795 lectures in Bristol, and Wordsworth reached similar conclusions in revolutionary France under the tutelage of Beaupuy, captain among the Republican forces. Coleridge had once planned to move to the new American Republic, which he assumed would be the ideal environment for realising human perfection through democratic decision making and living. If America were meant to be the ideal place for writing pantisocratic literature, would it not also be the perfect place for reading it as well? Many of Wordsworth's and Coleridge's early political sentiments can be traced in the 'Preface', and it is thus understandable how this text would have garnered a more favourable and immediate reception in a newly founded Republic. Wordsworth himself, in a letter to Henry Reed (19 August 1837), makes it clear that he considers his US audience to be among the ideal readers of the *Ballads*:

> It is gratifying to one whose aim as an author has been to reach the hearts of his fellow-creatures of all ranks and in all stations to find that he has succeeded in any quarter; and still more must he be gratified to learn that he has pleased in a distant country men of simple habits and cultivated taste, who are at the same time widely acquainted with literature. (Broughton 4)

Well before Wordsworth penned this letter, Dennie and Humphreys had taken it upon themselves to cultivate the taste of American readers of 'simple habits' by acquainting them with the poetry of the *Ballads*. Their reasons for doing so stem from a common belief in classical republicanism: both viewed their presses as ways to educate Americans, thereby creating good citizens of the Republic. At a time when the appearance and price of a publication carried a political charge, Humphreys' *Ballads* (which contained the complete contents of the 1798 and 1800 English editions) cost only a little over a dollar, or a day's wages for a labourer. In England, a labourer would have had to part with a week's wages to buy the 1800 London edition. All of the early English editions made luxurious use of paper space, printing only eighteen lines per page at a time when paper was so scarce that London periodicals were asking readers to contribute unwanted rags to paper mills, and offering monetary rewards for anyone who could find a new material for paper. The American edition has more than a hundred fewer pages than its English equivalent and, more importantly, the revolutionary poems appear in a new typeface. Humphreys' proposals for printing books confirm that he carefully saw to every aspect of the book's production; for instance, one of his 1803 proposals states, 'the following work is now in the Press printing on a handsome new Type purchased especially for the Purpose'.[18]

On 23 January 1775, the Pennsylvania convention 'resolved, unanimously that as printing types are now made to a considerable degree of perfection in Germantown; it is recommended to the printers to use such type in preference to any that may hereafter be imported' (Annenberg 28). In 1802, the typefounders Binny and Ronaldson had become, with Jefferson's encouragement, the largest typefoundry on the continent. American type in many ways corresponded with the aesthetic of the ballads in that it was meant to be simple in its style. This point is illustrated by an advertisement to the *Pennsylvania Mercury* in which the printers:

> beg leave to acquaint ... the public, that the types with which this PAPER is printed are of AMERICAN manufacture; and ....We are sensible that in terms of elegance, they are somewhat inferior to those imported from England, but we flatter ourselves that the rustic manufacturers of America will prove more grateful to the Patriotic age, than the more finished production of Europe.[19]

Like Humphreys' American eagle watermark, these new typefaces were an appeal to everyday people over aristocracy. These bibliographical symbols present a second set of signs and signifiers, a palimpsest that reinforces many of the tenets of the primary text, one that paves the way for a smooth reception of the poems and their printer in post-revolutionary America.

The typography of the English edition, to the contrary, worked *against* its content. The London *Ballads* did not represent a radical break with the past, typographically speaking: the early editions appeared in Caslon's 1734 typeface which looked antiquated compared with Bell's 1789 modern face. In America, where printing presses were abundant and paper was cheap and untaxed, print could more accurately be called the voice of the common person: newspapers of the time were replete with articles signed 'a Farmer' or 'a Citizen'. The simplicity of the *Ballads* was noted by John Sargent (later a Whig candidate for vice president) who was a twenty-three-year-old politician when the poems were published in Philadelphia:

> I remember when some of his [Wordsworth's] earliest (small pieces) appeared. They were so simple in their dress, so humble in their topics, so opposite to the pomp and strut of what had been the poetry of the times *immediately* preceding, that they were a good deal of a puzzle. Yet, it was manifest, even then, that they touched a kindred chord in the heart, and I remember a conversation about them *in the first four or five years of the present century*, in which their power was acknowledged. (Broughton 11)[20]

The political similarities between Jefferson's Declaration and Wordsworth's 'Preface' did not escape Humphreys' notice. Although he critiques
Jeffersonian Republicanism through the watermark of a Federalist eagle, he
is also sceptical of Hamilton's centring power in a strong federal government, a national bank and wealthy citizens. On this issue he leans more
towards Jefferson's desire to locate authority in the agrarian landowners
and states. Yet, Humphreys is also critical of Jefferson's notion of a nation
of property-owning farmers because, like Dixon more than a century later,
he is concerned as to whether or not the president and vice president will
protect *all* Americans. For Humphreys, the works he publishes (*Lyrical
Ballads* or *Hamilton*) represent his own political statement: they are voices
that he orchestrates to make a collective statement about civil liberties of
the disenfranchised taking precedence over increasing the power of the
privileged.

Humphreys targeted his text for consumption by Federalists, Republic-
ans, Quakers, and also by those interested in science and medicine. He
used his press to educate all Americans about scientific topics. Such a
readership found the *Ballads* interesting, insofar as many of the poems are
about unusual states of mind, particularly 'Goody Blake and Harry Gill',
which draws from Erasmus Darwin's *Zoonomia* (Darwin being Charles
Darwin's grandfather). Humphreys not only sold Darwin's *Zoonomia* and
Botanic Garden but he also kept his shop fully stocked with 'Genuine
Patent Medicines'. It is worth noting that among Wordsworth's American
visitors to his home in Rydal Mount were physicians, professors of science
and reformers who had read the *Ballads* and sought advice from the poet
on ways to ameliorate the conditions of the disadvantaged in their home
country. The conflation of Humphreys' audiences is represented by
George Bacon Wood, Philadelphia Quaker and professor of materia
medica at what is now the University of Pennsylvania, who in July
1836 visited Wordsworth. Humphreys himself had studied medicine at
this same university before he took up printing, and his publications make
manifest his continued interest in the acquisition and dissemination of
medical knowledge. Humphreys' decision to print *Lyrical Ballads* was not
arbitrary, nor was it governed solely by a quest for profit. He also felt it was
his duty as a publisher to issue literary 'vaccinations' against society's ills.
In his edition of the *Town and Country Friend and Physician*, he informs
his readers of 'his motives in handing . . . this plain and compact form to
the public: there is not a means in the hands of the affluent by which solid
comfort can be more . . . easily administered to the infirm and wretched,
than in the proper disposal of such books among them'.[21]

Humphreys viewed the *Ballads* as part of this ministry and advertised the collection of poems, along with other medical texts, on the last pages of the *Town and Country Friend and Physician* and other publications. As Wordsworth states in the 'Preface,' the ballads are concerned with portraying the human mind in a 'state of excitement' (*LB* 97). Many of the poem's speakers and subjects, such as the mad mother, have symptoms of what would now be diagnosed as clinical depression. The remedy recommended by Wordsworth and Coleridge, in poems such as 'The Convict' and 'The Dungeon', is communion with nature. Humphreys agreed with the concept of nature as an elixir of mental and physical health. One of his other publications is geared for those who are 'solicitous to improve their HEALTH, and to adopt the parental Hints of Nature rather than submit to the precarious Relief of Art' (*Town and Country* 323). Many ballads contain a celebration of nature that makes reading the poems therapeutic, producing a cathartic effect on the minds and emotions of readers. This reader–text dialogue is confirmed not only by Wordsworth's 'Preface' but also by Humphreys' *Town and Country Friend and Physician*, in which the author states: 'I recommend it [reading] as a medicine, which, by it's [*sic*] effects on the mind, will secure you from the attacks of some diseases which really originate there' (iii). In his discussion of 'Goody Blake and Harry Gill', Wordsworth reveals that 'the power of the human imagination is sufficient to produce such changes even in our physical nature as might almost appear miraculous' (*LB* 112). This aspect of Wordsworth's influence in America reaches its height in the mid 1800s in the work of Dorothea Lynde Dix; she was inspired by the *Ballads* to establish residential treatment for the mentally ill and disabled in beautiful, therapeutic natural settings, and to petition the Massachusetts legislature to enforce laws against those holding them in prisons, dungeons and other inhumane conditions.

In one set of advertisements in which Humphreys markets the *Ballads*, he notes that his publications are '[a]ll calculated to instruct and amuse, and to instil and disseminate those Principles which cement society, and on which its general Happiness is founded'.[22] Often Humphreys' means of producing this effect was by criticising American society in his publications. For instance, Wordsworth addresses the effects of the American Revolution on the mind in 'The Female Vagrant'. He wrote the poem when, according to him, 'The American war was still fresh in memory'.[23] This poem brought American readers into sympathy with British soldiers and families, who at the mercy of American forces witnessed 'Murder, by the ghastly gleam, and Rape' (*LB* Line 158). The *Ballads* and 'Preface' also

indirectly address other wrongdoings of the American military, particularly
the inhumane treatment of Native Americans. The thrust of Wordsworth's
prose and poetry would have both coalesced with and critiqued the ideas of
President Jefferson, who believed that his new Republic would be successful only if the balance of power were held by its farmers and planters and
those who earned a living through honourable toil.

Lyrical Ballads *and Democratic Principles*

Many of the *Ballads*, particularly 'Goody Blake and Harry Gill' and
'Simon Lee', promote a clear message of loving and helping thy neighbour,
a message with a particular resonance for a nation where Native Americans
were being forcibly removed from lands that would be worked by slaves.
Jefferson's Louisiana Purchase from Napoleon doubled the land size of the
United States, a move supported by Hamilton. This was land that Jefferson wished to set aside for his pantisocratic agricultural nation. However,
such a political gesture reverses the action of ballads such as the 'Female
Vagrant', in which the aristocratic master of the mansion buys or starves
out the cottage owners of the surrounding property. It is also possible to
read the poem with King George as the mansion owner and the Americans
as those being starved out by excessive taxation; or with Jefferson as the
villain buying out the parental land of the Native Americans who, as a
result of this purchase, were subject to genocide and forced west of the
Mississippi. (A similar property debate can be read into 'The Oak and the
Broom', particularly in the lines 'why should I wish to roam? / This spot is
my paternal home' (Lines 65–66)).

In 'The Complaint' and 'Ruth', Wordsworth portrays Native Americans
as lawless and savage, reinforcing stereotypes about them that are present
in the racist pseudoscience of Johan Friedrich Blumenbach, Samuel
George Morton and other phrenologists on both sides of the Atlantic.
The 'Preface' ruminates on how taste is formed by the mind from the
moulds of society's mores. In doing so, this document creates a process
that empowers the reader to identify the instances in which poetry (including that of the volume itself as well as that of its predecessors) can be linked
to pre-existing racist social norms, called into question, and seen to be at
odds with the invocation of equality of the 'Preface'. For instance, Wordsworth mentions that he accompanies 'the last struggles of a *human
being* . . . in the Poem of the FORSAKEN INDIAN,' and yet the poem
itself offers a stereotypical depiction of the very population it is seeking to
represent. (*LB* p. 98; emphasis added). Jefferson's *Notes on the State of*

Virginia outline a white supremacist taxonomy by placing European Americans above Native Americans, whom he places above African Americans. The portrayal of Native Americans in the *Ballads* seems to advocate Jefferson's notion that they and their land should be cultivated, and yet the portrayal of hereditary rights in the property issues of certain ballads offers a critique of an America, which is forcing Indians off 'its' land. When a group of Cherokee Indians applied to be citizens of the United States, Jefferson refused to grant them their property and this status, unless they stopped hunting and began to farm the land. In 1801, Humphreys published other works that championed the rights of Native Americans, arguing against what would become known as 'Manifest Destiny' by printing works such as Charles Crawford's *Essay on the Propagation of the Gospel, in Which There Are Numerous Facts and Arguments Adduced to Prove That ... the Indians in America Are Descended from the Ten Tribes.* This essay also targets those using Christianity to buttress the slave trade by advocating that the Gospel be taught to slaves and that the evil institution of slavery be abolished.

Humphreys' press also advocated universal equality, and was particularly concerned with African Americans, Native Americans and women. Humphreys published many texts written by and for women, including Jane Marcet's *Conversations on Chymistry* (1806), which she wrote expressly for 'the female sex, whose education is seldom calculated to prepare their minds for the abstract ideas of scientific language'.[24] Marcet continues to note that in writing the work she was often 'checked in her progress by the apprehension, that such an attempt might be considered by some ... as unsuited to the ordinary pursuits of her sex' (ii–iii). By publishing the works of women, Humphreys achieved more successful representation than did Jeffersonian America, where women had no political authority, or the literary republic of the *Ballads*, where women are at best former versions of the poets ('Tintern Abbey') and at worst mad mothers, potential murderers (Martha Ray), or spectral presences, such as Life-in-Death.

It is easy to see how the *Ballads* would have been read as making a very strong contribution to the ongoing debate over the democratization of rights as well as authorship. The best illustration of Wordsworth's contribution is the fact that his use of language is censured in Robert Rose's parody of Wordsworth's 'Preface'. Not only is this among the first American parodies of the *Ballads*, but it also predates all published English parodies as well. After Rose read the Ballads, he sent a parody entitled 'A Lyrical Ballad' to the editor of the *Port Folio*; the lampoon is prefaced by an explanatory letter: 'I never once had the idea that I was a poet', confessed Rose,

> till the other day, when I got a very pretty book to read, and found, that the author and I felt exactly alike. I always thought that to make verses and them like was right down hard; but it an't so at all. You wouldn't, perhaps, believe it, sir, but I declare I can write as fast as any of your correspondents; besides, what I write is so vastly natural, that I'm sure you'll like it. I'm sure its [sic] better than writing about things one don't understand. However, as it an't right to say too much for one's self, you shall have a specimen of my abilities.[25]

His preface parodies Wordsworth's and the politicised diction of the *Ballads*, and attempts to insinuate that the realms of poetical and political composition are beyond the grasp and language of the working class. Rose's parody is aimed not only at the English author of the *Ballads*, but also at the trends in American language to disrupt grammatical forms and invent new words and conventions. Like Sir Francis Jeffrey, Rose is also scolding Wordsworth for using the language of the working class. The text of Rose's preface is strikingly similar to minstrelsy, which misrepresented African Americans through crude imitation. The speakers of such songs hold nonsense discourse on matters of politics, presenting such issues as incomprehensible to black Americans. The parody is, thus, indicative of American anxiety surrounding opening up politics and poetics to all without regard to class or race. African American spirituals testified to the power of everyday language long before Wordsworth's 'Preface', and long after Wordsworth, *Hamilton* and other hip hop–based protest poetry and spoken word draw on the popularity of the genre and accessibility of the everyday lyrics to keep America accountable to its promises of equality.

Humphreys levelled many criticisms at Jeffersonian America on this issue; particularly in one publication, the author points out that 'if there be an object truly ridiculous in nature, it is an American patriot [Jefferson], signing resolutions of independence (and let me add equality) with one hand, and brandishing a whip over his affrighted slaves with the other'.[26] Humphreys also used works of fiction, such as Maria Edgeworth's *Popular Tales* (1804), to speak to the working classes. Edgeworth herself wrote that she chose the title of her book with the wish that the tales 'may be current beyond circles which are sometimes exclusively considered as polite'.[27] The tale 'The Grateful Negro' is about two neighbouring plantations (England and America), one run by a Mr. Jefferies (Jefferson), who considered slaves an inferior species, and the other by a Mr. Edwards (King George), who planned to emancipate his slaves. In a fictional gesture that prefigures the American Civil War, Jeffries's plantation is eventually burned and destroyed by a violent insurrection. This message had particular resonance with an America that had abolished the anti-slavery clause in the Declaration of Independence, so the Southern delegates would ratify the document. The Quakers had, in 1763, asked their members to 'keep their hands clear of giving encouragement in any shape to the slave-trade; it being evidently destructive of the natural rights of mankind' (Clarkson II. 54). In 1773 Philadelphia had, under the influence of the Quakers, succeeded in passing laws that prohibited the slave trade, and in 1780 Pennsylvania enacted the first gradual emancipation law in the history of America.

   In another of his publications, Humphreys prints an appendix that contains suggestions on passing laws to ameliorate the condition of slaves.[28] Thomas Jefferson heads the list of subscribers to this book, which proves Humphreys' civic humanism that sought to fight tyranny in any political party had made its way into the library of the slave-owning president, the very same one who had penned the anti-slavery clause in an early draft of the Declaration of Independence. Humphreys viewed books as the very things that 'cement[s]' society and this explains his Loyalist efforts to keep America from a revolution he thought would prove harmful. After the war, as a convert of the new American Republic, he enlisted his press in the philanthropic cause of buttressing at times and critiquing at others the directions in which Jeffersonian America was moving. What is of the utmost importance to students and scholars of Wordsworth and Coleridge is that he chose to publish *Lyrical Ballads* as a means of accomplishing this end. It is the crowning achievement of Humphreys' press that Isaiah Thomas, the most renowned printer-patriot of the Revolution, forgives him for his transgressions against the budding country and refers to him as a 'good and accurate printer and a worthy citizen'.[29] Wordsworth's reception in America is wedded to the bibliographical history of this text. As the production and advertising of the American edition attest, this 'earthly casket of immortal verse', politically speaking, 'had voices more than all the winds' (*Prelude* 1805 V. 164, 108). Through Humphreys' endeavours, Wordsworth was able to shake his red coat of English political associations and infiltrate the ranks of patriotic readers. The US texts and contexts created a unique backdrop for the politics and poetics of the *Ballads* and its principal author. The American edition is as politically and religiously charged as its overseas counterpart, and its affordability, portability and typographic simplicity were such that, more so than the early English editions, it corresponded to and realised Wordsworth's ideas and ideals as laid out in the 'Preface'.

Wordsworth's use of rhymed, metered ballads to give a voice to the voiceless places it on a continuum with Miranda's *Hamilton*; however, its failure to represent the disenfranchised accurately connects it both to Humphreys' fear about Jefferson's presidency as well as Dixon's about Trump's. In *Hamilton*, a diverse cast portrays the architects of a nation, and in *Lyrical Ballads*, the founding fathers of Romanticism seek to portray those who are marginalized. In New York, Pence was addressed by representatives of the 'diverse America' that he and Trump had been elected to serve. The *Ballads* as a house of representations is a house divided that raises questions about the ability of two privileged men to represent diverse voices, a question as relevant in 1798 as it is today. At the core of the *Ballads* and *Hamilton* is the belief in the power of poetry to effect change: 'we truly hope that this show has inspired you to uphold our American values and to work on behalf of all of us,' notes Dixon. If his words and Wordsworth's are placed in a call and response, they direct us to a specific 'spot of time': 'we're all here sharing a story of love' 'for this single cause, / That we have all of us one human heart' ('The Old Cumberland Beggar', Lines 145–146). The implied contract between the 'Preface' and the reader is the same as that between *Hamilton* and its audience, or that between the mariner and the wedding guest/reader. It is the one upon which Humphreys' civic humanism depends: that we will be the change, the subject and transitive verb that are missing from the phrase *e pluribus unum*. Miranda issues a call to action in Hamilton's last lyrical ballad, a toast to past, present and future Dreamers:

> What is a legacy?
> It's planting seeds in a garden you never get to see
> I wrote some notes at the beginning of a song someone will sing for me
> America, you great unfinished symphony, you sent for me
> You let me make a difference
> A place where even orphan immigrants
> Can leave their fingerprints and rise up
> I'm running out of time. I'm running, and my time's up
> Wise up. Eyes up
> . . .
> Rise up, rise up, rise up
> . . .
> I'll see you on the other side
> Raise a glass to freedom
>
> ('The World Was Wide Enough')

Endnotes

1 Transcript of the speech is available online: www.bustle.com/articles/196017-transcript-of-hamilton-casts-statement-to-mike-pence-doesnt-read-like-very-rude-harassment

2 Lin-Manuel Miranda, 'The Schuyler Sisters', *Hamilton: An American Musical,* Atlantic Records, 2015.

3 http://variety.com/2017/music/news/lin-manuel-miranda-on-trump-and-puerto-rico-i-dont-run-well-on-anger-1202594163/

4 Opening paragraphs of The Declaration of Independence, emphasis added. See: https://www.archives.gov/founding-docs/declaration

5 Maurice Annenberg, *Typefoundries of America and Their Catalogs* (New Castle, DE: Oak Knoll Press, 1994), 23.

6 Charles Inglis, *The True Interest of America Impartially Stated, in Certain Strictures on a Pamphlet Intitled COMMON SENSE. By an American* (Philadelphia: James Humphreys, 1776), viii. Emphasis added.

7 'Preface' to the *Port Folio* (1801), I. 1, front page.

8 Thomas Gravell and George Miller, *A Catalogue of American Watermarks 1690–1835* (New York: Oak Knoll Press, 1979), 27.

9 See Parts 3–5 of E. Digby Baltzell, *Puritan Boston & Quaker Philadelphia* (London: Routledge, 2017).

10 *Port Folio,* III. 36 (1 October 1803): 288.

11 Wordsworth's copy in the Wordsworth Library, Grasmere, is bound as two volumes, as is Stephen Gill's personal copy. Both have the American eagle watermark.

12 See Dorothy Kilner, *The Rotchfords; or the Friendly Counselor: Designed for the Instruction and Amusement of the Youth of Both Sexes* (Philadelphia: Humphreys and Groff, 1801), 322.

13 Thomas Clarkson, *Portraiture of Quakerism,* 3 vols. (London: Longman, Hurst, Rees, and Orme, 1806), II. 148. Wordsworth was made aware of his popularity with the Quakers by Clarkson, who gave him a copy of this book. I would like to thank Evan Radcliffe for bringing this text to my attention.

14 William Hazlitt, 'Mr. Wordsworth' from *The Spirit of the Age* (1825), in *The Norton Anthology of English Literature*, ed. M. H. Abrams, 6th ed., vol. 2 (New York: W. W. Norton, 1993), 441.

15 Leslie Nathan Broughton, *Wordsworth and Reed* (Ithaca: Cornell University Press, 1933), 59–60.

16 This watermark is reproduced here courtesy of the Wordsworth Library, Grasmere, with special thanks to Robert Woof and Jeff Cowton. The volume 1993, R13.1, from which this photograph has been taken, bears the following inscription: 'To Mr Wordsworth [,] this copy of the first American Edition of his poems – a proof of the early appreciation of them in the United States – is communicated by his affectionate friend (as it is his privilege to call himself) Henry Reed[,] Philadelphia[,] April 1839'.

17 *Port Folio*, II. 8 (27 February 1802): 62.

18 Joshua Montefiore, *Commercial and Notarial Precedents* (Philadelphia: Humphreys and Groff, 1803), 351.

19 This advertisement appears in the Pennsylvania Mercury for 7 April 1775.

20 John Sargent to Henry Reed, Washington, DC, 9 February 1839; second emphasis added.

21 James Humphreys, 'Advertisement', in *Town and Country Friend and Physician* (Philadelphia: Humphreys and Groff, 1803), iii–iv.

22 Patrick Kelley, *Elements of Book-Keeping* (Philadelphia: Humphreys and Groff, 1803), 208.

23 *Wordsworth and Coleridge: Lyrical Ballads*, ed. R. L. Brett and A. R. Jones, 2nd ed. (London: Routledge, 1996), 281.

24 Jane Marcet, *Conversations on Chymistry* (Philadelphia: Humphreys and Groff, 1806), ii–iii.

25 Robert Rose, 'A Lyrical Ballad', *Port Folio*, IV. 33 (Saturday 13 August 1804): 257–258.

26 John Harriott, *Struggles through Life, Exemplified in the Various Travels and Adventures in Europe, Asia, Africa, & America* (Philadelphia: Humphreys and Groff, 1809), 27.

27 Maria Edgeworth, *Popular Tales* (Philadelphia: Humphreys and Goff, 1804), ii.

28 Bryan Edwards, *The History, Civil and Commercial, of the British Colonies in the West Indies*, 4 vols. (Philadelphia: Humphreys and Groff, 1805).

29 Isaiah Thomas, *The History of Printing in America*, 2 vols. (Worcester, MA: I. Thomas, 1810).

CHAPTER 14

The Indigenous Lyrical Ballads

Nikki Hessell

From the early nineteenth century onwards, there was a canon of British Romanticism taking shape in the colonies, which mirrored that of nineteenth-century Britain, and in turn generated responses from indigenous intellectuals in the nineteenth and early twentieth centuries. The indigenous response to British Romanticism was, naturally, shaped by the British and colonial Romantic canon: lots of Byron, Burns, Scott, and Hemans, some Shelley, no Blake and only a little Keats. It was this version of Romanticism that settler and colonising populations took around the world and that became embedded in the new print cultures, libraries and school curricula of diasporic British communities across the globe. From those cultural sites, Romantic literature was then introduced to indigenous peoples, whose assimilation into a Western-style education system, sometimes voluntary but often forced, brought them into contact with the colonists' favourite texts.

Lyrical Ballads is manifestly interested in indigenous peoples, as we see in 'Ruth' and 'The Complaint of the Forsaken Indian Woman'. But were indigenous people interested in *Lyrical Ballads* when they first came into contact with them? Wordsworth and Coleridge featured somewhere in the middle of this list of colonial favourites, less popular than Byron and the other superstars of the nineteenth-century version of British Romanticism, but more established than Blake and other figures who remained marginal until their critical revival in the twentieth century. As a consequence, indigenous responses to *Lyrical Ballads* occur less frequently than responses to other Romantic authors and texts, and far less frequently than responses to the Bible, Shakespeare or John Bunyan. But Wordsworth and Coleridge's volumes remain an interesting intertext for indigenous print culture from the nineteenth century onwards.

In broad terms, indigenous responses to *Lyrical Ballads* take one of three forms: translation into an indigenous language; direct citation of Wordsworth's 'Preface', an individual poem, or the volume as a whole as a motivation for, or corollary to, political and literary efforts within one's own cultures; or an interaction with the broader concerns of *Lyrical Ballads*, such as the attention to common language, nature, childhood, everyday experience, traditional poetic forms and, especially, the development of an autobiographical voice. These responses generate interpretations of *Lyrical Ballads* that can change the way we read the poems today, and prompt us to ask new questions about the volumes and their place within the global Romantic tradition.

Translations: Lyrical Ballads *and Different 'Tongues'*

The creation of new, printed texts in indigenous languages was an essential aspect of the European colonial project in many parts of the world. Driven primarily by missionary activity and the need for Christian texts that could act as persuasive tools for conversion and religious instruction, colonial cultures of print generated orthographies, written alphabets and, ultimately, printed texts of the Bible, hymns and scripture. These texts constituted the first examples of indigenous printing in the Pacific and North America, but took their place alongside long-standing indigenous literacies in a sophisticated range of oral, artistic and performative modes. Indigenous peoples in other colonised regions already had written traditions in their own languages; this was especially true in India, where the earliest written accounts date back more than two thousand years.

While indigenous-language Christian texts were the priority of translators and printers in the British colonial world, they were by no means the only texts to be produced. A wide range of English texts was translated into indigenous languages, including many literary texts. And while missionaries and colonial administrators were among the first to produce printed texts in indigenous languages, they were not the only translators. Skilled bilingual authors were soon emerging among indigenous populations as a result of new colonial education systems. In Aotearoa New Zealand, the continental United States and in Hawai'i, for example, indigenous-language newspapers, many of them run and composed by Māori, First Peoples and Kanaka Maoli authors and journalists, produced an extraordinary range of original and translated text from the mid nineteenth century onwards. Indigenous populations were often highly literate in written languages, in addition to their advanced literacies in modes of communication other than writing.[1]

As material for literary translation in the colonies, *Lyrical Ballads* appears to have taken hold more strongly in India than anywhere else.

V. Bhagavantha Rao, for example, a teacher from the V. S. School in the southern Indian city of Tanjore, published a translation of 'The Rime of the Ancyent Marinere' in 1920. This translation, which makes use of a mixture of Sanskrit and Tamil, appeared as part of the 'Tamil Fine Reading Series'. Bhagavantha Rao's text offers some significant challenges to a purist reading of Coleridge's poem, or of *Lyrical Ballads* more generally. More significantly, he renders Coleridge's poem as prose. Bhagavantha Rao called his translation an 'explanatory' one, and part of the explanatory power of his version comes from reimagining Coleridge's poem not simply within the Tamil and Sankrit languages, but within their forms as well.

When Bhagavantha Rao is faithful to the content of the English text, he nevertheless introduces some small alterations that have a profound effect on how the poem is read, such as in the example of Coleridge's iconic lines on the crew's punishment of the mariner:

> And every tongue thro' utter drouth
> Was wither'd at the root;
> We could not speak no more than if
> We had been choked with soot.
>
> Ah wel-a-day! what evil looks
> Had I from old and young;
> Instead of the Cross the Albatross
> About my neck was hung.
> (*LB* Lines 131–138)

In place of Coleridge's lines, Bhagavantha Rao produces this description (translated into English here for clarity's sake):

> The temperature was so hot that the tongues of all the sailors were hanging out. We felt like the smoke was making us breathless and we could not talk at all. During all these difficulties, the sailors were bitter with me and saw me as the source of all the hardships they were facing today. They were angry and thought that my killing of the bird was the cause of all the difficulties we were facing. Oh! What to say, how everyone, young and old, was angry and talked to me harshly. They were so angry that they took off the rosary beads from my neck, threw them away, and instead they took and tied the body of the bird tightly around my neck.[2]

There are many small but meaningful changes introduced by Bhagavantha Rao. The rosary in place of Coleridge's cross opens up a sectarian dimension that is not present in the original poem, for example. Some alterations appear to diminish the emotional impact of the verse, such as the decision to replace the Gothic effect of the sailors' 'wither'd' tongues with the more prosaic image of the sailors' tongues hanging out of their mouths owing to thirst. Other alterations, by contrast, change the nature of the imagery, such as the suggestion that the albatross serves as a kind of noose, hung 'tightly' around the mariner's neck. A Tamil reader would be absorbing an understanding of Coleridge's poem that offered different insights and provoked different reactions from the original text.

More radical readings, however, emerge from the integration of Indian concepts and words into the text. Some of these changes to the original English involve significant alterations of meaning, and touch on the most iconic aspects of Coleridge's poem. There *is* a Tamil term for the albatross (*aṇṭaraṇṭap paṟavai*), but Bhagavantha Rao's bird is a *kinnara*, an angelic form with a human body and the face of a horse (7). As the mariner contemplates his sin while looking at the sea-snakes, Bhagavantha Rao introduces Indian spiritual concepts and rituals into the text:

> I also started thinking that a section of people were justified in saying that when people die, their progeny must do acts for purification of their souls like Srardham, Tharpanam, etc. for the sins which they had committed while they were alive, and before they reached hell, and also that the more they do those deeds the more it reduces the stay of those souls at hell. (71)

Coleridge's Christian message, and the literal and symbolic value of the albatross in the poem, are replaced with Indian notions of the supernatural, the spiritual and the afterlife. The mariner and the albatross, two iconic figures in English poetry, here take on Indian forms and act in Indian contexts.

Finally, the poem as a whole is used as the foundation for a concluding prose essay on Indian philosophy and spirituality, situating the lesson of Coleridge's poem in the context of beliefs in reincarnation and karma. 'The Rime of the Ancyent Marinere' becomes subsumed, in this translation, into a wider textual project, in which *Lyrical Ballads* is only one reference point. But the poem nevertheless provides significant material for considering religion, materiality, folklore and other concepts from within Indian thought. It gets recast, in Bhagavantha Rao's translation, as an Indian text, integrated with relative ease into a tradition to which it might seem, at first glance, irreducibly foreign. But this integration occurs alongside a parallel process in which the poem retains its original form and meaning. It is perhaps telling that there is an *additional* Tamil term for 'albatross' that appears to derive from Coleridge's poem: the term *talar kampaḷit tuṇi*, which refers figuratively to a handicap or hindrance. The albatross around the mariner's neck emerges as a global signifier for an inescapable impediment, but it does so alongside other, indigenised imaginings of the poem's significance and its form. The poem retains its original meaning and, simultaneously, develops new, local meanings across the colonised world.

Some of *Lyrical Ballads* appear to have received more attention than others in the flourishing print market of nineteenth- and twentieth-century India. 'Michael', for example, was translated into the southern Indian language Malayalam twice in the early twentieth century: once by C. P. Parameswaran Pillai in 1912, who had encountered Wordsworth's poem as an examination text in 1905, and then by Sasthamangalam P. Ramakrishnapillai in 1929.[3] Although both translations were faithful to Wordsworth's ballad, changes were introduced to help indigenise the text. The 1912 translation introduced a range of Malayalam names into the poem. Parameswaran Pillai explained that his aim was to 'give the whole thing a touch of naturalness' and therefore 'to give the story a Hindu garb'(iii). For that reason, he had renamed all the characters – Kelan (Michael), Koman (Luke), Nangu (Isabel) – as well as renaming Wordsworth's Green-head Gill as Āgasmēram, which he used as the poem's title. In his preface, he explained the decision to name the poem after its location, rather than its main character, as one driven by his Indian readers' tastes: 'it is my conviction', he wrote (without any further elaboration to clarify why he thought this) 'that the name Kelan, as the title of a book, will not be liked by most of my readers' (ii). He also adjusted the metre to suit his own language, in a decision that echoes Wordsworth's comments about metre in the 'Preface' to *Lyrical Ballads* (108–109), reconfiguring the poem in the *mandakranta vritham*, a metre he described as 'best suited to compositions of this kind on account of its slow and advancing measure' (ii). In the 1929 translation, Sasthamangalam P. Ramakrishnapillai scattered Indian references, so that the 'natural tune' (357) of Luke's gurglings as a baby are described as sounding 'as if mother nature's gentle fingers were / on the fine strings of the Veena' (Lines 393–394), an Indian stringed instrument. The oak (175) under which Michael and the villagers sit becomes, in Ramakrishnapillai's text, a banyan tree (558), while the young Luke's cheeks are no longer like 'Two steady roses' (189), but are instead 'the colour of hibiscus' (211). These indigenising changes were regarded by the translators and by some of their readers as enhancements to Wordsworth's original; the commentator R. Narayana Panicker said in his introduction to the 1929 translation: 'All the changes effected from the original are apt in their context, and have the effect of supporting and enriching it'.[4] To these translators and their readers, there was nothing especially foreign, or perhaps even especially original, about Wordsworth's poem; as Parameswaran Pillai wrote in his English-language preface to his translation, in reference to the mountain range that runs down western India, a character like Michael 'could every day be met with by all readers in many a village on this side of the Ghats' (iii). In instances like these, *Lyrical Ballads* could be malleable, easily adapted to times and places beyond its original moment and site of conception; the property of a global readership.

This adaptability extended beyond major poems like 'The Rime of the Ancyent Marinere' and 'Michael' to the wider *Lyrical Ballads* collection. In 1923, Pallath Raman, a lower-caste poet and essayist from Kerala, produced a volume of *Selections from Wordsworth*, which included several poems from *Lyrical Ballads* among its sixteen choices.[5] Like all of the translators discussed so far, Raman occasionally substituted local words for English ones; there are banyan trees, for example, in his versions of 'Lucy Gray' and 'The Pet Lamb, a Pastoral', although perhaps the most interesting example is his decision to rename Lucy Gray 'Malini', the Sanskrit word for 'fragrant' and a name with rich associations in Hindu mythology and history as the mother of the deity Ganesha.

But Raman also undertakes some significant repurposing of *Lyrical Ballads* in his selection in ways that radically reconfigure its shape. He selects 'The Tables Turned' for inclusion but not the poem to which it responds, 'Expostulation and Reply', for example. He also includes 'The Pet Lamb, a Pastoral', but cuts it in half, producing (without comment) two poems that are separated, in his collection, by two unrelated Wordsworth pieces. The two poems are called 'A Pure Love', with part one ending with line 32 of Wordsworth's original poem, and part two beginning with line 33. He begins 'Malini' with a line that has no equivalent in Wordsworth's poem ('To my eyes, Malini, you resemble the moonlight' [1]), but which links 'Malini' (and thus 'Lucy Gray') to the other 'Lucy Poems' in *Lyrical Ballads*, especially 'Strange fits of passion I have known', with its association of Lucy with the moon.

Lyrical Ballads could thus be used by indigenous translators in any way they saw fit. The poems were common property, to be adapted to local circumstances.[6] The translators expressed admiration for the poems but very little sense of deference. Their repurposings could modify such fundamental aspects as the ballad genre or the verse form, the rights of Wordsworth and Coleridge as original authors to control the meaning of their poems, the canonicity of specific versions, key images or moments in the verse that would seem necessarily central to a Western reader, and the moral lessons of the poems. These indigenous translations of *Lyrical*

Ballads did not merely transmit or imitate; they *indigenised*, taking what they needed from the texts and adding what they wanted. If indigenous writers did not see something worth translating in Wordsworth's and Coleridge's poems, it is likely that they simply did not engage with them in translation. Among the well-developed print literacies of Māori, Hawaiian, and some First Nations peoples, there do not appear to be any translations of these poems, although professional scholars' limited familiarity with these languages and literacies might have prevented accurate identifications to date. If it does prove to be the case that there is a genuine paucity of indigenous translations of Wordsworth's and Coleridge's poems, that is itself a response, and one that needs careful consideration in criticism on the global relevance of *Lyrical Ballads*.

Citations: Language and Literature

While the poems themselves might have undergone limited translation into indigenous languages in the colonised world, the ideas both expressed and symbolised by the volumes gained more traction in indigenous intellectual debates. The prefatory material surrounding translations, for example, often provided critical discussions of Wordsworth's 'Preface', its articulation of the role of nature, language and the poet, individual poems, and *Lyrical Ballads* as a whole. The luminaries who supplied complimentary forewords to the two 'Michael' translations discussed earlier, for example, offered detailed readings of the 'Preface' as a manifesto for indigenous poetry. Narayana Panicker translated into Malayalam for readers of the 1929 version of 'Michael' Wordsworth's opening remark that the 1798 *Lyrical Ballads* volume 'was published, as an experiment, which, I hoped, might be of some use to ascertain, how far, by fitting to metrical arrangement a selection of the real language of men in a state of vivid sensation, that sort of pleasure and that quantity of pleasure may be imparted, which a Poet may rationally endeavour to impart' (*LB* 95; Panicker viii). The scholar P. K. Narayana Pillai, meanwhile, explained to readers some of the composition history of *Lyrical Ballads* in his Malayalam-language introduction to the 1912 version, and offered a detailed description of the theories of poetry outlined in the 'Preface', focusing on Wordsworth's ideas about nature, ordinary people and rural life, and the role of common language in poetry.[7]

The translators themselves also used prefatory material to articulate and endorse Wordsworth's vision for *Lyrical Ballads*. Raman's understanding of Wordsworth, for example, was clearly shaped by the contents of the 1800 'Preface' to *Lyrical Ballads*. Although he made no direct reference to the 'Preface', Raman included a short explanatory sketch of Wordsworth that draws heavily on its philosophies and arguments:

> Wordsworth's principle is that poetry should be written in a simple, storytelling language. He was of the opinion that any creative work should be exactly what the author thinks about, and akin to conversing with another person, effortless and without using flourishes of language, and naturally emerging, and he himself strictly adhered to this principle. (1)

Although the early twentieth-century Māori translator Reweti Kōhere (1871–1954) does not appear to have translated any of *Lyrical Ballads* among his numerous translations of English poetry, he did name Wordsworth and Coleridge as two of the 'great literary figures of the English language' in his essays on English literature in the 1920s, and cited a definition of the relationship between poetry, the poet and land that connects with that expressed in the 'Preface': 'Many of the works of [these poets] have been embedded into the very essence of the land, along with their philosophies and their teachings, which continue to flourish and never fade'.[8]

These examples might seem deferential, but they were typically part of a wider argument about the value of indigenous literature and language, to which Wordsworth, Coleridge, the 'Preface' and *Lyrical Ballads* as a whole were harnessed. Indigenous commentators tended to link the concerns of *Lyrical Ballads* with their own local situations. In particular, it was the argument in the 'Preface' for the language 'really used by men' which, 'arising out of repeated experience and regular feelings, is a more permanent, and far more philosophical language' (*LB* 97), which spoke to indigenous authors and readers. One of the reasons why translations of Wordsworth and Coleridge flourished in southern India, for example, was the resurgence of interest in vernacular languages. In regions such as Kerala, Sanskrit had been the literary language for centuries, while the vernacular languages, such as Malayalam and Kannada, had not been considered appropriate for literary expression.[9] In other parts of the colonised world, indigenous languages had struggled to survive against the pressure of English-language printing, education and sermonising. *Lyrical Ballads* offered indigenous intellectuals one way to think through the poetic value of vernacular languages and call for their reinvigoration as literary languages. It was in this context that Indian commentators praised the translations of Wordsworth's and Coleridge's poems, not simply for their own merits, but for the role they would play as core texts of a linguistic revival. Thus R. Narayana Panicker extolled the 1929 translation of 'Michael' because it was necessary while Malayalam-language literature was 'undergoing a transformation'(ix), whereas Ulloor S. Parameswara Iyer wrote of Raman's *Selections from Wordsworth* that 'Translations of this nature are necessary for the absolute progress of literature in any language'.[10] B. M. Srikantaiah's translations of English poetry, published in 1926 as the *English Geethagalu*, were described as both '"The Lyrical Ballads" of Kannada literature' and as 'a guidebook for lyric poetry in Kannada', suggesting a connection between the original English poems, their translated forms and the longer traditions of indigenous language and poetry.[11] In these examples, *Lyrical Ballads* provided both a global reference point and a model for future literary and linguistic development.

As well as supplying the raw material for increasing the range of vernacular-language texts through the process of translation, *Lyrical Ballads* also offered a rationale for the value of original vernacular poetry. In the case of Indian languages, Wordsworth and Coleridge's collection was invoked as a parallel to a process already under way or perhaps even completed. R. Narayana Panicker, for example, drew parallels between the changes in English poetry signalled by *Lyrical Ballads* and the rise of vernacular poetry in Malayalam: 'After the age of Johnson, who was a giant among the giants of English literature, and his contemporaries, the same trend that occurred in the English literature occurred in Malaylam, following the age of the great Kerala Varma Valia Koithampuran, who for long years had dominated the horizon of Kerala's literary world' (vi).

In other parts of the colonised world, *Lyrical Ballads* offered a model for a literary and linguistic transformation that was still to come. Wordsworth's name was invoked when Kōhere exhorted his readers to record some of the oral literature that he felt was being lost: 'Our songs and our legends lie only with us, they lie only on our marae, they are not taught in the colleges of the world, therefore as a result our Māori culture is diminishing as our identity diminishes also; perhaps tomorrow is the time this [Māori literature] will be in the European books.'[12] George Copway (Kahgegagahbowh) (1818–1869), an Ojibwe author and minister who regularly peppered his writings with Romantic reference points, made a similar case when he linked the language of Ojibwe literature to the natural world and the environment in which such language was both formed and expressed. In a treatise on the Ojibwe language included in his 1850 work *The Traditional History and Characteristic Sketches of the Ojibway Nation*, Copway wrote:

> A language, derived, as this is, from the peculiarities of the country in which it is spoken, must, necessarily, partake of its nature. Our orators have filled the forest with the music of their voices, loud as the roar of a waterfall, yet soft and wooing as the gentle murmur of a mountain stream. We have had warriors who have stood on the banks of lakes and rivers, and addressed

with words of irresistible and persuasive eloquence their companions in arms.[13]

There was a revolution coming in indigenous languages and literary expression, these authors suggested, and one way to express the shape it would take was to link it to the similar poetic revolution in late eighteenth-century Britain.

Interactions: Memory and the Autobiographical Speaker

The texts of *Lyrical Ballads* and their specific theories of poetic composition are easier to map in indigenous contexts than the more ephemeral influences of voice and subject matter. There is a danger too in assuming that aspects of indigenous expression that resonate with Romantic ideas draw direct inspiration from British Romanticism and its foundational texts, when in fact we might simply be reading those aspects as Romantic because we are looking for signs of Romanticism. But the emergence of indigenous-authored autobiographies in the nineteenth and twentieth centuries presents a useful case study in a post-contact that was heavily influenced by Romantic ideas of memory, childhood and the autobiographical speaker's voice. While 'autobiography' as a broad concept could be identified and accommodated within pre-colonial indigenous epistemologies and literacies, the idea of a written, published, sole-authored story of an individual's life from cradle to grave owed a great deal to Romanticism and to Wordsworthian ideas of childhood and memory transmitted via colonial education systems.

Some indigenous readers might have encountered those ideas most directly in *The Prelude*, but that cannot be the case for George Copway, a contemporary of Wordsworth who was educated before the existence of the *Prelude* was known in Britain, let alone in the colonies. In his autobiography (1850), Copway offers readers autobiographical passages that connect not to the *Prelude*, but to 'Lines Written a Few Miles above Tintern Abbey', such as his description of himself as a child shaped by the natural world:

> I was born in *nature's wide domain!* The trees were all that sheltered my infant limbs—the blue heavens all that covered me. I am one of Nature's children; I have always admired her; she shall be my glory; her features—her robes, and the wreath about her brow—the seasons—her stately oaks, and the evergreen—her hair—ringlets over the earth, all contribute to my enduring love of her; and wherever I see her, emotions of pleasure roll in my breast, and swell and burst like waves on the shores of the ocean, in prayer

and praise to Him who has placed me in her hand. It is thought great to be born in palaces, surrounded with wealth—but to be born in nature's wide domain is greater still!'[14]

Both Copway and Rēweti Kōhere also take on the role of the Wordsworth-ian speaker of the autobiographical poems in *Lyrical Ballads* when they reflect on revisiting landscapes that they knew as children and as young men. But, unlike Wordsworth, who finds his former homes and hideaways largely unchanged, indigenous authors deploy the terms of *Lyrical Ballads* to describe the irrevocable environmental destruction that came with colonisation. Wordsworth can evoke a yew tree's 'gloomy boughs' as signs of a stable environmental history that outlasts individual human life (*LB* 'Lines Left Upon a Seat in a Yew-Tree', Line 24), or can revisit the banks of the Wye and see a natural scene that precisely mirrors his memory of it:

> The day is come when I again repose
> Here, under this dark sycamore, and view
> These plots of cottage ground, these orchard-tufts,
> Which, at this season, with their unripe fruits,
> Are clad in one green hue, and lost themselves
> Among the woods and copses, nor disturb
> The wild green landscape.
> ('Lines Written a Few Miles above Tintern Abbey', Lines 9–15)

Kōhere, by contrast, similarly singles out a tree as a site of memory, but it is a marker of absence, which he uses to lament the loss of native trees near his birthplace, destroyed by floods caused by settler deforestation of his tribe's land: 'All my life, I had known these trees, and one of them I had particular reason to remember. Now, my trees are gone—gone for ever. They were strewn on the beach, like dead soldiers on a battlefield.'[15]

Copway offers another politicised version of this sort of speaker when he discusses the abandonment of the spot where he was born:

> I remember the tall trees, and the dark woods—the swamp just gone by, where the little wren sang so melodiously after the going down of the sun in the west—the current of the broad river Trent—the skipping of the fish, and the noise of the rapids a little above. It was here I first saw the light; a little fallen down shelter, made of evergreens, and a few dead embers, the remains of the last fire that shed its genial warmth around, were all that marked the spot. When I last visited it, nothing but fir poles stuck in the ground, and they were leaning on account of decay. Is this dear spot, made green by the tears of memory, any less enticing and hallowed than the palaces where princes are born? I would much more glory in this birth-place, with the broad canopy of heaven above me, and the giant arms of the

forest trees for my shelter, than to be born in palaces of marble, studded with pillars of gold! (*Life, Letters, & Speeches* 73)

A number of comparisons could be drawn here to the imagined American landscapes in *Lyrical Ballads*, especially those in 'Ruth'. But Copway's authorial voice here is less like those of the American characters devised by Wordsworth and Coleridge, and more like that of a reoriented version of Wordsworth's own autobiographical speaker. Copway's description is studded with Wordsworthian diction and preoccupations: trees, birds, animals, the crumbling shelter, the 'genial warmth' of the fire, the emphasis on a 'spot' as both location and *lieu de mémoire*. But for Copway, this scene is reconstructed from memory, while the present-day site is one of decay and collapse. Wordsworth's comforting vision of revisiting a childhood haunt in *Lyrical Ballads* is evoked by indigenous authors in order to highlight its impossibility in colonised lands, in which it is replaced with the eradication of a personal and cultural history through the processes of colonial capitalism.

Alongside the connections to Wordsworthian diction and rhetoric, indigenous autobiographies also contain numerous references to their own poetic and creative traditions in ways that echo Wordsworth's call for an indigenous British poetic diction and form. Kōhere's autobiography is studded with *whakatauki* (proverbs), an art form in which he was an acknowledged expert, as well as a host of historical Māori stories.[16] Copway includes multiple references to Ojibwe songs, chants and literacies in his writings, which are usually directed at a Euroamerican audience that requires convincing about the validity of indigenous traditions.[17] If *Lyrical Ballads* is read as a late eighteenth-century revival and reinscription of much older literary traditions, indigenous to the British Isles, then these autobiographies behave in the same way, updating creative forms and mixing them with new generic and cultural influences. They contain the same in-built generic and literary hybridity that made *Lyrical Ballads* successful and influential.

Indigenous authors also include anecdotes in their autobiographies that mirror the encounters described in *Lyrical Ballads*. Some of these anecdotes seem almost entirely imagined from within the imagery and symbolism of Wordsworthian Romanticism, rather than within their original settings, such as Kōhere's account of a visit to Tolaga Bay, on the east coast of New Zealand's North Island, with its echoes of 'Simon Lee', 'The Old Cumberland Beggar' and 'Old Man Travelling':

> At the foot of a steep cliff on the island nestled a little hut, outside of which I noticed gooseberry bushes, laden with ripe fruit. Attracted by the noise of

our arrival, an old man, with gray hair and beard, came out of the hut. He was all alone in this lonely, but picturesque spot. With its owner, in his rustic clothes, standing at the door, the little hut added to the picturesque and romantic atmosphere of the spot. The hermit came towards us and inquired who we were. On being informed, he extended to us a warm welcome and a cordial invitation to help ourselves to the fruits in his garden. We, particularly I, were only too glad to accept the invitation. (*Autobiography* 53)

These autobiographical encounters are often homely and atmospheric, as in this example, but also attend to political concerns similar to those that absorbed Wordsworth and Coleridge. Sol Plaatje (1876–1932), an African author and founding member of the African National Congress, for example, writes about meetings with destitute people in his homeland in order to generate political sympathy for the plight of black Africans from his white (and mainly British) readers, in much the same way that *Lyrical Ballads* aims to provoke compassion for the dispossessed of late eighteenth-century Europe. Plaatje, another indigenous author steeped in the English literary tradition, includes descriptions of 'native mothers evicted from their homes [who] shivered with their babies by their sides' which echo the concerns of 'The Mad Mother', while the deaths of the livestock and, ultimately, the children of displaced families that he describes connect to the tragic accounts embedded in 'The Last of the Flock' and 'The Thorn'.[18] Plaatje's extended description of the eviction of the elderly Kgabale and the widowed Maria from their land captures the way in which the poetry of *Lyrical Ballads* might influence indigenous prose:

> the landlord is said to have set fire to Maria's thatched cottage, and as the chilly southeaster blew the smoke of her burning home towards the northwest, Maria, with her bedclothes on her head, and on the heads of her son and daughter, and carrying her three-year-old-boy tied to her back, walked off from the farm, driving her cows before her. In parting from the endeared associations of their late home, for one blank and unknown, the children were weeping bitterly. Nor has any news of the fate of this family been received since they were forced out on this perilous adventure. (82)

In his attempt to persuade British readers to use their political influence to help black Africans, Plaatje turns to a rhetoric borrowed from Wordsworth and Coleridge, not least because that was a rhetoric of emotional response to political events in which European readers were already steeped, thanks to *Lyrical Ballads* and Wordsworth's desire to 'excite thought or feeling in the Reader' (*LB* 113–114).

It is neither possible nor desirable to assert definitively that these aspects of indigenous autobiography come directly from *Lyrical Ballads*, or even from a more generalised Wordsworthian approach to self-expression. In the cases of Kōhere, Copway and Plaatje, there is a documented exposure to Romantic poetry, whether in Aotearoa New Zealand, the Great Lakes region of North America or the Cape Colony in southern Africa, which suggests the ways in which the lessons of *Lyrical Ballads* might have begun to influence indigenous intellectual development from 1800 onwards. It is questionable, however, why we would assume or want to create this kind of trajectory of influence. It has long been suggested that British Romanticism, and especially Wordsworth and Coleridge's volumes, coalesced in part as a response to their reading of the travel literature that arose from colonial experience of indigenous cultures. More radically for our theories of English literature and its global role, perhaps these examples suggest that *Lyrical Ballads* was not a parallel expression, but rather only ever an echo of indigenous tradition itself.

Conclusion: How to Do (Indigenous) Things with *Lyrical Ballads*

While these translations, citations and interactions are interesting, is important to query why *Lyrical Ballads* should matter at all to indigenous readers and writers. The New Zealand educationalist and author Bernard Gadd, editor of several literary anthologies for young readers, made this comment about his time as a teacher in Otara, a predominantly Māori and Pasifika suburb of Auckland:

> As head of the English department arriving in 1971 at Hillary College in Otara I soon found a need to provide literature for working class – and especially working-class Maori and Polynesian families – both school attendees, and school leavers and adults. The stocks of books I inherited at the school included stuff like Lyrical Ballads by Wordsworth and Coleridge.[19]

Describing material like Wordsworth and Coleridge's work as written for 'the Boss classes', Gadd went on to create new resources of homegrown material to interest his Māori and Pasifika students. This dismissal of 'stuff like Lyrical Ballads' partly reflects a move that has been replicated across the anglophone world, in which historical British literature is seen as less relevant than more contemporary local literature. The nineteenth- and twentieth-century indigenous authors discussed in this chapter perhaps offer a new perspective on a binary that sets a repressive colonial education system, typified by a text like *Lyrical Ballads*, against an authentic decolonised voice and mode of expression, in ways that Manu Samriti Chander has also highlighted.[20] Bhagavantha Rao, Raman, Copway, Kōhere and Plaatje form only a selection of indigenous authors who found something useful in *Lyrical Ballads*, but in ways that decentred and repurposed it according to indigenous needs, priorities and cultural values. Its poems and 'Preface', whether translated, cited or alluded to, are almost always present in indigenous texts as part of a more important local question, such as vernacular revival, the loss of indigenous lifeways, land and literature, or the need for sympathetic responses from white publics. It is in this conceptual space that *Lyrical Ballads* was made relevant.

Indigenous readings should certainly reformulate Western academic understandings of *Lyrical Ballads* and its significance. The shape of the volumes looks quite different from the perspective of indigenous readers, writers and translators. Poems which the academy has come to regard as important fade into the background, while 'minor' poems take centre stage. The sequencing of and relationship between different poems are reorganised. Poetic features such as the ballad form, rhyme, imagery and diction are indigenised, played down or set aside. The relatively stable thing that we call *Lyrical Ballads* – the volumes themselves, the values that they espouse, the political and literary events that they represent – come to feel much less stable once seen through indigenous eyes. More significantly, *Lyrical Ballads* comes to seem much less seminal than even contemporary revisionist interpretations have conceded. Perhaps, instead of seeing Wordsworth and Coleridge's text as sitting at the head of a global movement, or even working alongside currents in global thought, we need to explore more fully the possibility that *Lyrical Ballads* actually *begins* in indigenous understandings of literature, land and language, and work to recover a greater range of voices and examples from throughout the colonised world. The echoes we hear across centuries and continents might not be emanating from the Lake District; Wordsworth and Coleridge might rather have heard, and retransmitted, a sound that continued to reverberate throughout the indigenous world.

Endnotes

1 See, for example, Noenoe K. Silva, *Aloha Betrayed: Native Hawaiian Resistance to American Colonialism* (Durham and London: Duke University Press, 2004), 55.

2 V. Bhagavantha Rao, *Explanatory Translation of Coleridge's 'The Rime of the Ancient Mariner'* (Tanjore: Sri Ramanuja Vilasa Press, 1920), 13. The

translations of Indian language texts in this chapter are courtesy of linguists at the New Zealand Translation Centre.

3 C. P. Parameswaran Pillai, *Āgasmēram*, 2nd ed. (Thiruvananthapuram: Aksharalankara Printing Press, 1912); Sasthamangalam P. Ramakrishnapillai, *Michael* (Thiruvananthapuram: V. V. Press, 1929).

4 R. Narayana Panicker, 'Introduction', *Michael* (Thiruvananthapuram: V. V. Press, 1929), i–ix, v.

5 Pallath Raman, trans., *Selections from Wordsworth* (Madras: K. A. Kannan, 1923).

6 See Maureen N. McLane's work on the usefulness of ballads in *Balladeering, Minstrelsy, and the Making of British Romantic Poetry* (Cambridge: Cambridge University Press, 2008).

7 P. K. Narayana Pillai, 'Introduction', *Āgasmēram*, 2nd ed. (Thiruvananthapuram: Aksharalankara Printing Press, 1912), vi–xiii.

8 Reweti Kōhere, 'Nga Tangata Rongo-Nui o Te Pakeha' [The Famous People of the Pakeha], *Te Toa Takitini* (July 1924): 68–70; 68. Kōhere's comments throughout this essay, originally published in Māori, are here translated by Tai Ahu.

9 K. M. George, *A Survey of Malayalam Literature* (Asia Publishing House, 1968), 126.

10 Ulloor S. Parameswara Iyer, 'Introduction', *Selections from Wordsworth* (Madras: K. A. Kannan, 1923), n.p.

11 Vanamala Viswanatha and Sherry Simon, 'Shifting Grounds of Exchange: B. M. Srikantaiah and Kannada Translation', in *Post-Colonial Translation: Theory and Practice*, ed. Susan Bassnett and Harish Trivedi (London: Routledge, 1999), 162–181; 166.

12 Reweti Kōhere, 'Nga Kupu a Anaru Kaneki, Te Mea Nui Ake I Ana Miriona' [The Sayings of Andrew Carnegie Are Worth More than His Millions], *Te Toa Takitini*, (December 1931): 69–71; 71.

13 George Copway, *The Traditional History and Characteristic Sketches of the Ojibway Nation* (Boston: Benjamin B. Mussey, 1851), 125–126.

14 George Copway, *Life, Letters, & Speeches, George Copway (Kahgegahbowh)*, ed. A. LaVonne Brown Ruoff and Donald B. Smith (Lincoln: University of Nebraska Press, 1997), 73.

15 Rēweti Kōhere, *The Autobiography of a Maori* (Wellington: Reed, 1951), 15.

16 See for example Kōhere, *Autobiography*, 33–36.

17 See the chapters 'Their Legendary Stories and Their Historical Tales' and 'Their Language and Writings' in Copway, *Traditional History*, 97–136.

18 Sol Plaatje, *Native Life in South Africa* (1916) (Johannesburg: Picador Africa, 2007), 73.

19 Cited in 'Of Poetry and Politics,' *Dominion Post* (Wellington), 31 January 2009.

20 Manu Samriti Chander, *Brown Romantics: Poetry and Nationalism in the Global Nineteenth Century* (Lewisburg: Bucknell University Press, 2017).

Guide to Further Reading

A BRIEF SUMMARY OF EDITIONS AND RESOURCES FOR *LYRICAL BALLADS*

NOTE: The three main editions of *Lyrical Ballads* (1798, 1800, 1802) create problems for editors because of their evolving and accretive nature, forcing them to choose between editions and then to give a rationale for that choice (with the exception of the online edition below). Where 1798 is privileged, this is because it is the first edition seen as the only truly joint edition and the 'foundational text of early Romanticism . . . marking the culmination of a decade of revolutionary poetry' (Gamer and Porter 35). But 1798 does not contain the 'Preface' so cannot allow comparison of prose and poetic principles. Where 1800 is privileged this is because it contains the first publication of the 'Preface' as well as the second volume of Wordsworth's pastoral poems. Where 1802 is privileged it is as the most complete version with the additional extensions to the 'Preface'. See Gamer and Porter (Introduction 34–36) for a discussion of the challenges involved and survey of key editions over time.

Lyrical Ballads 1798 and 1802. Ed. Fiona Stafford. Oxford, Oxford University Press, 2013.

[This edition was chosen as the standard edition for this volume, mainly because of its easy accessibility for students but also because it provides good coverage of the two main volumes and the 'Preface' in its fullest version.]

Lyrical Ballads 1798 and 1800: William Wordsworth and Samuel Coleridge. Ed. Michel Gamer and Dahlia Porter. Toronto: Broadview Editions, 2008.

[As the title makes clear, this edition gives both of the earlier editions in full as well as some extremely useful appendices with a range of contextual information. Very useful for teaching. Seeks to range across editions in order to 'map this process of becoming' (36).]

Lyrical Ballads by William Wordsworth & Samuel Taylor Coleridge. A Scholarly Electronic Edition. Ed. Bruce Grave and Ron Tetreault. Romantic Circles and Cambridge University Press, August 2003.

www.rc.umd.edu/editions/LB/index.html [Accessed 19.03.2018]

[An extremely useful online resource. It presents all four editions of the poems: 1798, 1800, 1802, 1805 with dynamic collation. Perhaps digital editing represents the way forward for the kind of multiple edition text that *LB* represents.]

William Wordsworth Lyrical Ballads 1800. Ed. Jonathan Wordsworth. Poole and Washington, DC: Woodstock Books, 1997.

[Part of Jonathan Wordsworth's invaluable facsimile series: presents the two-volume 1800 edition as originally printed.]

'Lyrical Ballads' and Other Poems, 1797–1800 by William Wordsworth. Ed. James Butler and Karen Green. Ithaca: Cornell University Press, 1992.

[A major volume in the Cornell series tracing the collection through its entire corpus of seventy-eight surviving manuscripts and representing the process of the poem in full. The Reading Text is based on the printer's MS for *LB* 1800. Wordsworth's 'Preface' and Coleridge's contributions are provided in appendices.]

Lyrical Ballads: The Text of the 1798 Edition with the Additional 1800 Poems and the Prefaces. Ed. R. L. Brett and A R. Jones. London: Routledge, 1963; 2nd ed. 1991.

[Popular first modern edition to present two editions alongside each other, combining volume 1 from 1798 and volume 2 from 1800.]

PREVIOUS COLLECTIONS OF CRITICAL ESSAYS ON *LYRICAL BALLADS*

Campbell, Patrick. *Wordsworth and Coleridge: Lyrical Ballads: Critical Perspectives* London and Basingstoke: Macmillan, 1991.

Cronin, Richard ed. *1798: The Year of the Lyrical Ballads.* New York: St Martins' Press, 1998.

Gravil, Richard and Daniel Robinson. *Oxford Handbook of William Wordsworth.* Oxford: Oxford University Press, 2015. Contains three essays on *LB*; Daniel Robinson, 'Wordsworth and Coleridge's *Lyrical Ballads*, 1798', 168–185; Susan J. Wolfson, 'Poem upon the Wye', 186–203; Jason N. Goldsmith, Wordsworth's *Lyrical Ballads*, 1800', 204–220.

Jones, Alun R. and William Tydeman. *Wordsworth: Lyrical Ballads a Casebook.* London and Basingstoke, Macmillan, 1972.

Trott, Nicola and Seamus Perry, *1800: The New Lyrical Ballads.* Wiltshire: Palgrave, 2001.

Woof, Robert. *Towards Tintern Abbey: A Bicentenary Celebration of Lyrical Ballads, 1798.* Grasmere, 1998.

TEN INFLUENTIAL STUDIES TO READ ON *LYRICAL BALLADS*

Bialostosky, Don. *Making Tales: The Poetics of Wordsworth's Narrative Experiments.* Chicago: University of Chicago Press, 1984.

Blades, John. *Wordsworth and Coleridge: Lyrical Ballads.* London and Basingstoke: Macmillan, 2003.

Eilenberg, Susan. *Strange Power of Speech: Wordsworth, Coleridge and Literary Possession.* New York: Oxford University Press, 1992.

Glen, Heather. *Vision and Disenchantment: Blake's Songs and Wordsworth's Lyrical Ballads.* Cambridge: Cambridge University Press, 1983.

Jacobus, Mary. *Tradition and Experiment in Wordsworth's Lyrical Ballads (1798)*. Oxford: Oxford University Press, 1976.

Jordan, John E. *Why the Lyrical Ballads? The Background, Writing, and Character of Wordsworth's 1798 Lyrical Ballads*. Berkeley: University of California Press, 1976.

Levinson, Marjorie. *Wordsworth's Great Period Poems: Four Essays*. Cambridge: Cambridge University Press, 1986.

Magnuson, Paul. *Coleridge and Wordsworth: A Lyrical Dialogue*. Princeton: Princeton University Press, 1988.

Newlyn, Lucy. *Coleridge, Wordsworth and the Language of Allusion*. Oxford: Oxford University Press, 1986.

Parrish, Stephen, *The Art of the Lyrical Ballads*. Cambridge MA: Harvard University Press, 1973.

Roe, Nicholas. *Wordsworth and Coleridge: The Radical Years*. Oxford: Oxford University Press, 1988.

FURTHER READING FOR PART I: PART AND WHOLE

Abrams, M. H. *The Mirror and the Lamp: Romantic Theory and Critical Tradition*. Oxford: Oxford University Press, 1958.

Beer, John. *Coleridge's Poetic Intelligence*. London: Macmillan, 1977.

Bewell, Alan. *Romanticism and Colonial Disease*. Baltimore and London: Johns Hopkins University Press, 1999.

Butler, Marilyn. *Romantics, Rebels & Reactionaries: English Literature and Its Background 1760–1830*. Oxford: Oxford University Press, 1981.

Chandler, James. *Wordsworth's Second Nature: A Study of the Poetry and Politics*. Chicago: University of Chicago Press, 1984. 98–103.

Connell, Philip and Nigel Leask. *Romanticism and Popular Culture In Great Britain and Ireland*. Cambridge: Cambridge University Press, 2009.

Cook, James. *A Voyage Towards the South Pole and Round the World: Performed in His Majesty's Ships the Resolution and Adventure, in the Years 1772, 1773, 1774 and 1775*, 2 vols. London, 1777.

Duggett, Tom. *Gothic Romanticism: Architecture, Politics, and Literary Form*. Basingstoke: Palgrave, 2010.

Everest, Kelvin. *Coleridge's Secret Ministry: The Context of the Conversation Poems, 1795–1798*. Hassocks: Harvester Press, 1979.

Fulford, Tim. *Coleridge's Figurative Language*. Basingstoke: Macmillan, 1991.

Jordan, John E. 'The Novelty of the *Lyrical Ballads*' Bicentenary Wordsworth Studies in Memory of John Alban Finch. Ed. Jonathan Wordsworth. Ithaca: Cornell University Press, 1970. 340–358.

Kitson, Peter J. 'Coleridge, The French Revolution and The Ancient Mariner: A Reassessment'. *Coleridge Bulletin*, n.s. 7 (Spring 1996): 30–48.

Lee, Debbie. 'Yellow Fever and the Slave Trade: Coleridge's "The Rime of the Ancient Mariner."' *English Literary History*, 65 (1998): 675–700.

Lowes, John Livingston. *The Road to Xanadu: A Study in the Ways of the Imagination*. New York: Houghton Mifflin, 1927.

Magnuson, Paul. *Coleridge's Nightmare Poetry*. Charlottesville: University of Virginia Press, 1974.

Mayo, Robert. 'The Contemporaneity of the Lyrical Ballads.' *PMLA*, 69.3 (1954): 486–522.

McEathron, Scott. 'Wordsworth, Lyrical Ballads and the Problem of Peasant Poetry.' *Nineteenth Century Literature*, 54.1 (1999): 1–26.

McGoogan, Ken. *Ancient Mariner: The Arctic Adventures of Samuel Hearne, the Sailor Who Inspired Coleridge's Masterpiece*. New York: Carroll and Graf, 2003.

McKusick, James C. *Coleridge's Philosophy of Language*. New Haven: Yale University Press, 1986.

McLane, Maureen N. *Balladeering, Minstrelsy, and the Making of British Romantic Poetry*. Cambridge: Cambridge University Press, 2008.

Modiano, Raimonda. *Coleridge and the Concept of Nature*. London: Macmillan, 1995.

Newlyn, Lucy. *Wordsworth, Coleridge, and The Language of Allusion*. Oxford: Clarendon Press, 1986.

Newman, Ian. 'Moderation in the Lyrical Ballads: Wordsworth and the Ballad Debates of the 1790s.' *Studies in Romanticism*, 55.2 (Summer 2016): 185–210.

Robinson, Daniel. 'Wordsworth and Coleridge's *Lyrical Ballads*, 1798.' *Oxford Handbook of William Wordsworth*. Ed. Richard Gravil and Daniel Robinson. Oxford: Oxford University Press, 2015. 168–185.

Simmons, Clare A. *Popular Medievalism in Romantic-Era Britain*. Basingstoke: Palgrave, 2011.

St. Clair, William. *The Reading Nation in the Romantic Period*. Cambridge: Cambridge University Press, 2004.

Walford Davies, Damian. 'Diagnosing 'The Rime of the Ancient Mariner.' Shipwreck, Historicism, Traumatology.' Studies in Romanticism, 55 (2016): 503–536.

Ware, Malcolm. 'Coleridge's 'Spectre Bark': A Slave Ship?' *Philological Quarterly*, 40 (1961): 589–593.

Woodring, Carl. *Politics in English Romantic Poetry*. Cambridge, MA: Harvard University Press, 1970.

FURTHER READING FOR PART II: SUBJECTS AND SITUATIONS FROM COMMON LIFE

Bainbridge, Simon. *British Poetry and the Revolutionary and Napoleonic Wars*. Oxford: Oxford University Press, 2003.

Bewell, Alan. *Wordsworth and the Enlightenment: Nature, Man, and Society in the Experimental Poetry*. New Haven: Yale University Press, 1989.

Bialostosky, Don H. *Making Tales: The Poetics of Wordsworth's Narrative Experiments*. Chicago: Chicago University Press, 1984.

Brooke, Hopkins. 'Wordsworth, Winnicott, and the Claims of the 'Real." Studies in Romanticism, 37 (1998): 183–216.

Brown, Bill. 'Thing Theory.' in *Things*, ed. Bill Brown. Chicago: University of Chicago Press, 2004.

Clancey, Edward W. *Wordsworth's Classical Undersong: Education, Rhetoric and Poetic Truth*. Houndmills: Macmillan, 2000.

Danby, John F. *The Simple Wordsworth: Studies in the Poems, 1797–1807*. New York: Barnes and Noble, 1960.

Fry, Paul H. *Wordsworth and the Poetry of What We Are*. New Haven: Yale University Press, 2008.

Galperin, William. 'Wordsworth's Double-Take', *Wordsworth Circle*, 41.3 (2010): 123–127.

Gill, Stephen. *Wordsworth's Revisitings*. Oxford: Oxford University Press, 2011.

Glenn, Heather. *Vision and Disenchantment: Blake's Songs and Wordsworth's Lyrical Ballads*. Cambridge: Cambridge University Press, 1983

Graver, Bruce Edward. *Wordsworth's Translations from Latin Poetry*. Chapel Hill: University of North Carolina Press, 1983.

Illbruck, Helmut. *Nostalgia: Origins and Ends of an Unenlightened Disease*. Evanston: Northwestern University Press, 2012.

Leadbetter, Gregory. 'Wordsworth's Untrodden Ways: Death, Absence and the Space of Writing.' *Grasmere, 2011: Selected Papers from the Wordsworth Summer Conference*. Ed. Richard Gravil. Penrith: Humanities-Ebooks, 2011. 103–110.

Luckhurst, Roger. *The Trauma Question*. London: Routledge, 2013.

McKusick, James C. '*Lyrical Ballads* and the Natural World.' *Wordsworth's Poetry and Prose*. Ed. Nicholas Halmi. New York: W. W. Norton, 2014.

Mitchell, W. J. T. 'Empire and Objecthood.' *What Do Pictures Want? The Lives and Loves of Images*. Chicago: University of Chicago Press, 2005.

Newlyn, Lucy. *William and Dorothy Wordsworth: 'All in Each Other.'* Oxford: Oxford University Press, 2013.

Perry, Seamus. 'Coleridge, Wordsworth, and Other Things.' *The Wordsworth Circle*, 29 (1998): 31–41.

Piper, H. W. *The Active Universe: Pantheism and the Concept of Imagination in the English Romantic Poets*. London: Athlone Press, 1962.

Robinson, Daniel. 'Wordsworth and Coleridge's *Lyrical Ballads, 1798*.' *The Oxford Handbook of William Wordsworth*. Ed. Richard Gravil and Daniel Robinson. Oxford: Oxford University Press, 2015. 168–185.

Roe, Nicholas. *Wordsworth and Coleridge: The Radical Years*. Oxford: Oxford University Press, 1988.

Shaw, Philip. *Suffering and Sentiment in Romantic Military Art*. Farnham: Ashgate, 2013.

Sheats, Paul D. *The Making of Wordsworth's Poetry, 1785–1798*. Cambridge, MA: Harvard University Press, 1973.

Simpson, David. *Wordsworth, Commodification and Social Concern: The Politics of Modernity*. Cambridge: Cambridge University Press, 2009.

Trott, Nicola. 'Wordsworth's Loves of the Plants.' *1800: The New 'Lyrical Ballads.'* Ed. Nicola Trott and Seamus Perry. London: Palgrave, 2001. 141–168.

Walker, Eric C. *Marriage, Writing and Romanticism: Wordsworth and Austen after War*. Stanford: Stanford University Press, 2009.

Wolfson, Susan J. *The Questioning Presence: Wordsworth, Keats, and the Interrogative Mode in Romantic Poetry*. Ithaca: Cornell University Press, 1986.

FURTHER READING FOR PART III: FEELING AND THOUGHT

Bailey, Quentin. *Wordsworth's Vagrants: Police, Prisons, and Poetry in the 1790s*. Farnham: Ashgate, 2011.

Brooks, Cleanth. 'Wordsworth and Human Suffering: Notes on Two Early Poems.' Eds. Chandler, James. *An Archaeology of Sympathy: The Sentimental Mode in Literature and Cinema*. Chicago: University of Chicago Press, 2013.

Fay, Jessica. *Wordsworth's Monastic Inheritance: Poetry, Place, and the Sense of Community*. Oxford: Oxford University Press, 2018.

Glen, Heather. *Vision & Disenchantment*. Cambridge: Cambridge University Press, 1983.

Hilles, Frederick W. and Harold Bloom. *From Sensibility to Romanticism: Essays Presented to Frederick A. Pottle*. New York: Oxford University Press, 1965.

King, Joshua, "The Old Cumberland Beggar': Form and Frustrated Sympathy', *The Wordsworth Circle*, 41 (2010): 45–53.

Lowe, Brighid. *Victorian Fiction and the Insights of Sympathy: An Alternative to the Hermeneutics of Suspicion*. London: Anthem, 2007.

Manning, Peter. *Reading Romantics*. New York: Oxford University Press, 1990.

McGrath, Brian. 'Wordsworth, 'Simon Lee', and the Craving for Incidents', *Studies in Romanticism*, 48 (2009): 573–582.

Parrish, Stephen Maxfield. *The Art of the Lyrical Ballads*. Cambridge, MA: Harvard University Press, 1973.

Ratcliffe, Sophie. *On Sympathy*. Oxford: Oxford University Press, 2008.

Richey, William. 'The Rhetoric of Sympathy in Smith and Wordsworth.' *European Romantic Review*, 13 (2002): 427–443.

Simpson, David. *Wordsworth, Commodification and Social Concern: The Poetics of Modernity*. Cambridge: Cambridge University Press, 2009.

Wordsworth's Historical Imagination: The Poetry of Displacement. London: Methuen, 1987.

FURTHER READING FOR PART IV: LANGUAGE AND THE HUMAN MIND

Jacobus, Mary. *Tradition and Experiment in Wordsworth's 'Lyrical Ballads.'* Oxford: Clarendon Press, 1976.

Land, Stephen K. 'The Silent Poet: An Aspect of Wordsworth's Semantic Theory.' *University of Toronto Quarterly*, 42 (1973): 157–169.

O'Donnell, Brennan. *The Passion of Metre*. Kent, OH: Kent State University Press, 1995.

Parrish, Stephen. *The Art of the 'Lyrical Ballads.'* Cambridge; Harvard University Press, 1973.

Regier, Alexander and Stefan H. Uhlig, eds. *Wordsworth's Poetic Theory: Knowledge, Language, Experience*. Basingstoke: Palgrave Macmillan, 2010.

Sheats, Paul. *The Making of Wordsworth's Poetry, 1785–1798*. Cambridge: Harvard University Press, 1973. Sykes Davies, Hugh. *Wordsworth and the Worth of Words*. Cambridge: Cambridge University Press, 1987.

Wolfson, Susan. *Formal Charges: The Shaping of Poetry in English Romanticism*. Stanford: Stanford University Press, 1997.

Romantic Interactions: Social Being and the Turns of Literary Action. Baltimore: Johns Hopkins University Press, 2010.

FURTHER READING FOR PART V: A GLOBAL *LYRICAL BALLADS*

Bate, Jonathan. *Romantic Ecology: Wordsworth and the Environmental Tradition*. London: Routledge, 1991.

Bewell, Alan. *Romanticism and Colonial Disease*. Baltimore: The Johns Hopkins University Press, 1999.

Fraser, Robert. 'School Readers in the Empire and the Creation of Postcolonial Literary Taste.' *Books without Borders. Vol. 1: The Cross-National Dimension in Print Culture*. Ed. Robert Fraser and Mary Hammond. Basingstoke: Palgrave, 2008. 89–106.

Fulford, Tim, *Romantic Indians: Native Americans, British Literature, and Transatlantic Culture, 1756–1830*. Oxford: Oxford University Press, 2006.

Fulford, Tim and Kevin Hutchings, eds. *Native Americans and Anglo-American Culture, 1750–1850: The Indian Atlantic*. Cambridge: Cambridge University Press, 2009.

Fulford, Tim and Peter J. Kitson, eds., *Romanticism and Colonialism: Writing and Empire, 1780–1830*. Cambridge: Cambridge University Press, 1998.

Garrard, Greg. *Ecocriticism*, 2nd ed. London: Routledge, 2012.

Gupta, Abhijit and Swapan Chakravorty, eds., *Print Areas: Book History in India*. Delhi: Permanent Black, 2004.

Hessell, Nikki. *Romantic Literature and the Colonised World: Lessons from Indigenous Translations*. Basingstoke: Palgrave, 2018.

Joshi, Priya. *In Another Country: Colonialism, Culture, and the English Novel in India*. New York: Columbia University Press, 2002.

McKenzie, D. F. 'The Sociology of a Text: Orality, Literacy and Print in Early New Zealand.' *The Book History Reader*. Ed. David Finkelstein and Alistair McCleery. New York: Routledge, 2002. 205–231.

McKusick, James C. *Green Writing: Romanticism and Ecology*, 2nd ed. New York: Palgrave Macmillan, 2010.

McLane, Maureen N. *Balladeering, Minstrelsy, and the Making of British Romantic Poetry*. Cambridge: Cambridge University Press, 2008.

Ottum, Lisa and Seth T. Reno, eds. *Wordsworth and the Green Romantics: Affect and Ecology in the Nineteenth Century*. Durham, NH: University of New Hampshire Press, 2016.

Paterson, Lachy. 'Print Culture and the Collective Māori Consciousness.' *JNZL: Journal of New Zealand Literature*, 28.2 (2010): 105–129.

Richardson, Alan and Sonia Hofkosh, eds., *Romanticism, Race, and Imperial Culture, 1780–1834*. Bloomington: Indiana University Press, 1996.

Round, Phillip H. *Removable Type: Histories of the Book in Indian Country, 1663–1880*. Chapel Hill: University of North Carolina Press, 2010.

Sellers, Stephanie A. *Native American Autobiography Redefined: A Handbook*. New York: Peter Lang, 2007.

Silva, Noenoe K. *Aloha Betrayed: Native Hawaiian Resistance to American Colonialism*. Durham: Duke University Press, 2004.

Somerville, Alice Te Punga, Daniel Heath Justice, and Noelani Arista, eds. 'Indigenous Conversations about Biography', *Biography*, 39.3 (2016).

Viswanathan, Gauri. *Masks of Conquest: Literary Study and British Rule in India*. London: Faber and Faber, 1990.

Wiley, Michael 'No Place on Earth / Can Ever Be a Solitude: *Lyrical Ballads*, Hartleianism, and a World of Places.' *Global Romanticism: Origins, Orientations, and Engagements, 1760–1820*. Ed. Evan Gottlieb. Lewisburg: Bucknell University Press, 2014. 80–90.

Index